Ambassadors of Culture

TRANSLATION | TRANSNATION

SERIES EDITOR **EMILY APTER**

KIRSTEN SILVA GRUESZ

Ambassadors of Culture

The Transamerican Origins of Latino Writing

PRINCETON UNIVERSITY PRESS

PRINCETON AND OXFORD

Copyright © 2002 by Princeton University Press
Published by Princeton University Press, 41 William Street,
Princeton, New Jersey 08540
In the United Kingdom: Princeton University Press,
3 Market Place, Woodstock, Oxfordshire OX20 1SY

All Rights Reserved

Library of Congress Cataloging-in-Publication Data

Gruesz, Kirsten Silva, 1964–
    Ambassadors of culture : the transamerican origins of Latino writing / Kirsten Silva
Gruesz.
      p.   cm. — (Translation / transnation)
    Includes bibliographical references and index.
    ISBN 0-691-05096-1 (acid-free paper) — ISBN 0-691-05097-X (pbk. : acid-free paper)
    1. Hispanic American literature (Spanish)—History and criticism.   2. American
literature—19th century—History and criticism.   3. United States—Relations—Latin
America.   4. Latin America—Relations—United States. I. Title. II. Series.

PQ7070 .G78 2002
860.9′868073—dc21

                                              2001021485

British Library Cataloging-in-Publication Data is available

This book has been composed in Minion

Printed on acid-free paper. ∞

www.pup.princeton.edu

Printed in the United States of America

10 9 8 7 6 5 4 3 2 1

10 9 8 7 6 5 4 3 2 1
(Pbk.)

Consagrado al recuerdo de mis antepasados y antepasadas

Hay muertos que alumbran los caminos

Dedicated to the memory of my forefathers and foremothers

The dead light the way

CONTENTS

> Su negocio cobró vigor cuando para su sorpresa, empezó a
> recibir periódicos de California, de Trinidad, Colorado, de
> Laredo, de Nuevo México, y de partes que ni sospechaba
> hubiera gente mexicana. . . . ¿Y los papeles? Se encontraban
> en el aire. ¿De dónde eres? De la tierra señor.
>
> *[His undertaking grew strong when to his surprise he began to
> receive newspapers from California, Trinidad, Colorado, Laredo,
> New Mexico, and from places where he never even suspected
> there were Mexicans. . . . And the papers? They had vanished
> into thin air. Where are you from? From the land, sir.]*
>
> —Aristeo Brito, *El diablo en Texas / The Devil in Texas*

Among contemporary Latino narratives, there are few visions of history
as unrelenting as Brito's *The Devil in Texas*, a multiperspectival novel in
which generation after generation struggles with the burden of memory.
The nineteenth-century progenitor, Francisco Aranga, puts his faith in
the power of the word. He summons all the defenses of his legal archive
to defend the citizenship status of his fellow *tejanos* after the Treaty of
Guadalupe-Hidalgo, and begins a newspaper to protest the depredation
of their properties and rights—noting with wonderment that his modest
little publication is not alone in that vast zone once known as New Spain
and now called, vaguely, "the West." Instead, he is part of an invisible
web of Spanish speakers and readers linked by common political interests
and a shared taste for the clumsy sentimental verse produced by local
poets and featured in those papers. But Aranga's effort fails. The printing
press is shut down, the legal appeals wither, and the written word crumbles
into the dust that plagues the windswept, desolate border town of
Presidio, persisting only as oral memory, and the imagined community

of a reading public stretching from the Pacific to the Gulf of Mexico disappears along with it. When Brito's final narrator takes up the family story again in the 1970s, in the final pages of the novel, it is with the hope of reconstructing that community by writing—through them, for them, with them—a revisionist history of the land that English speakers had arrogated to themselves as "America."

Like Brito and many others, I am haunted by these traces, and by the ways in which early Spanish-language periodicals published in what is now the United States might have reflected or shaped the identities of those who lived in their communities, both literate and nonliterate. The fact that there *were* publications in Spanish in the United States during the nineteenth century will be surprising enough to most readers; the claim that they might contain important, even crucial, ways of understanding the world will require some serious buttressing. I am even more interested in what these textual traces might tell us about the historical conditions of contemporary Latino subjectivity within the United States, at a moment when those who claim origin in a Spanish-speaking country or commonwealth are approaching one-quarter of the nation's population. Yet the methodological problems of proposing to locate the "origins" of Latino writing in the nineteenth century are immediately apparent: Spanish-language cultural productions such as the fictional Aranga newspaper—even supposing all copies of it have not crumbled into Texan dust—are no more numerous than those of many other language groups, and the total population of Spanish speakers in the United States during this period is sometimes regionally large, but nationally quite small until the Mexican Revolution. Furthermore, the dynamics of exile, dispossession, colonization, and immigration that have brought the patchwork category of "Latino" into its contemporary state, and that conspire constantly to reshape it, vary intimidatingly over the populations claiming Mexican, Puerto Rican, Cuban, Dominican, Salvadoran, Honduran, Nicaraguan, Guatemalan, Panamanian, Costa Rican, Venezuelan, Chilean, Peruvian, Argentinian, Ecuadoran, Bolivian, Uruguayan, and Paraguayan backgrounds—and these national categories do not even begin to take into account differences of class, race, indigeneity, or gender.[1] What, after all, would a Texan-Mexican *ranchero* of 1840 have had to say to an enslaved Afro-Dominican at the same historical moment, and why should a first-generation mestiza schoolchild living in Los Angeles be assumed, in the year 2001, to attach any value whatsoever to words they might have thought or said?

Precisely because of the impossible diversity of the term

"Latino"—and its status as a fictive construct of the late twentieth century, given dubious authority by the machine of the state—archival work on nineteenth-century texts of this sort has tended to stick close to a specific nation (or better yet, region) of origin. Rosaura Sánchez, for instance, closes her exemplary analysis of the long-suppressed testimonials of the *californios* with the admonition that "we are compelled to respond to that past in the degree that it is a measure of the future," but she warns against any too-easy identification of elite subjects like Mariano Vallejo as early "Chicanos," insisting on a strongly historicized understanding of his particularly class- and race-based identity, further located within a region he once governed.[2] Although I have sought to be equally rigorous in placing the subjects of this study within historically specific forms of affiliation, I have also tried to test out the possibility of a meaningful commonality of the idea of Latino expression, even before the term was invented. In so doing, I deliberately risk anachronism in order to pose larger questions about how the anxiety of a Latino future drives readings of its past. Suzanne Oboler's thorough dissection of the invented category "Latino" moves finally toward this observation: no matter what their origin, "Latinos have been racialized such that they experience the effects of invisibility in social and political institutions."[3] One of those institutions is, of course, literary history itself, and the national-pedagogical complex that relies on it to produce definitions of what is "American." Thus, one fundamental directive of this book runs parallel to the revisionism inherent in the Recovering the U.S. Hispanic Literary Heritage (RUSHLH) project: to refute the claim that there is no meaningful literary presence of Latinos or of the Spanish language within the United States before the middle of the twentieth century.

But there is more to be done than simply recuperate the historical presences behind the fictional ghost of Francisco Aranga. Whatever else may be said about the nineteenth-century Latino subjects I describe here, they were constituted not only by the cultural and linguistic forms of their Hispanophone place of origin, but by those of the Anglophone United States as well. As I contend, Latino subjectivity is produced in no small part by the web of political maneuvers designed to control, or to acquire outright, the territories Spain had once claimed in the hemisphere. Sometimes in tandem with the state's actions and sometimes in protest against them, Anglo-American writers helped create a cultural logic of desire and repulsion, of projection and rejection, toward Latin America in general and toward Mexico and Cuba—closest to the U.S. vision—in particular. That logic revolved variously around "Spanishness," "Indianness," and related general notions of aristocracy, Catholicism, civilization, free will and self-possession, heteronormative visions of the national family, and the integrity (or lack of integrity) of racial categories. Although some of the more significant fashioners of these ideas of Latin Americanness are or were once prominent figures in U.S. literary history, their writing on this subject has been neglected as well—and so it seemed to me necessary to reconstitute some of the mainstream currents of thought within or against which Latinos have had to position themselves. Likewise, since the exiles, immigrants, and dispossessed citizens I discuss here all had a primary affiliation with another nation (or, in the case of Cuba and Puerto Rico, a national ideal), the history of Latin American projections and rejections of the United States enters importantly into this analysis, although the archival and perhaps conceptual limitations inherent in my location in the U.S. academy will be apparent to readers there.

This book ultimately argues, then, for a strong revision of literary-historical narratives of the U.S. national tradition that render the Latino presence ghostly and peripheral. More than simply encouraging an additive process of restoring lost texts from the Spanish borderlands to the canon, this revision requires a nongenealogical view of Latino identity grounded in a larger web of transamerican perceptions and contacts. Each chapter opens with a scene of transamerican literary exchange that I take as emblematic, and goes on to unroll a fabric of relationship—literary, political, social—that contains and enables that scene. The chapters are episodic, proceeding in a roughly chronological order from the 1820s to the 1880s, but certain events and figures are threaded throughout the whole, reemerging from time to time as unifying reference points. Chapter 1, "'Alone with the Terrible Hurricane': The Occluded History of Transamerican Literature," lays out a methodological justification for the project, beginning with my choice to discuss print culture. Rather than seeking to reproduce the privilege of print, and the structures of European colonialism and domination with which its history in the Americas is enmeshed, I try to redefine publishing, circulation, and reading as performance contexts, in which subjects possessing a broad range of literacies can participate. Because of its brevity, mobility, association with the voice, and status as a prestige genre, I focus particularly on lyric poetry—the most common literary genre to be published in fugitive periodicals, as well as the most likely to be translated. With regard to the Spanish periodical literature of the borderlands in particular, I see poetry as occupying a middle ground of literary production, a kind of vernacular formation whose value lies in its openness of access to authorship. Authorship serves as a form of political engagement within both national and regional contexts; when they venture into transamerican thinking by traveling or translating other American poems, writers perform an act of cultural ambassadorship. I defend the apparent imitativeness of many of these vernacular productions, seeing imitativeness as a form of asserting one's agency as a cultural producer. Besides retracing the hemispheric travels of texts through periodical and book publishing, I try to imagine the living publication that is the memorized poem. "Latino writing" thus indicates not only authorship but a whole range of expressive practices strongly affiliated with oral and performance tradtions.

Chapter 2, "The Chain of American Circumstance: From Niagara to Cuba to Panama," begins with the figure of Maria Gowen Brooks "going Cuban"—her translucent gowns and tropical adornments marking a transformation into María del Occidente—in her self-chosen exile in Matanzas. Like many of her contemporaries, Brooks saw the emergent colonies of the New World as mutually foreign but possessed of a fluidity that hinted at the possibility of an eventual unified identity: a perception crystallized in the Monroe Doctrine of 1823 and in classic poetic declarations of Americanism by Andrés Bello and others. Such statements initially cluster around a group of sublime landmarks acknowledged by poets and aesthetic travelers both North and South to be the very source of shared American uniqueness—Niagara Falls and the pyramids of central Mexico, for example—and their invocation of a "lost" indigenous past. Bryant's translation and propagation of "Al huracán" and another widely known poem by José María Heredia "Niágara," indicates his interest in attributing moral value to sublime American landscapes, as he himself does in "The Prairies." Heredia, as he relocated to Mexico, helped establish both a national print culture and a way of imagining a common Latin American identity, but he did so by popularizing a potentially dangerous trope: that of the nation enslaved by its colonizer, the republic in chains. Although Heredia supported the abolition of slavery, when his early death helped transform him into an iconic martyr to the cause of Cuban liberty, other nationalists would take up this figure in disturbingly paradoxical ways. I conclude chapter 2 by returning to María del Occidente's tropical fantasies in light of the Escalera revolt of 1844, a violent suppression of Afro-Cuban mobility that would be revisited many times over the course of the century.

Chapter 3, "Tasks of the Translator: Imitative Literature, the

Catholic South, and the Invasion of Mexico," charts the rise of a type of Hispanophilic ambassador of culture who projected a virtuous feminized identity on the Catholic "South," even as the United States prepared to intervene possessively into Mexico and the Caribbean. This ambassadorial role is often played out through the popularization of translation and a cosmopolitan ethos of poetry, which seeks to reconcile imitation with the nationalist desire for originality. A nexus of transamerican contacts, Longfellow embodies a kind of commitment to the translative mode that echoes in the work of other diplomat-poets such as Rafael Pombo and Olegario Andrade. Longfellow's *Evangeline*, significantly revised by its Chilean Spanish translator, suggests that his popularity was accomplished largely by appropriating forms of sentimental nationalism previously associated with women; I link this phenomenon to the rise of an aggressive expansionist movement in the United States that increasingly projected feminine attributes onto Latin America (and its racialized citizens) to argue for intervention and rescue—or conquest—of that terrain. I trace responses to this gendered revision of the fraternal language of the Monroe Doctrine on the eve of the invasion of Mexico in 1846, reading poems by Whittier along with editorials in the Spanish periodicals *El Clamor Público* of Los Angeles and *El Bejareño* and *El Ranchero* of San Antonio, elaborating on their literary aims, translation theories, and practices.

Chapter 4, "The Mouth of a New Empire: New Orleans in the Transamerican Print Trade," is centered in New Orleans, the mouth of the Mississippi River linking the original U.S. territory to its new West, as well as the capital of an important triangle of trade connecting the northern states to South America and the Caribbean. It was also the locus of many troop movements to, and most press coverage of, the Mexican War. During (and briefly after) the war, a significant Spanish-language print community flourished in New Orleans and was best embodied by *La Patria*—one of the most successful Spanish-language papers in the United States. Walt Whitman's participation in the New Orleans print sphere in 1848 links him to *La Patria*, and I revisit the critical controversy over Whitman's politics of continental expansion through a reading of his early journalism and poetry composed in that city. New Orleans was also home to the Cuban rebel poets known as the *Laúd del desterrado* group after the anthology they published together. This community of writers, including José Agustín Quintero, Pedro Santacilia, and Miguel Teurbe Tolón, enabled a number of Texan-Mexican-Cuban connections and coalitions even as it increasingly lost its voice in the national controversies over Cuban annexation and the filibustering expeditions of Narciso López and others. Quintero, in particular, emerges as a paradoxical figure whose subject position shifts as he takes on multiple affiliations to Cuba, the Confederacy, and the Union.

Chapter 5, "The Deep Roots of Our America: Two New Worlds, and Their Resistors," begins with a counterpart to Whitman in New York: Rafael Pombo, the Colombian diplomat, poet, and translator whose long stay in the United States was punctuated by his increasing mistrust of U.S. activity in Central America during the search for a canal zone. The chapter then turns to interrogate more deeply borderlands print culture as an index of larger transamerican sentiments and historical developments, drawing examples from the continent's geographical extremes: *El Nuevo Mundo* of San Francisco, published 1860–64; and *El Mundo Nuevo/La América Ilustrada* of New York, 1871–75. I read the work of the exiled Mexican poet Isabel Prieto against the backdrop of multiethnic San Francisco, where former Mexican citizens confronted an influx of Latin American and Yankee fortune-seekers along with a small group of refugees from Maximilian's Mexico. Both Prieto's work and Pombo's was later published in *El Mundo Nuevo*, founded by Cuban exiles who established a partnership with popular press mogul Frank Leslie to distribute an ambitious illustrated weekly throughout the hemisphere. The paper drew attention to the cause of Cuban independence through coverage of the execution of poet Juan Clemente Zenea, the inheritor of Heredia's mantle as well as the lover of celebrity writer-actress (and crypto-Jew) Adah Isaacs Menken. The chapter closes with a return to New Orleans, where Zenea's former co-conspirators struggled with their increasingly subordinate racial and class position during Reconstruction, by way of Guillermo Prieto, the Mexican politician and *poeta nacional* whose 1877 *Viaje a los Estados Unidos* describes his stay with Quintero and his visit with Bryant, and presciently speculates on the future of U.S.-Mexican relations. A final coda, "The Future's Past: Latino Ghosts in the U.S. Canon," summons a deathbed letter from Vallejo to Longfellow in order to speculate on the significance of these cultural expressions, both from the borderlands and from urban and cosmopolitan avenues, in the context of later anti-imperialist Latin American exile writers—chief among them José Martí—and in light of contemporary debates about Latino identity and citizenship.

The chapters of this book thus oscillate internally between readings of English and Spanish texts, and between centers and peripheries of cultural and political power. Since the *movement* of subjects and communities is a central theme, I frequently discuss transamerican travels and translations. But such a structure risks falling into easy binaries of North-South, English-Spanish—a risk I try to guard against by calling attention to exceptions and contradictions, and by interweaving poems and essays that claim membership in a more or less stable "tradition" with obscure texts recovered from periodical archives, which disrupt the stability of such national canons. This does not suggest that I have presented anything like a complete panorama of transamerican and Latino cultural production during the period. Indeed, the swift pace at which new portions of the Spanish-language archive are being uncovered means that the gaps in my study will grow more obvious over time. I attempt whenever possible to give the stage to female, mestizo, mulato, black, and indigenous writers, but the nearly universal disenfranchisement of these groups during the period means that the vast majority of the voices recorded in print are those of white men, and generally those of a privileged class—a fact I can only underscore, not redress.

A penultimate word about language: I give original Spanish quotations precedence in the text, providing deliberately unpolished, "literal" translations (recognizing how problematic the term is) alongside the originals. In so doing, I seek to make this study accessible to as wide an audience as possible; but I also open myself up to inevitable protests over the fidelity of those translations of convenience. That is precisely the point: to push Anglophone readers into grappling seriously with Spanish as an essential literary language of the United States. The translations in brackets, then, should not be taken as encouragement to let the eyes skip over the original, but as a provocation to engage with it to the best of the reader's ability. In a very few cases, where cognate words are strong and the meaning seems obvious, I leave the Spanish to stand alone. I have also regularized nineteenth-century orthography in both English and Spanish, except where the original spelling may offer clues about the historical articulation of a term (e.g., "México-Tejanos" rather than "mejicanos"). Finally, for what ought to be obvious reasons, I eschew the use of "American" as an adjective meaning "of the United States"; if the alternative—the abbreviation "U.S." positioned adjectivally—seems awkward, so at first did many now-familiar interventions into common usage, such as the feminine third-person pronoun, which quietly seek to correct unnoticed hegemonies of language.

In Borges's classic fiction "Pierre Menard, autor del *Quijote*," the minor symbolist poet conceives of a method to "arrive" at the writing of that novel without copying it—to learn Spanish intimately, to reclaim

Catholicism, to fight in the Crusades, to forget everything he knew about the intervening centuries of European history, to *become* Cervantes; Menard ultimately rejects this method as being "too easy." My aims must seem similarly audacious: to reject the hegemonic map of America and its traditional locations of centers and margins of culture; to reconsider the nature and quality of imitation in literary expression; to recapture the experience of individual readers and writers with poetry, amply defined; and to reclaim Spanish as a literary language of the United States. There is also a Borgesian quality to my method. As often as not, my emphasis falls on the ephemeral, the accidental, the peripheral; on crumbling pieces of newsprint, letters, and other evidence of the material presence of the word. Like these objects, its insights will be fugitive—but not, I hope, in vain.

ACKNOWLEDGMENTS

Although it seems counterintuitive to begin by thanking an institution rather than a person, my presence in the intellectual sphere would be unthinkable without the agency of Swarthmore College, to which I am indebted for financial support as well as a deeper kind of validation. As a graduate student in Comparative Literature at Yale, the serendipitons accident of being enrolled simultaneously in courses with two great teachers, Roberto González Echevarría and Richard Brodhead, led me to explore the then dubious prospect of transamerican literature. Few traces of the dissertation they supervised remain in this book, but a discerning reader will detect their subterranean influence on it. Vera Kutzinski, who was also an early supporter, has generously read many versions of this project over the years, and it has benefited greatly from her sharp critical instincts.

As I made the transition into archival work, I was helped by numerous librarians and archivists far more experienced than I at the University of California at Santa Cruz and Berkeley; the Bancroft and Ethnic Studies Libraries at Berkeley; the Houghton Library at Harvard; the Williams Research Center of the Historic New Orleans Collection; the New York Public Library; Yale University; Tulane University; the University of Texas at Austin; and the Biblioteca Nacional José Martí in Havana. Permission to reproduce materials from the Maria Gowen Brooks Papers in the Manuscripts and Archives Division of the New York Public Library (Astor, Lenox, and Tilden Foundations), as well as materials from the Longfellow Collection of the Houghton Library, Harvard University, is gratefully acknowledged.

Students and colleagues at Yale and Harvard, at the College of William & Mary, and ultimately at the University of California at Santa Cruz were instrumental in asking the probing questions that prodded me to rethink what I meant by "literature of the Americas." I learned a great deal from students in my courses in Latino/a and Chicano/a literature, in particular. The wide-ranging and thought-provoking conversations I had with my colleagues across disciplines at Santa Cruz helped this project gestate; I am particularly grateful to the Center for Cultural Studies for sponsoring the Inter-Americas Research Cluster as well as a number of stimulating conferences and speakers. I thank the lively intellects of Chris Bongie, Chris Breu, Maria Elena Caballero-Robb, Louis Chude-Sokei, Jonathan Freedman, Susan Gillman, Jennifer Gonzalez, Adalaine Holton, Curtis Márez, Lourdes Martínez-Echazábal, Michelle Morton, Juan Poblete, Ricky T. Rodriguez, Shirley Samuels, Shelley Stamp, and Adriana X. Tatum. I am indebted to student research assistants who were part of the project at various points: Jill Baker, Thomas Hill, and especially Gloria Chacón. I also had invaluable support with the devils of word processing from Kathy Durcan, Verónica Higareda, and Cheryl Van de Veer. Not least, I received financial support from several institutions: a summer research grant from William & Mary, annual research grants from the University of California at Santa Cruz, and a President's Research Fellowship from the University of California.

Audiences at numerous conferences of the American Studies Association, the Modern Language Association, and the American Comparative Literature Association as well as at UCLA, Stanford, and the University of Michigan offered helpful comments on various portions of this work. Ken Price, besides teaching me a good deal about Whitman, brought me into the fold of a community of scholars working on the Dickinson and Whitman Electronic Archives; conversations with Martha Nell Smith, Ezra Greenspan, Ed Folsom, Jay Grossman, Ellen Hart, Marta Werner, Stephanie Browner, and the participants in our annual retreat helped me think not only about poetry but about the transiency of technologies of the word. I have been consistently inspired by meetings of the Recovering the U.S. Hispanic Literary Heritage project, and by the Latino/a scholars across generations I have met there, particularly Jesse Alemán and John M. González. José David Saldívar generously offered his enthusiasm and support at various junctures.

Finally, I want to thank my editors at Princeton University Press—Mary Murrell, Fred Appel, and my superb trilingual copyeditor, Kim Mrazek Hastings—for patiently shepherding this project to completion.

"Always a web, always a knit of identity," Whitman writes, and the dear friends who have endured my absorption in this project for many years are deeply woven into it: Rachel Berwick, Joshua Dienstag, Jim Flint, Betty Lilley, Alva Noë, Iván Núñez Cuesta, and Nancy Watzman, among others. Finally, although this is an originary debt, I can only begin to express my gratitude to my extended family for their support and tireless good humor over the years. I thank my parents Dave and Cheryle; my brother Carl and his family; and my cousins, *abuelos*, aunts, and uncles for reminding me how privileged I am to be anchored in a loving family.

Ambassadors of Culture

I

"Alone with the Terrible Hurricane"
The Occluded History of Transamerican Literature

> La tormenta umbría
> En los aires revuelve un océano
> Que todo lo sepulta . . .
> Al fin, mundo fatal, nos separamos;
> El huracán y yo solos estamos.[1]

Near the beginning of the century in which nationalism in the Americas assumed its fateful form, the Cuban-born writer José María Heredia penned these lines from "En una tempestad: Al huracán," which was first published from his political exile in New York City in 1825. A few years later, the editor and poet William Cullen Bryant translated "The Hurricane" and another poem for publications he edited, from which they were liberally reprinted around the country for the next several decades. A partial inventory of the subsequent appearances of original and translation is both telling and tantalizing. In 1854 *DeBow's Review*, an adamantly proslavery monthly in New Orleans, cited Heredia as an example of the high accomplishments of Cuban culture in order to support its argument that the rich island was languishing under Spanish rule and would be better served by U.S. governance. Across town, the Spanish-language weekly *La Patria*, which had raised one of the sole protests in New Orleans against the expansionist war on Mexico, used Heredia to stir up the sentiments of Cuban expatriates in favor of the Spanish empire and against such foreign influence. In far-off San Francisco, *El Nuevo Mundo*, an urbane daily paper published for the city's Mexican and Chilean elites, used an epigraph from "Al huracán" to introduce an original poem comparing the French intervention in Mexico to Spain's continuing grip on Cuba, thereby making Heredia's struggle a corollary to their own. "Al huracán" was also reprinted in various anthologies and newspapers in Mexico, where Heredia had lived out the rest of his short life; when Bryant visited Mexico City in 1872—perhaps the only yanqui of the period to be received there with genuine popular enthusiasm—his translation of the poem was distributed in broadside. Finally, in the flurry of enthusiasm for pan-Americanism that swept the United States after its acquisition of an empire in the Pacific and the Caribbean, the Bryant-Heredia exchange was resurrected in at least three anthologies as an example of the fraternal ties that allegedly bound the hemisphere. In the U.S.-occupied San Juan of 1903, Francis (Francisco) J. Amy made this pairing one of the centerpieces of his curious textbook, *Musa bilingüe*, which sought to foster "the intellectual Americanization of Porto Rican youths" through parallel readings of English and Spanish poems. One Professor Brau contributed an introductory apostrophe that makes clear the civilizing mission that an education in the English language and its high culture is meant to have for Puerto Rico:

> The task of directing our social destiny having devolved onto the great republic of Washington, she has brought us, in the folds of her revered flag, the irradiation of her democratic spirit; but alas! the spirit without the speech can accomplish no redemption. . . . This means that perfect homogeneity does not exist between directors and directed, owing to divergencies in language which must be done away with by both. . . . Take this book; study its cohesion, analyze its component parts, fathom its syncretism that blends together the intellectual genius of two empires to which you are bound.[2]

Amy's book of facing-page poetic translations is presented as the path toward a desirable cultural "syncretism" that would bow to an inescapable political reality: the exchange of a new "empire" for the old. Despite *Musa bilingüe*'s hopeful gesture at the mutual education of English and Spanish speakers, their relationship is as unequal as that of "directors" and "directed." Brau continues, revealingly, "without voice it is impossible to call for help, and we are virtually mute, since we find no one to understand us." Translated language follows, if not precedes, the accomplishment of *traslatio imperii*, the movement of empire. And the voice of that power now speaks in English. Puerto Rico, as Brau senses, is alone with the hurricane, the naturalizing force of U.S. culture that occludes all things behind its own forceful presence.

What ties together these discrete uses of a poetic text, jointly expressed as "original" and "translation" by two politically engaged writers who despite their former fame today seem antique, relegated to the peripheries of academia? As the early publishing history of "Al huracán" suggests, the ideal of a transamerican culture—of a bridgeable, thinkable communion between the Anglophone and Hispanophone worlds—is rooted in a revolutionary and cosmopolitan Romantic ethos that Bryant and Heredia, whatever their differences, shared. But this ideal was from the beginning beset by the powerful engine of U.S. territorial expansion. By the time of the "neighborly" U.S. occupation of Puerto Rico and Cuba at the turn of the century, it had disintegrated into a strained awareness of the structural imbalances between the former colonies of the hemisphere—imbalances that encouraged the more overt forms of U.S. domination that would be perfected (and tiresomely repeated) throughout the course of the twentieth century. "The spirit without the speech can accomplish no redemption," Brau writes, reiterating the nineteenth-century commonplace that speech—and heightened literary speech in particular—might do what mere economic forces and political proclamations could not: transform subjects into citizens, and strangers into compatriots. This utopian will of the word is generally recognized as a corollary project to nation-building.[3] Yet the relationships of imagined community at this time also extended across porous and contested national boundaries to establish and strengthen other alliances: between slaveholding interests in the U.S. South and their Cuban partners and rivals in the sugar trade; between radical republicans from Mexico and the Caribbean who made New Orleans a convenient locus from which to plot the overthrow of Spanish and European colonial powers; or between liberal procapitalist coalitions across Greater Mexico from northern California to Veracruz's Caribbean port—to mention just the examples offered by "Al huracán." Transnational alliances all, and yet they also gesture toward a slowly evolving Latino presence within this national sphere. Nor does "transnational" adequately describe the relationship of disparate groups of Spanish speakers living in the United States to each other. The sense of confraternity, whether deeply felt or merely wished for, might explain how Heredia's tropical storm came to be offered as entertainment for the relatively conservative californio population of San Francisco.

This longstanding Latino presence, which has grown in both quantity and visibility at the edge of a new millennium, invites us to revisit the history of transamerican cultural contacts. It encourages us to take seriously the possibility that the divergences between English and Spanish that Professor Brau sadly noted might in fact eclipse a common tradition—common without being unitary or imperially reductive; common, perhaps, in the very nodes of their divergence. This tradition is currently accessible to us in two forms, each contained within a particular discipline and its knowledge structure. The first is the archival preservation of the written traces of Hispanophone communities in zones of border contact such as New Mexico, California, and Texas, and in urban spaces of great ethnic diversity such as New York, Chicago, New Orleans, and Los Angeles. This is the record currently being identified and preserved by one of the most ambitious such efforts ever of its kind, the Recovering the U.S. Hispanic Literary Heritage project. The assemblage of this vast archive is made meaningful through the lens of an implicit ethnic genealogy; that is, it aims to produce knowledge about the historical contributions of different Latino populations to their particular communal identity (as Chicanos, Puerto Ricans, Cuban Americans, or under the larger umbrella of "Latino") and to U.S. culture at large.[4] The second way in which we might consider the common history of Anglophone and Hispanophone American culture invokes the larger frame of transamerican and transatlantic cultural contact: networks of publication and transmission; relationships of patronage, influence, and translation; and the institutions of pedagogy, canonization, and official sanctification that allow texts to live or die in the public imagination. Such contacts fall within the scope of comparative literature, which has historically been seen—at least within U.S. studies—as a footnote to the more pressing issue of the national imagination.[5] To the extent that these two frames differ—for at certain points, they do not—both are essential components of a cultural history of the Americas, and need to be simultaneously rendered visible. Such a vision is necessary not only to provide a historical grounding for contemporary Latino identity but to imagine a new form of U.S. cultural history in general: one that would unseat the fiction of American literature's monolingual and Anglocentric roots and question the imperial conflation of the United States with America.[6]

Although written by a Cuban—more accurately, a discontented Spanish subject with ties of birth and property to Cuba, who cemented these into a Byronic aura of political idealism and longing—"Al huracán" does not signify exclusively in the context of that nation's tradition.

Nor does it figure solely in the development of an ideally unified Latin American culture, along the lines of José Martí's vision of *Nuestra América*. Rather, each of the poem's appearances in periodicals from rural or urban border spaces contextualizes local issues of autonomy and agency by placing them in broader contexts, and marks lines of affiliation that now might be called "global" or "diasporic," without the postmodern simultaneity that is usually implicit in such terms.[7] Each iteration of the poem can be understood as a social performance, a summons to discrete groups of readers who impose on it the filters of their own positioning within the transamerican sphere, and create if not a "new" poem, then a distinct transaction of it. The travels of a written work such as this one may seem less historically resonant than the movements of troops, tribes, or tourists across the hemisphere, particularly since the historical record of reception is relatively thin. We can only speculate on the full range of the text's movements; its presence in a publication from San Francisco or from Santiago de Cuba hints at—but never fully documents—the ways in which it was heard, understood, or misunderstood in those places, and passed along to others in the form of an imitation, a few lines lifted or memorized, or a distant echo. In the pages that follow, I want to fill in some of these forgotten transactions and speculate on the missing, invisible ones.

In traditional literary history, the textual transmissions that matter are those that take place between canonical figures: Emerson's letter of blessing to Whitman, or Sarmiento's argument with Bello over American language differences, to cite two emblematic examples. A more historicist approach might single out a scene of transmission that seems to represent some larger cultural pathology, for instance, General Winfield Scott telling William H. Prescott that Prescott's *History of the Conquest of Mexico* had inspired him on the field, and urging him to write a sequel that would glorify the new "conquest" of the country by Scott's forces.[8] My effort here is to broaden the range of textual movements that we consider vital and meaningful. This process involves, in part, a movement away from canonical scenes of transmission and toward an expanded set of texts that we take to be relevant. More profoundly, however, it involves an amplification of the domain of the term "American" into other languages and other spaces aside from the obvious centers of political and artistic activity. How do we codify the relationship between a famous poet like Heredia and an all-but-anonymous literary citizen like the editor in San Francisco in a way that will illuminate the cultural values distinct to the immediate world of each, as well as the ones they shared?

A striking aspect of early Spanish-language periodicals published in the continental United States, as I hinted earlier, is the prominent place of belles lettres in them. Poetry and criticism, composed by both unknown and well-known writers, appears much more often than does serialized fiction. Far from being isolated records of local sensibilities, such publications consistently referred to other periodicals in distant places, reprinting pieces from them, taking issue with their editorial stances, or simply mentioning them as reassuring proof that their readers were not stranded in a linguistic desert. The global sphere, in other words, was as important to these organs as the local one, and thus the significance of the work they published was inseparable from an overlapping set of larger cultural contexts: the forsaken *patria* with which most of the local readers identified; the Hispanophone world as a whole; and the Anglophone United States that surrounded them. Nicolás Kanellos and Helvetia Martell have usefully divided early Latino print culture into the exile press, the immigrant press, and the "native Hispanic" press, but these categorizations, as Kanellos and Martell acknowledge, are rarely exclusive, and the distinctions are particularly difficult to make in the nineteenth century.[9] More specifically, the existence of a borderlands literary culture seemed to beg pressing and much understudied questions about the place of a form of heightened or ritualized speech like poetry in the daily lives of a whole range of nineteenth-century readers of English and Spanish—from the barely literate (who might "possess" a text read aloud to them despite this handicap) to the hypereducated (for whom reading certain kinds of poetry represented their mastery of certain prestige discourses: rules of diction, meter and syllabification, intertextual references). Although many studies in both U.S. and Latin American literature have interrogated fiction's role in the construction of certain forms of identity—gender, citizenship, local and racial affiliations—we know little of the ways in which poetic and belletristic language might have influenced individual lives and community movements. Poetry's prominence in these readily available media forces us to rethink general assumptions about the pristine aesthetic "removal" of lyric and to consider its potential role in shaping larger ideological formations as well as influencing the ways in which individual readers and writers mapped their lives. That project, in turn, compels us to unloose—at least imaginatively—the geographical and linguistic boundaries traditionally associated with the history of U.S. national culture. The peregrinations of "Al huracán" call for a new geography of American literary history that emphasizes its formation within and around a culture of the Americas.

Geografía Nueva: An Alternate History
of the American World System

A historicized rendering of this transnational space must consider, first, the social networks through which literary information is circulated, beginning with the nature and degree of literacy among various social classes and stretching to include the highest forms of cultural consecration: the academy, high-prestige publishing houses, state patronage, and so on. Pierre Bourdieu attempts to sketch this context by establishing a set of economic and cultural factors that determine the relationships between writers or artists (cultural producers) and the dominant class wielding economic and political power. He describes this relationship spatially in terms of the adjacency of the field of cultural production, which creates and circulates symbolic capital, to the field of power, which distributes economic capital. By plotting various coordinates on these overlapping fields—low/high profitability, strong/weak consecration from established arbiters of culture, high/low artistic autonomy—Bourdieu is able to identify provocative connections between the market, the state, and various kinds of art in a nuanced way that demonstrates the increasing alienation of intellectuals from the field of power during the nineteenth century, while also revealing the points at which they colluded and cooperated with it.[10] Literary-historical scholarship that draws from Bourdieu, or from the similarly influential notion of the "public sphere" derived from the work of Jürgen Habermas, generally uses these models to illuminate the development of a national cultural identity, as democratic ideas and definitions of community are traded into familiarity through the currency of words within the public sphere enabled by a strong print culture.[11] These claims are grounded in data about the history of book and periodical publishing such as that gathered by Ronald Zboray in his overview of the antebellum period in the United States. Zboray suggests that the mass of low-cost periodicals and books that flowed through newly improved trade routes down the Mississippi, through the Ohio River valley, and along the Erie Canal were just as important in affirming shared values among different parts of the nation as they were in producing the period's noteworthy economic expansion. Zboray's metaphorical borrowings from the atlas of trade—his vision of a nation intellectually (if not politically) unified by the traffic in print culture—relies on a model of center and periphery analogous to the federal system. Certain key cities (Boston, New York, Philadelphia) were sources of printed goods, which worked on their readers to build national cultural affiliations, while a string of far-flung small towns received these goods and their urban ideologies. But such cities never limited their trade relationships to the peripheries of the nation; they exchanged intellectual goods with other national capitals as well. Examples of a transnational traffic in words, such as the peregrinations of "Al huracán" via Heredia, Bryant, and their diverse readers, call for new interpretations of the history of print and the relationship of the field of cultural production to other fields of power and influence.

One model for such a comparison derives from liberal historian Herbert Bolton, who in 1932 famously argued for a common history of the Americas, whereas another arises more recently from the world-systems model of Immanuel Wallerstein. The Bolton thesis relies on a suggestive list of similarities: the fact that following the wars of independence (1808–26 on the southern continent, excluding the Caribbean islands), native-born property-holders in all the American nation-states struggled to escape European colonial domination; most inherited economies based on slave labor and their attendant paradoxes; and all confronted a residual indigenous presence by imposing internal colonial structures based on racial and linguistic divisions. Yet to the eyes of later historians, these similarities pale next to the sheer diversity of national experience in the hemisphere, not least the gaping disparity between their modes of economic development. The United States by 1820 had a coherent political economy built on competitive capital and by 1870 was already making a transition into monopoly capital, whereas Latin American nations largely continued in dependent economic relations with Europe. Thus, such comparative histories seemed destined, at best, to conclude that Latin America was slow or deficient next to the Anglo world in fostering democratic institutions and economic "progress"; at worst, to downplay the increasing role of the United States itself in the relations of external dominance that hampered Latin American self-determination.[12] In contrast, Quijano and Wallerstein's 1992 essay "Americity as a Concept" gives the hemispheric thesis an inverted focus by arguing for the common significance of the Americas to the rest of the world: "the creation of this geosocial entity, the Americas, was the constitutive act of the modern world-system . . . there could not have been a capitalist world-economy without the Americas."[13] Shifting the focus definitively from global political relations to economic ones, they identify such historical events as the violent territorial expansion of the United States into the rest of the continent, and its imitation of European colonial relations later in the century, as points that require transnational investigation focusing on relations of capital.

Likewise, comparative literary studies that rely on the superficial similarity of historical "themes" suggested by the Bolton thesis, rather than the complex imbrications of power and influence in the Americas, seem to exist in an odd vacuum. The traditional disciplinary model of Goethean *Weltliteratur*, with its emphasis on personal relationships of influence and a shared Greco-Roman tradition, has yielded remarkably little fruit in this context, as attested by Stanley T. Williams's 1955 *The Spanish Background of American Literature* and Luis Sánchez's 1973–76 *Historia comparada de las literaturas americanas*, virtually the only efforts in this field for many years.[14] Only when we draw back from their emphasis on national literary traditions and turn toward more global patterns of migration, diaspora, and exile does a transamerican cultural history begin to make a serious argument for its usefulness, and a phenomenon like "Al huracán" can become intelligible through its own geometry of distribution, reception, and influence. Illustrating the possibilities of such a cultural history, Hortense Spillers remarks that "the historic triangular trade [in African slaves] interlarded a third of the known world in a fabric of intimacy so tightly interwoven that the politics of the New World cannot always be so easily disentangled as locally discrete moments." She goes on to produce an insightful reading of an artifact of culture produced and distributed—like any other form of capital—within that triangle.[15] Hers is just one of numerous recently proposed cultural geographies that challenge the primacy of the nation, like Paul Gilroy's "Black Atlantic" stretching from London to Georgia and to Santo Domingo and Jamaica; or Joseph Roach's "circum-Atlantic" performance trajectory dotted by New Orleans, the Antilles, West Africa, and London. The history of print culture and its role in certain forms of acculturation, then, is narratable with reference to maps other than the national: the links between Mexico City and late-century Santa Fe, New Mexico, for instance, are as significant in describing the flow of ideas and expressions that create communities of thought and feeling as is the cultural traffic between Boston and Springfield, Illinois.

In a parallel move away from the national frame, an emphasis on the borderlands, and their incomplete and contested assimilation into the nation-states that claim them, has dominated the "new Western history" for the past two decades. Following Bolton's rejection of Frederick Jackson Turner's national-destinarian terminology of the "frontier," this new history emphasizes local relations of conflict and cooperation among ethnic and linguistic communities, and the relative autonomy and hetero-geneity of their cultural practices with respect to national centers. Such critical formulations as Gloria Anzaldúa's "borderlands/*frontera*," José Limón's "Greater Mexico," José David Saldívar's "*transfrontera* contact zone," and Walter Mignolo's episteme of "border gnosis" all echo this fundamental reformulation.[16] Viewed from the destabilizing perspective of the borderlands, both the map and the history of "America" look unarguably different. Yet the critical potential of borderlands theory lies not merely in its insistence on local expressions of difference or resis-tance, but in the implicit dialogue with the national that it calls forth: the very concept of the border is unintelligible without the nation. Such a theory needs to ask not only how the community of San Antonio may have maintained an identity as part of Greater Mexico long after its incorporation into the United States, but how that identity may have simultaneously altered other forms of U.S. nationalism. It would consider not only New York's central role in shaping a national culture during the nineteenth century, but its simultaneous development (described in vivid detail in Mary P. Ryan's recent *Civic Wars*) as a "border city" with a polyglot, chaotically changing, and ambivalently assimilated society.

Perhaps the most important application of this dual frame of border/nation has to do with issues of canonicity. As I suggest in the closing pages of this book, the challenge posed by the changing demo-graphics of the United States is not so much to accommodate Latinos to an existing national tradition, but to reconfigure that tradition to acknowledge the continuous presence of Latinos within and around it. That presence—like the systematic eradication of indigenous peoples and cultures in the service of continental expansion—acts as a repressed national memory, but one that is well on its way to an uncanny return. Part of what has been repressed in the United States is its location within a hemisphere *also* known as America (or, to inflect it with an appropriate Spanishness, América), a name it has appropriated synechdochically unto itself. This imperial conflation of America with the United States operates both spatially—imagine the surgically isolated silhouette of the forty-eight contiguous states, indelibly imprinted into the minds of school-children—and temporally, as certain events are chosen over others to emblematize turning points in a shared national memory. The conven-tional landmarks of nineteenth-century history offer instructive exam-ples: the rise of Jacksonian individualism as the prominent expression of "national character"; the debates over sectionalism, slavery, and expan-sion that led to the Civil War; and the triumph of urban industrial cap-

italism toward the end of the century are widely taken as the key interpretive clusters through which political and social life are to be understood. They are crucial not only to historiographic debates about the
period, but to broader paradigms of contemporary literary history and
American identity as well.[17] We could, however, as readily focus on pivotal moments in the history of the United States as it belongs to the Americas and stage them in ways that are equally suggestive of significant
patterns in intellectual and cultural life: the origins of the Caribbean
slave-and-sugar trade at the beginning of the century; the Monroe Doctrine of 1823; the eastern demand for land that resulted in Texas's independence and, eventually, the U.S. invasion of Mexico in 1846; the
rampant filibustering in Central America and the Caribbean that began
in the 1850s, motivated both by the engine of territorial expansion and
by U.S. desires to control a transcontinental waterway; the systematic
disenfranchisement of formerly Mexican californios and tejanos of their
citizenship rights under the Treaty of Guadalupe-Hidalgo during the
1870s and 1880s; the uneasy standoff of the first Pan-American Congress
in 1889 and the U.S. interventions in Puerto Rico, Cuba, and Panama
that followed. Thus, the bulk of this study occupies itself with an alternative version of the "American Renaissance" of the late 1840s and
1850s, and sees the subsequent decades not through the lens of the Civil
War and Reconstruction but in terms of the development of U.S.
expansionism.

   This alternate set of emblematic moments in nineteenth-century
history both follows on and challenges another recent trend in literary
and cultural criticism: the argument that the development of canonical
U.S. literature cannot be separated from the climate of its transformation
into an imperial state. Modernist culture, according to this thesis, must
be read within the context of the push for global influence and colonial
counterstruggles unleashed in 1898.[18] However, as William Appleman
Williams points out, 1898 might be a convenient watershed for discussions of a U.S. empire—the point at which they spilled into daily discourse—but the history of U.S. interventionism begins with a small
military landing in what is now the Dominican Republic a full century
earlier.[19] Although "imperial" may be a problematic term, it is useful for
describing certain modes of relations, both political and cultural, that
developed in an uneven but recognizable way over the course of the
century as Manifest Destiny was transformed from slogan into reality and
as private and public institutions from the North increasingly sought to
constrict Latin American sovereignty. I begin this study in the 1820s,

despite the wealth of texts written in the colonial period in Latin America that might offer interesting comparison to works like Barlow's *Columbiad*, because it happens to coincide with several events of hemispheric significance. During 1823 alone, Iturbide's short-lived Mexican empire came to an end, lifting the crown off the eagle on the national flag and restoring the country to an unstable democratic rule; the reforms to colonial policy in the Caribbean that had been hopefully begun by liberal delegates to the Spanish Cortes were quashed, bringing Cuban hopes for self-government to an end; and Félix Varela, one of the key fashioners of Caribbean revolutionary thought, fled in exile to New York. Andrés Bello, the foundational Bolivarian poet and legislator, published in Caracas his *Gramática de la lengua española destinada al uso de los americanos*, a prescription for cultural and linguistic unity that would prove as influential as the grammar Nebrija published in 1492, the original imperial year. The year 1823 also marked the inception of the Monroe Doctrine. Whatever fraternal rhetoric may have marked Monroe's famous speech decrying European interference in the hemisphere, that protective claim was contorted, slightly more than two decades later, into a justification for President James K. Polk and congressional warmongers, both Whig and Democrat, to occupy Mexican territory on thin pretext. Entrepreneurial plans for a transatlantic passage were first activated during this decade as well: the Colombian government considered a request for a canal concession as early as 1821, while the U.S. Atlantic and Pacific Canal Company began plotting a Nicaraguan route in 1825. Recent studies like that of Fredrick Pike have demonstrated in detail the way judgments about the lack of "civilization" among Spanish Americans, anti-Catholicism, and racial stereotyping about Indians and mestizos migrated freely through nineteenth-century Anglo-American discourse from one hemispheric context to another, even when the places were as vastly different as the Mosquito Coast and Buenos Aires.[20] At the same time, however, these events did not unfold without significant protest from within the United States about its evolving tendency toward an imperial politics in the hemisphere, particularly in the early 1850s, when a concern over the sovereignty of other nations and their borders entered the consciousness of many writers, both prominent and obscure. That protest was largely caught up in, and to some extent muffled by, more immediate questions of abolition and separatism, but anti-imperial concerns returned in full force by the end of that century, when Mark Twain, for instance, mustered all his authority to denounce U.S. policy in the Philippines.

Just as these developments profoundly affected the formation of national culture in the United States, so too did they influence Latin

Americans. The key texts advocating cultural autonomy at the turn of the century—Darío's late political poems, Rodó's *Ariel*, and Martí's *Nuestra América*—make the recognition and rejection of this imperial power their core epiphany. For all the ways in which Latin America, as its intellectuals have pointed out for years, has suffered as the local testing ground of U.S. experiments with extranational power, its role in the past and future shaping of U.S. identity narratives remains disturbingly understudied and undertheorized. Given the increasing proportion and significance of Latinos to the nation's body politic—whether as assimilated citizens, as a largely invisible underclass, or as binational workers—this neglect seems even more irresponsible. The geographies of reception and influence that I pose here seek to stretch the silhouette of U.S. national identity—in both its spatial and temporal dimensions—out of recognizable shape, making way for a transnational historical framework that will accommodate the peculiar subject-position of Latinos from the nineteenth century to the twenty-first. My aim is to retrace the movements of texts, ideas, and politics across the map of an enlarged America and to consider the ways in which what happened outside U.S. borders on that map affected its development as a nation. Veering from the *Weltliteratur* path, I aim to be "comparative" in a way that explicitly respects the different political, social, and economic trajectories of the United States, the numerous nations of Latin America, and the regional bodies whose experiences may have been out of step with any of these national patterns.

Citizen, Ambassador: Stations of Literary Representation

A textual experience, for my purposes here, comes into being within a broadly conceived geography of America and within smaller, discrete social spheres as well: the fields of production and reception, the state's privileging of literacy, the cultural institutions that assign values to work based on judgments of taste and moral or political utility. What is the role of an individual writer or reader in these spatial matrices—and what does it mean to be an "author" in a distinctly transamerican sense? The transnational exchanges within print culture can, of course, be described through the movements and actions of persons as well as material objects like periodicals, books, or the translation of a particular poem. Sometimes the movement of an individual through America gets recorded as a travel narrative, with all the appropriative dangers that James Clifford,

Mary Louise Pratt, and others have associated with that form. One well-known example is Richard Henry Dana, whose *Two Years before the Mast* and *To Cuba and Back* shaped antebellum biases about the indolence of California Mexicans and Indians, and Cuban Spaniards and mulato and *negro* slaves, respectively. But the effects of personal contact with a geographically expanded sense of America can be seen in less obvious genres than the travel narrative. It becomes visible, for instance, in the poetry of former Bostonian Maria Gowen Brooks, who adopted Cuba as her home and renamed herself María del Occidente, a daring self-fashioning that allowed her to figure Cuba both as a precapitalist paradise of sensuality and as a liberatory space in which her erudition—dismissed and suspect in patriarchal New England—could find fuller expression. There are inverse cases of such Anglo-American appropriations too, in which the United States becomes the space that is experienced as exotic and strange. Guillermo Prieto, the prominent Mexican politician and writer, commingles lyric and travelogue in his *Viaje a los Estados Unidos por 'Fidel,'* which gains satiric punch through its deliberate undoings of American norms. In other cases, the individual encounter with an alternate American space occurs in a more mediated fashion—through an interlingual correspondence, a translation, or an imagined vision triggered by other books. Emily Dickinson's "Colors from Vera Cruz," Bret Harte's mock-Spanish *leyenda*, "Yerba Buena," and the Mexican poet Mercedes Salazar's ode to Panama (figured as a woman cinching the canal like a belt around her tiny waist) are only a few examples from the later nineteenth century of the poetic exoticizing of what one has never seen. A third kind of encounter applies to the residents of border regions in the United States: those who underwent involuntary shifts of citizenship after the war with Mexico, or those who consciously chose a new affiliation—like the former *mejicana* María Amparo Ruíz de Burton, an officer's wife in Washington, or the Cuban/Confederate poet José Agustín Quintero—but continued to grapple artistically with their primary identifications with that space of home.

Not surprisingly, the individuals whose acts of reading, writing, and publishing initiated the transamerican encounters that I discuss here resist simple characterization by nationality. Many were exiles, expatriates, im-/emigrants, or determined cosmopolites. Others seem, in a way, hypernational: iconic figures rendered representative of a country, celebrated in patriotic engravings and statues now superannuated, both aesthetically and ideologically. Many of these writers served in diplomatic posts, while others used their outreach beyond the community or region as its own kind of ambassadorship, mediating between local and global spheres of culture. During this period these two apparently distinct categories of affiliation, the national and the cosmopolitan, readily melt into air: "national" poets who rarely left their native region often indulged in the wish to be an exile, to be from elsewhere (Henry Wadsworth Longfellow is a prime example), whereas universalist cosmopolites, in turn, found themselves cast as necessary components of national canons and identities—sometimes apparently in defiance of logic (Andrés Bello, for instance, was virtually deified in Venezuela, although his birth there preceded its existence as a nation and he spent most of his life in England and Chile). Such apparent paradoxes of affiliation attest to a larger problem of Romantic nationalism in all its incarnations. Postrevolutionary writers who consciously worked to establish a national culture distinct from that of the colonial power were forced to acknowledge the inherent limitations of originality—the fact that most of their tools of analysis and expression were extranational rather than indigenous. The writers most aware of this paradox, most creative and conscientious in their responses to it, are often those who resist identification by nationality even though the nation itself may have developed a strong investment in them, as the example of Bello suggests.

Finally, then, writers can appear within the transnational sphere in a wholly imaginary but nonetheless powerful way, as ambassadorial icons of national cultures. The conditions of authorial celebrity created during this period are heavily informed by nationalistic desires, and when writers or works are identified as particularly "national"—a phenomenon that occurs frequently—they are made available as a kind of export product, one in which other young nations may take an intense interest. The cults of Longfellow, Cooper, and Stowe in nineteenth-century Latin America, or the cult of Neruda in the United States in the late twentieth, are examples of such exportation. Put differently, the question of what it means to be a cultural producer in a transnational context ultimately engages questions of political representation. The Romantic-era search for the national author whose writing would best represent "our" essential values and character (a process one also sees at work in the contemporary context of ethnic writers) sought to compress a complex web of meanings into a single icon of cultural mastery. What interests me here is not whether such well-known writers were indeed "representative" but how they performed the ceremonial rituals associated with that popular (and sometimes institutional) expectation. The problem of authorial representation is germane to forgotten, marginal, and local writers as well. In what ways do self-ordained poets who have achieved some minor fame claim to stand in for their readers, offering their lyric voice as exemplary? How are social, linguistic, or racial differences between author and reader suppressed—or heightened—by such a process of representation? These questions are particularly pressing with regard to the artistic pretensions and achievements of borderlands periodicals, in which the polarities of Spanish and English languages, of European and indigenous traditions, both attract and repel each other. What do we make of a mestizo in frontier Santa Barbara, California, adopting the pseudonym of Dantés (Dante) to publish his parodic yet admiring imitations of Euro-American high culture? Such an act seems to reinscribe existing hierarchies, yet it also poses a challenge to the very process of canonization and consecration.

Dantés, and thousands of virtually unknown writers like him, freely appropriated one of the existing roles of the cultural producer within the social field: the position of the Man of Letters, that legacy of the Enlightenment who claimed the ability to shape notions of taste in the service of collective moral ends. I use this category here in distinction to that of the intellectual, an oppositional figure who claims an autonomy for culture outside the influence of social and political power.[21] In Latin American literary criticism, Angel Rama has influentially argued that the important positions that the *letrado*, the administrative functionary, occupied during the colonial era left a strong imprint on national print cultures after independence; urban editors, reviewers, and figures who controlled writing continued to reflect a strongly conservative interest in the order of the state, even when their social leanings were liberal.[22] If the early United States lacked the same entrenched class of cultural gatekeepers (to the dismay of the aspiring writers in organs like the *North American Review*), the great publishing boom that began in the 1840s brought with it a great demand for a new class of writers and arbiters of writing, creating distinct "cultures of letters" located in the urban publishing centers of Boston, New York, Philadelphia, Chicago, and—with less visibility but equal importance—spread throughout Virginia, Ohio, and Louisiana.[23] Even the editor of a small local newspaper, however, creates a smaller version of this sphere of letters in relation, to which he stands as arbiter and ambassador. The possession of letters, in other words, is a form of capital not held exclusively *in* the capital. The Man of Letters (a position occasionally, but not frequently, occupied by women) validates his own authority through a tradition of taste and prestige understood to be the culturally dominant one, whose designated representative he declares himself to be and which he is constantly representing—explaining, interpreting, supporting—to readers who participate in it only partially. Alternately, however, he also stands in for his readership, representing interests, and values, their knowledge before the tribunal of Tradition. The first might be called a "top-down" model of cultural transmission; the second, a "bottom-up" model. Yet they can exist in more or less dialectical relation, as in the case of Gertrudis Gómez de Avellaneda, who made skillful use of the Spanish Bourbon court's fascination with its exotic colonies in order to sell herself as a uniquely Cuban writer—and then parlayed that Spanish stamp of approval into a level of prestige and popularity in Latin America completely unprecedented for a woman. The liberal agenda pursued by most of these cultural ambassadors was never intended to level social hierarchies but rather to redistribute the cultural capital of European-style high art by "Americanizing" it and by promoting institutional programs that would spread both basic and specialized literacies in the dominant national language. A more radical agenda—questioning and destabilizing that system of status and symbolic power itself—surfaces only rarely. The institutional status to which such individuals aspired is legible in the phrase "ministers of culture," one frequently used to describe influential critics, writers, and editors; the term conveys the same kind of implied didactic-moral responsibilities as a minister or priest would have for his flock. For instance, J. M. Gutiérrez, the first poetic anthologist of Latin America, closes his 1846 introduction to *América poética* with a description of the ideal poet and his audience. The poet is "sacerdote de las musas, cant[a] para las almas inocentes y puras" [priest of the Muses, he sings for pure and innocent souls]. More mundanely, however, he speaks to a specific readership in America consisting of "esa familia escogida de pensadores y de ciudadanos intachables" [that select family of thinkers and of irreproachable citizens]. Rufus Griswold's 1842 apostrophe to *The Poets and Poetry of America* likewise observes: "It is a gratifying fact that nearly every thing in the poetic manner produced in this country is free from licentiousness, and harmless, if not elevating in its tendencies. Thus far the distinguishing characteristic of American poetry is its moral purity."[24]

The collusion—both rhetorical and actual—between nineteenth-century letrados and institutions like church and state located more squarely within the field of power has generally been held against them. (This despite the fact that the presumed political affiliations of "patrons" and "patronized" are often misleading: populist Whitman enthusiastically backed the U.S. war on Mexico, whereas patrician Longfellow strongly opposed it.) Violently rejecting "compromised" art and embracing the fiction of the autonomous intellectual, various forms of poetic modernism in particular have gone to great lengths to bury the Man of Letters. Literary histories from the early twentieth century onward reflect this bias, which is often rhetorically cast as a rejection of the "feminized" poet-priest. Hence one of my concerns here is to trace not only the relative access of women to the sphere of literary ambassadorship, but the gendering of the category itself.[25] This eventual rejection of the authority of the letrado, which we have inherited, recalls the Protestant refusal of priestly mediation in favor of direct contact with God. To see through and beyond this rejection requires a certain suspension of judgment in favor of an analysis that would simply assess the representational abilities of the letrado in a given geographical and social context, testing the conditions under which his attempted moral mediation works or fails to work. Playing on the double meaning of "minister," I want to substitute a statist metaphor for a religious one and consider the Man of Letters as an ambassadorial role. An ambassador's authority comes about secondarily; it resides in the political authority s/he represents rather than being intrinsic to the ambassador's own self. To be an ambassador of culture involves reporting and representing, but not enforcing, the authority of that idealized realm of prestige knowledge in a place where it does not rule —whether in the hinterlands or in a cosmopolitan space where many value systems come together in chaotic plurality, as they did in American cities. The rhetoric of ambassadorship insists on literature's place within a public sphere, where definitions of citizenship, identity, and policy are debated. A number of the writers in this study held diplomatic posts, which was a common enough occupation for letrados in newly independent Spanish America. Rafael Pombo, whom I discuss in chapter 5, was a member of the Colombian diplomatic legation in New York and Washington during early negotiations over a transatlantic canal, all the while publishing poems and translations. In other instances, writers acted as distinguished visitors whose presence elicited strong feelings about the national culture they represented, as with Bryant's visit to Mexico in 1872.

Borrowing this term from the diplomatic sphere suggests the inherently interested, ideological nature of such transamerican exchanges. It is important to recall here that the cult of letters, and the institutions it supports, is strongly implicated in the European conquest of the indigenous Americas, as Walter Mignolo's *The Darker Side of the Renaissance* demonstrates exhaustively. Turning to the nineteenth century, Mary Pratt's study of travel literature's role in imperial conquest lists several roles associated with European contact with "new" geographies—the navigator, the conquistador, the scientific explorer-collector—and suggests that each was also an instrument in the service of the imperial age's hunger for raw materials to produce capital.[26] Like these vocational types, the American ambassador is inevitably caught up in the tendency to naturalize Euro-American (criollo) values, including the expansion of networks of capital (frequently, in Latin America, British or French ones). At the same time, however, the figures in this study were much more attuned to the political and cultural presence of the rest of the hemisphere than most of their compatriots, so to see the work of the cultural ambassador as no more than an ongoing complicity in imperial acts is to oversimplify the case. The very presence of an ambassador implies a prior act of mutual recognition. My opening example from Francis(co) Amy's bilingual teaching text—"without voice it is impossible to call for help"—indicates that translation and ambassadorship are closely related functions, as both mediate between linguistic and cultural systems. Both are also charged with making the voice of a particular polity (or author) heard when that voice would otherwise be mute before a foreign audience. Pombo's case poses a particularly convoluted circuit of ambassadorial representation: in "representing" Colombia to the United States, he also refracted that host nation to the audience back home through his translations of Longfellow and Bryant, so that the roles of poet and diplomat became hopelessly entangled. The ambassador's constant performance—the way he shifts from role to role and takes on different identities, the suggestive connections between public poetry and oratory—gestures at one of the generative contradictions of ambassadorship. The demands of the time put a premium on the hasty building of national identities, and the cultural ambassador obligingly sets out to represent the national body by codifying through metaphor and figurative language its cultural identity, its specificity. Yet the most significant measure of his success at doing so is external: only when audiences outside the national sphere recognize and applaud his construction of the national essence does it become, for him, truly valid. Translation is a measure of this external validation. Most of the letrados in this study made at least one attempt to translate poems by Heine, who expressed the German national spirit in a fashion thought to be exemplary and reproducible in other national contexts. The search for national writers in the early nineteenth century is always also a search for a Representative Man to take his place in the world pantheon—one thinks of the figurative plaster busts of "good gray poets" now forgotten—but this gesture is as cosmopolitan as it is national.

The spheres within which the cosmopolitan ambassador of culture moved—nationally distributed periodicals, urban publishing centers, influential universities and salons—might seem very remote from everyday practice on the American borderlands, where cultural expression was less literacy-based. But the structures of literary and moral value advanced by these self-appointed ministers were not monolithic; the farther one went from urban institutions of authority and validation, the more elastic and accessible the role of the "taste-maker" became. Editors on the border, as I suggested earlier, became small-scale ambassadors of culture, speaking to the local community on behalf of world culture at large and representing their readerships before that wider audience, scattering their own newspapers like seeds across the country and the globe. Ultimately, the choice to write poems, translations, or criticism of poems was, for writers situated on the peripheries of political and cultural influence, less an experiment in raw self-expression than a symbolic claim on larger forms of authority. Although the work of Gómez de Avellaneda, Bryant, Heredia, Longfellow, and others was (at least once) widely known whereas the work of local periodical poets remains as stubbornly obscure as it always was, popular memory and the academic canon have largely forgotten both bodies of poetry. By bringing these local ambassadors into dialogue here with the better-known Men of Letters on various national scenes, I hope to erase some of the stigma of derivativeness attached—to different ends and degrees—to both groups. For this is the final paradox of the citizen-ambassador: despite the stature that appears to accompany the ambassador's position, his is a peculiarly self-abnegating kind of authority, since it derives from a relationship of secondary representation. This may imply a kind of personal impotence or a vicarious relationship to experience—the image of the benevolent but naive poet locked in his study that Whitman and Martí savaged with such delight— or it may signal a kind of creative gift that is secondary, derivative. The taint on such secondariness has much to do with the American fetish of originality—a historically specific literary value and one to which I return in later pages.

The Transamerican Archive: Poetry as Daily Practice

My effort to reconstruct a portrait of these varyingly empowered ambassadors of culture, and the local and global communities they addressed, calls forth an archive that is large, eclectic, and by definition incomplete. It relies on material evidence such as records of book and periodical publishing and distribution; personal letters between readers and writers; reviews, editorials, and anthologizing practices to irradiate the lyric poems that are my primary focus. Given that my interest in this body of transamerican writing has to do with its ideological works, this choice of genre might seem odd: poetry on the whole has been largely neglected in recent historicist analyses of nineteenth-century literary culture, presumably because of its apparent removal from the daily life of readers and the political evolution of nations. Scholars are accustomed to think of lyric as at best opaque about, and at worst completely detached from, its informing contexts of collective identity and power.[27] Certain forms associated with public performance—such as patriotic odes, heroic elegies, and folkloric epics—more readily invite critique based on their political content, but the lyric "I" seems by definition to reject its access to a communal imaginary in favor of idiosyncratic experience. In the oral tradition, the first-person stance is either effaced or rendered generic and representative in the greater service of articulating a common tradition, as in the folk ballad; printed lyric, in contrast, vacillates between the extremes of complete idiosyncracy and the myopic assumption that its subject position is universal.[28] But if the gestures made within the lyric seem primarily individualistic, the field in which such works are written and disseminated is not. One innovative American comparatist, Roland Greene, speaks out against the post-Romantic assumption that "lyric poetry is personal by nature, and social or political only occasionally, indirectly, or at removes," arguing that because lyric is a "widely adaptable literary technology," it registers the events around it in a particularly nimble way.[29] Moving out from the colonial period of which Greene writes, I want here to place the genre within a historicized map of developing cultural tensions and affinities in postrevolutionary America without reducing it to the sum of these effects.

It is a commonplace that as late as the beginning of the nineteenth century, poetry reigned both as the prestige genre of high-cultural literary production and as one of the most familiar forms of expression in popular life—especially insofar as it intersected with hymnody and the ballads that were vestiges of an oral culture, "lyric" in its musical sense. It is just as widely agreed that by century's end, the novel came to supplant poetry in both spheres, the consecrated and the commodified.[30] This division of high and low cultures, as one might guess, is excessively schematic; readers during the period could and did make fine gradations between different kinds of poetry, their functions and aspirations. Given the high degree of mutual borrowings between the two supposedly distinct levels (the vogue of Romantic "balladry" among philologically trained writers, for instance), we could adapt for poetry Lawrence Levine's observation about Shakespearean drama: that for most of the century it occupied an inchoate place on the cultural hierarchy and was claimed by a whole range of audiences of varying tastes, until the rise of English Literature as a profession at the end of the century resacralized it as the sole possession of an educated elite. The polarization of the poetic field into an arcane "high" and a crassly commercial "low" would be finalized when modernist criticism severed any remaining links with the idea of the popular poet. Although we lack a comprehensive study of the global distribution of poetry along the lines that Franco Moretti provides for the European novel, if we accept Moretti's claim that market forces drive literary genres to seek symbolic hegemony by dominating a central locus of production and dooming writers on the periphery to underdevelopment and dependence, the lyric poem seems better positioned to resist such centralization.[31]

During the period when poetry occupied multiple locations in the cultural field, its historical connections with both folk and elite traditions were invoked in institutional projects to impose literacy in a dominant language as a condition of full citizenship. Zboray, like many other contemporary scholars of the history of literacy, traces a process through which "the printed word became the primary avenue of national enculturation": "Orality emphasized the local present. By contrast, type was well suited to the work of constructing a national identity; imprints simply endured unmodified beyond the exigencies of time and space. The same text could go everywhere and encourage (but not decree) a common reading experience. In their eminent transportability, the books, periodicals, and ephemera of the period differed little from other goods produced by the economic upsurge."[32] However, the functional literacy rate in the United States in 1850 was probably less than 60 percent of the population as a whole, despite census claims—much touted abroad—to a 95 percent rate.[33] The spread of literacy was also uneven in Latin American nations, which on the whole began to provide universal public education in the 1870s (earlier in Chile), though there is too much variation to generalize. Mexico's 1895 census showed a national basic literacy rate in Spanish of 14 percent, but it ranged from a high of 38 percent in Mexico City to lows of 6–7 percent in heavily multilingual, indigenous states like Chiapas, Oaxaca, and Guerrero. Nonetheless, of the six cities in the New

World with populations greater than 100,000 in 1825, four—Mexico City, Havana, Rio de Janeiro, and Bahia—were in Latin America, so the sheer numbers of readers and potential readers there is impressive.[34]

The concept of "transitional literacy" developed by medieval scholars influenced by Walter Ong provides a more useful way to codify the variable skills and needs of American reading communities of the nineteenth century. It assumes that "the conditions 'orality' and 'literacy' are the end points on a continuum through which the technology of writing affects and modifies human perception." When written texts are understood to reflect points along that continuum, rather than proof of writing's utter dominance, critical attention shifts from the conditions of authorship to "the ability of the reader and the function of the manu-script," along with "the conditions under which the physical text was received."[35] Joseph Roach's suggestion that we replace the worn distinc-tion between oral and written expression with a performative notion of "orature" (a term he borrows from the Kenyan novelist Ngugi wa Thiong'o) responds even more directly to the alliance of literacy with power, insisting that orality and literacy "have produced one another interactively over time." Orature describes constantly shifting ways of performing texts—written, memorized, and spontaneous alike: "in this improvisational behavioral space, memory reveals itself as imagination."[36] The portrait of reading as a direct, one-on-one encounter between a well-educated writer and an equally educated, leisured reader settled on a cozy sofa is merely the most widely mythologized among many possible scenes. Besides this fully equipped reader, we should imagine others who might fail to grasp every nuance of a text and the referential milieu in which it is embedded: native speakers who are still learning the written language through reading; children and nonnative speakers whose com-mand of even the oral language is limited; and people who are being read *to*, for whom the experience of listening to the written word evokes not only daily speech but the connotations of religious ritual or certain occa-sions of communal celebration in which they are accustomed to forming a listening audience. All these groups form part of the community of a text's interlocutors, and each brings to the experience a slightly different set of expectations and reading practices. Just as nineteenth-century peri-odicals passed through a number of hands, with the buyer sharing a single copy with multiple individuals, the words printed inside them passed through a number of minds.[37]

Conclusions about how a given reading public thought about poetry are usually drawn from contemporary criticism, in the form of manifestos, reviews, and introductions to anthologies like those of Gutiérrez and Griswold. Yet those works aimed to critique and reshape current practice, not to catalog it, so they give a limited portrait of what was actually thought and said about poetry—particularly since, with book purchasing out of reach to so many readers, much of it was distributed in periodicals ranging from self-consciously literary monthlies, to the middlebrow illustrated newsweeklies, to the thousands of general-circulation newspapers aimed at both national and local audiences. On the pages of a periodical, in particular, a poem is staged among competing articles, editorials, and other pieces, set against the noise of announcements and advertisements. The possibilities for transmitting poems under such a dynamic model are numerous: reading aloud between lovers or confidantes; inscribing and sharing albums of handwritten and printed poetry, a hobby particularly associated with young women; reading to the family circle; reading within the institutional setting of the schoolroom; reading to groups like the *sociedades literarias* in the New Orleans of the 1850s or the New York of the 1880s; and even, as the existence of cigar-factory *lectores* in south Florida at the turn of the century suggests, reading in the workplace.

The notions of transitional literacy, orature, and performance also call into question the commonly assumed division between the static individualism of the printed lyric, on one hand, and the performed collectivity of the oral ballad, on the other. Since not all the published poems that adapted skeletal forms from European high culture were equally "learned"—they called forth different levels of language skills and interpretive dexterity—we can place them not only along a scale of transitional literacies, but within a set of socioliterary practices that likewise ranges from popular to learned and from lightly to densely referential, with a good deal in between. They also flout the Romantic model of lyric poetry as a private, individual experience of communion, which prizes originality and the authentic voice of the individual to such a degree that it renders inaudible a whole chain of listeners and interlocutors. The critically validated way to read poetry may have involved acts of meditative contemplation, careful rereading and parsing, and finally aesthetic judgment, but nineteenth-century audiences could do many other things with a poem: read it once and toss it aside; copy or clip it into a scrapbook, album, or another newspaper; or commit it to memory. Of course most of the record of how people did read, or absorb what was read to them, is virtually invisible, except through reviews and in rare cases diaries.[38] However, the task of recovering a sense of poetic performance and interpretation is made somewhat easier by the conventionality of so much of this verse: the imitation, repetitiveness, and tendency toward cliché that render it uninteresting according to the critical standards prevalent in the academy for the last two centuries, but quite revealing about the shared values and assumptions that were naturalized as universal aesthetic and moral laws.[39] Formula, repetitiveness, and mnemonic tools like syllabification and rhyme recall printed lyric's primordial connection to oral traditions. Thus, the conventionality of many popular poems might be understood not as signs of their failure to meet the standards of consecrated artistic practice, but as features that allow a wide range of readers/auditors from different points on the literacy continuum to understand, enjoy, and repeat these verses.

This attunement to the conventional leads me to consider several lyrics that nearly any critic of the time would have dismissed as substandard. The task here is not to separate genuine poetry from doggerel, or the authentic compositional work of genius from "poetizing," but rather to discover what went into the making of those values and judgments, whether in the academy or at a powerful journal, around the family fireside or on the street. Popular judgments about poetic value were more overtly concerned with a poem's pragmatic effects than were those of the academy or the journal, but even learned observers found moral or political value in a popular vision of poetry as an elevated or ceremonial language by which communal feelings were commemorated, or personal feelings shared. They spoke of the functional quality of that language as well as its simple musicality. The interest in exhuming competing critical visions lies not so much in the details of controversies in poetics like the debate over the trochaic substitution, but in the way such arguments shaped national canons and pantheons. The regulations of form, like a prescriptive grammar, empowered an elite few to establish the conditions of value and the principles of exclusion and inclusion into the guild of poetic technicians. The ever-changing and variably enforced rules of poetic practice served, in other words, to control access to authorship, although in an era of uncontrolled growth in publications, such gatekeeping could never be absolute.

Vernacular Authorship, or the Imitator's Agency

This question of access—both to publication venues themselves and to the possibility of cultural consecration—is key to the consideration of agency for dispossessed writers and their communities. The exclusionary qualities that lyric poetry seems to have—that is, the rarified, costly form of cultural literacy required to master forms and references of a certain density—is counterbalanced by its democratic and equalizing aspects. Highly portable, readily translated and memorized, poetry was and is the genre through which an aspiring writer can most easily enter the literary field. Although studies of oral and folk tradition prize the nonprofessional, untutored creative spirit, when it comes to published work, the bias against poetic amateurism in print runs deep. Yet given its considerable capacity to attract nonprofessional writers, lyric poetry may be thought of as a vernacular genre. I use "vernacular" here not in the linguistic sense nor in the traditional literary one, in which a writer selectively adopts localisms and dialect speech for novel effect—Whitman's slangy repetition of "so long!," a term borrowed from New York street youths, or José Hernández's renditions of gaucho speech in *Martín Fierro*. Rather, I employ the term to shake off the negative connotations of "amateur" writing, suggesting instead a verbal analogue to vernacular architecture and similar forms of material artisanry.[40] Like the nonprofessional artisan, the vernacular poet works within conventional patterns in ways that are understood to be blunt and unrefined, for they are primarily created to be used by, and to give pleasure to, the family or community for whom they are made. Their works are not fully describable as "folk" practices, since the traces of ideas and aesthetic contests already in public circulation are readily visible in them (e.g., books of house blueprints inspiring country carpenters). Although rustic forms of language, like Whitman's or Hernández's, can be used in vernacular poetry, I mean the category to be broader, for such poems often deploy perfectly "proper" speech that is carefully wrought and even showily built, with features like baroque paraphrasis and elaborate rhymes—the equivalent of gingerbread cornices—boasting of the artist's dexterity. Vernacular authorship works according to different assumptions about composition and motive: its aim is not to outdo previous achievements or to establish new standards of taste, but to make a new impression from a known template. This view of the authorial vocation lies far from the Romantic/Bloomian notion of composition as the private, titanic struggle of genius with tradition. But it reflects the lived reality of the nonprofessional author: unlike fiction, poems could be written and revised in a matter of moments or hours. Since conventions of form and content are both a shorthand and a shortcut, imitation plays a far more central part in this kind of writing than does the desire to "make it new."

Insofar as the vernacular writer's imitative practice presumes a relationship of substitution, surrogacy, and vicarious claims to authority, it is similar to ambassadorship—and with that comparison, the gaping social divide between the spheres of national versus local influence, of the sanctioned versus the excluded, begins to dissolve. Although the ambassadorial arbiters of culture, steeped as they were in Romantic ideology, hardly thought of imitativeness as a poetic virtue, they were, as I mentioned earlier, profoundly interested in translation: Chapter 3 establishes that the relationships between North and South American letrados were often, owing to distance and the difficulties of travel, limited to exchanges of admiring letters and round-robin translations. In presenting a "foreign" text to their own linguistic community, however, they were engaged in a profoundly political act. Bryant, again, offers a telling example. Having set out for Spain as a representative of his own country, he returned to the United States with a sense of obligation to act as a cultural ambassador on behalf of Spain, informing a suspicious Anglo-American elite that both the culture and the empire were crucial to understand without prejudice. Rather than another translation, he offered a "rendition" of a Spanish poem written in what he took to be the communal lyric voice. He described the poem thus: "It is not 'from the Spanish' in the ordinary sense of the phrase [i.e., a translation], but is an attempt to put into poetic form sentiments and hopes, which the author frequently heard, during his visit to Spain, from the lips of the natives."[41] Bryant needs to insist that the voice is not his own but a borrowed one for which he is merely the mouthpiece; yet his ventriloquy implies an act of translation, since the broadly summarized Spanish "sentiments and hopes" the poem expresses have been quietly rendered into English. Bryant's "rendition" is at once an act of appropriation—claiming a voice that belongs to another—and a gesture of authorial self-effacement in the service of a hoped-for solidarity between Spain and the United States, to be brought about by the sheer force of his linguistic will. Less directly, the ambassadors of culture also rode the waves of a series of literary vogues in favor of one European poet or another—Byron, Heine, Dante, Hugo—during which translation was a necessary precursor to informed criticism. Translating poetry was widely regarded as a kind of apprenticeship to the vocation: a coming-of-age for younger poets yet to prove themselves, or a ritualized form of homage to an important influence. Struggling with a double burden of originality that stemmed from their intellectual moorings as Romantics and their political engagement as Americans, these writers' debates about rendition, paraphrase, and translation necessarily invoke deeper issues of originality and influence, imitation and license.

Although the trope of origins and originality is one of the hoariest in American studies both North and South, it offers a way to project the problem of imitation and secondariness onto specific geographies. These tensions of cultural authority with regard to Europe emerge again within the national context as an anxiety about controlling language and culture along its peripheries, in places far from the urban center, as we shall see. In this light, translation practices on the border become newly interesting in the way that they map hierarchies of language onto location. The Argentine critic Nelly Richard has proposed, with regard to the colonization of thought in Latin America, that the spatial nodes of center and periphery represent kinds of cultural authority as geographical locations: "Center and periphery sealed their historic relation of hierarchy and dependence in the dyad original/copy which the dogma of cultural colonization transcribes: the original as first and only meaning deposited in the center (the model); the copy as mimetic reproduction in subordinated language; the model as original whose value lies in the supremacy of the origin according to the foundational hierarchy."[42] The peripheral and marginal realm—for the purposes of this study, the vernacular writer lacking the means, language, racial or gender qualifications to gain access to symbolic power on a larger scale—inhabits a subordinated language; yet even the "central" figures who can claim such access as arbiters of culture are trapped within a relationship of secondariness.

Richard follows the lead of other critics of this colonial logic, urging that we undo its hierarchy of original and copy by locating texts from the periphery whose imitativeness cloaks an underlying, subversive act of parody. Certain instances of poetic imitation, then, may represent something more than "mimetic reproduction in subordinated language": imitation is not a relationship of simple dominance and submission, but rather involves a complex selection process of taking what is useful from the model being copied, and leaving the rest. If we are to take seriously the literary production of the disenfranchised, we must also take seriously their tendency toward imitation as something more than a sign of consenting domination to the forces of cultural hegemony. In listening so intently for a formally innovative and original voice, we deny the disenfranchised author one of the very things she had originally sought out: the kind of cultural authority that arises from similitude, from having effectively (or even ineffectively) identified oneself with language forms that signify power. My emphasis on the dynamics of performance with regard to the transmission of poetry among differently enabled "readers" is an attempt to show how particular texts and authors—that is, their currency as icons of cultural authority—were highly adaptable to the demands of varied audiences. The learned and the newly literate, the socially well positioned and the marginally working-class alike received poems and imitated, memorized, reread, rejected, rewrote, or otherwise appropriated them. We understand inadequately how the disenfranchised read culturally validated writers and works that did not "represent" them; yet the appropriation of the words of the powerful by the relatively powerless strikes me as an act that has inherent political interest.[43]

2

The Chain of American Circumstance
From Niagara to Cuba to Panama

> *Happy climate, I exclaimed, what a power dost thou possess*
> *of throwing a bright misty veil over every obtrusive recollection!*

—Dalcour, the French-Cuban planter, in María del
Occidente's *Idomen*

Meditations on Niagara: Transnational Pilgrims and the American Sublime

To virtually every observer in the early nineteenth century, Niagara Falls
encoded the very essence of the New World sublime, the difference inherent in American nature that allowed it to rival European civilization.
What the bison was to Jefferson's rebuke of Buffon, Niagara was to
American poets and painters—indigenous proof that the continent could
compensate for its lack of history with sheer dramatic force. The prolif-
eration of celebratory works about Niagara in the first half of the century
is nothing short of astonishing.[1] Yet this vision of Niagara begs a fundamental question about the boundaries of Americanness, for unlike other
natural sites that would come to be placed in the service of celebratory
nationalism (e.g., the Columbia River, the Rockies, and ultimately the
Grand Canyon), the splitting of the falls into Anglo-Canadian and Anglo-
American sides lends it more properly to use as an *inter*-American icon.
This symbolic potential is exemplified not only by the long history of

peace conferences and expositions pointedly located there, but also by the attraction of the place for foreign visitors with a pilgrim spirit. Latin American traveler-observers, in particular, seemed to feel a particular burden to put Niagara on the itinerary of even the shortest visits to the North, just as Yankee artists from Frederick Church to George Catlin would trek through the Andes to Mount Chimborazo, up the Amazon and the Orinoco, or through the spectacular volcanic ruins and tropical mountains of Mexico.[2]

Despite the hope during the early republican period that native subjects like the falls would inspire a truly original native literature, the great Niagara poem, it seemed, never did appear. In 1901, when a national canon was already well in place, one critic would attribute "the remarkable fact that the greater American poets have not attempted to describe Niagara" to the theory that "the greater the gift of expression . . . the more impotent *in its presence* the poets have felt." Indeed only Lydia Sigourney, among all the well-known U.S. poets of the period, wrote Niagara poems; the dozens of others listed in Charles Dow's definitive bibliography form a catalog of the obscure and forgotten, "a gentle warning to the too eager expression of words which so often hide rather than reveal thought."[3] So it seems ironic that some of the most prominent nineteenth-century poets of Latin America—including José María Heredia, Gertrudis Gómez de Avellaneda, Vicente Riva Palacio, Manuel Carpio, Rafael Pombo, Guillermo Prieto, Juan Antonio Pérez Bonalde, and José Martí—memorialized the "Niagara moment" in some significant way. Niagara's power to invoke New World commonality while suppressing its more blatant nationalist appropriations has an analogue in the psychodynamics of the genre: like other objects of contemplation experienced within the mode of the Burkean sublime, Niagara Falls provoked complex meditations on the veil of forgetting and the loss of language that, though on the surface antithetical to the raw patriotism behind the cult of American nature, form an important part of that cult.[4] These explorations of the limits of consciousness, prompted by Niagara's terrifying sense of proximity to death, generate fundamental questions of personal and poetic identity. To work the complexities of Niagara as an emblem of the central linguistic and cultural divide of America, I turn first to one of its most liminal figures: Maria Gowen Brooks, "María del Occidente," a Bostonian by birth and Cuban by choice.

Even among the dozens of forgettable poems about the "great Cataract," Brooks's "Stanzas to Niagara" have been shrouded in the same "bright misty veil" that surrounds her life and career in general. The poem was written sometime before 1843, when it appeared near the end of her autobiographical novel *Idomen*; it was also reprinted in a Niagara souvenir book and in Read's *Female Poets of America*. Here, and in the anthologies of her champion Rufus Griswold, she appears as a rarified creature of acknowledged learning but odd temperament. Following the conventions of American epic discourse, the "Stanzas" begin with an apostrophe to the Muse, seeking a classical blessing on the strange new world: she begs the "spirit of Homer" to "touch the fervid tongue / Of a fond votaress kneeling on the sod" near Niagara. The poet also invokes "Nature's God" in these opening lines, a deism reinforced at the end of the text when an angel—a kind of cosmopolitan traveler "who had been / O'er earth and heaven"—pronounces Niagara the "wonder of this western world, / And half the world beside!" This confident judgment repeats and legitimates the speaker's own earlier claims. Although it partakes of the full set of conventions governing the Niagara ode—the revelation of God in nature, the pride imparted to America by its grandeur, the deadly power of the falls and the humbling difficulty of describing it—the poem departs from them to offer instead a meditation on suicide. The speaker compares the changing rainbows of the waters to the brilliant colors of a dolphin in his death throes. This recollection is cut short by a tourist's excited observation ("Look, look!") as first a swan, then an eagle, lured by the calmness of Lake Niagara's waters too close to the "fatal brink," are swept into the rapids and perish. Seduced by the aesthetic power of this scene, the poet is tempted to follow them:

> Terrific—but, oh!—beautiful abyss!—
> If I should trust my fascinated eye,
> Or hearken to your maddening melody,
> Sense—form—would spring to meet your white foam's kiss,
> Be lapped in your soft rainbows once, and die.

What is imagined here is an erotic dissolution of individual consciousness into the welcoming "soft kiss" of the waves—a sentiment that would be difficult to find in the more conventional pieties of Sigourney's Niagara lyrics. The fantastical quality of the angel, the allegorically suggestive birds, and the oddly out-of-place dolphin that appear in this poem suggest that Brooks is wholly uninterested in the problem of realistic representation of the falls and is moving instead toward one of Poe's fantastical landscapes. But her footnotes to the poem dictate otherwise: she documents cases of eagles and swans being caught in the rapids in order to prove that her lines are true to naturalistic observation. Another note glosses the image of the dying dolphin's skin changing color, claiming that she has herself observed this on Caribbean voyages. The dolphin's hues color the ever-changing rainbows of the falls with a suggestion of death's seductive beauty—a train of associations that is furthered, in the novel, by the context of the passage in which the poem appears. Pressed by her guide to compose something to commemorate their voyage, the heroine presents him with this poem "tied with riband of pea-green and lilac—colours most predominant in the dolphin while dying, in agony to himself, but *in beauty and pleasure to those around him*—the colors of the Dolphin and of the Falls of Niagara."[5] This rather morbid keepsake suggests that the mysterious power of Niagara can best be portrayed with reference to the natural history of the Caribbean, which somehow conveys a more intimate acquaintance with death and beauty—the two are linked—than the suppressed tones of the North can express. It is a theme to which the poet would return again and again.

More than any other Anglo-American poet of the time, Maria Gowen Brooks saw herself as a poet of the New World. The early promise, domestic sufferings, and ultimate "Cubanization" of María del Occidente contain the makings of a melodramatic novel of the type that, later in the century, would bring other women writers the fame she openly coveted but never achieved. Van Wyck Brooks, in *The Flowering of New England*, compares her usefully to Longfellow in terms of her ambitions to write poetry that was both deeply cosmopolitan and responsive to the felt burden of American newness.[6] Born Abigail Gowen into a family of modest wealth and culture in 1794, she was reported to have memorized much of the Western canon, to be conversant in several languages, and to have composed her own verses by the age of nine. Like Margaret Fuller, she was intellectually indulged by a father who ran in Harvard circles; unlike Fuller, however, she lost that support when she was orphaned and, at fourteen, engaged to her guardian, a widowed merchant named John Brooks. Brooks, who had two children, married her as soon as she finished school. He was forty-nine, she was sixteen, and the marriage was not a happy one—particularly after Brooks lost his fortune in speculations related to the War of 1812. With two of her own children to support, Maria (she had legally changed her name in the first in a series of self-refashionings) published her first book, the woman-centered *Judith, Esther, and Other Poems*, in 1820 with the hope of making money, but her husband's death in 1823 brought a different kind of opportunity. An uncle who owned a coffee plantation near Matanzas invited her to relocate to Cuba, and not long afterward she inherited the plantation, raised her sons there, and cultivated her career. In an age that increasingly valued authorial personality, she took the pen name of María del Occidente and created a romantic self-image, retreating to a classical cupola in the garden and wearing gauzy white gowns of her own devising and passionflowers in her hair.[7]

When Brooks's first collection was published, she seemed well poised to capitalize on the vogue of "feminine" poetry that would bring attention and fame—though within conscripted limits—to figures like Sigourney, Elizabeth Oakes Smith, Elizabeth Ellett, Anne Lynch, and Frances Osgood during the 1830s and 1840s. Brooks, however, failed throughout her life to translate those abilities into sales and status despite a bold willingness to seek help from well-placed patrons. The first canto of the Orientalist epic Zóphiël, or the Bride of Seven, published in Boston in 1825, is prefaced with a lament about the difficulties women of "genius" have in finding the time to write and in getting their due as artists. Indeed, it took four more years for her to complete the manuscript, and another four to find a publisher for it. Robert Southey took an interest in the project and shepherded it to publication, praising it as "the most passionate and imaginative of any poem ever written by a female," while Rufus Griswold echoed the praises of London's Quarterly Review and Fraser's in an 1839 piece in the Southern Literary Messenger, where he characterizes her work as "a bijou in our American literature."[8] Despite such support from two of the most powerful critics on either side of the Atlantic, as one of her contemporaries recounted to biographer Zadel Barnes Gustafson, "It was all useless. The American people seemed to be joined in a conspiracy not to read 'Zóphiël.'" Brooks herself wrote to Griswold in 1843, "I do not think that any effort of my humble imagination can be 'too elevated' or even elevated enough for the better part of the public as it really is in these North American States, but I absolutely know, that my little works have been nearly suppressed by the vilest impositions which can possibly be practiced."[9]

Brooks's next production was Idomen; or, The Vale of Yumuri, serialized in the Boston Saturday Evening Gazette in 1838 and published in book form in 1843. Idomen is a prose romance set in Cuba and studded with descriptive details of the island's natural history, learned footnotes, meditations on the ethics of suicide, and short lyrics supposedly written by the title character, a doomed female genius whose life bears no small resemblance to Brooks's. Unhappily married too young but fortuitously widowed, Idomen leaves the United States for Cuba, where she blooms as woman and writer; she then follows her love to Canada, where she twice attempts suicide when that love goes awry. The novel weaves back and forth between these climatic extremes, juxtaposing passion with stoicism, tropical lushness with icy clarity. Brooks is interested in dramatizing the process of writerly creation as well; the Niagara scene near the end is significant because it marks the heroine's creative reawakening as she recovers from her suicide attempt and makes her way back to Cuba. Leaving the fairy-tale snows of Quebec where her fickle lover lived, Idomen is nearly unable to manage the seduction of death she feels at Niagara Falls, which endangers her "self-possession." Her ability to compose the poem suggests a potential integration of her northern and southern identities (the Canada/Cuba binary): Niagara is "the wonder of *half* a world," the western hemisphere. Yet only back in the tropics does her poetic gift finally flourish. Although dozens of accounts of Cuba by Anglo "health tourists" and would-be entrepreneurs appeared during the 1850s—including those by literary figures of some stature like Richard Henry Dana (*To Cuba and Back*, 1859), Julia Ward [Howe] (*A Trip to Cuba*, 1860), and N. P. Willis (*Health Trip to the Tropics*, 1853); and William Cullen Bryant's letters to the *Evening Post* describing his first Cuban adventure, collected in his *Letters of a Traveller; or, Notes of Things Seen in Europe and America* (1850)—*Idomen*, which is full of travelogue, was perhaps the first to make a serious descriptive effort. At the time of Brooks's death of a tropical fever in 1845, she had reportedly completed another epic, *Beatriz, the Beloved of Columbus*.[10]

The aestheticization of death that occurs in "Stanzas to Niagara" (with its dying dolphin sacrificed for the viewer's pleasure), alongside the Orientalist and Hebraic mythography of *Zóphiël*, aligns Brooks's poetry with a Byronic Romanticism never very popular in the United States but central to writers of the period in Spain and Latin America. Her attraction to the exotic marks her as tellingly out of step with most conceptions of a U.S. poetic tradition, as exceptional as Poe—who would himself become a pivotal influence, via Baudelaire, on Spanish *modernismo*; and a more important poetic progenitor outside the United States than in it.[11] Whereas Poe's imagination of the rest of the hemisphere narrowed into the vaguely Patagonian landscape with which he ends *The Narrative of Arthur Gordon Pym*, María del Occidente and her genius heroine insist on an understanding of the American sublime that superimposes Niagara and the Caribbean on each other. This is the trajectory, too, of a far better-known poet who followed her path, in reverse, at around the same period: the Cuban-born José María Heredia y Heredia, called by Martí and others "el primer poeta de América" largely on the grounds of his ode to Niagara.[12]

Martí's celebration of that poem, in a famous speech delivered in New York in 1888, defines "America" in a similarly transnational way—perhaps intentionally, for an English translation of Heredia's "Niágara" had a fairly wide circulation in the United States through the efforts of William Cullen Bryant, who had also called it "the best which has been written about the Great American Cataract."[13] The translation, which was generally attributed to Bryant and on which he at least collaborated, appeared in the *United States Review and Literary Gazette*, the quarterly that Bryant coedited from 1826 to 1827 before he abandoned Boston for New York and mainstream journalism at the helm of the *Evening Post*. The translation was probably better known than any other Spanish American poem: it appeared in various anthologies and textbooks, including John Pierpont's *National Reader* from 1827 to 1836 and a number of Niagara souvenir books.[14] Bryant later translated "The Hurricane" and published it in 1828 in the annual *Talisman*, edited by an anonymous coalition of prominent New Yorkers including Bryant himself. Since Bryant also contributed a number of his own poems and one of his few prose fictions, "A Story of the Island of Cuba," to the *Talisman*, the translation was often misattributed as an original poem of his own composition.

Bryant's interest in Spanish-language literature and in the history and culture of Spanish Florida, Mexico, and Cuba, sustained over decades but most intense during his early career, has helped fuel the notion that Bryant and Heredia—although they never met—led in some sense parallel lives. They each chafed under the influence of a powerful, conservative father (a Federalist for Bryant, a criollo loyalist for Heredia) and had an adolescent conversion experience to revolutionary Romanticism; both wrote most of their famous poems before the age of twenty-five; and both translated numerous canonical works from the other's Old World tradition. Bryant briefly lived with a Spanish family in New York, socialized in their musical and artistic circles, and later took Spanish lessons with his wife and daughter from the famous writer and phrenologist Mariano Cubí y Soler.[15] Altogether he translated about twenty poems from Spanish. He had a keen interest in liberatory struggles elsewhere in the hemisphere and wrote several minor poems about them ("El 2 de mayo," "The Damsel of Peru," "Lament of Romero") as well as editorials in the *Post*. Although Latin America was only one of his political interests and Spanish one of his five languages, he maintained stronger emotional and cultural ties there than any of his peers, visiting Cuba in 1849 and again in 1872 on his way to Mexico.[16] Both became pioneering figures in a national literary culture. Bryant, who forged the *Post* into the most influential liberal newspaper in the country, epitomized the politicized man of letters in midcentury New York City—not coincidentally, the first important site of Spanish-speaking print culture and exile politics in the United States Heredia founded a short-lived Spanish paper, *El Habanero*, as soon as he arrived in Philadelphia, and after relocating to Mexico from New York started three significant journals there—*El Iris, Miscelánea*— and *Minerva*, becoming "the progenitor of Mexican print culture."[17] Both advocated the rights of workers, opposed slavery, and spoke out against ethnic particularism, supporting cosmopolitan values by publishing their correspondence from abroad in newspapers and by publicizing works of global literature. After entering public life, both men wrote fewer, and less interventionist, poems. Following his early death in 1839, Heredia too was transformed into a transnational subject, ritually invoked as a symbol of Cuban-Mexican commonality.

Thus each member of the Brooks/Heredia/Bryant trinity enacts a particular kind of hemispheric imaginary, processing their notions of the American sublime in a way that evades simple North/South dyads. Brooks juxtaposes the pastoral scenes of Canada, Cuba, and New England; Heredia, the urban spaces of Matanzas and Havana, Philadelphia and New York, Toluca and Mexico City; and Bryant, the publishing centers of Boston and New York, Mexico City, and Havana. These itineraries of the circulation of texts and persons were closely bound to material and political developments—as routes of trade and labor, as sites of corporate and geopolitical desire. The possibility of annexing or "acquiring" Cuba, first expressed by Jefferson, was still an open question in 1823 and would remain so for decades. The rhetoric of the natural sublime, whether originating at Niagara, the Andean heights, or the Amazonian jungle, also fed efforts to convert nature into a commodity; from 1820 to the mid-1840s, the first phase of relations between the postindependence American republics, the key hemispheric markets in sugar, coffee, cacao, fruit, and guano were opened.[18] Although the development of inter-American trade and its particular methods of corporatizing agriculture, land, and labor are not my primary areas of focus here, they underlie the events that shape each poet's imagined geography and the values with which that geography gets inflected. Those political currents include, most importantly, U.S. expansionism toward the West and the southeastern seas; Spanish protectionism against French and

British interests in the Caribbean; the growth of abolitionist movements in the United States and Cuba; the Mexican struggle to consolidate its far-flung republic after proclaiming independence in 1821, which resulted in rebellions all along its northern borderlands and in the Yucatán; and the beginnings of efforts to build a transoceanic passage either through Colombia's Panamanian extension, by linking Lake Nicaragua with the Pacific, or through one of several routes in Mexico. Governing this shifting set of events was a series of increasingly interested (if not openly imperial) interpretations of the Monroe Doctrine, part of a presidential speech delivered in 1823—the same year in which Heredia arrived in Boston on the first leg of his triangulated exile, and in which Maria Gowen Brooks first sailed for Cuba. By the time expansionism came to dominate U.S. politics in the mid-1840s, the polar extremes of Cuba, Niagara, and western Mexico represented to many the endpoints of a projected "Empire of Democracy," as Whitman would later describe it. The transamerican sense of space that Brooks, Heredia, and Bryant helped shape was thus not synchronic: it played into a whole set of desires, many of them contradictory, about the direction of the American future, and their works were inevitably interpreted in the context of those desires.

But the temporality of transamerican space could gesture importantly backward as well. The three poets participated intently in their age's fascination with a pre-Columbian past, and integrated those nationalistic anxieties into their conceptions of the American sublime. Heredia's "Las sombras" [The Shades], "En un teocalli de Cholula" [In a Temple Pyramid of Cholula], and Bryant's "The Prairies" summon a lost, but partially recoverable, indigenous culture out of the landscape. Although Brooks's *Beatriz, the Beloved of Columbus* is lost, the subject suggests a similar romanticizing of the Cuban past: the island claimed to have been the site of Columbus's first landfall and boasted that his remains were in the Havana cathedral. Despite the forward-looking rhetorics of post-revolutionary American nations in the 1820s through 1840s, then, the American sublime that lent itself to effusions of national pride was also fraught with connotations of mourning, grief, and racial guilt. Pondering the sublimity of the vast, "new" landscape almost inevitably led poets of the Americas to contemplate death, often by way of elegizing the pre-Columbian Indian past—as *Jicoténcal*, a historical novel published in Philadelphia in 1826, would do as well. Although the subject of early national treatments of indigenous persons and legends is too vast to treat here in full, I want to touch on the aspect that posits the natural sublime as a suppressive force, as a rationale for collective forgetting. As numerous recent critics have suggested, the gesture at hermetically sealing the indigenous world in the past is closely allied with racialized efforts to contain the threat of Indian sovereignty.[19] But sublime repression is also allied with an even more pressing social issue for the American nations: the future disposition of African slaves and of indigenous American peoples, and of the institutions that bound them, which haunts these three writers in different ways.

The Cuban Star over New York: Heredia's Translated Nationhood

José María Heredia was, like Brooks and Bryant, a prodigy. At the age of sixteen, while studying law in Mexico City, he composed "En un teocalli de Cholula," a long meditation still considered one of his greatest works. Returning to Havana the following year, he started his own journal, *Biblioteca de Damas*, and befriended Domingo del Monte, who would become one of the most important intellectual figures in Cuba. Inspired by struggles in Greece and South America, he and del Monte joined a secret revolutionary society, the Suns and Rays of Bolívar. One of his first poems to be published, "Oda a las habitantes de Anáhuac," appeared in an album celebrating Mexican independence printed in Philadelphia; it endorses Bolívar's earliest vision of a federation of Spanish American states.[20] While living in Matanzas with his family and boldly circulating incendiary poems with titles like "La estrella de Cuba" [The Cuban Star], he was denounced as a conspirator against the colonial government, and in late 1823 he fled the island aboard the brigantine *Galaxy*, bound for Boston and what would become a lifelong exile. He was about to turn twenty. Generations of Cuban exiles have identified strongly with the lines he wrote in New York, in "A Emilia":

Tan sólo escucha de extranjero idioma	*[He hears only the barbarous sounds*
los bárbaros sonidos: pero al menos	*of a strange language: but at least*
no lo fatiga del tirano infame	*he isn't dogged by the insolent noise*
el clamor insolente, ni el gemido	*of the infamous tyrant, or the moan*

del esclavo infeliz, ni del azote	*of the unhappy slave, nor the crack*
el crujir execrable, que emponzoñan	*of the awful whip, which poison*
la atmósfera de Cuba. ¡Patria mía,	*the atmosphere of Cuba. My country,*
Idolatrada patria!	*my idolized country!]*[21]

Settling soon afterward in the Hispanophone community of New York, he taught Spanish to make a living and associated with *independentistas* like José Antonio Miralla and Padre Félix Varela, who had also fled Cuba in exile and was a foundational figure in the Spanish-language press in the United States for the next thirty years.[22] He penned "Niágara" on a June trip upstate in 1824. The colonial government condemned him, in absentia, to permanent exile, moving him to write more inflammatory verses urging Cuban independence, which were published in book form in 1825 by Behr and Kahl and distributed from New York as far as Mexico and Colombia. Later that year, complaining that his fragile health was compromised by northern winters, Heredia left New York for Mexico; his "Vuelta al sur" [Return to the South] celebrates his return to the tropical zone. (Ironically, the city of Toluca, where he would make his home, is situated at a high elevation and he also suffered frigid winters there.) Settling into a busy and highly visible political and cultural sphere in central Mexico, Heredia began his three literary periodicals and edited various daily newspapers; founded an institute of arts and sciences; staged dramas about imperial Rome that made thinly veiled reference to the Spanish "Caesar" in Cuba; married into a prominent Mexican family; and was elected to the Mexican legislature only to have his election challenged on the basis of his questionable citizenship. He was initially a friend to Santa Anna, but later a critic of his autocratic ways. In 1836, disillusioned by Mexican political instability and ill with tuberculosis, he humbled himself before Cuban captain-general Miguel Tacón, renouncing his early proindependence activities and asking to visit his mother after thirteen years of separation. He was granted a stay of three months, during which time he was pointedly snubbed by the island's reformists, including his old friend del Monte, who tarred him as a "fallen angel" for renouncing his earlier beliefs. On his return he took over the literary section of the *Diario del Gobierno de la República Mexicana* but was forced to give it up for his health. He died in 1839, at the age of thirty-five.[23]

Heredia's "Niágara," which was widely admired and has held its place in the canon, both disproves the Anglocentric claim that there has been no great Niagara poem and illustrates why U.S. audiences were unable to accept it as such despite Bryant's accolades. Like Brooks's ode, it pays due homage to the Niagara conventions: the overpowering contrast between the serene surface of the river and the treacherous falls; the felt proximity of death; and the dwindling of Man next to such vast natural forces, which suggest the presence of a God. But unlike Sigourney's or Brainard's Niagara poems, Heredia's work allows the subject of nature's nation to set off a more abstract mediation on his own consciousness and the way it was shaped by nationality. The speaker begins from a damaged position; the muse he invokes in the first lines has not visited him in some time.[24] But the sight of Niagara's "sublime terror" prompts a sudden recovery of that lost inspiration, and the next stanza reaffirms our sense that the wounded self is the real subject of the ode: "Yo digno soy de contemplarte" [I am worthy to contemplate you], he says, because he has always eschewed the mundane in favor of "lo terrífico y sublime" [the terrifying and sublime]. As proof, he recounts a previous encounter with the sublime that seems to offer the closest analogy to the Niagara experience: a tropical storm on the ocean, during which "amé el peligro" [I courted danger], thrilling to the excitement of the waves that tossed his small boat in the air over a yawning vortex below. Not even that hurricane, he continues, could provide the rhetorical apparatus to describe Niagara—the terrible din, the nauseating depth of its abyss, the dizzying speed with which water dashes against rocks.[25] In the third stanza, Heredia's attempt to describe the undescribable turns to compare the thousands upon thousands of waves that pass over the rapids to the din of his own mind. The force of Niagara confounds and confuses thought itself.

Heredia takes what might be a standard scene of the Anglo-Germanic sublime and Americanizes it, revisiting the Caribbean comparison of the hurricane in the fifth stanza with a reflection on his own act of perceiving: "Mas ¿qué en ti busca mi anhelante vista / Con inútil afán? ¿Por qué no miro / Alrededor de tu caverna inmensa / Las palmas ¡ay! las palmas deliciosas" [But what does my longing eye seek / With pointless eagerness? Why don't I see / Surrounding your immense cavern / The palm trees, Oh! the delightful palms]. Like one who sees the face of his beloved in every mountain pass, the speaker's perception is affected by preexisting conditions—in this case, his exile, which burnishes the memory of a previous landscape into the scene before him and inscribes Cuba onto Niagara. A standard move in sublime poetics—the poet confronting the limits of his own ability to speak—is here given a specifically political origin. The recollection of a palm tree sets off a whole series of contrasts between North America and the Caribbean: the native "rustic pine" suits Niagara's "terrible majesty," while the royal palm, myrtle, and "delicate rose" seem frivolous in comparison, inspiring only "mezquino deleite" [petty pleasures]. This contrast of sublime and picturesque initially seems puzzling, since it appears to denigrate the same Cuban flora that represent all that the exile claims to miss so terribly. But he explains the reason: an experience with the Niagaran sublime creates "el alma libre, generosa, fuerte" [the free, generous, strong soul]. "En otros climas" [in other climes], such picturesque pleasures have attracted "execrable monsters" who do not believe in the God who manifests himself in the sublime. The list of their crimes begins with impiety, but it does not end there; because of them, the natural beauties of Cuba itself are endangered:

Los campos inundar en sangre y llanto,	*[To drench the fields in blood and tears,*
De hermanos atizar la infanda guerra,	*To provoke brothers into an awful war,*
Y desolar frenéticos la tierra.	*To frenetically desert the land.]*

With the desolation of the picturesque landscape of home so complete, a bit of sublime transcendence is in order: "Por eso te buscó mi debil mente / En la sublime soledad" [So my weakened mind sought you out / In the sublime solitude. The crisis of wordlessness signaled at the beginning of the poem has been solved by a confrontation with the prospect of self-immolation, through the painful recollection of scenes previously repressed. The movement here prefigures and inspires Neruda's *Alturas de Macchu Picchu* (1948) in its meditation on political and personal healing through the sublime.

"Niágara" constructs a delicate pyramid of analogies between nature and consciousness, between theology, language, and politics, so when it moves on in the penultimate stanza to introduce another topic—the loss of love—it seems to risk excess. "Nunca tanto sentí como este día / Mi soledad y mísero abandono / y lamentable desamor . . . ¿Podría / En edad borrascosa / Sin amor ser feliz?" [I never felt as I do today / My solitude, my miserable abandonment / My lamentable coldheartedness. . . . Can one / In a stormy age, / Be happy without love?]. The speaker fantasizes about the imaginary woman who could end his solitude, thinking that her beauty would be enhanced by her terror at seeing the falls (which would presumably strengthen her character and insulate her from the temptations of the picturesque, making her a fit companion). But the "delirio" of this erotic daydream inevitably leads back to the all-permeating Caribbean consciousness: "¡Ay! Desterrado, / Sin patria, sin amores, / Sólo miro ante mí llanto y dolores!" [Oh! Exile, / without a country, without love, / I see before me only weeping and pain!]. As one of the few rhymes in this torrent of free *endecasílabo* lines, this couplet stands out. By equating the lack of love with absence from the homeland, Heredia inaugurates a thematics of eroticized nationalism, of *poesía civil interna*, that anchors a distinct tradition of Latin American poetry to come.[26]

In the end, then, "Niágara" is just as concerned with describing the condition of Cuban exile as it is with its ostensible natural subject. Yet it takes the sight of the great falls, its unfamiliar flora and foreign terrain, to liberate the muse and unleash his repressed consciousness of his own desolation, which is in turn an analogy for the current spiritual and political impoverishment of the island. The speaker "needs" the northern setting to invoke the inspirational terror of the sublime, but he also needs its emptiness in order to realize through contrast the two things he lacks: Cuba and love, which together mean home. This consciousness comes at a price; it provokes a dark brooding about death and the impermanence of poetic memory in the final lines, and as in Brooks's lyric, there is a trace of suicidal fascination with going over the brink.[27] But if "Niagara" is mainly a mirror in which the lost homeland is reflected, does that make this poem simply an inverted case of the imperialistic travel tale, written *about* a place without being *of* it? What place, in short, does North America have in Heredia's poetics?

Heredia's first impressions on entering Cape Cod in November 1823 suggest that he experienced the United States as the same kind of utter void as Poe's southern "whitescape" in *Pym*:

> Vi con horror lo que es invierno. Un río estaba ya helado. Todo el campo parecía consumido por un incendio reciente. No se ven ni un hombre, ni un animal, ni un insecto. . . . Creía que me hallaba con Milton en la inmensa soledad donde se alza el trono de la muerte. Sin duda este funesto cuadro resfrió mucho el entusiasmo con que saludé la tierra de libertad en que se abre un asilo inmenso a todos los oprimidos de la tierra. . . . Acabaré esta carta y me pondré a revolver periódicos de que no

entiendo una sílaba. A no ser por la observación curiosa del traje y modo de estas gentes, me devoraría el tedio en este aislamiento absoluto.

[I saw with horror what winter is. A river was already frozen. The whole countryside seemed as if consumed by a recent fire. Not a person, not an animal, not an insect was to be seen. . . . I felt that I'd found myself with Milton in the immense solitude where the throne of Death sits. Doubtless this depressing picture greatly chilled the enthusiasm with which I greeted the land of freedom, which offers asylum to all the oppressed of the world. . . . I'll finish this letter and set myself to looking at newspapers I don't understand a single syllable of. If it weren't for my curious observation of the clothes and manners of these people, I would be eaten up with boredom in this utter isolation.][28]

By the time he undertook the Niagara voyage, though, Heredia saw the U.S. landscape and language not as an absence but as a presence. As a language instructor and translator, he styled himself an ambassador of Hispanophone culture for the Anglophone world, prefacing the 1825 New York edition of his *Poesías* with notes for English speakers on the correct pronunciation of Spanish as well as a bilingual introduction. He also published a Spanish translation of Daniel Webster's oration on the battle of Bunker Hill, adding a specific paragraph about its potential lessons for Spanish American patriots.[29] When Heredia moved to Mexico, he repeated this mediation in the opposite direction, publishing his own translations of Tytler's multivolume *Lessons of Universal History* and Scott's *Waverley*. As an editor, he advocated a cosmopolitan and left-Romantic agenda, arguing that doses of Byron and Rousseau, Campbell and Moore would stabilize Mexico's bumpy democracy with enlightened republicanism. Knowing English was a necessary component to such a progressive sensibility: in an essay defending Byron's politico-poetic engagement while condemning his "moral failings," Heredia suggests that when English, "idioma de hombres libres" [the language of free men], is as well known in the new American nations as French, their literary sensibility will greatly improve. He apparently kept up on northern publications in both Spanish and English, as his reviews of Philadelphia imprints indicate.[30] As the intermediate leg of his triangulated sense of the possibilities of nationhood, Heredia's experience of the United States evolved from a simple opposition between the frigid North and the passionate tropics.

None of Heredia's prose writings about the United States were available to English readers, though they might have been as salutary as de Tocqueville's or Dickens's; a handful of his poems, however, were.[31] The version of "Niágara" that appeared in the *United States Review* is suggestive about what U.S. readers were prepared to accept from the other America. Bryant admitted in a letter that "The translation from Heredia is not *wholly* made by myself and therefore I have not felt justified in putting my name to it."[32] Nonetheless, for years the translation was attributed to Bryant, and even included in some editions of his collected poems, so I want to consider the collaborative translation not as an authorial product but as a cultural performance, a transaction of a poem coded as both foreign and familiar. The translation is weaker than Bryant's "Hurricane" in terms of linguistic accuracy; there are errors in both literal and figurative meanings, and unexplained excisions. But simply to call it flawed is to miss the point that it reveals more about the host culture than about the original. The most glaring loss that occurs in the transformation of "Niágara" into "Niagara" has to do, strangely enough, with the poem's relation to an American sublime aesthetic that was, as we have seen, a common reference point among U.S. artists and critics. The English version throughout avoids the word "sublime," which appears three times in the original; this absence is even more striking given that it is a translator's dream word—a perfect bilingual homonym. Indeed, the English avoids the very concept of the Longinan/Burkean sublime. Heredia's invocation of "lo terrífico y sublime" is reduced, somewhat bathetically and euphemistically, to "Nature in her loftier moods." A line in the early recollection of being drenched at sea by a storm, "palpitando gocé" [trembling, I felt joy], meant to demonstrate the speaker's dark affinity for deadly close encounters with nature and therefore his worthiness to approach Niagara, becomes the sunny cliché "I have been touched with joy."

On the whole, the translation chooses overwrought exclamations over Heredia's carefully controlled bursts of alternating emotion and restraint. The English version opens, for instance, with "My lyre! Give me my lyre!" (a line that calls to mind a bad declamation of *Richard III*) for the significantly less hysterical "Templad mi lira, dádmela" [Tune up my lyre; give it to me]. Throughout, the English uses more exclamation points than strictly called for. It goes Wordsworthian without leave: the speaker of the translation says he has been intrigued by nature "from my early boyhood," a reference completely absent from Heredia's simple "siempre," forever. More damning is the sapping of the center of the original's vital energy—the loss of the Cuban homeland, and specifically the chaotic, potentially bloody political scene that keeps it off limits. (Perhaps in this leeching of the political, too, the translators unwittingly recall the later Wordsworth.) This process begins in the first stanza, where the force that has robbed the speaker of his will to create poetry, "la mano impía" [the impious hand], a vague but suggestive reference to some external authority like the colonial court that sentenced him to exile, is rendered merely as "sorrow." Lines 78–80, which lambast the "execrable monsters" who have drenched the fields of Cuba in bloody warfare—an unfortunately prescient vision of the Ten Years' War—are excised entirely in the most glaring of the transmission's several small omissions.

This apparent effort to sublimate the sublime, as it were, and in general to depoliticize the poem may help explain one of the translator's more puzzling choices: to use "mind" consistently for "alma" rather than "soul" or even "spirit," since the latter terms would, presumably, have been not only more accurate but more intelligible within the popular sentimental vein of Anglo-American poetry to which the translation otherwise gestures. This choice has particular consequences in line 70— which, as I suggested earlier, marks a key turn in the poem, rationalizing the sublime terror of the falls through its contrast to the deceptively picturesque pleasures of the Caribbean. This is where Heredia makes his exhortation for free, strong souls to stand up against petty tyrants; the translation renders "el alma libre, generosa, fuerte" as "generous minds," which next to the liberatory ring of "el alma *libre*" has all the force of a sparrow's wingbeat. The final toning-down of the original occurs with the civic-erotic vision of the penultimate stanza. The English version envisions the woman chastely "clinging to my side" rather than "sostenerla [en] mis amantes brazos" [holding her in my loving arms]; more importantly, it moves away from the sense of living in a difficult historical moment that prompted this vision. The line "¿Podría / En edad borrascosa / Sin amor ser feliz?" is rendered "Alas! / How can the impassioned, the unfrozen heart / Be happy without love?" and the reference to the current uncertain, stormy era disappears. Although the translation astutely recalls the quality of frozen speechlessness with which the poem begins, and hints that the writing of the poem represents an emotional and artistic thawing-out, it does so at the expense of the haunting of history and the ideal of revolution.

To North American readers, Heredia's juxtaposition of the palm and pine, his turn from the immediate scene of Niagara to the remembered scene of Cuba, must have seemed puzzlingly digressive; some editors (Francisco Amy, for instance) trimmed these stanzas even further. The revolving door of successive analogies in "Niágara," the constant moving from art to religion to nature to homeland and love, probably struck genteel audiences as not only excessive but unfashionably pessimistic.[33] It is tempting to draw the conclusion that this translation marks the beginning of a particularly bad habit on the part of U.S. readers of Latin American texts—of failing to see how the erotic and domestic realms are deeply imbricated in the political. Yet at the same time, Heredia's effortless shift from the sublime landscape to the eroticized patria and the resulting desire to share both with a soulmate strongly anticipates Whitman, and reminds us what it was about Whitman that reached such a receptive audience in Latin America. Bryant's judgment that the poem was the best that had been written "about" Niagara Falls is—like the translation itself—a kind of friendly suppression, tailoring the content selectively to better suit an audience either uninterested in or unable to imagine the full ramifications of its message.

Yet the tendency to read "Niágara" selectively is not limited to U.S. audiences, for nearly two centuries of Cuban readers have downplayed its scientifically informed treatment of a specific northern landscape in order to magnify its Cuban content.[34] His poems are said to be the source, for instance, of the star on the national flag (from "La estrella de Cuba"); the royal palm tree on the national shield (from the "palmas deliciosas" in "Niágara"); and the slogan "Morir por la patria es vivir" [To die for the homeland is to live]. But Heredia was also a profoundly transnational subject, who spent relatively few years in Cuba itself. Even as a child, his parents—who themselves had fled to Cuba from Santo Domingo during the Haitian revolutions—took him from one bureaucratic outpost to another in Florida and Venezuela, tracing out a path in the trans-Caribbean world whose circuit he would complete with his passage through the North American ports and through Veracruz, Mexico's opening to the Caribbean. As a journalist and public figure in later life, Heredia would become the first of many Cubans to play an important role in Mexican history (I discuss another, Pedro Santacilia, in chapter 4). His prospectus for *El Iris* makes plain the magazine's larger Americanist aspirations: "pondremos en común de nuestros lectores en estado de apreciar los progresos y la marcha de las letras en Europa y América. Es inútil decir que las producciones americanas atraerán de preferencia nuestra atención" [We will make all our readers reach a common state of appreciation for the advances and progress of letters in Europe and

America. It hardly needs to be said that American productions will attract our preferential attention].[35] It thus seems appropriate that his poems focus as much on oceans as they do on bordered lands, and that his most unequivocal statements on Cuban identity were written aboard ship. Heredia's life offered testimony to a world of transamerican connections and potentials as they developed and receded; he developed them within a governing belief that this New World was matched to a democratic ideology, a destinarianism that was alternately hopeful and pessimistic. Increasingly, his attention—like Bryant's—was drawn away from the poetics of the sublime landscape and toward the indigenous past so prominent in Mexico.

Republics in Chains: From Bryant's Prairies to the Mexican *Meseta*

Readers of Whitman tend to mark the prematurely continental shape of his vision of an America stretching "over the Texas and Mexican and Floridian and Cuban seas" as unprecedented in poetry—as a particularly Whitmanian invention springing from his contact with John O'Sullivan and the Young America group. But one of Bryant's best-known works, "The Prairies," outlined the same geographical imaginary two decades earlier. Written five years after Bryant published the two Heredia poems, "The Prairies" revisits similar terrain. The vastness of the western frontier, like the incomprehensible force of Niagara's waters, becomes an occasion for human humbling: "Man hath no power in all this glorious work." "The Prairies," however, moves quickly from the sublime to the picturesque, claiming that these "Gardens of the Desert," "for which the speech of England has no name," reveal the linguistic and naturalistic particularity of the New World.[36] Like Heredia confronting Niagara for the first time, Bryant can only think to compare it to an ocean (the wind in the grass is like a wave in its "gentlest swell"). The crucial moment comes when he begins to speculate on the force behind this motion, identifying it as a transcontinental wind:

> Breezes of the South!
> Who toss the golden and the flame-like flowers,
> And pass the prairie-hawk that, poised on high,
> Flaps his broad wings, yet moves not—ye have played
> Among the palms of Mexico and vines

Of Texas, and have crisped the limpid brooks
That from the fountains of Sonora glide
Into the calm Pacific—have ye fanned
A nobler or a lovelier scene than this?[37]

"Breezes of the South!" constitutes virtually the only apostrophe in the poem. In this section, the breezes become the speaker's interlocutor, as if they are taking the positions of North and South in a staged debate. The rhetorical question "have ye fanned / A nobler or a lovelier scene than this?" contains a not-so-subtle challenge, marking the natural beauty and "nobility" of the prairies as a source of pride; the "golden and the flame-like flowers" recall the lush, bright glories of the southern tropics and even outdo them. From what "South" did Bryant imagine these breezes came to Illinois? The far frontier of Illinois that Bryant visited in 1831 was only a few hundred miles east of Mexican territory, along a border that had been agreed on but a decade earlier in the Adams–de Onís Treaty; and it was substantially east as well as north of the "fountains of Sonora" he invokes. The more likely "South" to Illinois was the Gulf of Mexico below New Orleans, also a recently acquired territory that was the gateway to possible Caribbean expansion. Thus this stanza encourages a mutability in territorial boundaries, both to the west and to the south of the United States, and indeed most recent readings of "The Prairies" have focused on the vanishing-Indian story preceding this passage, with its implicit endorsement of Manifest Destiny. David Baxter even labels Bryant one of the master architects of the nation's "sudden, dramatic giant step to the Pacific" because of his strong editorials supporting a bill to establish military outposts in Oregon as early as 1826.[38]

But the conquest of foreign time in "The Prairies" is as significant as the conquest of foreign space. The same southern breezes that infuse the prairie with movement bring the waft of an unseen history to the speaker's imagination. Guiding his horse along the awe-inspiring landscape, he is moved to imagine the ground beneath him filled with bones: "Are they here— / The dead of other days?—and did the dust / Of these fair solitudes once stir with life / And burn with passion?" He then enters into a dialogue with the "mighty mounds," conjuring a vision of a pastoral people who had occupied the prairies prior to the Plains Indians. In the long section that follows, which occupies the bulk of the poem, Bryant spins an elaborate (and thoroughly specious) description of the peace-loving "race" who had inhabited this area long before the Greeks, a society that domesticated bison like cattle and ox.

"All day this desert murmured with their toils": they sang, danced, and courted, meeting nineteenth-century definitions of "civilized" peoples. The mythical Mound Builders were lovers and artists, occupations of the leisured Golden Age; with their "forgotten language and old times, / From instruments of unremembered forms" they "Gave the soft winds a voice"—suggesting that those "breezes of the South" might yet carry the echoes of their lost voices and language, infusing a "new" world with a classical history. Even in the remotest Rockies, the Indian "rears his little Venice"; although bison no longer roam the prairies, "yet here I meet / His ancient footprints stamped beside the pool."

Then, he imagines dramatically, "The red man came— / The roaming hunter tribes, warlike and fierce, / And the mound-builders vanished from the earth." If the Mound Builder theory propagated by Benjamin Smith Barton helped justify the extermination of the more "barbaric" peoples who had supposedly supplanted them, as Ralph Miller suggests, then the poem too advances a progressivist theory of civilization.[39] All that remains of their classical civilization and architecture, the speaker notes mournfully, are grave mounds, the old city walls, and what he takes to be platforms for worship. Bryant depicts the scene of the conquest of the Mound Builders by the "Red Men" with a zeal that seems excessive for a pacifistic onlooker. Five lines detail the battle for the "city" in bloody detail, with the settlement "heaped with corpses" and vultures flocking "to those vast uncovered sepulchers." The gory scene prepares for the romantic turn to come: "Haply some solitary fugitive" escapes the massacre and is spared by the conquerors, showing that even the most "barbaric" people have an instinctive compassion: "Man's better nature triumphed." But this reassurance too is called into question, for even after the captive's redemptive intermarriage with a daughter of the "Red" tribe, he cannot forget "the wife / Of his first love, and her sweet little ones / Butchered, amid their shrieks, with all his race." This fantasy-within-a-reverie owes much to sensational Indianist literature, of which there was no shortage in antebellum prose—but Bryant's unswerving depiction of genocide is unusual in a poetic text.[40] The scene starkly asks us to ponder central questions in political philosophy, about the nature of civilization and the lifespan of empires, as the invocation of the Greeks had earlier suggested. The next stanza responds directly to those questions:

> Thus change the forms of being. Thus arise
> Races of living things, glorious in strength,

And perish, as the quickening breath of God
Fills them, or is withdrawn. The red man, too—
Has left the blooming wilds he ranged so long . . .

These lines neatly distill what Lucy Maddox and others have rightly pointed out was a common justification for the Indian removal policy that crystallized in 1830: a Christianized historical progressivism that argued that the time was ripe for Indian cultures to be superseded by a more advanced civilization, ranking agricultural societies as more advanced than nomadic ones.[41] Bryant's categorization of the Mound Builders as pastoral and the Red Men as nomadic warriors follows this hierarchy of values when it imagines future settlers placidly raising bees and walking to church across the now-empty prairies; those settlers, he implies, will in some sense reinstate the values of the peaceful civilization of America's past.

Both the terrors of the past and the sublime extension of the frontier are thus domesticated in "The Prairies." The endless space of the wilderness will become manageable as soon as it welcomes "that advancing multitude / Which soon shall fill these deserts." But the poem ends with a profound uncertainty about whether these projections of past and future are as well grounded as they seem, and with a recognition that the landscape of the present is the only truly accessible one:

All at once
A fresher wind sweeps by, and breaks my dream,
And I am in the wilderness alone.

That final line bears an unmistakable resemblance to Bryant's choice to end his translation of Heredia's "Hurricane" by excising the final stanza, thereby giving emphasis to these lines:

And I, cut off from the world, remain
Alone with the terrible hurricane.[42]

"The wilderness," like "the hurricane," returns the solitary prairie wanderer in the end to the undomesticated sublime that each term embodies. Finally, the theory of cyclical history haunts the poem with the unsettling possibility that this natural cycle by which "forms of being" rise and fall might engulf the coming Anglo-American empire, too, in its turn.[43]

Bryant and Heredia drew from the same well in their thinking about cycles of empire, conquest, and revolution in the New World: the histories of the Aztec and Incan empires and the Spanish conquest, which attracted a great deal of attention in the new republics, particularly in the

United States and in Mexico, which already boasted a long histo-riographical tradition. Bryant's gesture toward the south suggests that his fantastical depiction of the conquest of the pacific Mound Builders by the bellicose Red Men might have resonated for antebellum audiences with accounts of other pyramid-builders—Aztecs, Mayans, Incans. Although William Hickling Prescott had yet to publish his *Conquest of Mexico* (1843) and *Conquest of Peru* (1847), which powerfully shaped Anglo-American attitudes toward Latin America, interest in Aztequiana was already building.[44] Barton's theory of the Mound Builders as a distinctive and more advanced race than contemporary Indians addressed white anxieties over what they bemoaned as a lack of organized civilization in northernmost America. Their presence was summoned to compensate for the classical age that Spanish America possessed but Anglo-America lacked. Thus Bryant describes the Arcadian life of the Mound Builders as an analogue of classical Greece. Although the pastoral "gardens" of "The Prairies" seem to fit within the trope of American utopianism (Adamic man creating Eden in the wilderness), there is a specifically Spanish American resonance to its central theme.[45] "The Prairies" depicts a binary contrast of "races" and social organizations in a way that resembles less the Roman empire supplanting the Greeks than it does the Aztecs dis-placing the Toltecs, and consolidating their empire with blood against other tribes like the Tlascalans. (The story of Doña Marina, as Prescott elaborates it romantically in *The Conquest of Mexico*, recalls Bryant's lone survivor of the peaceful race who intermarries with the conquerors.) Nor was central Mexico the only "south" entering the peripheral vision of Bryant and his Hispanist peers. In "A Story of the Island of Cuba," which he probably heard from his neighbors the Salazars and published in the *Talisman* next to his translation of "The Hurricane," he retells a Gothic Indian tale set in preconquest days that plays on an already conventional dramatic contrast between the peace-loving Ciboneys and Tainos and their fearsome nemeses, the Caribs. So the Indian theme in "The Prai-ries" draws on his and his readers' perceptions of the Caribbean theater as well.

If a melded MexiCuba forms Bryant's notion of the South, and that South is full of artistically generative similarities and contrasts to his own country, this is apparent in yet another of his contributions to the *United States Review* in 1827: a lengthy review of the anonymous Span-ish-language novel *Jicoténcal*, possibly authored by Félix Varela, which had been published the year before in Philadelphia.[46] The piece seems part of a pointed campaign to assert the quarterly as an influential, cosmopolitan journal, perhaps in contrast to the more prestigious *North American Review*: "We have been principally induced to notice this book on account of its belonging to the Spanish literature of America" (336). The review includes Bryant's own 1200-word translation of a scene from the novel, an apparent sign that Cubí's language tutelage was paying off. He notices, astutely, that the novel invites comparison between the heroic rebellion of the Tlascalan cacique Jicoténcal (also rendered Xicoténcatl) against the Spaniards, and the nineteenth-century struggles against Spanish "despotism" in the Americas. Both the novelist and the reviewer comment admiringly on native revolutionary heroes willing to lay their lives on the line for the patria. Bryant further encourages the analogy by advocating the didactic uses of fiction and suggesting that *Jicoténcal* might be profitably used to teach the values of heroism and autonomy in Spanish America: "Next to the public journals the readiest and most effectual way a writer can take to disseminate his opinions on these subjects [civil rights and religious freedom], is by ingeniously mingling them with the contents of works of fiction . . . [novels] are the surest instruments of political conversion" (337). As Bryant retells the plot of *Jicoténcal*, he is careful to distinguish between the virtuous "race" of Tlascalans, whose realm is pastoral—well governed, "fertile and populous"—and the Mexicas (Aztecs), "whom they hated and whose power they had long defied and resisted" (338).[47] He summarizes the character of Cortés, who makes an alliance with the Tlascalans only to betray them, as "greedy, treacherous, and cruel without bounds" (343). The easy analogy between past and present struggles against the Spanish becomes further confirmation of the Hegelian theory of the rise and fall of empires and races: reading *Jicoténcal* seemed to give him source material for his exploration of the same idea in "The Prairies."

The final three pages of Bryant's review depart from the subject at hand to generalize more openly about the nature of just government and the present condition of the Spanish American republics. The revolutions there, he suggests, constitute a kind of vindication of the virtuous Tlascalans on the part of the criollos, who wage on their colonizer wars as destructive as those by which they were conquered:

> It is natural to compare the character of these wars, undertaken for such different purposes. If ever a war can have a favorable effect upon the morals of a people, it must be one for national liberty; and if any war can debase and degrade its character more than another, it must be one of rapine and plunder. (343)

Here, then—in the Spanish American context—he expresses a solution to the troubling paradox raised in "The Prairies": if empires rise and fall in natural succession, what is to insulate current democratic regimes in America against the same inevitable process? Only democratic pedagogy—and literature. Jicoténcal, Bryant says, models a moral character worthy of Washington, Paine, or Bolívar;[48] he "opposed the alliance with Cortés, because he foresaw from it the destruction of the liberties of his nation, and the degradation of his race" (339). Thus Bryant excuses whatever excesses the Spanish American revolutions might have committed by looking ahead to the improved moral climate that will greet the second generation as they take lessons from such revolutionary heroism:

> It might almost seem as if a nobler race of men had grown up in these countries [i.e., Spanish America]. In the midst of their political storms, they have taken care to found institutions for the purpose of forming the minds of those, who are soon, under better auspices, to take the place of the men who threw off the Spanish yoke. (344)

Again, one "race" is naturally superseded by another, as the necessary violence of an initial stage of revolutionary conquest gives way to a higher, dominant peace. But as in "Niagara" and "The Prairies," this confident theory of historical succession is unsettled by the possibility of its own failure, and by the acknowledgment of such failures in the past.

Bryant's most productive period as a poet corresponds to the moment in which the very nature of neighborliness in the New World was being encapsulated in the form of an official governmental attitude, although that formalization was not immediately apparent as such. Initially slow to recognize most of the southern republics, the United States finally sketched out a vision of the Americas as neighboring space in the form of the Monroe Doctrine. The importance of this document comes not from its original conception, which is ambiguous, or from its early reception, which was tepid, but from the increasingly pointed interpretations of the doctrine through policy in subsequent decades. In his annual presidential speech to Congress in December 1823, Monroe approached the issue of Latin American independence indirectly, by way of the more immediately pressing threat of Russian, French, and British land claims on the western and southern extremes of North America. He employs a language of proximity in regard to "these continents": "with the movements in this hemisphere we are of necessity more immediately connected," suggesting that neighborliness endows nations with certain rights. From this proceeds first the anticolonialism clause, which proclaims

> that the American continents, by the free and independent condition which they have assumed and maintain, are henceforth not to be considered as subjects for future colonization by any European power.[49]

The right to be free from colonization rests on the past and future actions of recently liberated peoples. "Assuming" independence is not sufficient; it must also be "maintained." This is an important point in that it assumes nations are agents, responsible for their own success or failure. To affirm that responsibility, he posits the second key clause, nonintervention:

> It is impossible that the allied powers should extend their political system to any portion of either continent without endangering our peace and happiness; nor can anyone believe that our southern brethren, *if left to themselves*, would adopt it of their own accord. (emphasis mine)

The relationship hinted at in Monroe's statement is thus based on both familial ("our southern brethren") and geographical forms of proximity. Bryant's review of *Jicoténcal*, written just a few years afterward, echoes the important statements of the doctrine: it speaks out against European intervention in the Americas and characterizes the northern and southern republics as neighbors. Bryant, however, implies that the U.S. role is less that of enforcer than of sympathetic exemplar, withholding judgment on the false starts of democracy elsewhere in faith that the South will eventually come to resemble the North, for "in such a contest of an oppressed nation with its despotic masters, its character cannot fail to elevate and purify itself. . . . Those who lived through our own Revolution, witnessed this process" (344). Bryant makes no claim to exact similitude, but he heartily endorses the virtues of proximity:

> One case which tends greatly to improve the character of a people thus struggling for liberties, is the *relation* in which it stands to the nations that surround it. If that struggle take place in an enlightened period of the world, it cannot fail to learn from its *neighbors* many important truths . . . it sends out its inquiries, observes and compares the institutions of other nations, and profits by the lessons of their experience. (345; emphases mine)

Although this passage seems paternalistically directed at the "younger" republics, one cannot help but wonder whether the benefits of relation do not extend in both directions for Bryant, whose efforts to imagine the scope of the continent plunge him uneasily into a sense of being in the wilderness—or in the hurricane—alone. He seems relieved at having southern "neighbors" in the overwhelming task of "civilizing" America. The Monroe Doctrine, which transfers to other nations the right to self-determination on which U.S. political discourse is founded, suffers from the same paradox that underlies that discourse: the conflict between the freedom of individuals (or nations) to be "left to themselves" and the rights of their neighbors with which they are potentially in conflict. The overpowering sense of aloneness with which "Niágara" and "The Prairies" end suggest that both of these meditations on national community are profoundly ambivalent about the potential consequences of self-determination.

Heredia likewise turned to Mexico for neighborly consolation in exile and for intellectual and poetic analogues with which to address the colonial situation in Cuba. His interest in Mexico's indigenous history, and the lessons it might have for a future empire of freedom, began as early as his student days. "En un teocalli de Cholula" begins, like "The Prairies," by locating the natural beauty of the former pyramid site within hemispheric space:

¡Cuánto es bella la tierra que habitaban,	*How beautiful is the land in which*
Los aztecas valientes! En su seno	*the valiant Aztecs lived! In its bosom,*
En una estrecha zona concentrados,	*concentrated in one narrow zone,*
Con asombro se ven todos los climas	*you see, surprisingly, every climate there is*
Que hay desde el Polo al Ecuador.	*between the Pole and the Equator.*

This geographical stretch centers the valley of Mexico as a kind of condensed essence of the entire New World. As in "Niágara" and "The Prairies," the speaker makes a solitary voyage to a sublime site and is visited by visions of a bloody past. He climbs the Choluteca pyramid and watches night fall over the "volcán sublime," meditating pensively on the "ley universal" [universal law] that empires must eventually fall. Imagining scenes of ritual sacrifice on the pyramid, he interprets the Spanish conquest as a kind of punishment for the Aztecs' use of slave labor, concluding that "la raza presente y la futura" [the past race and the future one] must absorb this historical lesson or suffer similar consequences. (Mexico's 1821 Constitution had outlawed slavery, though not peonage; here again Heredia may have been more concerned with Cuba, whose incredible wealth during this period—its exports were valued more highly than those of the entire nation of Mexico—was so dependent on slave labor that it seemed impossible to end.)[50] But his treatment of the Aztecs is at the same time highly sympathetic; he praises their great architectural and cultural achievements, and invokes heroic individuals who resisted conquest, as he would do again in the urgent 1822 "Oda a las habitantes de Anáhuac." Increasingly, he integrates Nahuatl names and terms into his poems, prefiguring a move that *indigenista* writers would make much later in the century. When del Monte wrote Heredia from New York to upbraid his friend for doing too many translations and to urge him to mine "those incredibly ancient archives of Tenochtitlan," which ought to "inflame the ardent imagination of the bard of Niagara," Heredia had already responded with "Las sombras," a poem he probably drafted in New York.[51]

"Las sombras" represents Heredia's most interesting use of the Mexican past. His imagination piqued by reading the heroic colonial histories of the Aztec empire, the speaker makes a pilgrimage to a solitary high point (Chapultepec, the spiritual center of Mexico City and a former burial place of emperors). Like the Bryant persona in "The Prairies," he imagines the past resurrecting itself before him, filling the air with the voices of "mil espectros pálidos y fríos" [a thousand pale, cold ghosts]. The "shades" of the title are the great indigenous rulers of the Americas, both heroic and ineffectual, who enter the nineteenth-century democrat's troubled moment and, in successive dramatic monologues, denounce warfare and tyranny, and project a future in which the contested land will again be peacefully settled by industrious farmers. "Las sombras" opens by mimicking the voice of "proud despotism," which claims that

"El orbe todo entre cadenas gima,	*"In chains the whole world turns,*
Y el hombre hundido en servidumbre odiosa	*And Man is beaten down in hateful servitude, kissing*
La mano bese que feroz le oprima . . ."	*the cruel hand that oppresses him."*

The tyrant claims not only that oppression is natural, but that the servant loves to be mastered—and this is what the poem tries to rebut. Mournfully agreeing that America remains frustratingly servile, the speaker turns to Moctezuma, Ahuitzol, Cuitlahuatzín, and Guatimozín (from the Mexican world), Axayaca, Atahualpa, Manco Capac, and Tupac Amaru (from the Andean), and finally Guaycaypuro (leader of a confederation of tribes that repelled the Spanish in Venezuela). In keeping with his vocation as an editor and man of letters, Heredia's direction in this poem is clearly, in part, didactic, anticipating Martí's famous injunction in *Nuestra América* to study indigenous history rather than "the Greece which is not ours." Of all the ghostly shades, Moctezuma has the loudest and (nearly) the last word—which seems appropriate, since the present-day speaker summons forth this dream-vision from the seat of the former emperor's power. Moctezuma complains that his glory was once sung "del raudo Chagre al Niágara" [from the raging Chagres to Niagara Falls], but now his "infeliz América" must struggle to achieve its own liberation.[52]

Where "The Prairies" linked past and future scenes of pastoral glory, "Las sombras" uses the sublime perspective offered by a view of American nature to establish a past tradition of resistance that might galvanize present and future freedom-fighters, ultimately giving lie to the tyrant's claim that by nature some are meant to be enslaved. Whereas Bryant had already moved into the postindependence moment of territorial consolidation, Heredia still clung to one of the preferred metaphors of revolutionaries North and South: that the absence of perfect liberty is equivalent to slavery. As his poems on American history range from indigenous resistance to the Spanish conquest to Washington's triumphant crossing of the Delaware to celebrating the Fourth of July or the triumph of Bolívar, Heredia draws from the same limited lexicon, dominated by terms like *libertad, esclavitud, opresión,* and *tirano.*[53] Bryant, too, encourages the continuing use of the metaphor with regard to Spanish America at the end of his review of *Jicoténcal:*

> We should never fear, therefore, that too much of our
> sympathy will be given to an oppressed and suffering people,
> struggling to break the long-worn *chain of its bondage,* since we
> may be certain that, ere the struggle is at an end, that sympathy
> will be amply deserved. The pity we at first give to its
> misfortunes will, at length, grow into admiration for its moral
> qualities. We shall see it laying aside the vices of its *servitude,*
> because it has no longer any occasion for them, and assuming
> the virtues of a free nation, because its condition calls them
> forth. War is, without doubt, under all circumstances and all

aspects, a tremendous evil, but it is, perhaps, the best school in which the character of a nation, emerging from *slavery and degradation,* could be formed. . . . What would become of such a nation if its *chains* were to be taken off quietly, and it were at once permitted to govern itself, without the apprehension of danger from its old *masters* to serve as a *bond of union* . . . ? It would hardly be ruled, at first, more wisely and equitably under the new system of things, than under the old. (345–46; emphases mine)

Heredia and Bryant's shared representations of colonial government as a form of slavery, of the need for heroic individuals to break their colonial chains, and of the virtue inherent in such a struggle do not constitute innocent metaphors. For the United States and Cuba in particular, these metaphorical usages were situated within an increasingly tense and problematic crisis in the transnational economy having to do with the future of chattel slavery.[54] Moreover, the centrality of an individual nation's agency—its ability to "maintain" its independence, in the language of the Monroe Doctrine—allows distinctions to be made between neighboring peoples according to how "servile" they seem. By the mid-1840s, this moral distinction would be interpreted as a justification for the morally superior "free" nation to violate the noninterventionist clause of the Monroe Doctrine. Its discourse of civic freedom and the need to break the "chains" of the colonizing power's "enslavement" conflicts with the same nation's desire to stretch itself out territorially.

The very forms of temporal and spatial proximity that Heredia and Bryant try to establish between the Americas—a common history of cyclical oppression and liberation, a common claim to experience of a New World sublime, and a common republican destiny—generate equally powerful forms of mutual rejection, largely related to the material (as opposed to rhetorical) presence of institutionalized slavery. The geopolitical ramifications of the "Santo Domingo moment," the stages of the revolution in Haiti, and the 1844 Escalera uprising in Cuba, as Eric Sundquist has shown convincingly, made a deep impression on U.S. intellectuals.[55] Roughly simultaneously with the publication of *Jicoténcal* and Bryant's doomed attempt to portray the Spanish American nations sympathetically in the United States, the affirmation of American proximity expressed in the Monroe Doctrine met its first real challenge. Bolívar's grudging invitation of the United States to a hemispheric conference of nations in Panama set off months of wrangling between Congress,

President John Quincy Adams (who made no secret of his dislike for all things Spanish) and Secretary of State Henry Clay. Objections to a U.S. presence at the 1826 Panama Congress centered around racial discomfort at the presence of Haitian leaders at the table as well as the alarm of sugar traders, who were preoccupied with rumors that Colombian and Mexican leaders were supporting liberationist activity in Puerto Rico and Cuba. Adams's eventual charge to the Panama representatives, therefore, emphasized not the possibility of building economic and political coalitions or the revolutionary work still to be done in the hemisphere, but the rights of existing commercial interests to maintain the "peace and security" of the islands.[56]

Heredia, observing from Mexico in *El Iris*, interpreted this as an abandonment of Cuba, and responded by translating and glossing Adams's message to Congress about the Panama meeting. He endorses the anticolonial and antiinterventionist passages of the Monroe Doctrine as "noble y lleno de dignidad, y sus ideas . . . dignas del jefe de la nación primogénita de la gran familia americana" [noble and full of dignity . . . its ideas are worthy of the head of the nation that is the primogenitor of the great American family]. However, he blasts Adams's refusal to support Cuban independence as a betrayal of his personal and national revolutionary heritage:

> ¡Hijo de John Adams, la causa de América estará
> comprometida, mientras Cuba no sea libre, a pesar de tu
> política temerosa!
>
> *[Son of John Adams, in spite of your timid policies, the cause of
> America will be compromised until Cuba is free.]*[57]

Heredia takes particular umbrage at Adams's statement that Cuba cannot yet manage independence because of its "heterogeneous" population, which he recognizes as a euphemism for "racially mixed." This is hypocritical, he points out, given the million-plus slaves in the southern United States. Yet he apparently fails to see the remark about racial heterogeneity as a veiled reference not only to Caribbean *mestizaje* but also to the suspect racial stock of the Spanish creoles themselves. The familial sense of disappointment he expresses here (and which other independentistas will echo in the coming decades) contains its own blindnesses, perhaps based on the selective vision with which he viewed the country during his exile. In a letter describing his impressions of a pleasant summer day on Lake Erie, he had written that for once "no sentía la mano de hierro que apretara mi corazón en los campos de Cuba cuando me acordaba que su riqueza venía del sudor, de la sangre tal vez de tantos miserables esclavos" [I didn't feel the iron hand that would squeeze my heart in the Cuban countryside when I'd remember that its riches came from the sweat—perhaps the blood—of so many miserable slaves]. What he cannot see—because he has so much invested in imagining the North as a peaceful, orderly opposite to his vision of Cuban chaos—is the economic interdependence of the northern states with the southern slavocracy.[58]

Heredia did not live long enough to witness some of the strikingly paradoxical events that proved that the metaphor of colonial government as enslavement was all too fungible—the importation of Mayan slaves to work the sugar plantations in the Caribbean, beginning in 1850, for instance.[59] Nor was he alive at the time of the most jolting challenge to the fraternal image of the American republics that he propagated in his prose and poetry: the U.S. annexation of Texas in 1845 and the war that followed. By the 1840s, when Bryant helped found the Free-Soil Party, many liberals had come to see national expansion, in terms of both population and territory, as the only way to brake the growth of the slave economy. This concern outweighed the republican value of self-determination and the rights of a people or nation to be "left to themselves." Bryant's reversal of his initial objections to the Mexican War is a tragically revealing case of this dilemma; it required that he suspend his own politico-ethical convictions against expansion at the expense of Indian lives and international boundary rights, as I detail in the coming chapter. Cuba played an ambiguous part in this liberal predicament. It was both a site of expansionist designs through annexation and the ultimate site of what northerners most feared and despised in the slavery system: the southernmost South, in a sense. During the galvanizing period of the 1830s and early 1840s, Brooks too was caught between the conflicting imperatives epitomized by Cuba. As she refashioned herself from a mere visitor, an impoverished Boston Brahmin, into a poet of Cuba, María del Occidente distanced herself from her origins by an increasing allegiance to criollo attitudes about slavery while clinging tenaciously to the revolutionary right to self-determination.

_____

Vistas del Infierno: The Racial Dilemma of María del Occidente

The interamerican moment of the Panama Congress coincided with Maria Gowen Brooks's maturation as a poet, and this is also the time of her transformation into María del Occidente—itself a suggestive name in light of contemporary visions of the westward course of empire. She published the first canto of *Zóphiël* in Boston in 1825 and returned to Cuba to finish it, which she accomplished in 1829. Little biographical information survives to illuminate her responses to political developments involving her country of birth and the one that brought her fortune and a new identity, but she was surely attuned to those events to some degree. First, she inherited substantial property, including a coffee plantation, and would have been directly affected by the new dominance of the sugar aristocracy in Cuba during the 1830s. Second, her son Horace attended West Point (she had petitioned Washington Irving and the Marquis de Lafayette for help in getting him admitted) and served first in the Seminole Wars in Florida and then in the Caribbean. Third, surviving correspondence with George Ticknor, the leading Hispanist in the United States, suggests some ongoing contact with the Harvard circles with which her father had associated.[60] Her *cafetal*, San Patricio, was located near Matanzas, which was a hub of criollo literary and revolutionary activity in the 1830s and 1840s; the relatively short distance to Havana was served by regular steamboat. If she had had contact with the literary circles in Matanzas—contemporaries claimed her Spanish was fluent—she may well have brushed against del Monte and his liberal circle, or read the important periodicals he helped publish, *La Moda o el Recreo del Bello Sexo* and the *Revista Bimestre Cubana*. A minor character in *Idomen* is named del Monte.[61] Brooks's final years in Cuba witnessed both the liberation of the press under Tacón and a series of slave uprisings and abolitionist agitation that culminated in the Escalera revolt and the trial of its suspected conspirators, notably the tremendously popular poet Plácido (Gabriel de la Concepción Valdés).

What degree of "Cubanization," and more importantly what vision of *cubanidad*, does her work express? Earlier, I suggested that "Stanzas to Niagara" measures out a cosmopolitan geography of the New World that transcends national boundaries; Idomen's visit to Niagara represents a transition point between the two disparate but related extremes of wintry Quebec and the perpetual summer of northwestern Cuba.[62] Most extensively in *Idomen* but as early as *Zóphiël*, Brooks tries to normalize Cuba as a focal point for the literary imagination. Brooks's attachment to footnotes is evident in each of her three surviving books: in an intimate, engaging tone that often seems at odds with the formality of the work, the authorial persona shares details of her life, shows off her learning and linguistic capabilities, and presents firsthand observations of botanical and horticultural facts about the New World settings she describes. Cantos 2–6 are signed from various places on the island where they were composed, and the final canto of *Zóphiël* opens with an ode to twilight passing over "the luscious landscape" of Cuba as it "glows o'er wave, sky, flower, and palm-tree tall." The zeal with which Brooks annotated her poems and prose suggests her strong desire to claim a place in the library of Western culture. In the 1879 edition of *Zóphiël*, for instance, the notes take up 56 pages of six-point type, compared to 189 pages of eight-point text, with only about five stanzas to the page.[63] Like passages from Melville (whom she resembles perhaps more strongly than does any other female writer of the period), these notes flourish in their very digressiveness, taking on a life of their own. For example, this note follows a reference to a grove of young trees in which the heroine, Egla, shelters herself sleepily:

> It is impossible for those who never felt it to conceive the effect of such a situation in a warm climate. In this island, the woods, which are naturally so interwoven with vines as to be impervious to a human being, are in some places cleared and converted into nurseries for the young coffee-trees, which remain sheltered from the sun and wind till sufficiently grown to transplant. To enter one of these "semilleros," as they are called, at noonday, produces an effect like that anciently ascribed to the waters of Lethe. After sitting down upon the trunk of a fallen cedar or palm-tree, and breathing for a moment the freshness of the air and the odor of the passion-flower—which is one of the most abundant and certainly the most beautiful of the climate—the noise of the trees, which are continually kept in motion by the trade-winds; the fluttering and various notes (though not musical) of the birds; the loftiness of the green canopy (for the trunks of the trees are bare to a great height, and seem like pillars supporting a thick mass of leaves above); and the soft, peculiar light which the intense ray of the sun, thus impeded, produces,—have altogether such an effect, that one seems to forget every thing but the present, and it requires a strong effort to rise and leave the place.[64]

The rapturous language of this note has almost the same distracting effect as the *semillero* it describes.

Zóphiël is nominally, at least, an epic about a melancholy fallen angel's love for a Jewish maiden, Egla, during the Babylonian captivity. The angel, Zóphiël, six times protects Egla (who does not wish to marry but keeps getting forced to do so) from sexual ravishment by entering her bedroom and invisibly slaying the bridegroom on their wedding night. Just when Egla is about to capitulate to Zóphiël's seductions, he is confounded by the archangel Gabriel, who is determined that Egla should meet and marry her destined mate, with whom she will restore the Hebrew empire. Zóphiël, in the end, seems to be redeemed by this experience—and by the deeply homosocial love bond he shares with his patient friend, Phraërion. But for all its cosmopolitan and biblical gleanings, *Zóphiël* presents itself as a work grounded in the Americas, recasting Orientalist conventions within a particularly Caribbean light and locating them within a New World geography and history. Toward this end, the poem offers its opening "Hail Muse" to Columbus, who is invoked as the artist's protector and spiritual progenitor, as the notes make clear: "The remains of Columbus are preserved in the cathedral at Havana . . . these stanzas were written on the same coast, about seventy miles distant" (205).[65] Although *Zóphiël* is set in the Near East, its landscape is West Indian: Egla rests in lush floral bowers, and the ocean is always nearby.

More strikingly, perhaps, is the fact that *Zóphiël*'s plot describes the redemption of a captive people from slavery, and makes use of one of the global abolitionist movement's favorite analogies for the predicament of Africans in America: the Egyptian and Babylonian captivities. Not surprisingly, however, the slavery portrayed in the poem is highly abstracted from any scenes of labor, for Brooks uses the metaphor more directly to argue against the "captivity" of loveless marriage and the entrapment of women deprived of property rights. The poem's prescient feminist consciousness is often striking, and has attracted some interest among contemporary critics for its outright eroticism and feminist leanings.[66] She speaks of the Euphrates as the river near which the "first mother awoke" and discusses her research in matriarchal religions; she hails the "Daughter of God" and Sappho in her "Invocation"; her youthful lyrics on Judith and Esther celebrate the strength of female will. The title character of *Idomen* resists being "sold into wifehood" to a local planter (69), preferring to maintain her autonomy, though her later suicide attempts suggest the difficulties of maintaining such autonomy in a patriarchal world. And in the 1825 preface to *Zóphiël*, Brooks explains the difficulty of finding time to write when a young mother, and describes herself as "the slave of Fate," identifying with prisoners under the repressive colonial regime in Cuba: "Alas! How many, in the flower of youth and strength, perish in the loathsome dungeons of this island, and, when dead, are refused a decent grave; who, in many instances, were their histories traced by an able pen would be wept by half the civilized world." It is all the worse, she suggests, to be the "slave of fate" if one is an artist or a sensitive woman.[67]

At the same time, Brooks also acknowledges the obvious material embodiments of this captivity metaphor that surround her in Cuba:

> Every nation, however rude, has, as it has been justly observed,
> a taste for poetry. . . . In the place where I now write labor
> several hundred Africans of different ages, and nations, the
> most debased of any on the face of the earth. I have been
> enabled to observe, even in this last link of the chain of
> humanity, the strong natural love for music and poetry. Any
> little incident which occurs on the estate where they toil, and
> which the greater part of them are never suffered to leave, is
> immediately made the subject of a rude song which they, in
> their broken Spanish, sing to their companions; and thereby
> relieve a little the monotony of their lives. I have observed these
> poor creatures, under various circumstances, and though,
> generally, extremely brutal, have, in some instances, heard
> touches of sentiment from them, when under the influence of
> grief, equal to any which have flowed from the pen of
> Rousseau. (16–17)

Despite the Romantic racism of this passage, it does not deny the reality of inescapable forced labor (the "monotony" of the lives of the "poor creatures" who are "never suffered to leave" the plantation).[68] By the time *Idomen* was composed a decade later, however, Brooks's tone had changed to outright apologism. *Idomen* extends *Zóphiël*'s concern with the injustice of "imprisoning" a sensitive artist within proscribed female roles. The character of Idomen—gorgeous, talented, and untimely wed to an unsympathetic older man—is such a victim; when Niagara inspires her to write verses again, it is a sign of her recovery from the romantic obsession that had led her to attempt suicide. Her return to the Cuban climate also promises blooming health and renewed creativity, for the kind French planter Dalcour takes her under his wing and encourages her to write, unfettered by wifely servitude. Unfortunately, malicious gossip about her relationship with Dalcour brings on Idomen's mysterious final illness, and after her death a convoluted found-manuscript structure introduces us to her life and her poems, which are "seemingly the conception of a master" (210). The double entendre here is irresistible, since Brooks—a plantation owner herself—went to great lengths to avoid seeing herself as a "master" in the other sense of the term.

Both in the preface to *Idomen* and in its Cuban passages, bondage is presented as a lamentable but unavoidable condition in a world that will always be unequal. Brooks also claims that slavery is unrelated to race because whites are kept as slaves in Asia, and "that servitude or slavery which every poor person is condemned to suffer" afflicts all nations (xix). Every human being is fitted for some natural station, just as the dolphin is suited only for warm waters; she thus claims that Africans are well suited for both the climate and the work of the West Indies.[69] Like Las Casas (whom she cites as an authority), Brooks uses this biological argument to defend vigorously the rights of indigenous peoples in the Americas. She writes to Southey in 1837 that, although her son had served in the military in the guerrilla campaign against the Seminole resistance, she supports "those unfortunate Indians . . . though many whites have been murdered I cannot forbear a wish that the same brave man [Oseola] had sufficient power and wisdom to protect his oppressed brethren, and organize into a nation of all the wretched tribes that remained of them." A poem called "The Oration" published in the *Boston Saturday Evening Gazette* in 1838 purports to record the last speech of a great Indian chief arguing for "an Indian state," supporting his case with both rhetorical and affective power (he is killed for sport by a boorish trapper). The poem's footnotes defend Brooks's claim that "of all beings in the wide universe I know of none so much wronged as the unfortunate Indians of the New World."[70]

Despite this attachment to an ennobling (though hardly unproblematic) view of indigenous Americans—a view that recalls Child and Sigourney—in later writings Brooks takes on the tenor of proslavery apologists like William Gilmore Simms and Augusta Evans Wilson to defend the enslavement of Africans in sentimental terms: "Nourished for many years by the labors of ebony fingers, no one can possibly feel for the Negro a sympathy more pure and intense than the writer of these observations" (*Idomen*, xvi). She claims that she was present at all the births and deaths on her cafetal; that she "responded to their evening orisons" and "knelt to heaven, at the dreadful sound of the lash, and prayed, in an agony, to the God of mercy and justice." But then she insists that the sound of the lash was never heard on her own estate— "otherwise, who but a *fiend* could endure to live long in the midst of them?" (xvi). These prefatory pages seem determined to forestall a degree of criticism and moral outrage that she apparently expects, even though *Idomen* makes no claim to be "about" slavery, and only one black character in it has a name. "Incompetent to meddle with any great political question, the relatress of the story of Idomen can only say, that the happiness of the first pair, before their expulsion from their native garden, can seldom be more fully realized than on a flourishing coffee estate, where the sable laborers among its fruits and flowers, are directed by wisdom and benevolence" (xiii). Brooks seems very well aware that her story of Cuba will be read (at least in Boston) within the context of that "great political question," and her claim of incompetence is undermined by the ingenuity of her apologia—which is based, as this sentence suggests, on portraying life on the coffee plantation as a model of just government and as an Edenic paradise for both whites *and* blacks. In the novel, beautiful African women adorned with jewelry and bright clothing of their own design sing, dance, comb their children's hair, and care for their (miraculously intact) families; African men respectfully seek their master's wise opinion about their family troubles.[71] The only work we see takes place when Benito, the majordomo, brings in trays of exotic fruits, each of which is carefully described in Brooks's attentive footnotes. By the end of the novel, the German narrator who has been hearing the story of Idomen, Herman Albrecht, goes Cuban himself, deciding to devote his life to the study of "man in his natural state" among the Africans who live in such Rousseauvian bliss. The "throbs of the heart," he has concluded, "are felt, with equal fullness, by the slave in his palm-covered hut, amid the fruits and perfumes of Cuba," as by a European prince beneath a silk canopy (216–17).

The repressive effort required to construct this outrageous fantasy shows its strains as early as the vision in the preface of a woman crying and begging someone to spare the whip—a vision that gets denied just as swiftly as it had been invoked: "otherwise, who but a *fiend* could endure to live long in the midst of them?" Brooks clearly does not relish seeing herself as a fiend; yet she is also, just as clearly, enamored of Cuba and determined to attract the world's attention both to its fascinations and to her own talents. It is revealing, then, that the Cuban landscape is strongly associated with the power of repression. In the note to *Zóphiël* cited previously, Brooks had described the shady grove of coffee trees as having "an effect like the waters of Lethe," and the very opening lines of *Idomen* suggest that the tropical climate acts as a kind of drug to induce serene forgetfulness: "Let him who sighs for death, come hither; a light veil will soon be spread over all the scenes of memory" (1). Dalcour, later, will characterize the climate as a force that draws a "bright misty veil over every obtrusive recollection" (44). Idomen's two suicide attempts involve laudanum, a potion for forgetting. The suicide plot in *Idomen* is thus not as unrelated as it seems to the long passages of Cuban travelogue, and the "conversion" of Albrecht that consumes the final pages, otherwise inexplicably, with his impressions of slave life. In the preface, Brooks claims that she has written this book in order to explain more compassionately the despair that drives some to suicide, and expresses the hope that "When every stream of this 'New World' has been navigated, and when roads are cut through all its forests, it may be that some being, *even of this hemisphere,* may abstract himself, a little, from the charms of gold, ease, and notoriety; and turn his power and reason to the kindly purpose of saving the forms of those he loves from *what even thought dares not dwell on*" (viii, emphases mine). The "unthinkable" is a reference to suicide, but it suggests other unimaginable subjects as well— that is, the repressive effort it takes to argue forcefully on behalf of women, Indians, and unjustly subjugated people, on one hand, while painting African chattel slavery as a natural and benevolent institution, on the other. A few pages later, this link is made utterly clear: "the sooth-ing and direction of such feelings as sometimes impel to self-immolation, would add more to the sum of earthly happiness, than *even* the breaking of the bonds of those blacks who labour under masters" (xii, emphasis mine).

Brooks seems forever caught between the appeal of forgetting and the fear of being forgotten, of having her works go unread. *Idomen,* like *Zóphiël,* encourages a comparison between women and slaves: Al-brecht's other goal, at the end of the novel, is to redact Idomen's papers and get her poems published, to "give my country the outlines of this unknown being of the New World" (210) who had not been able to realize her "genius" (187) because of shortsighted attempts to chain her in conventional forms of femininity. Paradoxically, Cuba—the first land of slavery the author knew—represented Brooks's ticket to precisely this kind of liberation. Inheriting the cafetal fantastically resolved the pressing problem of supporting herself and her sons after the death of her penni-less husband. It bought her the leisure to write, the capital to travel to Europe, and the freedom to reject offers of remarriage. Small wonder that she shrugged off New England ways and took on the racial privileges and paradoxes of the Cuban criollo class who saw liberation from colo-nial "slavery" as necessary while dismissing the abolition of chattel slav-ery as impractical. To escape one form of slavery was to endorse another.

However idealized and racist her work may be, Brooks's treatment of Cuba is still more astute, more detailed, and more sympathetic toward Cuba and Spanish America in general than other Anglo-American treatments of the time. There are signs of recognition that her gauzy portrait of Cuban society is not an accurate reflection of the times. The manuscript that Albrecht redacts is dated 1827, implying that the events in the novel took place at least several years earlier (219).[72] Throughout the novel and elsewhere she denounces the relentless pursuit of money over art, culture, and human values. And a provocative letter to Griswold dated 24 July 1844, reprinted in part in his *Female Poets*, suggests that Brooks's last known poems were composed against the backdrop of the volatile events surrounding the Escalera conspiracy in 1844. Brooks writes: "On the seventeenth of April (1844) this poem was conceived and partly executed, in the midst of a dearth such as had not for many years, been known in the island of Cuba. A late attempt at insurrection (in the same island) had been followed by such scenes and events as could not otherwise than call forth thoughts and hopes of a future existence even if private sorrow had not before awakened them." The poem she mentions is an elegy to her dead son Edgar, "Ode to the Departed: Con Vistas del Cielo"; in the same letter, she mentions a companion piece titled "Con Vistas del Infierno" conceived at the same time and employing the same unusual stanza, which she claimed as her own invention.[73] Although I can find no trace of the second poem, the Dantesque pairing of "Views from Heaven" with "Views from Hell" suggest that they respond in tandem to the questionable future aroused by current events in Cuba. Throughout 1843 there had been a series of slave rebellions in and around Matanzas, and in early April—around the date Brooks gave for her first draft—the free mulato Plácido was arrested as a conspirator and imprisoned for six months. The following year marked the beginning of a series of brutal government repressions especially severe in Matanzas, and Plácido was executed on 28 June 1844, less than a month before the July completion of the "Heaven" poem.[74]

Surely, the northwest of Cuba must have seemed particularly hellish to a plantation owner that year—even one bent on repressing her participation in its cause. Moreover, if María del Occidente was at all a reader of Cuban poetry, then the execution of the most famous poet in her hometown could not have seemed anything but tragic, whatever her opinion of his guilt or innocence may have been. At the very least, the public whippings and torturous interrogations of Afro-Cubans in connection with Escalera would have made it impossible not to hear the

sound she hoped never to hear. Barring the discovery of further manuscripts, there is no way to tell what Brooks's "view from Hell" might have
been; her letter can only refer indirectly to scenes as so unsettling that
they "could not fail to call forth thoughts and hopes of a future existence." It is not inconceivable that she might have caught a glimpse of
the scene that Heredia, too, had tried to repress before the sight of
Niagara released it: a scene of blood covering the picturesque countryside, the cost that her own liberty extracted from others. Bryant sees it in
the prairies, the haunting of the past, but he shoos away those ghosts to
will himself in the wilderness alone. For Brooks's "Con Vistas del Cielo"
expands, at some length, on her theory that angels and the spirits of the
dead walk the earth, and some will even dash their hands "'gainst blood-
stained ground" to save human souls from purgatory. She ends the poem
with this plea:

> Sprites, brothers, manes, shades, present my tears and prayers![75]

The obscuring mist over Niagara and Cuba, along with the "shades"
of the American past that had haunted Heredia, Bryant, and Brooks in
turn, appear again in the following chapter as the veil of language in
translation.

3

Tasks of the Translator
Imitative Literature, the Catholic South,
and the Invasion of Mexico

> So little interest is felt here in this shabby and disgraceful
> war with Mexico, that the New Orleans paper in our
> Reading Room has not been out open for the past two
> weeks. I met W. Salas, who expressed his great disgust at
> our Republic's so wantonly breeding ill blood between itself
> and a sister Republic. Good old man!
>
> —Longfellow in his journal, 27 May 1846

"A Mist of Lurid Light":
Translation Practice in the Americas

Wedged between an article celebrating Harvard College and a review of a
linguistics tract in the January 1849 issue of the *North American Review*,
the most elevated publication of the antebellum period, is a lengthy and
surprisingly well informed treatise titled "The Poetry of Spanish America." Like Bryant's review of *Jicoténcal*, this essay by William Henry
Hurlbert shows an unusually respectful attentiveness to a Latin American
cultural presence that would continue to be ignored in the North for the
rest of the century.[1] A survey, with translations, of poets from Sor Juana
to Plácido, the article argues for "serious observation" of Latin America
instead of the filters of romantic expectation that Anglo-Americans of the
time brought to it. Hurlbert begins with a sharp blast of invective against

the intellectual closed-mindedness of Spain, and its imposition of those limitations on "the Western paradise" of its American colonies. Speaking hopefully of the southern revolutions and praising their educational initiatives, he makes the following plea for the attention of his readers:

> Spanish America, at the present hour, looms up to us on the far horizon of the political world in a mist of lurid light, which veils her from the general gaze about as effectively as the darkness of her old estate. Her condition, her destinies,—these are problems too much unheeded, and yet unsolved. Those of us, who, like the Javanese, consider gold-color the perfection of beauty, go down in ships to her borders, to bring back hoards of patriot doubloons, and strange stories pleasant to hear, of *tertulias*, and mantillas and unlimited combs, and beggars on horseback (dismal types of their country's career); but very few persons have bestowed any serious observation and thought on the character and resources of these mysterious tropical nations, with whom it is the "manifest destiny" of our country to be more and more connected, and who, with such magnificent powers at their disposal, have as yet played so trifling a part in the great world drama. (130–31)

This passage registers an ironic contempt for Anglo fortune-hunters, comparing them to island "primitives" enthralled by the glimmer of gold, as well as for adventure-tourists seeking "strange stories pleasant to hear." Those who go south in search of sources for picturesque literary appropriation in the form of mantillas and mystery will find what they expect, but not—he suggests—the real thing. Yet at the same time, Hurlbert blunts his critique by falling into the same language of the South as an exotic feminine space when he promises to peer beyond the veil, to reveal "her true character and resources." Hurlbert, like Brooks, treats Latin America (and more specifically Cuba, to which he devotes the bulk of the essay) as a local Orient, even as he insists that his readers imagine their national identity increasingly linked to the rest of the hemisphere.

The scare quotes around "manifest destiny" offer a political context for that insistence, yet Hurlbert's portrayal of potential unions within the Americas is ambivalent. He employs the same language of occlusion as does Melville in describing the *San Dominick* in "Benito Cereno": as a veiled woman whose true features are difficult to make out in the "mist of lurid light."[2] The mysterious figure, in both cases, seems to provoke both fear and longing. If Spanish American space is, for Hurlbert, shrouded in a Gothic darkness, poetry promises to be its light: the lyrics he has chosen to translate for the essay have "helped us to discover the presence, amidst the shadows and vile noises of South American life, of nobler thoughts and higher aims than her politics have yet developed" (131). The end of the article repeats the sentiment that there are "some flashes of poetic light above the general darkness":

> those revolutionary countries, whose literature we have
> supposed to consist chiefly of *pronunciamientos* and military
> harangues, do really contain the germs of a vigorous intellectual
> life,—germs which promise the development of a purer, a more
> stable society. Like those ancient palaces and temples of their
> country, which the growth of the wilderness has hidden for
> centuries from the eyes of man, these best sons of Spanish
> America are, indeed, surrounded by an overwhelming
> multitude of the ignorant, the vicious, and the miserable. (159)

Combining diverse figures and images from all over the continent into a generalized landscape of "ancient palaces and temples" covered by dense tropical "wilderness," Hurlbert's language of veiled secrets, of ancientness, and of hidden profundities mirrors Anglo-Protestant notions of Catholicism at the time—which, as Jenny Franchot has demonstrated, held a dual fascination and repulsion for many antebellum writers.[3] Both passages appeal to the Catholic South to allow the northern lights of art and reason to penetrate its occlusion, even as they register their own desire for it. Given this rhetorical tie between Spanish America, Catholic mystery, and the feminine, it is not surprising that Hurlbert begins his biographical case studies by singing the praises of Sor Juana Inés de la Cruz. Tracing her life in some detail, he mourns that "her nation and her age" did not allow Sor Juana to develop her talents more fully.[4] He then admits that he has not found a contemporary Mexican poet worthy of following in her footsteps, despite his reading in various literary publications:

> When Mexico shall be fairly incorporated into our glorious
> confederacy, we may perhaps feel it to be a patriotic duty to fill
> up the *lacunae* of our information; at present, however, the
> indefinite boundaries of our country forbid the prosecution of
> such a purpose, and we therefore pass to Yucatan, which may
> possibly be electing her representatives at Washington while we
> are inditing these words. (135)

Hurlbert's article was written *after* the 1848 Treaty of Guadalupe-Hidalgo had clearly settled those "indefinite boundaries," but as his reference to Yucatán reveals, the legacy of the war with Mexico was an open season on the possibility of other territorial acquisitions in the hemisphere. Yucatán, which had more than once asserted its separate identity from the central Mexican government, was at this moment involved in the bloody and repressive Caste Wars of 1847–53, and some members of the beleaguered white minority in Mérida were seeking U.S. annexation as a protection against further racial violence.[5] Yet, Hurlbert's hint of a possible acquisition of further parts of Mexico may well be ironic, lampooning the Democratic proponents of Manifest Destiny and their overwrought notions of a "glorious confederacy"; the emphasis on *fairly* "incorporating" Mexico casts an ambiguous light on the justice of the treaty. Indeed, his discussion of Mexican culture moves against the patriotic tide, shying away from the glorification of military conquest: "we gladly turn from the 'wild war-drum' of the Aztec priest, and the loud *réveille* of the American conqueror, to listen to the gentle singing of the Mexican nun in her quiet, consecrated cell" (135). The past and present noise of masculine display, of Aztec ritual and Yankee military parades, are equated and dismissed as so much barbaric clamor in comparison to the "singing" of true poets.

Despite the timely references to Mexico and Yucatán, it is really Cuba, "that Garden of the West," that signifies the center of his cultural interest in Spanish America:

> In this island, so richly endowed with material gifts, we find the
> noblest and loftiest poets of Spanish America, men of true and
> universal sympathies, of high aspiration, and noble character,
> whose souls are fired with great ideas and unselfish hopes,
> whose poems are not of stereotyped sentimentalities, tender or
> terrible, but manly outpourings of serious feeling, full of a
> genuine, high-toned enthusiasm for great and generous objects.
> (137)

Hurlbert's enthusiasm for Cuban thought and sentiment, over and above any interest he might have in its resources, recalls and even outpaces Bryant's. He continues, "it is strange, indeed, that so little should be known among us of an intellectual and spiritual life so nearly allied to the best thought and feeling of our own country, and it is surely time for us to extend our free and respectful sympathy to the people from whom such men as Heredia, Milanes, and Placido have sprung" (138). His treatment of Heredia, with partial translations of several of his poems (and praise of Bryant's "Niagara" and "Hurricane"), runs for five pages; of Plácido, seven. He assumes his audience to be already familiar with Plácido's "martyrdom . . . in an unsuccessful attempt to vindicate his rights" (145). Hurlbert translates a handful of the Matanzas poet's lyrics, and includes enough comments from other readers in English and Spanish to indicate that he was as conversant as anyone with the life, work, and already substantial myth of Plácido. Hurlbert's references indicate that, during and perhaps after his visit to Cuba, he had access to its major literary publications of the time, including the *Aguinaldo habanero* and the *Aguinaldo matancero*, gift books published to highlight the literary culture in Havana and Matanzas respectively; he concludes that "much agreeable poetry may be found in the Cuban journals" (156). The sentimental cult of Plácido, the first important newspaper poet of Cuba, had been largely spread through the mechanics of print, and Hurlbert seems well aware of this.[6]

If Plácido's anguished addresses to his wife and mother epitomize the "manly outpourings of serious feeling" that Hurlbert endorses, in both its Mexican and Cuban sections his review adapts the general tendency to feminize Latin America by seeing its feminine qualities as positive—even idealized. In a passage praising José Jacinto Milanés for his "reverence for the true greatness and worth of woman" and his "deep sense of the wrongs" done to them, Hurlbert remarks that North American writers would do well to emulate the sentimental poet. Milanés, he says, speaks to Woman "in the language of brave and aspiring sympathy . . . as to the friend and equal of man, with strong, heartfelt appeals to her better nature calling her to break her chains of servile ignorance and indolent luxury, and to labor in her own blessed sphere, with her God-given energies of love and faith, for the redemption of her country and her race" (143–44). Although Hurlbert's reference to a Christianized "sphere" of domesticity suggests that he is working very much within conventional ideals of true womanhood, his emphasis on female "bravery" and "equality" also gestures toward the revolutionary metaphor of "breaking the chains" of colonial slavery. Thus he not only encourages a view of women as competent actors in the process of their own individual liberation; he validates the struggle for self-determination of feminized Latin American nations as well.

Such an insistence on agency sets Hurlbert apart from the mass of U.S. commentators around the time of the Mexican War, for although the gendering of Spanishness and nationhood in the Anglo-American imagination has deep roots, this conflict intensified it, with Mexicans depicted as either emasculated or outrightly feminine.[7] Without straining to find direct political consequences of such metaphoric acts, they are clearly allied to a range of assumptions that would influence policy: a general notion of natural feminine weakness, for instance, might reinforce the judgment that other American nations have failed to "maintain" their own liberty, in the Monroe Doctrine's language. This perception of political weakness, in turn, encourages the production of self-justifying visions of necessary intervention on the part of stronger powers, like the "chivalrous defense" of Texan independence against Mexico that pervaded discussions of its annexation as a state. Even (or perhaps especially) in sympathetic observers like Hurlbert, there is a growing tendency to distinguish among Latin American nations as among a set of feminine stereotypes: for instance, to imagine Cuba as a virtuous woman in need of rescue from her brutish governors while sexualizing Mexico as a "dark lady" whose territorial body seemed provocatively available.[8] These two geographical fronts—the near Caribbean, and the Mexican border from the Rio Bravo to northern California—were, as I suggested in the preceding chapter, crucial but ill-focused horizons in the Anglo-American imagination of its central place in the hemisphere throughout the 1840s and 1850s. As I hinted there, sympathetic "neighborly" responses to Latin America on the part of U.S. intellectuals hit squarely on the dilemma of expansion: to those who found slavery repugnant but interracial society difficult to imagine, colonization of some sort seemed a likely solution, either by resettling American blacks in Africa or by diluting their presence in the nation through Anglo settlement of the West and Southwest on a massive scale. Either response required a moral justification for the inevitable displacement of the existing inhabitants of those lands—and the period between Zachary Taylor's deliberately provocative order of his troops across the Nueces River into Mexican territory in January 1846 and the explosion of the *Maine* in Havana harbor in 1898 shows an increasing ability to provide such justifications. The old discourse of the Americas as a neighborhood of fraternal republics, with a shared identity as former colonies that had claimed and maintained their independence, gave way to an Anglo-American vision of Spanish America (and eventually the Spanish Pacific) as a group of potential colonies of its own. Such a shift in rhetoric and policy required its own high-level veilings and occlusions.[9]

    This tension between past and present meanings of colonialism plays out in the development of literary culture in the Americas in numerous ways over the course of the century. It enters into the well-known paradox of early American expression, caught between the desire to be "original"—to shrug off the master's yoke through loud and obvious forms of difference—and the need to be authorized to take the master's place by supplanting him on his own terms. Across the hemisphere, as I detailed in chapter 1, the call for an originary language and literature was being made in tandem with the rise of print culture, even on the peripheries of the ephemeral, underpopulated "nations" of Texas and California, which nonetheless fostered a geographically delimited sense of communal cultural identity. The core debate of this process centered on a balance between innovation and imitation: how much of this nascent culture ought to spring "natively" from the land, and how much could be guiltlessly borrowed from extranational sources. The same social groups that continued to locate cultural capital in European letters tried to foster a distinctly American culture by rifling through indigenous and folk traditions to translate literally or figuratively into other generic forms. In the next two chapters, I distinguish between two principal modes of nineteenth-century poetic production: "translative" and "originary," typified in the United States by Longfellow and Whitman respectively. Though falsely schematic, this distinction helps reconnect the linguistic sphere to the social one by examining the relationship between translation and transculturation. My aim is not to recapitulate the argument, originating in Goethe and finding its most popular recent avatar in Gloria Anzaldúa, that a bilingual writer "translates" a culture's ideologies along with its language, but to think through the relationship of translation to national state formation in the nineteenth century.[10] Although rarely discussed in this context, this argument over poetics took place against the traumatic backdrop of U.S. expansion to the west and to the south.

Spanish-language print communities in places like California, Texas, Florida, and New Mexico as well as the foreign-language press of New York, Philadelphia, and New Orleans were brought into being by local editors and publishers who acted as small-scale arbiters of culture. Like their analogues in the very centers of cultural power, the cosmopolitan translators of the borderlands were forced into a similar awareness of the problem of colonialism and language. Not only did periodicals on the borderlands, as elsewhere, reprint, plagiarize, and translate other's literary (and quasi-literary) pieces in order to fill column space; but issues of translation played a vital role in the very mission of the newspapers' nonliterary functions, arbitrating between two linguistic worlds that the

Spanish speakers frequently experienced as hostile. Those whose citizenship and identity had been redefined by the outcome of the war on Mexico became in some sense colonial subjects, for whom language was an instrument of power. Wherever located, then, the American translator is always positioned as a cosmopolitan—one who thinks globally, even when writing locally, but she or he must balance the competing claims of each sphere of influence.

Henry Wadsworth Longfellow, by far the best-selling U.S. poet during the nineteenth century, staked his career on the belief in a universally intelligible poetic center, and in translation as the common route to it. As the first consequence of that idea, he devoted more attention than had even Irving or Bryant to the process of translation, rendering foreign works intelligible to U.S. audiences as a way of teaching them the rudiments of cosmopolitanism. Another result ensued: his translations and paraphrased "traditions" from both Old and New World sources rode on the heels of his own work's popularity, and as a result reached readers spread across a wide range of social classes.[11] Longfellow had begun his career as a translator of Spanish and French instruction books for use in the first modern language courses to be taught at Bowdoin College, and his translation of *Coplas de Manrique* was highly praised when it was published in 1833. During the early years of his career, between 1832 and 1837, what he published was almost entirely translations. Even after the success of his first collection of original verse, *Voices of the Night*, in 1838, he continued to issue a number of translations through the 1840s, slowing down for some years and picking up with the massive project of translating *The Divine Comedy* in the 1860s.

From his youthful travels in Spain to his reception of visiting Latin Americans *de cierta clase* at Craigie House, Longfellow was an avid consumer and (re)producer of the Hispanic cultural tradition. His youthful decision to learn Spanish was pragmatic in many senses: he needed to prepare for his teaching position at Harvard; he cast himself as a successor to Washington Irving; and his father, though skeptical about the choice of a literary career, felt that Spanish might be an important trade language in case that career failed.[12] Aside from the *Coplas*, Longfellow translated Cervantes's *Novelas ejemplares*, the exiled liberal José de Espronceda's *El estudiante de Salamanca*, and several short poems by contemporary writers, including two by the prominent Cuban translator and anthologist Rafael Mendive. He also made notes for never-written verse romances recounting the drama of colonial greed at the San Luis Potosí mines in Mexico and the ongoing Argentine struggle against the Rosas dictatorship, inspired by Sarmiento's *Facundo*.[13] His imaginative engagement with *hispanidad* was not only appreciated but returned with interest by Latin American readers: measured by number of published translations and critical attention, Longfellow's works were disseminated in Latin America at a rate unsurpassed by any other U.S. author until the French-inspired vogue of Poe challenged that supremacy at the end of the century.[14] Although many of the originators of Latin America's national literary canons were avid readers and rewriters of all sorts of cosmopolitan figures outside the Spanish-speaking world (most of them French), Longfellow's writing appealed equally to pious conservatives like Juan de Dios Peza (known as the Mexican Longfellow) and anticlerical social engineers like Sarmiento. His other Latin American translators, who total nearly one hundred, include Miguel Antonio Caro and Rafael Pombo, two key arbiters of Colombian national culture; Bartolomé Mitre, poet and president of the short-lived United Provinces of the Río de la Plata; Pedro II, emperor of Brazil; and José Martí himself.

The perceived value of translation, as opposed to original composition, varied over the course of the century. On both continents, educational practice for elites gradually shifted from the classical emphasis on *paraphrasis* and *aemulatio*, methods that saw literal translation from Greek and Latin as an important training step in composition, toward a positivistic emphasis on self-mastery and translation as an apprenticeship in the modern languages of commerce.[15] The most influential letrados in Spanish America and the Caribbean during the century produced self-consciously nationalist texts right alongside their translations: Juan Bautista, Alberdi, José Eusebio Caro and his son Miguel Antonio, Juan Clemente Zenea, José María Róa Bárcena, Carlos Guido y Spano, Juan Antonio Pérez Bonalde, and Olegario Andrade lead a long list of writers who were politically as well as poetically active, and who devoted significant proportions of their literary labor to the practice of translation. At first glance such translation would seem ill suited for the task of American nation-building through shared literary experience, insofar as it continued to affirm the authority of European high culture, the "parent" of what Bello, Sarmiento, and Caro persistently referred to as the unruly mongrel tongues of America.[16] But their American improvisations on Romantic themes helped maintain the cultural capital associated with the colonial letrado class, which remained heavily invested in the authority of poetic laws in general, even as tastes in that genre fluctuated. As Angel Rama states, "Even poets helped construct the ideological framework of Latin American society . . . until the vogue of positivistic modernization in the late nineteenth century . . . they regarded poetry as part of the common patrimony of all *letrados.*"[17] Although its power waned as access to literacy widened, the letrado class of the postindependence period maintained virtual control over the key institutions of cultural reproduction—school and university systems, patronage publishing—that they had held as functionaries during the Spanish regime. The limited function that the letrado performed for the state was to model a regulated national language, whether through overtly patriotic and public genres like the ode and the occasional lyric, or within apparently apolitical texts expressing private sentiments of home, love, and loss.

The fact that the resulting national cultures in nineteenth-century Latin America bore the strong impress of French literature would occasion a modernist backlash, beginning with Martí's famous dismissal of them, in *Nuestra América,* as frock-coated imitation Parisians, comically out of place in their own countries. A glance at Emilio Carilla's list of Latin American Romantic-era translators goes on for pages with versions of Hugo, Lamartine, Byron, Longfellow, and the German lyricists (most of them read, in turn, in French translation); the French influence was so strong that numerous writers spoke out against the corrupting influence of French on American Spanish.[18] Most of those poet-translators are now lumped together as at best precursors to any truly Latin American expression. In the twentieth-century narrative of literary development, the vogue of "translated" sentiments from elsewhere gives way to the telluric originality of Darío and Neruda, and the cosmopolitan class cedes its privilege to a more democratic globalism (in the form of international socialism or anti-imperial *arielismo*).

The same general pattern applies in the United States, although the lettered class there was affiliated less with state bureaucracy, acting more as a secular priesthood wielding a benevolent authority over its readers. Longfellow in particular, with his strong associations with the family and the most prestigious university in the country, served as a kind of national high priest of culture—particularly in his role as translator, borrower, and imitator of the world's "traditions" (a word he often used to assign his poems to a genre). Just as the early church had unified its Babel of devotional languages in the lingua franca of Latin, Longfellow, as the appointed translator with access to the sacred "original" texts, produced in anthologies like *The Poets and Poetry of Europe* and *Poems of Places* a liturgy for a catholic American sensibility. It is precisely this image of Longfellow as a missionary of culture that has doomed him, along with most of the Latin American poets who claimed him as a fellow traveler, to exile from the canon in both Americas. Carilla ruefully comments in his definitive *El romanticismo en la América hispánica* on the cult of Longfellow: "Nowadays it pains us to admit it—not the admiration itself, but the magnitude of that admiration. However, we must surrender in the face of the evidence."[19] Just as nineteenth-century U.S. poetry tends to be reduced, in anthologies, to the innovations of Whitman and Dickinson, "telluric" Latin American works like the gaucho ballad *Martín Fierro* have long since eclipsed the work of the generations of poet-critics who made more than sixteen different Spanish translations of Longfellow's "Psalm of Life."[20] In the Americas context, modernist literary history poses translation as *imitatio*, plain and simple: the antithesis, and enemy, of poetic originality and the genuinely critical sensibility assumed to go with it. To later generations of writers and critics, the era's fondness for translation was precisely what seemed damningly derivative about figures like Longfellow and Caro. But this modernist rejection of the translative school was accompanied by a solidification of certain theories about translation. Retracing that history, Lawrence Venuti argues that by the end of the nineteenth century, transparency and invisibility had become installed as the dominant values for Anglo-American translations. The cult of authorial individuality, along with the increasing scientism of the age, contributed to the consensus that translation is "a second-order representation: only the foreign text can be original, an authentic copy, true to the author's personality or intention, whereas the translation is derivative, fake, potentially a false copy." Yet, paradoxically, "translation is required to efface its second-order status with transparent discourse, producing the illusion of authorial presence whereby the translated text can be taken as the original . . . translators playact as authors, and translations pass for original texts."[21] Venuti's analysis shows this fetish of invisibility to be historically determined and mutable, and constructs an alternative practice based on Friedrich Schleiermacher's distinction between "reader-friendly" and "author-friendly" translations. In Venuti's interpretation,

> Schleiermacher allowed the translator to choose between a *domesticating* method, an ethnocentric reduction of the foreign text to target-language cultural values, bringing the author back home, and a *foreignizing* method, an ethnodeviant pressure on those values to register the linguistic and cultural difference of the foreign text, sending the reader abroad. . . . Foreignizing translation signifies the difference of the foreign text, yet only

by disrupting the cultural codes that prevail in the target language. In its effort to do right abroad, this translation method must do wrong at home, deviating enough from native norms to stage an alien reading experience.[22]

In the spirit of the French translation theorist Antoine Berman, Venuti finds in this "foreignized translation" an ethics of preserving cultural difference that clashes sharply with the domesticating, transparency-oriented theories of translation solidified in England and the United States by modernist prejudices and practice. Tracing this commitment to "abusive fidelity" back to the universalism of Dryden and Tytler, he links such an emphasis on domestication to class and racial anxieties, and to strategies of ethnolinguistic containment expressed in colonial missionary activity and an Arnoldian scorn for popular culture.[23]

"Foreignizing" translation in the mode of Schleiermacher was not inattentive to the problem of enlisting language in nation-building: to the contrary, it promoted the interests of bourgeois nationalism. Yet it met a hostile reception in England. As an example, Venuti describes the ambitious efforts of the pedagogue Francis Newman to oppose "the English regime of fluent domestication" with a German-inspired populism, aiming to reach "the *unlearned* English reader" of Dickens and the daily newspapers with his new translations of Homer. Newman chose the ballad form, as "the archaic English form most suitable to Homeric verse," and consciously archaized his vocabulary even as he expurgated and otherwise adapted the *Iliad* to suit Victorian values: "what was foreignizing about Newman's translations was not their morality, but their literary discourse, the strangeness of the archaism . . . [which] deviated from current usage and cut across various literary discourses, poetry and the novel, English and Scottish."[24] Newman and Longfellow were in many respects kindred spirits: not only did Newman assign *Hiawatha* to his Latin classes for translation exercises, but Newman's most damning critic—Matthew Arnold—used *Evangeline* as a negative example of how one ought *not* to write Homeric hexameters in English. As the high priest of poetic translation in the United States and one of its most accomplished Germanists, Longfellow had assimilated not only Schleiermacher's theory of translation, but those of Goethe, Schlegel, Novalis, and the rest of the German Romantic school.[25]

Longfellow's sense of mission regarding the role of translation in the development of national literatures is evident in his work as an anthologist. He undertook the Herculean task of compiling *The Poets and*

Poetry of Europe in 1843, just after returning from an extended stay on the continent and marrying his second wife, Fanny Appleton, who collaborated with him on the massive anthology.[26] He wrote to his friend the German radical Ferdinand Freiligrath that he conceived of the book as a response to the successful anthology formulas of that most ardent literary nationalist, Rufus Griswold, adapting the syntax of Griswold's titles and the material appearance of his books to different ends:

> I agree with you entirely in what you say about translations. It is like running a plough share through the soil of one's mind; a thousand germs of thought start up (excuse this agricultural figure) which otherwise might have lain and rotted in the ground. Still it sometime[s] seems to me like an excuse for being lazy, like leaning on an other man's shoulders. I am just beginning the publication of a volume of Specimens of foreign poetry, being a selection of the best English translations now existing from the Anglo-Saxon, Icelandic, Danish, Swedish, German, Dutch, French, Italian, Spanish, and Portuguese. The object of the book is to bring together in one volume what is now scattered though a hundred and not easily got at. The volume will be of the same size and appearance as Griswold's Poets and Poetry of America. I shall write the introduction and Biographical notices. Most of the translations, of course, will be by other hands.[27]

Longfellow is reacting against what he perceived as an American tendency toward provincialism, reinforced by the excesses of cultural nationalism manifested by Griswold and others.[28] The anthology seeks to make obscure texts then available only to scholars (and to those with the leisure and privilege to learn languages and to travel in Europe) universally accessible: the eight hundred-page book features the work of four hundred poets in ten languages. This profoundly democratizing move was underscored by Longfellow's desire to have a multitude of "hands," of different translators, represented in it. In the new age of mass-marketed books, *The Poets and Poetry of Europe* was hugely successful; nothing of its kind had appeared in England or the United States before 1845, and its publisher, Carey and Hart, was more middlebrow than the elite Ticknor and Fields house where Longfellow published his own works. In 1879, he would launch an even more ambitious project with Houghton Mifflin—the thirty-one-volume *Poems of Places*—which is organized according to a kind of colonial itinerary. It begins with England and

Wales (volumes 1–4); proceeds through Ireland, Scotland, and Scandinavia (volumes 5–8) through the rest of continental Europe (volumes 9–18); then moves by way of Greece to Turkey, Russia, and Asia (volumes 19–23) and Africa (volume 24). The remaining volumes swing back toward the Americas, beginning with New England (volumes 25–26), proceeding into the "Middle," "Southern," and "Western" states (volumes 27–29), and ending with "British America, Mexico, and South America" (volume 30) and "Oceanica" (volume 31). The final volumes seem to signal potential directions for the future course of the western—that is, the American—empire.[29]

Do these anthologies constitute, in Schleiermacher's division, an effort to "domesticate" foreign texts or to "foreignize" the target language and increase its receptiveness to cultural otherness? As an exercise in influencing the national schoolroom, the anthology would seem to do the former; yet elsewhere Longfellow suggests that understanding other cultures through translation must precede any "native" expression. In a satirical passage about national literature in the cotemporous novel *Kavanagh*, Longfellow endorses this Goethean notion through the character of the schoolmaster Churchill: "As the blood of all nations is mingling with our own, so will their thoughts and feelings finally mingle in our literature. We shall draw from the Germans, tenderness; from the Spaniards, passion; from the French, vivacity,—to mingle more and more with our English solid sense. And this will give us universality, so much to be desired."[30] Both Longfellow's fundamental faith in the need for writers to look outside the Anglo-American tradition to prevent a dangerous myopia, and his deeply Romantic ambivalence about the status of translation as a "secondary" form of creativity are evident in the preceding letter to Freiligrath. There he wavers between seeing translation as a "plough" that enables creative fertility and as "an excuse for being lazy." Throughout his life Longfellow continues to express a Germanic attentiveness to the tantalizing (im)possibility of a faithful translation, as he continues to invest at least one-fourth of his productive energy into translative enterprises. He expresses sharp criticism for those translators who think "that what the foreign author really says should be falsified or modified, if thereby the smoothness of the verse can be improved. On the contrary I maintain . . . that a translator, like a witness on the stand, should hold up his right hand and swear to "tell the truth, the whole truth, and nothing but the truth."[31] "Smoothness," then, is never the highest value in his linguistic economy. A "foreign" cast to a translation, even if it impedes transparency and flow, will promote rather than detract from its ability to communicate the sense of the original. To put it in terms of Schleiermacher's tradeoff, Longfellow seeks to accommodate the writer, not the reader. Though not generally a self-promoter, he wrote in a notebook that his *Divine Comedy* was "exactly what Dante says, and not what the translator imagines he might have said if he had been an Englishman."[32]

In part, Longfellow achieved the foreignizing effect through scholarly practice, for instance by affixing an introduction about Spanish devotional practice to his *Coplas de Manrique,* as a reminder of the kinds of cultural gaps that required the reader's effort to grasp and respect. With the Dante translation, too, he made his American audience feel most "at home" in the surrounding apparatus of the book rather than in the translation itself. His *Inferno,* though aimed at the general market of educated readers, provides as many notes as text. Many are simply pedagogical, providing historical background and explaining classical and biblical allusions, but some serve no other purpose than to identify this as a work for American readers: mentions of the Medusa in Canto IX, Ariadne in Canto XII, and the monster Geryon in Canto XVII lead to notes about Hawthorne's various fictionalizations of these mythic figures, while a note to Canto XIV refers to *The Scarlet Letter.* Longfellow glosses a reference to the horizon in Canto XXVI with a long quote from Alexander von Humboldt's *Personal Narrative of Travels to the Equinoctial Regions of the New Continent* describing his first glimpse of the Caribbean sky, in which the explorer in turn imagines what Columbus must have thought of it. Thus Longfellow inserts his reader in a chain of observers of the New World who now reverse the gaze of Europe by returning to its foundational visions and texts. He seems aware that as Americans they cannot help but superimpose their own landscapes on what they see, but he sets limits on their ability to domesticate the original itself.

Longfellow's *Divine Comedy* (1865–67), Bayard Taylor's *Faust I* and *II* (1870, 1871), and William Cullen Bryant's *Iliad* (1870) and *Odyssey* (1871) were the most ambitious and high-profile translation efforts attempted by U.S. writers in the nineteenth century.[33] All were conceived as popularizing, but not domesticating, experiments in a distinctly American spirit. The wife of Longfellow's publisher, James T. Fields, reported on a dinner in 1870 at which he and Taylor shared ideas about translating. "Longfellow advanced the idea that the English, from the insularity of their character, were incapable of making a perfect translation. Americans, French, and Germans, he said, have much larger adaptability to and sympathy to the thought of others. He would not hear Chapman's Homer or anything else quoted on the other side, but was zealous in enforcing this argument. He anticipates much from Taylor's version of *Faust.* All this was strikingly interesting, as showing how his imagination wrought with him, because he was arguing from his own theory of the capacity of the races, and in the face of his knowledge of the best actual translations existing today." Here Longfellow claims for Americans an enlarged "adaptability" and "sympathy" for foreign patterns of thought, and uses this as license to stray far from the homogenizing English translation practice, epitomized by Arnold.[34]

Taylor's rendition of *Faust*—the first complete translation by an Anglo-American—was ultimately criticized for his adherence to the Germanic theory of foreignizing. Convinced that he needed to reproduce the syntax of the original as well as its meter, Taylor gave his English German word order—a fact that has led most critics, including even his sympathetic biographer, to agree that "there seems to be an overabundance of inversions in it. They mar the sense of naturalness in the work and give it a foreign flavor."[35] Both Taylor and Longfellow, then, violated the principle of invisibility, an aesthetic value that seeks to conceal the seam or the difference of translation and thereby to reinforce the monoglossic dominance of the national language into which they are translating. They offered up their translations with the explicit instruction that they be read as alien, as exemplary expressions of some other national or tribal Being. The irony here is that Taylor, whose career represented an equally populist but more peripatetic version of Longfellow's domestic cosmopolitanism, expressed a stronger desire than Longfellow to invent a native idiom for New World poetry. His early works during the 1840s seize on the Mexican part of the continent as a field "yet untouched in the fast-spreading domain of American literature," as he wrote to the enthusiastic expansionist Evert A. Duyckinck. His narrative poem *Ximena, a Romance of the Sierra Morena* was published in 1844, before he had traveled anywhere; after his travels to California during the gold rush came *El Dorado, or Adventures in the Path of Empire* (1850). As that title indicates, Taylor anticipated Whitman in his identification of the Spanish Southwest and the West as future territory for the United States to dominate both politically and culturally. When Taylor published his "Ballads of California" in the *New York Tribune,* they were slyly presented as "translations from the Spanish by a gentleman of St. Louis."[36]

Taylor was not alone, however, in his simultaneous engagement with expansive nationalism and respectful cosmopolitanism. He exemplifies the paradox of the nineteenth-century translator's burden: to authorize new American language uses through contact with the foreign and alien, while insulating against the excesses of cultural nationalism and monoglossia. Translation brings out every anxiety that writers schooled in the Romantic cult of originality might have about belatedness and secondariness. That anxiety can also be read in terms of sentimental discourse, for translation theory is historically shot through with a problem of gender: the perceived secondariness of translation relates, in a very general way, to a hierarchy of value that equates a masculine original with a feminine "copy," as Sherry Simon argues.[37] Just as Longfellow's position as a masculine sentimental figure confounds such gendered spheres, his *Evangeline* in its English and Spanish versions disrupts the hierarchy of original and copy.

Ecos de México: Whittier, Longfellow, and the Case against Expansion

The years between Bryant's "The Prairies" and Hurlbert's remark that his readers ought to take an interest in the culture of the Spanish American nations "with whom it is the 'manifest destiny' of our country to be more and more connected" were eventful in hemispheric history. Texas's declaration of independence from Mexico in 1835 and its eventual incorporation into the Union began a souring of U.S.-Mexican relations that culminated in diplomat John Slidell's disastrously double-handed attempt to purchase California and New Mexico in the fall of 1845, which finally boiled over into a provocative confrontation between Taylor's troops and Mexican forces in territory long claimed by Mexico in late April 1846. The twenty-months' war that followed, involving a full-scale invasion of central Mexico by land, a siege of the capital and its principal port, and a military expedition across the far western portion of the continent to Santa Fe, radically changed the balance of power in the Americas, arguably turning the United States into an imperial power and modernizing the practices of warfare and war journalism.[38] Initially William Cullen Bryant took a strong stand against the annexation of Texas; an editorial in 1836 warned that the United States would join "those spoilers of nations, whose examples we are taught as republicans to detest" if it intervened in Mexico's dispute with the newly declared Texas Republic. As late as May 1846, after the official declaration of war and the calling-up of volunteers set off a national war mania, Bryant continued to argue that military involvement in Mexico would be "vexatious and expensive and slow," and that waging war on a sovereign neighbor would "cheapen" national morality. But his strong Free-Soil sympathies brought him reluctantly to support President James K. Polk, and he threw the *Post*'s editorial support in favor of the war, robbing the national press of what would have been an influential voice of resistance against it.[39]

In opposition to all the patriotic boosterism of the war, however, there was a small but steady protest movement against the invasion of Mexico, mostly among northern abolitionists like Charles Sumner, Theodore Parker, and William Lloyd Garrison. The ardent poet of abolition John Greenleaf Whittier found the Mexican War offensive mainly as a provocation on the part of slaveholding interests; he rallied hard against the annexation of "slave Texas."[40] But he was also aware, as were Garrison and Thoreau, that Mexico's territorial integrity and fundamental rights as a nation were at stake, and in two well-known poems responding to the war he portrayed Mexico as a wronged woman, adapting the strategy of sentimental writers like Lydia Maria Child who cloaked political questions about the rights of the downtrodden in the language of Christian piety. Whittier, an autodidact, was not much of a translator, but several of his poems imitate the foreignizing method of alienating U.S. culture from itself. He, like Longfellow, was fond of the ballad form and frequently adapted "legends" from other countries to reflect on political issues near to his heart. "The Angels of Buena Vista" was written for the abolitionist paper Whittier edited, the *National Era*, appearing on 20 May 1847, shortly after the siege of Veracruz, the rout at Cerro Gordo, and the uncontested occupation of Puebla. The poem was widely reproduced and illustrated, and occasioned one of the more popular and durable myths of the war.[41] It begins with a perspective from the enemy's side, showing "our Ximena" cowering in fear in her own home as the "fearful whirlwind" of the battle of Buena Vista takes place outside her door. Rushing out after the battle to find her lover dead, she turns instead toward another wounded soldier, noticing with initial horror "the Northern eagle shining on his pistol-belt." She nurses him anyway, and he dies in Ximena's arms dreaming that she is his mother. She in turn casts

> "A bitter curse upon them, poor boy, who led thee forth,
> From some gentle, sad-eyed mother, weeping, lonely, in the
> North!"[42]

Ximena, aided with other "noble Mexic women," goes on to tend the wounded soldiers of both sides alike, "and the dying foeman blessed them in a strange and Northern tongue." The appeal to Christian ideals of womanhood is clear; the invasion and burning of the heroine's sacred space of home is meant to stir readerly outrage and sympathy in equal measure. Conventional as "The Angels of Buena Vista" may be, it manages a neat manipulation of readerly assumptions: seen from Ximena's privileged perspective, the enemy is not a nation but simply an amorphous place called "the North," as undifferentiated as the mysteriously veiled South invoked in Hurlbert or Melville. There are no more specific adjectives anywhere in the poem to mark the invading force as "Yankee" or "American." The northern soldiers and their language are made to seem foreign and out of place, emphasizing the strangeness and unnaturalness of this scene of war. In Whittier's abolitionist poetry in general, "the North" naturally represents the polestar of freedom, while the South represents barbarity. Here, however, he allows a potentially dangerous slippage in that geography of sentiment.

By the time the imbalanced war was won, Whittier transferred the feminine qualities he associated with vulnerable Mexico to the territories it had surrendered. In "The Crisis," which according to the epigraph was "written on learning the terms of the treaty with Mexico" and first published in the *National Era* on 30 March 1848, Whittier gives his version of the transamerican geographical sublime, unrolling a panorama that begins in the mountains and follows "the circles of our empire" to California. But his version of the genre, in contrast to Bryant's, envisions a tragic future:

> O vale of Rio Bravo! Let thy simple children weep;
> Close watch about their holy fire let maids of Pecos keep;
> Let Taos send her cry across Sierra Madre's pine,
> And Santa Barbara toll her bells amid her corn and vines;
> For lo! the pale land-seekers come, with eager eyes of gain,
> Wide scattering, like the bison herds on broad Salada's plain.[43]

Painting Mexico as feminine and infantilized allows him to argue sympathetically that the land will suffer from the advent of the greedy, "pale land-seekers"—the strange-looking "Saxon," as he puts it later in the poem. Yet he also seems resigned to the acquisition of territory he had once feared, saying that the western lands are "Forever ours! for good or ill, on us the burden lies." Still holding out hope for a positive end to the fight in Congress to prevent the extension of slavery into the new West, he moralizes for several further stanzas on the evils of slavery, concluding with a utopian vision of the "Northern pioneer" (no longer portrayed as a greedy acquisitionist) setting out "to wed Penobscot's waters to San Francisco's bay." Here, like Whitman in "By Blue Ontario's Shore," he imagines a national romance of reconciliation taking place through the body of the continent as its two extremes are "wed."

By far the majority of popular literary culture surrounding the war on Mexico, however, was jingoistic and celebratory, as Johannsen's book amply demonstrates. Whittier's didactic work always attracted its fair share of critics, but the more mainstream Longfellow—who, unlike Whittier or Taylor, never wrote topical verse outside his early "Poems on Slavery" and possibly "The Arsenal at Springfield"—responded to the events of the moment far less directly. In several ways, however, *Evangeline: A Tale of Acadie*, his first successful long poem, reflects the ethical questions surrounding invasion, territorial colonization, and displaced populations that confronted every newspaper reader in the country during the year in which it was composed. Longfellow's journal entries during the writing of the poem provide suggestive connections between the writing of the poem and the news from the Mexican front. He began the poem in early 1846, having been given the idea by Hawthorne. An entry on 21 January 1847 juxtaposes conversations with William Prescott, who probably knew more about Mexico than anyone else in Cambridge, and work on *Evangeline*. On 17 February he notes, "Wrote description of the prairies for Evangeline. In the evening began with Mr. Corwin's excellent speech against the war. Then Kendall's Santa Fé expedition."[44] Finishing the poem later that month (and immediately starting in on *Kavanagh*), he continues reading Kendall on New Mexico ("I longed to go there") and reporting on the war news in his journal. When *Evangeline* was finally published on 30 October 1847, the war was all but over, with Scott's troops occupying the capital. Like "The Angels of Buena Vista," it responds to contemporary issues of territorial expansion and expulsion through a sentimentalized female figure who represents her wronged nation.

Among the first readers of *Evangeline*, even those who expressed skepticism about the author's controversial choice to use hexameters agreed that the poem neatly fulfilled two literary desiderata of long standing. Praised for its moralizing narrative of pious patience and heroic self-abnegation, it also seemed to qualify as the long-awaited American epic, with lengthy descriptive passages that scrolled through the expanding panorama of the continental landscape. The combination of classical meter with contemporary sentimental romance moved the critic for *Littell's Living Age* to call it "the most perfect of domestic epics, the Odyssey of the nineteenth century," with its heroine playing both Odysseus and Penelope.[45] As the very notion of a "domestic epic" implies, the exiled character of Evangeline combines masculine fortitude with feminine self-abnegation, developing a version of Heredia's civic eroticism and—more importantly—providing an alternative to the traditional epic of Arms and Men, in the midst of the largest mustering of volunteers and the most massive movement of weaponry yet to occur in North America. A historical event, the British invasion of French settlements in the Bay of Minas under dubious pretext in 1755, spurs the plot into motion, and Longfellow's Evangeline—like Whittier's Ximena—suffers the loss of her betrothed in a way that seems designed to provoke outrage. Although Evangeline's story is set nearly a century earlier, her path follows that of the national growth of the United States, from the far North of small yeoman farmers, to the Louisiana territory acquired by Jefferson, to the West of the Catholic missions and the "Spanish cowboys." Like many Longfellow poems, it combines aspects of the cultural-nationalist agenda with that of the cosmopolitan. The story it recounts is "translated" from the whispers of the ancient pines of Nova Scotia, and presumably from the native French of the characters; in the second section, the heroine's wanderings are punctuated by a series of interpolated poems and stories told by Indians, trappers, and her confessor/companion, Father Felician.

Evangeline emplots a familiar pattern of sentimental narrative: an orphaned girl is cast out of the pastoral realm of her beloved home and exiled from her extended family in order to learn the lessons of endurance and heavenly compensation for worldly loss. As the poem's continuing half-life in French Canada and Cajun Louisiana suggests, however, that family plot is readily adaptable to a kind of national allegory. The lifelong separation of Evangeline Bellefontaine from her lover, Gabriel Lajeunesse, stands in for the unassimilable psychic loss that results from the forced exile of the Acadians from their "natural" home.[46] Longfellow deploys the abolitionist's strategy of portraying a political problem as a domestic one, so that the removals come as an outrage against the sanctity of the family. As the village of Grand-Pré burns under the watch of British soldiers, Acadian mothers and children are wrenched from each other on the beach and sent toward different ships, exacting a pathos similar to the slave-auction scenes in *Uncle Tom's Cabin* and portraying the army's burning of crops and homes as a senseless destruction endemic to war. Evangeline's aged father dies of grief at that very moment, suggesting the erasure of Grand-Pré's past and threatening the continuity of its traditions. But it is Youth (as Gabriel's surname, Lajeunesse, suggests) who absorbs the real blow of the tragedy, as Evangeline relives that initial loss over and over again through the tragic near-misses of her search for Gabriel. The poem does not simply thematize territorial removal and the unassimilable loss of exile; it enacts them on the body of Evangeline. "Something there was in her life incomplete, imperfect, unfinished."[47] She—like Ximena—must be content with letting her motherly instincts flow elsewhere, nursing not enemy soldiers but patients dying in a yellow fever epidemic, where she at last discovers Gabriel again, only moments before his death.

Like all exiles who carry a memory of their home country that is frozen in the moment of their leave-taking, Gabriel and Evangeline in this reunion scene are oddly stranded between two contradictory time frames: they act as if nothing has changed in the beloved in the decades since their parting. But their meeting also provides a necessary narrative of closure, assuring them (and us) that time *has* gone on without them, and that neither will be left to wander in limbo like the spurned lover in one of the Indian ghost stories Evangeline is told. The community of Grand-Pré itself suffers a similar temporal ambiguity: Longfellow's version of Acadian history is firmly grounded in the archive of real events, as admiring reviewers noted, but is also depicted as timeless and outside the realm of history. The poem locates itself in the mythical ground-zero time of medieval epic, the "mournful tradition" "still sung by the pines of the forests," and the anachronistically peaceful Acadians maintain a closed, self-reliant ethnic community where all "dwelt together in love . . . free from fear, that reigns with the tyrant, and envy, the vice of republics. . . . / There the richest was poor, and the poorest lived in abundance" (22). The Acadians are made into mythic *Volk*, heightening the pathos when the British ships, harbingers of modernity, leave the bay triumphantly, "bearing a nation, with all its household gods, into exile, / Exile without an end, and without an example in story" (61). The "nation" loses its coherence outside Grand-Pré, for the Acadian resettlement in the exotic South is presented as a series of patently false notes: touched by the ominous "Spanish fever" in Louisiana, Basil (who had nearly led an armed uprising against the British invasion) becomes a happy cowboy sporting a sombrero. As Basil remarks about his lovelorn son, those who mourn the past have no place in the present. Gabriel departs for the West because "He at length had become so tedious to men and to maidens, / Tedious even to me" (78). With that, the plot threads that involve the other villagers drop from the poem's design. If the Acadians eventually accept the violently progressive force of history, Evangeline resists such acceptance to the end, with her stubborn fidelity to her first love and to the original village community.

Because Evangeline's fate (perpetual exile) is thus separated from that of the Acadians (awkward assimilation), Longfellow's rendering of the tragedy as a principally personal, affective one might seem cagily depoliticized. The same emotional economy that dictates Evangeline's remarkable restraint on Gabriel's deathbed dictates the redirection of political conflict as well. The first part of the poem continually solicits sympathetic outrage on the part of the reader through repeated references to legal documents; but that outrage—like the revolutionary anger of the Acadians—is just as consistently defused. After the British soldiers trap the village's men inside the church to tell them that their lands have been seized, Basil Lajeunesse rises, "with his arms uplifted," to protest, "Down with the tyrants of England! We never have sworn them allegiance! / Death to these foreign soldiers, who seize on our homes and our harvests!" But "the merciless hand of a soldier" strikes him "upon the mouth, and dragged him down to the pavement"—a censorial silencing repeated by Father Felician, who enters and redirects their impulse toward rebellion into prayer. The men later emerge from five days' imprisonment in the church singing hymns: a remarkable displacement of emotion that is described as a translation ("their souls, with devotion translated"). What might strike some readers as a too-easy acceptance, on the part of the Acadians, of a tyrannical takeover simply naturalizes Evangeline's "lesson" about the redirection of emotion on a collective scale. Yet Basil's pacifistic leadership—which the poem seems to endorse—stands in opposition to President Polk's declaration of war speech, which invoked the Monroe Doctrine to claim that U.S. troops needed to occupy Texas to protect the homes of settlers against the tyrannical Santa Anna, and to guard against the possible British threat that might ensue if that nation came to the aid of the Mexicans.[48] The fictional Acadian response here implicitly rebukes Polk, who bellicosely ignored the Mexican government's statement that they would consider any troop movement south of the Nueces River to be "an act of war."

Finally, the epilogue, which directs its panoramic eye first at the lovers' graves in Philadelphia and then at the site of old Grand-Pré, encircles its readers within specific national geographies that implicate them in the poem as well. As the closing lines remind us, A(r)cadia had to make way for the ascendance of "another race, with other customs and language": that is, for the British colonizers to whom Longfellow's readers were linguistically and genealogically linked. The timelessness of the racialized Acadian community gets usurped by the progressive time frame of U.S. nationhood, which has as its point of origin another historical rupture: the colonists' rebellion, in turn, against the very same British forces who had usurped the "nation" of Grand-Pré. U.S. readers had to create contexts in which to interpret the events of 1846 and 1847, which resulted in a near doubling of their nation's territory and a new and troubling set of problems in political ethics to consider. For some, the parallel scheme of *Evangeline* might have prompted satisfaction at having avenged the moral outrage of the British invasion a century earlier. But others might have more gloomily asked—as did Longfellow and many of his fellow members of the New England intelligentsia—whether their nation's behavior toward Mexico was any more defensible than the expulsion of the Acadians from their Eden, or whether its results would be any less tragic.

Converting *Evangeline* to *Evangelina*

Besides its resonance with immediate political questions, *Evangeline* was one of the most popular stories about Catholicism to circulate in the nineteenth-century United States: though trained on centuries of mistrust of Spanish Catholics expressed in the historical Black Legend and fueled by popular Gothic romance, Protestant audiences experienced an exotic thrill in reading about Evangeline's antique piety.[49] Its priest and heroine were certainly portrayed with sympathy, although Evangeline wears her Catholicism but lightly—at no point does she appeal to the saints, light candles, or make offerings—perhaps a sanitizing gesture on Longfellow's part to shield her from the more vicious accusations of cultishness many associated with Catholic devotional practice. This sympathetic treatment may also help account for the fact that it was by far the most popular of his works in the Spanish-speaking world, which produced no fewer than twelve translations of *Evangelina*. Though not the first, perhaps the best known of these renditions was done by a Chilean, Carlos Morla Vicuña, and published in New York in 1871 with the help of Rafael Pombo, who was himself an enthusiastic Longfellow translator.[50] Longfellow's contemporary critics, both foreign and domestic, tended to repeat the claim that his cosmopolitan poetry, so well informed by history and tradition, expressed "universal" sentiments—meaning, of course, values held by powerful groups of literate elites. Latin Americans, in particular, referred to such universality as *catholic* feeling, mingling the sacred and secular resonances of a term very deeply embedded in the Spanish language—one that was, not incidentally, at the core of some of the most highly charged conflicts between *conservadores* and *liberales* during this turbulent century. Longfellow's appealing catholic sensibility is the main theme of Morla's preface, which argues that the intent of the poem is to bring about a rehabilitation of "la fé en todas las grandes y nobles cualidades del corazón humano y una comprensión más católica, más vasta y más liberal de las ideas cristianas" [faith in all the grand and noble qualities of the human heart, and a broader, more catholic, and more liberal understanding of Christian ideas].[51] He acknowledges the author's Protestantism, but emphasizes that it has a strong underlying "sentimiento moral" (xii), and praises it as the long-awaited realization of the "poema descriptivo americano" that both continents have awaited (viii). Both English and Spanish critics, then, zeroed in on *Evangeline* as a necessary text, one they expected would be at the foundation of a literary canon original to the New World; but each group contorted its vision of the other's dominant religion to counterbalance its own needs and anxieties.

Morla goes on to suggest that *Evangeline* is really about hemispheric history. In giving his capsule history of the Acadian removals, Morla deviates from U.S. commentators by claiming that religious persecution, rather than territorial expansion, was the main cause of the British "atrocities" there. By adding details about other expelled Acadians who found refuge in Santo Domingo or Guiana, he inserts the tragedy of Grand-Pré into the larger history of Spanish America as a place of tolerance and refuge. He translates it, in other words, into the language of Catholicism, resulting in a version that (although "faithful") produces a distinctly different reading of American history and subjectivity than that produced in the English *Evangeline.* He foregrounds the character of Father Felician, and rests his proof of the poem's elevated moral sensibility in a part of the text that U.S. commentators largely ignored: the brief mention of Jesuit missionary activity in the western territory (part 2, section 4). Those scenes, according to Morla, most fully achieve the Americanist literary agenda because they depict "the Catholic mission, which was the vanguard of civilization . . . the venerable, fatherly priest who presides over it . . . the innocent savages fascinated by the sweetness of religion" (x). Morla plays to the sensibilities—and prejudices—of *his* audience, making Longfellow the heir of the French Catholic apologist and novelist François-René de Chateaubriand: the two, he writes, are "organismos igualmente finos" (xi). Morla was not the only Spanish reader to find in Evangeline a whitened version of Atala. *El Mundo Nuevo*, a biweekly published in New York but distributed throughout Latin America, devoted a lengthy article to Morla's translation, claiming that the poem represents "el más alto en la aún escasa y poco variada literatura de los Estados Unidos. *Evangelina* es la primera obra americana donde se describen, con tanta exactitud y sentimiento poético, como en los siempre admirables aunque un tanto envejecidos escritos de Chateaubriand, pre- cursos y apóstol del género, los grandiosos y sorprendentes aspectos de la naturaleza de este nuevo Continente" [the highest point yet reached in the literature of the U.S., which is still scanty and little varied. *Evangeline* is the first American work which describes the grand, surprising aspects of Nature on this new continent with the same exactitude and poetic senti- ment as the ever-admirable (if somewhat old-fashioned) writings of Cha- teaubriand, precursor and apostle of the genre].[52]

Translation's power to catholicize a Protestant text is most appar- ent in the climactic passage, in which Evangeline, an aging Sister of Mercy in a Philadelphia hospital, seems to have succeeded in redirecting her love for Gabriel into love for others in need ("he was not changed, but transfigured"). In the original, she accomplishes this sublimation with a certain Yankee impecunity: "so was her love diffused, but . . . suffered no waste or loss" (99). Dedicating herself to the sisterhood is presented as a natural extension of her psychoreligious maturation, a way of taking responsibility for her own unruly emotions. Like any number of fictions of the period, *Evangeline* argues for emotional self-restraint as a form of internalized discipline, containing her "unsatisfied longing" and returning "its waters . . . back to their spring" to recycle her erotic loss into a spiritual gain. Evangeline Bellefontaine thus opens the gate for those novelistic heroines who model the sentimental ideal of growing beyond tears, learning to master desire (the great skill of, among others, "Little" Evangeline St. Clare in *Uncle Tom's Cabin*, another emotional steward who redistributes her disciplinary wealth among the poor in spirit).[53] The *Mundo Nuevo* reviewer sees Evangeline's psychological response to the loss of Gabriel differently: "Su corazón lacerado por tan implacable infortunio busca al fin reposo en el seno de la religión, toma el manto de hermana de la caridad. El poeta protestante no vacila en rendir homenaje de respeto y simpatía a esa noble y dulce institución católica" [Her heart lacerated by such implacable misfortune, she finally seeks solace in the womb of religion, taking the mantle of a sister of charity. The Protestant poet does not hesitate to render due respect and sympathy to that noble and good Catholic institution]. English readings, in other words, tend to interpret the deathbed scene as the epitome of Protestant self-regulation; Spanish ones, as affirmation of the solace to be found in Catholic institutions.

In the original, when Evangeline finally discovers Gabriel, she is suddenly overcome by

> All the aching of heart, the restless, unsatisfied longing,
> All the deep, dull pain, and constant anguish of patience!
> And, as she pressed once more the lifeless head to her bosom,
> Meekly she bowed her own, and murmured, "Father, I thank thee!"
> (104–5)

This climactic stanza exemplifies everything that modernist poetics has rendered unreadable about Longfellow. If it draws up too abruptly for a modern reader—the deflating final line seems a very limited outlet for the enormous emotional buildup of a thirty-years' search—it was precisely the touch that its first audiences, both English and Spanish, most admired. Hawthorne, who asked his son to read the poem aloud during his final illness, affirms this scene as his favorite.[54] Opines the *Mundo Nuevo:* "Esta escena final está trazada por Longfellow con notable sobriedad. Dura un instante, y es por lo mismo más patética y desgarradora" [Longfellow treats this final scene with notable sobriety. It lasts but an instant, and is all the more pathetic and wrenching for it]. However, in Morla's rendition, which carefully reproduces the assonance and alliteration of the English lines, the emotional tenor is different:

> Aquel inquieto, inextinguible anhelo,
> Esa pena profunda y siempre activa,
> Esa angustia constante y sin consuelo,
> Y ella, al besar la inanimada frente,
> 'Gracias, o Padre!' exclama humildemente.
>
> [*That restless, inexhaustible longing,*
> *That deep and always active pain,*
> *That constant anguish without consolation:*
> *And she, upon kissing the lifeless forehead,*
> *Exclaims humbly, 'Thanks, O Father!'*
>
> (111)

Without the original version's "constant anguish of patience," the text seems less relentlessly insistent that Evangeline maintain her calm self-restraint under even the most impossibly trying circumstances. The emphasis falls less on the magnitude of her built-up pain than on the idea that suffering is a constant, something "deep and always active"; and thus her final gesture, a reverent kiss on the forehead, seems less exaggerated than the grand Pietà in which Longfellow poses her.

Certainly, one would not want to lay too heavy a burden on these short passages to "prove" something as sweeping as a difference in Catholic and Protestant modes of regulating the subject. But a Catholic reading of the scene would not insist on seeing it as the final test of Evangeline's capacity for self-regulation and therefore (to some degree) of her salvation; the less insistent energy in the Spanish version may reflect this. In any number of ways, as I suggested earlier, Morla catholicizes both the text and its author. Where Longfellow simply describes the "ethereal beauty" that "shone on her face and encircled her form" after confession, Morla embroiders, "A veces con profundo desconsuelo / que hay sombras en su espíritu imagina / y santa luz que desvanezca el duelo / Pide al confesionario Evangelina" [Sometimes, with a deep anxiety / that imagines there are shadows in her soul, / Evangeline asks the confession / for the holy light which clears away pain] (10). She calls her confessor not "Father," but the more intimate "padre mío" or "antorcha mía" [my torch]. Yet, Morla does not use tokens of Catholic mystery to signify the Gothic, as Longfellow does: the English "ancient cathedrals of cypresses" becomes "como un cenotafio los crespones / en el silencio sepulcral" [the cypresses stood like gravestones / in sepulchral silence]. When Evangeline's search for Gabriel deludes her into believing for an instant that he has appeared in front of her, Longfellow psychologizes this moment ("it was the thought of her brain that assumed the shape of a phantom"), whereas Morla ascribes her belief that she will someday find him to the strength of her faith in God: "Una visión celeste, encantadora, / De Evangelina el corazón levanta; / Las sombras de su noche aterradora / Disipa luminosa la fé santa / De que Gabriel alienta en ese clima / Y hacia él por instantes se aproxima" [A celestial, enchanting vision / lifts Evangeline's heart, / The shadows of the terrifying night / are dissipated by the luminous, holy faith / That Gabriel breathes in this place / And that she draws closer to him with each moment] (44). In Morla's version, her passion does not need to be displaced into a saving religious practice; rather, her religious practice is a natural extension of her eroticism.

To readers in 1847, the original *Evangeline* spoke to some of the most pressing issues of the moment: the ethics of territorial acquisition in the Americas; the displacement of pastoral communities in the course of empire; the compatibility of Catholic and Protestant ways of life. To the extent that it shadows the events of the Mexican invasion, Longfellow's vision of the Acadians, though sympathetic, is also highly problematic. It deracinates the potential conflict posed by the entry of mestizo Catholics into a dominant Anglo-Protestant society, making its model Catholics inoffensively white and French-speaking.[55] As in "The Angels of Buena Vista," religious and racial differences are minimized so as to intensify readerly identification with an idealized feminine figure who fits within the confines of U.S. domestic ideology. Morla, in contrast, emphasizes in his commentary as well as his translation the accomplishments of Catholic missionaries in the New World. He expresses nostalgia for the power of Catholicism to unify vast territories, if only symbolically. To the *Mundo Nuevo* reviewer reading *Evangelina* in 1871, the poem serves as a kind of spur to encourage future writers in South America:

> No hay en español un buen poema *descriptivo americano*. . . .
> ¡Si Longfellow encontró tanta pincelada nueva y brillante
> colorido, para enriquecer la literatura inglesa describiendo este
> continente, qué tesoros no encontrarán los hijos de la
> naturaleza de los trópicos y de la cordillera de los Andes, si
> quieren pintar con la pluma, en una lengua como la nuestra,
> que Longfellow hubiera deseado hablar para dotar nuestra
> literatura con cosa que tanta falta le hace como un poema
> completo!

> [*There's no good* descriptive American *poem in Spanish*. . . . *If
> Longfellow found so many new brushstrokes and brilliant
> colorings to enrich English literature by describing this continent,
> what treasures the sons of the tropics and the Andean range might
> find if they set out to paint with their pens, in a language such as
> ours, what Longfellow himself would have wanted to say—it
> would give our literature something it sorely needs: a complete
> poem!*]

The reviewer, though writing from New York, is long past any sense of a shared hemispheric culture; his agenda is politely separatist and even chauvinistic, as his comment on Morla's choice of a meter for the translation indicates. Claiming that Longfellow's Virgilian hexameter lines would not have seemed so surprising or innovative in Spanish verse, in which twelve-syllable lines are common, he maintains that Morla "resolved to write his translation in the most demanding and difficult meter" so that it would require of him the same level of technical virtuosity as the original. Because of that decision, "Longfellow's verses *gain* from being masterfully transported into a well-rounded, well-formed *octava*": the translation thus represents more of a feat than the original composition. In the context of this review's call for an American literature to match its sublime landscape, seeing translation as a gain rather than a loss constitutes an intriguing reversal of the hierarchy between primary and secondary forms of expression.

In the Vernacular: Translation on the Border

Translations and quasi-translated "traditions" like *Evangeline* may have helped shape antebellum responses to foreign subjectivity, but the problem of language was felt in a much more immediate way by border dwellers in the Spanish-speaking Southwest and Far West, newly expatriated and repatriated by the Treaty of Guadalupe-Hidalgo. There, language might convey or deny one's access to political and legal influence, as communities were reshaped by the migration of individuals and capital from northern states. The maxim that language is power took on a particular resonance from 1848 to 1880, as former Mexican citizens found themselves increasingly outnumbered at maintaining their customs and property.[56] In this context, the roles of editors of Spanish publications, as local ambassadors of culture, were manifold: to arbitrate the linguistic and cultural gap between Anglo and Spanish cultures; to maintain some continuity with the icons of the formerly dominant culture (or, perhaps simultaneously, to encourage gentle assimilation into the new); to defend Spanish speakers against a system that often used language as a form of racialization and exclusion. If, as I have tried to argue, nineteenth-century debates over translation theory help describe a range of Anglo-American responses to "foreigners" who became suddenly more proximate, then the translation practices of these new participants in the national compact ought to be revealing because of their sudden positioning as marginal subjects within this representational economy.

Printing presses came to Texas in 1813 and to New Mexico and Spanish California in the 1830s, marking the origins of a Spanish-language print culture involved in disseminating religious and political treatises, agricultural and ranching information, and small-circulation newspapers for the benefit of the literate minority among the mostly mestizo settlers, church and military personnel.[57] According to journalistic historian Tom Reilly, U.S. military authorities suppressed the independent Spanish periodicals during the war with Mexico. Other sources, however, suggest that these papers offered a subversive voice of protest. The paucity of extant copies of such periodicals during 1847–48 makes this question difficult to settle.[58] In any case, a good number of Spanish periodicals survive from the subsequent three decades, during which the monologic fate of the border territories was still far from assured: the dispossession of the former Mexican citizens' property, and their general decline in influence due to immigration and assimilation came about slowly. *Hispanos* in New Mexico, for instance, continued to have a good deal of political self-determination. Prominent among the borderlands periodicals prior to 1880—when Spanish print culture would multiply— are *El Clamor Público* of Los Angeles (1855–59) and *El Bejareño* and *El Ranchero* of San Antonio and Bexar County, Texas (1850s). Although these journals do not necessarily share consistent political views (the San Antonio papers were continually sparring with each other over who best represented "los intereses del pueblo tejano"), they responded with equal outrage to the advent of the anti-"immigrant," anti-Catholic platform of the Know-Nothing Party during the restive 1855 elections. *El Bejareño* was the most assimilationist of the three; it began its first issue with an editorial statement that, despite the violence of the last few decades, tejanos were better off as U.S. citizens because the Mexican government was so poorly run. The editorial predicted (overoptimistically, as it turned out) that their children would be treated equally in schools and would learn English "sin perder el idioma de Cervantes" [without losing the language of Cervantes].[59] Nonetheless, the paper published a satirical *corrido*, "A mi paisano" [To My Countryman], which attacked, in separate stanzas, each of the major English-language newspapers from Galveston to El Paso for obstinately misleading the innocent "México-Tejano."[60]

The more durable *El Clamor Público* was ambitious, politically daring, and far-reaching in its vision of a distinctive Spanish-speaking community, evolving out of the English-language *Los Angeles Star* to become an independent voice that spoke out vigorously against what it saw as racially prejudiced courts trying Mexican land claims.[61] Under its youthful editors, José Elías González and Francisco P. Ramírez, *El Clamor Público* reversed the association of foreignness and ignorance with Mexican Californians. In an issue covering the elections, the paper sharply castigates recent Anglo-American arrivals in the state for their lack of hospitality toward "los diversos pueblos de la América española, de esos pueblos cuyos individuos debieran ser considerados por los Norte-Americanos de California como hermanos e hijos de una misma familia" [the diverse peoples of Spanish America, whose individual members should be considered by California's North Americans as brothers and sons of one and the same family].[62] Ramírez again invokes the familiar fraternal metaphor of the revolutionary heritage shared by the whole hemisphere, only to deploy it cagily against common usage—emphasizing not the positive achievements of the revolutions but their shared failures:

> Si el raíz de los males que sufren los nuevos Estados de la América, es la ignorancia profunda que se observa en las masas populares, el objeto de mayor importancia de que puedan ocuparse los hombres que están a su cabeza, no puede ser otro que civilizarlas, mejorar poco a poco su condición intelectual, moral y física.
>
> [If the root of all the evils suffered by the new States of America is the profound ignorance that can be observed in the popular masses, the most important thing its leading men can occupy themselves with is to civilize the masses—to work toward improving, little by little, their intellectual, moral, and physical condition.][63]

With this ambiguous reference to the "Estados de la América," which invokes both the individual states of the Union and the nation-states of Spanish America, the writer redefines "the masses" by class and educational level, rejecting ethnicity and language as markers of one's status as "civilized" or "uncivilized." Here, and when Ramírez defends the periphrastic construction of el idioma de Cervantes, he sounds remarkably like Mariano Vallejo or the neomexicano writer José Escobar, two prominent defenders of the rationalist and high-cultural legacy in Spanish.[64]

Like Bryant, Horace Greeley, or any number of other newspaper editors of the age, Ramírez sees "the eventual enlightenment" of all non-literates as the highest good imaginable, and sees print culture as the primary agent of this enlightenment. While this agenda undoubtedly reflects a class bias arising from the Mexican elite's historic degradation of indigenous oral cultures, in the context of the increasingly virulent racism of post–gold rush California, it constitutes a necessary defense strategy—an exaggerated denial of the Anglo-American stereotype of

Spanish speakers as "scarce more than apes," living in a cultureless darkness.[65] A poet himself, Ramírez predictably favored the orderly laws of classical poetic genres as a cornerstone of this redemptive literacy. *El Clamor Público* boasted of its literary aims in the self-description on its masthead: the first issue, dated 19 June 1855, is subtitled "Periódico Independiente y Literario"—an interesting combination of an adjective describing a political stance ("independent") with one that describes its content ("literary"). By 1856, Ramírez had amplified the subtitle to "Periódico de noticias, religión, política, literatura, descubrimientos, poesías, comercio y anuncios." Thus, as an integral part of its social defense mission, *El Clamor Público* took on the task of training its readership in the stylized pleasures of *culto* life—with a front-page article in volume 1, issue 7 about the French symbolist poet Gérard de Nerval, for instance. As disparate as the content and the community may have seemed, Ramírez's definition of the literary was broad enough to encompass doggerel, satirical notes about women, and other "subliterary" genres, suggesting that the values he associated with "educated people" were porous and that he was well aware of the editor's mandate to reflect popular tastes as well as attempt to shape them. The apparent elitism of his aesthetics, in other words, is cross-cut (as is Longfellow's) with a strong populism, an attempt to make the cultural capital understood to be latent in literary classics available to a wide audience.

Moreover, Ramírez encouraged his readers to acquire this cultural capital by publishing numerous local authors. In its regular corner of "Poesías Escogidas," *El Clamor Público* frequently published anonymous or initialed poems, many of which Luis Torres, in his important study, has identified as the work of Angelenos.[66] Some of their efforts to create visibly original or "native" adaptations of conventional poetic language and imagery are unintentionally comic: "El ángel de amor," for instance, introduces a New World simile with the praise, "es esbelta tu cintura / Como el tallo de la palma" [Your waist is as slender/ As the stalk of a palm tree].[67] However, the very conventionality of such lyrics lent them to use in the construction of an active community of commentary and interpretation; no doubt more than a few readers tried to decipher the identities of local muses named only as "N." or "La señorita M. R. L." Equally significant is the fact that these poems exist in dialogue on the page with more overt representations of local political concerns. The "Poesías Escogidas" column regularly appeared on page 3, next to legal notices that potentially had a great bearing on the community's well-being. In the adjoining column to "El ángel de amor," for instance, is a listing of the judgments arrived at in the most recent meeting of the Farwell Commission, which mediated californio land claims. The physical proximity of these two sections serves as a reminder that periodical poetry suggests dynamic acts of reading that are not closed off in an isolated sphere of literary experience, as a book of poetry is; the reading experience is shaped by its topical context. In another issue, the "Poesías Escogidas" column features the highly conventional anonymous poem "La cautiva," which plays on the fantastical, eroticized theme of a young princess kidnapped by pirates who killed her father and stole her from her mother. Although living in a house of gold and pearls, she laments her exile, unable to forget la patria, and is comforted only by

> Un dulce presentimiento   *[A sweet presentiment*
> Que nunca en el alma muere   *That will never die, in my soul,*
> Me dice que espere, espere   *Tells me, wait, hope—*
> Volver a mi patria al fin!   *To return to my country at*
>   *last!]*

No details further clarify the setting of this vaguely Orientalist poem; there is no hint of a concrete description of place beyond an empty beach where the captive contemplates her misery. But the very abstraction of the scene renders it highly suggestive in the context of *El Clamor Público.* It universalizes the sense of exile and loss common to every class of Mexican-American in Los Angeles, whether a laboring immigrant, a struggling store owner, or a well-to-do *ranchero.* The seemingly fantastical literary theme of piracy overflows into the rhetoric of Ramírez's editorials, which frequently denounced judicial discrimination against Mexicans and the appropriation of their property as "piratical."[68]

Judging from notices in their advertising section, the editorial staffs of Spanish-language publications frequently hired themselves out as translators to supplement their precarious incomes. In a broader sense, both the individual contributors and the paper as an institution served as cultural mediators, translating between legal discourses and culinary customs as well as languages. A humorous article titled "Pankekes, tortillas y pan" describes the competing temptations of "Señor BREAD" and "la tortilla, la enemiga más terrible del pan francés" [the tortilla, the fiercest enemy of French bread]. Acknowledging the appeal of the occasional doughy white roll, it warns against a loss of authentic *sabor* among the productions of local cooks, and advocates governmental enforcement of tortilla-making skills so that their products do not become "apankekada" [pancakey]. With such code-switching and linguistic play, the article

explores the manifold dimensions of cultural mixing in a way that anticipates the range of Spanish-English dialects in contemporary California.[69]
But while such forays into bilingualism were relatively rare, translation
played an important part in the installation of *culto* literary values; one
issue reprints the preface to Victor Hugo's latest work, which "we" have
translated especially for our readers.[70] Ramírez, then, sought to instruct
readers in the rudiments of a cosmopolitan identity transcending Los
Angeles or their province of origin in Mexico, partly through such literary translations and partly through the common practice of newspaper
exchange (*El Clamor Público* cited sources such as New York's *Sun* and
the Spanish *El Mensajero Semanal; L'Abeille,* the leading French paper in
New Orleans, translated into Spanish; and *El Mercurio de Valparaíso,* in
Chile). The paper's regular juxtaposition of previously published poems
by noted writers with local, vernacular texts may complicate attributions
of authorship, but that very confusion also helps bolster the authority of
local producers, reinforcing the significance of their efforts by putting
them on the same plane as international luminaries. Indeed, one issue
features an announcement of an international poetry competition sponsored by the University of Guadalajara, encouraging local poets to enter.[71]

In other issues, "Poesías Escogidas" included an unattributed
translation of Byron's "The Dream," and a poem by Gertrudis Gómez de
Avellaneda lauding a fellow Cuban poet. That pairing is also suggestive,
in that the focus of the paper's cosmopolitan education was sometimes
more narrowly directed at forging a broadly *Americanist* identification:
an occasional poem, like Gómez de Avellaneda's, was given the subhead-
ing "Literatura americana." For example, the 31 July 1855 issue featured
a selection from the Puerto Rican *costumbrista* Manuel Alonso's "Cuadros
de costumbres en la isla de Puerto Rico: Un casamiento gíbaro" [Pictures
of Customs on the Island of Puerto Rico: A Country Wedding]. Another,
"Todavía un himno" [Still, a Hymn] by the Venezuelan Abigaíl Lozano,
describes the treachery of a changeable lover (introduced with an
untranslated epigraph from Byron); this transamerican text appears on
the page next to a longer prose piece, "La ciudad de la Habana, descripta
por un Anglo-americano" [The City of Havana, Described by an Anglo-
American], that was apparently translated into Spanish by a member of
the paper's staff.[72] The multiple links in this chain of observation are
dizzying: a provincial angeleno translating a travelogue by an urbane
Anglo, with all his or her expectations and prejudices about the riches of
Cuba, for an audience that was in all likelihood equally ignorant of the
dazzlingly exotic tropics yet increasingly made aware of their own con-

nection to Cuba and Puerto Rico through a common language and parent culture emphasized by Ramírez's editorial selections.

El Clamor Público was far from the only Spanish-language newspaper to shape an implicit, incipient Americanist consciousness. My survey of approximately 250 poems appearing in fifteen different nineteenth-century borderlands periodicals revealed that among those attributed to authors roughly contemporary to the period, ten are Mexican; seven Spanish; six Cuban; four New Granadan/Colombian; two Venezuelan; two Argentine; one Guatemalan/Salvadoran; one Chilean; and one Peruvian.[73] This is in addition to the occasional poem or dramatic excerpt from the Siglo de Oro (Cervantes, Rioja, Calderón), the Latin American colonial period (Sor Juana, Alonso de Ercilla), or the translations from Lamartine, Hugo, Béranger, Byron, Longfellow, Moore, Heine, or other foreign poets—roughly 10 percent of the total. (The remainder are unsigned, signed with initials or unidentifiable names, or can be credibly attributed to local editors.) This is far from an exhaustive study, in the absence of the more complete catalog being gathered by the Recovering the U.S. Hispanic Literary Heritage project, but it suggests the range of transnational print communities into which local literate populations were inserted. Such juxtapositions encourage broader affiliations among readers without eliding differences among Spanish American nations and cultures. Indeed, to some extent they magnify difference in order to educate local readers about other national "types," such as Alonso's Puerto Rican gíbaro—paving the way for the commodification of a regionalist costumbrismo in the latter part of the century. The liberal interest among many editors of such periodicals in fostering a cosmopolitan identity among global Spanish speakers, and their defense of Spanish against the local dominance of English, never reaches the radical end of promoting an open system of linguistic power in which suppressed indigenous languages and dialects might be validated. But the juxtaposition of artifacts of elite culture next to evidence of the legal and social precariousness of Mexican Americans in Los Angeles on the pages of El Clamor Público surely brought home to its readers that language was not a neutral tool in those political conflicts; rather, it lay at their very foundation.

Debates over translation in the nineteenth century were centered around competing views about whether to work toward preserving the foreignness of the original text (as Longfellow, following Schleiermacher, believed) or toward assimilating it into the target language, slipping silently and invisibly across the linguistic border. The first approach has the effect of estranging the target language and the cultural values it contains and reflects; it renders the familiar foreign. Likewise, a fundamental task of editors in the Spanish-speaking peripheries was to mark English as the "foreign" tongue, and to interrogate the beliefs naturalized in Anglo-American linguistic and social usage. Against the backdrop of nineteenth-century expansionism, which increasingly portrayed things Spanish as feminized and weak, this view of translation fell out of favor in an Anglo-American literary culture ever more absorbed by its efforts to be "original." The efforts of Longfellow and others to dignify translation as a creative literary activity would likewise come to be stigmatized as imitative, secondary, passive. And, ironically, embattled Hispanophone arbiters of culture in the United States would begin their long campaign to protect "the language of Cervantes" from the very forms of creative bilingual hybridization that were already appearing in Ramírez's publication, fearing that if they did not do so, Spanish would become flaccid, diluted, or *apankekada*.

4

The Mouth of a New Empire
New Orleans in the Transamerican Print Trade

> *Nations ten thousand years before these States, and many*
>   *times ten thousand years before these States,*
> *Garner'd clusters of ages that men and women like us grew up*
>   *and travel'd their course and passed on,*
> *What vast-built cities, what orderly republics, what pastoral*
>   *tribes and nomads,*
> *What histories, rulers, heroes, perhaps transcending all others,*
> *What laws, customs, wealth, arts, traditions . . .*
> *What of liberty and slavery among them, what they thought of*
>   *death and the soul,*
> *Who were witty and wise, who beautiful and poetic, who*
>   *brutish and undevelop'd,*
> *Not a mark, not a record remains—and yet all remains.*

—Walt Whitman, "Unnamed Lands"

New Orleans, Capital of the (Other) Nineteenth Century

When contemporary New Orleanians press a comparison between their city and Paris, it is to magnify the French influence that continues— nearly two centuries after Napoleon sold off the land of King Louis—to be its most marketable commodity. Touted as the most exotic place one can travel domestically without crossing an ocean or a border, the city's tourism industry buys and sells good times *(laissez les bon temps rouler)*, old times (le Vieux Carré), and a temporary escape from time (one official nickname is the City That Care Forgot). But my borrowing from Walter Benjamin's famous essay intends, rather, to invoke a different simulacrum of Paris: el París hispano, the distant center of much of Latin America's intellectual life well into the twentieth century. To a lesser degree, New Orleans too, became a significant locus of Hispanophone literary activity for the Caribbean and more generally for the Americas, anchored by land to the better-known exile metropole of New York but in many ways worlds apart from it. Antebellum New Orleans seemed, to its wide range of Hispanophone visitors and permanent residents, a model space in which heterogeneous interests could functionally coexist, whereas New York—as I argue in chapter 5—increasingly came to signify for them an insuperably strange one. The mediating figure between these two cities is Walt Whitman, a poet indelibly associated with New York, but one who also spent three months in New Orleans precisely when the Hispanophone print community wielded its greatest influence, when a multitude of visions of Manifest Destiny and national expansionism were hotly contested. Because Whitman is a key figure in the construction of U.S. identity as a form of "imperial selfhood" (to use Quentin Anderson's term) that incorporates racial and linguistic difference into itself, his work has generated particularly intense criticism among Latin Americans.[1] In this chapter, I will intervene in this ongoing debate by placing Whitman within the context of this multilingual space and in particular of its Spanish-speaking community.

Since its incorporation into the United States by the Louisiana Purchase of 1803, New Orleans has enjoyed a reputation as the country's most linguistically and racially diverse city, with its once-substantial population of *gens libres de couleur* and its vital French culture disrupting dominant codes of national affiliation to create hybrid cultural spaces and alternative aesthetic possibilities. The tremendous influx of Anglo-Americans from the North during the 1830s, as well as a flood of immigrants from Ireland and Germany in the late 1840s and 1850s, altered the balance of power of the once-dominant Creole class without really displacing them. The population self-identifying as "Creole" had incorporated a good number of Spanish speakers during the thirty years of Spain's rule, and afterward Louisiana became a destination of choice for refugees from Cuba and Santo Domingo fleeing the chaos of the Haitian revolution.[2] Like Havana, to which it bears a more than superficial resemblance, the port of New Orleans was a nexus of trade in goods and slaves, smuggling, piracy, capital ventures, in- and out-migration, troop movements, filibustering adventurers, and travel between the eastern United States and points southward. Midcentury New Orleans was, fundamentally, a Caribbean city, strategically positioned within the transportation and communications system of the Gulf of Mexico's half-moon, linked to Cuba, Puerto Rico, Santo Domingo, and Mexico's Gulf Coast and Yucatán. Opening its mouth to the major inland shipping route on the North American continent, the Mississippi, it became the most significant point of transit between the northeastern states and the western territories; as such, it had the fourth largest population among U.S. cities and was its second busiest port.[3] Joseph Roach nicely describes it as "a circum-Caribbean cosmopolis with old family fortunes and colonial architecture already in various stages of decay (more like Venice, say, than Dodge City), through which the commerce of the nation's regions and the world's nations passed."[4] Roach's *Cities of the Dead* illumines New Orleans as a space in which African ritual practices, distilled through their peregrinations across the Atlantic, were absorbed by the sponge of a dominant Anglo-American culture through a process he labels "surrogation": a process of domestication, whitening, and concealment. Such instances of transculturation occurred in tandem with patterns of commercial exchange—most notoriously, traffic in the emblematic commodities of sugar and slaves, although one could add cotton, tobacco, salt pork, and coffee with perhaps less symbolic richness.[5] Whereas Roach focuses on performances of music and movement that preserve African communal memory through surrogation, my emphasis in this chapter falls on the traffic in information and the way Hispanophone print culture impressed itself into subsequent polemics—and poetics.

Expatriates and emigrés from around the Caribbean and Spanish America would have found New Orleans the least alienating city in the nation—for, besides the substantial population of Spanish speakers, most of their educated classes knew French and could get by without speaking a word of English. Accordingly, in the years following Mexican independence, many of the liberal enemies of Iturbide and then Santa Anna went into exile there, including José Antonio Mejía and Valentín Gómez Farías (from 1834 to 1835 and again in 1840–45). From New Orleans, they raised funds and volunteers to aid the Texan revolt against his centrist regime, although both later participated in various Mexican governments; Gómez Farías reluctantly served as Santa Anna's vice-president during the years of the U.S. invasion.[6] Later, the exiled ex-governor of Oaxaca, Benito Juárez, lived in the city for nearly two years, where he made a living rolling cigars (or, by other reports, selling fish in the French Market) while plotting the 1854 Plan de Ayutla with Melchor Ocampo and other key figures of the Reforma.[7] Equally significant were the constant comings and goings of Cubans—loyalist tradesmen with a strong allegiance to the mother country as well as separatist agitators such as Cirilo Villaverde, author of the classic antislavery novel *Cecilia Valdés* and one of Plácido's defenders; and a group of poets who would likewise use literature to foment sentimental outrage when they published the pathbreaking anthology *El laúd del desterrado* [The Exile's Lute] in 1858: Pedro Santacilia, Leopoldo Turla, Miguel Teurbe Tolón, and especially José Agustín Quintero, whose eventual integration into southern culture I discuss toward the end of the chapter. Like the French-speaking Creoles, with whom they shared a neighborhood in the French (as opposed to "American") Quarter of the city, these exiled writers identified nostalgically with a homeland that, for them, became frozen in time the moment they left it. Although the path of *Evangeline* had led to a new Acadia in western Louisiana, the plight of Longfellow's heroine held sentimental resonance for this group. The French and Spanish together forged a community somewhat oppositional to Anglo-American dominance, but at the same time, as the sectional conflict over slavery intensified, other alliances developed between the Cuban separatists—most of whom were doubtful that slavery could or should be abolished on the island—and the southern slaveholding aristocracy. Quintero's later service to the Confederate government is a prime example. The movement toward Cuban annexation attained its greatest strength among both U.S. and Cuban constituencies with the Narciso López filibusters of 1850–51, which were in turn strongly affected by the outcome of the Mexican invasion. Finally, New Orleans was the favored launching point for southern-led filibustering in Central America as well: one of its prominent citizens, Pierre Soulé, masterminded several filibustering expeditions while his political rival, John Slidell, was responsible for the disastrous 1845 attempt to purchase California cheaply from the Mexican government.[8]

What unites all these figures is the vibrant polyglot print culture in New Orleans, which reached global as well as local and national audiences. The first Spanish-language newspaper in the United States, *El Misisipí*, was founded there in 1806, and prior to the Civil War at least twenty-three periodicals in Spanish were published in the city, making it the undisputed capital of Hispanophone print production (New York, the nearest contender, had only thirteen).[9] Most of these papers, like their

English counterparts, came and went leaving few traces, but among those that survive one can trace the shifts we have already witnessed in Spanish American attitudes toward the rising Anglo-American world order. *El Telégrafo*, in 1825, praised the freedom of speech to be found in the new republic, in contrast to the autocracy and chaos of Europe. The longer-lived *L'Abeille/The Bee* and its ideological opponent, *L'Avenir du Peuple*, both printed Spanish-language sections throughout the 1830s; by 1840 nearly half the contents of the latter were in Spanish. The Democratic *Abeja* strongly defended both Creole and cosmopolitan interests, claiming to be "batallando contra estas gentes" [battling those people] who, in their view, wanted to exclude from the city and country "él que no habla y piensa como ellos"[whoever does not speak or think like them]. The Hispanophone papers were even international in scope: for at least the first six months of 1844, the venerable liberal weekly *Diario del Gobierno de la República Mexicana*, once edited by José María Heredia, was published in New Orleans—a case of an institution, rather than an individual, in exile. Villaverde founded a paper called *El Independiente* in New Orleans in 1853, of which no copies survive; it probably looked much like *La Verdad*, a separatist organ based in New York from 1848 to 1852 that evolved into *La Revolución* as its editors moved away from their earlier support of annexation.[10] But the printed artifact that has left the most textual traces was *La Patria*, which—with two name changes—was consistently published for six years, from 1845 to 1851. Within its pages, competing visions of cubanidad and mejicanidad were imagined and fiercely defended against and through each other, interpellated through transactions with a yanqui culture whose imperial designs were becoming increasingly readable over this decade and a half.

New Orleans occupied a crucially central point within U.S. print culture as well. Since the city was a logical transfer point for settlers, supplies, and arms moving westward into Texas, New Orleans journalists were also the primary filters of news of the Lone Star Republic from the 1830s onward. The war with Mexico was the first to be covered by modern journalistic techniques in the Americas, and the highly competitive New Orleans dailies thrived on their proximity to the center of action and officer's gossip; they developed an impressive communications infrastructure of express couriers via horse, steamboat, and railway as well as the rudimentary but fast-spreading technology of the telegraph. The Whig *Picayune* also put its own reporters on the field, foremost among them its founder, George Wilkins Kendall, who would later write a popular illustrated history of the war.[11] The press competed to see who could get dispatches from the front most quickly to the Northeast, which earned them considerable respect among even the chauvinistic New York papers, which often reprinted them verbatim. The hawkish views of the *Picayune* and the *Delta* reflected those of most of the Anglo-American citizenry of New Orleans, who—with their economy bolstered by the large-scale movement of men and *matériel* passing through the city— became the nation's most enthusiastic backers of the war. However, it was *La Patria*, with its reporters inside and outside Mexico and with access to other Spanish-language sources, that frequently scooped the other New Orleans papers, and its updates were widely disseminated; however, the editors' distinctly antiexpansionist perspective on the war was not.[12]

Founded as *El Hablador* by Victoriano Alemán and the Louisi-ana-born Eusebio Juan Gómez in 1845, *La Patria* was the most ambitious and ultimately significant Spanish-language publication in the United States during the period, read apparently even by President Polk.[13] First published as a triweekly, then briefly as a daily, and finally biweekly, *La Patria* was listed as one of the five largest-circulation papers in the 1850 city business directory.[14] At first it was printed at the offices of J. L. Sollée, but the editors eventually bought a press and established an office of their own at 68–70 Exchange Alley. Although circulation figures are as difficult to estimate as the number of Spanish speakers in antebellum New Orleans, the paper at its height claimed a subscribers' list of eight hundred and aimed to expand to reach a Spanish-speaking audience in the United States alone that it estimated at thirty thousand.[15] At the out-set Gómez and Alemán were openly optimistic and idealistic about the influence they hoped the journal would have. The tone of those early issues of *El Hablador* is self-consciously literary, indeed verging on the precious, as in their first New Year's editorial, begging for subscribers: "nuestro principal objeto es el de poner al *Hablador* tan cuco, que no haya hombre, mujer, joven ni vieja, niño ni anciano, blanco ni negro, grande ni chico, que no se enamore hasta los tuétanos de él" [our pri-mary object is to make the *Hablador* so adorable that there won't be a man or woman, youth or elder, child or old man, white or black, big or small, who won't fall in love with it right down to the marrow].[16]

When the paper was retooled as *La Patria* in January 1846, it had a new subtitle: *Organo de la población española de los Estados Unidos*, and a more solemn editorial voice.[17] This would seem to suggest that the paper was directed at Spaniards, yet a self-advertisement reprinted in every issue that spring implies that the adjective describes language, not nationality. The editors repeatedly stressed that "La población española de Nueva Orleans es indudablemente la más variada de cuántas existen no sólo en esta ciudad sino en toda la Unión" [the Spanish population of New Orleans is undoubtedly one of the most diverse not only in this city but in the whole of the Union]. This diversity, they felt, would extend the paper's reach. In the next paragraph, the editors speak of the necessity of having a paper to represent the interests of "las poblaciones Hispano-Americanas," by which they seem to mean those who intended to live for the long term among *los americanos*; "hoy, que vemos ante nosotros un brillante porvenir" [today, we see before us a brilliant future].[18] At some point during 1847, the front-page masthead became visually more provocative, featuring an image of a seated man before an inkwell (an emblematic *letrado*) flanked on his left by a U.S. flag with the banner of Spain behind it, and similarly on his right by the flags of the United States and Mexico. Accordingly, news items from west of New Orleans (Mexico and Texas) and from its east (Spain and its Caribbean empire) vie for importance with news from the northeastern United States. Only by turning toward each of these cardinal points could *La Patria* fulfill its stated mandate to report "todo aquello que concierna a nuestra nación" [everything that concerns our nation], for—as the three flags suggest—that patria is a no-man's land, a nonspecific site of an as yet undefined identity. If the newspaper's title refuses any final affiliation with one particular country, its implicit definition of the homeland becomes more and more oriented toward linguistic rather than statist connotations: "no es menos para todas las Américas donde se conserva aún, y donde se conservará siempre el hermoso idioma castellano" [it's intended as well for *all* the Americas where the beautiful Castilian language is preserved, and always will be]. By mid-1846, this print community was already well shaped: *La Patria* advertised that it had seven sales agents in bookstores and publishing offices in New Orleans; one each in Terre aux Boeufs, Baton Rouge, Mobile, and St. Augustine; two each in Havana and Matanzas; one each in Trinidad, Puerto Príncipe (now Camagüey), and Santiago de Cuba; and throughout Mexico and the Yucatán—in Veracruz, Mexico City, Jalapa, Orizaba, Puebla, Tampico, Mérida, and Campeche. Later issues listed sales offices in San Antonio, Matamoros, Corpus Christi, and New York.[19] Both the imagined and the material realms circumscribed by *La Patria*, then, encouraged a dual identification with the transnational space of Spain and Latin America as well as with fellow Spanish speakers repatriated to—or at least established in—the United States. Its circulation map represented the possibility of a specifically Latino vision uniting communities spread very widely across North America on the basis of their shared language and culture.

Gómez in particular seems to have occupied a relatively mobile position with respect to the Spanish and English spheres of influence. In 1846, he was nominated as General Winfield Scott's field interpreter, and quickly commissioned as a lieutenant colonel in the U.S. army. Almost immediately, however, there were allegations that he had leaked secret plans divulged in a meeting with Scott to the Mexicans, and his appointment was suddenly rescinded on the grounds that the Louisiana-born editor of *La Patria* was "un-American": he was, ironically, a man without a patria.[20] As Reilly retraces them, relations between this "órgano de la población española" and the sphere of Anglophone journalism grew increasingly strained—even to the point where their mail deliveries of international newspapers were apparently stolen—as Alemán and Gómez maintained an antiwar stance. From the beginning, well before Taylor's troops had began their march to Texas, Gómez and Alemán expressed outright suspicion of U.S. designs on the rest of the hemisphere and particularly on northern Mexico: "La extraordinaria facilidad con que se ha concluido y celebrado la anexión de Tejas; la poca o ninguna resistencia que ha hallado el pueblo Norte-Americano en esta agregación, ha hecho que el Gobierno como los demás individuos que componen esta grande Unión, hayan llegado a figurarse que todo lo pueden" [The astonishing ease with which the annexation of Texas was brought about and celebrated, and the little or no resistance to this annexation that the North Americans have encountered, has brought it to pass that the Government, like the rest of the individuals who compose this great Union, has come to believe that it can do anything it wishes].[21]

La Patria's coverage of the war can be only incompletely represented since a crucial year, 1847, is missing, but a representative sampling of editorials during 1846 and 1848 shows that Gómez and Alemán maintain a consistent rhetoric about its aims and probable political consequences, stressing (as Heredia had done) the contradiction between the theory of U.S. republicanism and the practice of interventionism. On 4 June 1846, shortly after the declaration of war, they write that after a relatively long period of postrevolutionary peace, "se ve la mitad del Nuevo Mundo envuelta en una guerra lastimosa y poco provechosa" [we now witness half the New World involved in a shameful and less than advantageous war]. They argue that the invasion of Mexico is a violation of the nation's founding principles: "entonces rechazaban a los invasores y resistían al tirano opresor que trataba de dominarlos cruelmente: pero hoy se nos presenta el reverso de la medalla, y esta gran nación que tachaba siempre la injusticia de los usurpadores, sigue las huellas y los malos ejemplos de otras naciones dominadas por la tiranía y la injusticia" [at that time, the United States repelled the invaders and resisted the tyrannical oppressor who tried to dominate them cruelly: but today we see the reverse side of the coin, and this great nation, which has always criticized the injustices of usurpers, is now following the steps and the bad examples of other nations dominated by tyranny and injustice]. As great admirers of republican principles, "no podemos ver con indiferencia que despojándose de su sinceridad y sanos principios, adopte el pueblo de los Estados Unidos doctrinas tan contrarias a las de su institución. . . . La guerra con Méjico . . . se llevará a cabo de la manera más sangrienta, es una guerra injusta y peligrosa a la Unión Norte-Americana" [we cannot look on with indifference as the people of the United States, robbing themselves of their sincerity and their healthy principles, adopt doctrines so contrary to their founding. . . . The war with Mexico . . . will be brought about in the bloodiest possible manner; it is an unjust war and dangerous to the North American Union].[22]

La Patria was not only alone in the New Orleans print community in opposing the war—it was also in the strange company of northern abolitionists, and they supported the plantation system that was the economic motor of the deep South and of Cuba—although they did not fabricate fearful scenarios of racial violence or amalgamation in the way that some other southern periodicals did. Although self-identified as a Whig paper, La Patria preferred relentless analysis to partisan politics, acknowledging the political instability in Mexico and spewing abundant criticism of Santa Anna. Very early on it saliently identified a psychological motive in order to explain the enthusiasm of average citizens toward the invasion of Mexico: a sense of restless, romanticized adventurism surpassing the more obvious economic and territorial gains. "'Marchemos a la ciudad de Méjico,' dicen los americanos, creyendo que tan fácil es el hacer como el decir. . . . Bien se sabe que la mayor parte de los que se empeñan en llevar a cabo la guerra lo hacen guiados por la necia esperanza de que han de hallar innumerables riquezas en las minas, y ricas alhajas en los templos, que tratan de loquear en el momento que lleguen a ellos. ¡¡Qué ilusión!! ¡Qué moralidad!" ["Let's march all the way to the City of Mexico!" the Americans say, believing it's as easily said as done. . . . It is well known that the majority of those who insist on prosecuting this war are guided by the ridiculous hope that they are going to find untold riches in the mines, and rich jewels in the temples, talking this nonsense as soon as they get there. What a fantasy! What morality!].[23]

Even after the end of the war, Gómez and Alemán continued to reiterate their interpretation of the founding fathers' interdiction against launching wars to "conquistar territorios, o quitar a otras naciones los que las pertenecen" [conquer territories or take from other nations the territories that belong to them]. Yet on the same page, they endorse the Whig presidential ticket, which featured the popular Mexican War hero Zachary Taylor, which must have stuck in their collective craw. But the alternative—a Democratic Party splintered along sectional lines, with the Free-Soil Party's strong connections to northern abolitionists—was too interested in pursuing "la anexación de la Isla de Cuba, el Canadá y lo que ha quedado a los mejicanos de las Californias" [the annexation of the island of Cuba, Canada, and what remains to the Mexicans of the Californias]; a graphic box on top of the editorial read, in various decorative typefaces, "Cass, Cuba, California, Canada" to scare off readers from voting for the Democratic candidate, Lewis Cass.[24] Thus La Patria encouraged its readers to see events in the hemisphere not as national issues but as part of the global distribution of postcolonial power, pointing out similarities between what had happened in Mexico—a territorial "purchase" forced on a weakened, divided, impoverished nation in order to further U.S. expansionist ends—and what might occur in Cuba, which had been the object of purchase offers for three decades. Though they joined other papers in condemning as "barbarous" the Mayan Indians who rebelled against the Yucatecan elites when the Caste Wars broke out, they supported central Mexican governance of the fractious state rather than encouraging U.S. intervention—a tactic enthusiastically backed by some in Congress. Although expansionists such as John O'Sullivan had been spreading the gospel of continentalism and a "Caribbean empire" for some time, La Patria pointed out this commonality to mobilize a defensive sensibility in its readership, broadening the geographical imaginary of individuals toward a more unified political agenda based on opposition to U.S. incursion into Spanish America.

If Gómez and Alemán, like all newspaper editors during this highly partisan era, envisioned their mission as a form of political activity, they never lost sight of its broader aim of cultural ambassadorship—particularly of the need to react against the harsh stereotyping of their "race" that the war had encouraged by convincing Anglo-Americans that Spanish speakers were as lettered, diverse, and intelligible as they—if not more so.

Antes que se publicara *La Patria*, la opinión general que se tenía en los Estados Unidos de los Españoles . . . era en extremo desfavorable según lo probaban los escritos que casi diariamente aparecían en los periódicos del idioma nativo. Y aun nosotros mismos hemos tenido la ocasión de afirmar esa opinión durante nuestros viajes en esa época por los Estados del Sur, Este, y Norte, y desde 1845 hemos estado combatiendo las más denigrantes ideas que se veían manifestadas en los periódicos de la Unión.

[Before La Patria *began publishing, the general opinion in the United States of Spaniards . . . was extremely unfavorable, according to the writings that appeared almost daily in the Spanish periodicals. And we ourselves have had the opportunity to verify this judgment during our travels through the states of the South, East, and North, and since 1845 we have been fighting against the most denigrating ideas that one sees manifested in the newspapers of the Union.]*[25]

In addition to this resistant and corrective activism, for a brief period in 1848 Gómez and Alemán struck out in a novel direction. They enlisted a Dr. Matthewson, formerly editor of a paper in Veracruz called *El Genio de la Libertad*, to edit a new English section for *La Patria*. Although many Spanish papers initially evolved out of sections in established English ones, this reverse trajectory appears to have been a first in the history of Latino journalism. The prospectus for the newly bilingual paper published on 14 April classifies English as a necessary language because of its practicality, and Spanish as the language of reason and aesthetics:

In presenting to the public this miniature specimen number of *La Patria* in the English and Spanish language, we shall state, in as brief a manner as possible, the prominent imperatives that induce us to make the change, and the principal advantages that are likely to result from it. There have been causes in operation for some time past, are in operation now, and will continue in operation hereafter, which will in the future materially affect our relation, not only with Mexico, but in all probability with the people of Spanish America. The intercourse between the English and Spanish inhabitants or races of the Western Hemisphere is, in a political and commercial, as well as in a social and moral point of view, becoming every day more intensely interesting, and hence it is of the utmost importance for them to study and understand each other's language in order to live in peace and harmony as occupants of the same Continent, and members of Great Republics. This useful and desirable object can be attained, to a certain extent, through the medium of our paper; for the leading articles will appear in each number both in English and Spanish, and the translations will be rendered as literal as the spirit of the language will admit. Our English subscribers will, therefore, have the opportunity of becoming familiar with the Spanish language in all its native beauty, simplicity, and uniformity; and our Spanish subscribers will have a like opportunity of becoming familiar with the English language, which, though Lord Byron calls it the

> —Harsh northern, whistling, grunting guttural
> Which we're obliged to hiss, and spit, and sputter all,

yet, is unsurpassed, if not unequaled, in its practical application to useful purposes.

As Francisco Amy's textbook for the "Americanization of Porto Rican youths" would do much later, this bilingual experiment envisions facing-page translations as an instrument of painless assimilation; yet in this case the assimilation is to be mutual. The target is not simply the subject population but both the "English and Spanish inhabitants or races of the Western Hemisphere." Moreover, its plea for mutual comprehension takes place within the dominating context of the paper's tradition of imposing an unrepentantly Latin American perspective on local events. This distinguishes it from the manifestos of liberal northern Hispanophiles like Long-fellow, Bryant, and Hurlbert that we saw in previous chapters. Here, English is the alien language, an imported British "grunting guttural" one is obliged to maintain as a commercial lingua franca. This English prospectus (which only *seems* like an awkward translation; it does not appear in Spanish) insisted that the paper would continue to be "independent and impartial," "neutral but not passive" in politics. That month, the English page praises the appointment of Stephen Kearney, who had marched across the southwest to occupy New Mexico, as the new governor of Veracruz; yet it also describes the war as "the North American *invasion*," in keeping with *La Patria*'s traditional usage. The experiment with the dual-language edition lasted only a few months, for reasons that seem self-evident.

Not surprisingly, the paper's defense of hispanidad clearly brought them at times into adversarial relations with other local papers: the *Delta*, the *Picayune*, and later the *Crescent*. One pointed article titled "Sobre la corrupción de la prensa periódica" [On the Corruption of the Popular Press] castigates

> periodistas que pasan en sociedad por hombres sensatos, y que se cree están en su sano juicio porque redactan un periódico *en inglés*, que bien visto, es la simpleza más grande del mundo, cuando se hace por los medios ordinarios o *de costumbre* en los Estados Unidos, los cuales consisten en recortar trozos de aquí y allá y llenar así columnas enteras. Naturalmente unos hombres que no saben hacer otra cosa que redactar un papel con *tijeras* y *almidón*, en el momento que se ven obligados a salir de su esfera y tomar la pluma para tratar de un asunto de gravedad, desbarran como locos, y dicen más disparatos que palabras; ¡y cuidado que los señores ingleses necesitan bastantes palabras para decir pocas cosas!
>
> *[journalists who pass in society as sensible men, and who believe that they have great judgment because they edit a newspaper* in English—*which, seen properly, is the simplest thing in the world when it's done the ordinary or* customary *way in the United States, which consists of cutting up pieces from here and there and filling entire columns this way. Naturally, some men who don't know how to do anything else besides edit a paper with* scissors and paste *start talking nonsense like crazy men as soon as they have to leave their little sphere and take up a pen to deal with a serious matter, or they fire more shots than words—and watch out, because Englishmen need plenty of words to say very little!]*[26]

The English language is associated with imitation (cut and paste) and excess (taking too many words to say too few things). English—at least as practiced by journalists—tends toward mere linguistic accumulation rather than quality; it even encourages militarism ("más disparatos que palabras"). Gómez and Alemán's critique of a particular linguistic prejudice—the reflexive tendency of those who possess the dominant language to assume that theirs is the only language of persuasion and art—does not undo their complicity in upholding racialized chattel slavery, but it does indicate a powerful awareness of the workings of less obvious forms of domination and subordination.

The Fertile Crescent: Whitman's Immersion in the "Spanish Element"

One of the practitioners of "scissors and paste" journalism who earned Gómez's scorn was the exchange editor at the *Crescent*—an obscure Brooklynite named Walt Whitman, who arrived in New Orleans at the very height of *La Patria*'s influence. Just as New Orleans was a crucial geographical gateway between the Americas, the figure of Whitman has served, at least during the twentieth century, as the very emblem of the attractions and pitfalls of a transamerican poetics. From the mixed admiration of Martí to the sharp critique of the Mexican González de la Garza, who memorably labeled him "racista, imperialista, antimexicano," Whitman's continental vision and rhetoric of inclusion have elicited polar extremes of attraction or repulsion among Latin Americans (to Neruda, for instance, Whitman's "chants democratic" prefigured the Chilean's own effort to reproduce the voices of working men and women). Readings of Whitman influenced by these Spanish American perspectives have brought the international industry of Whitman criticism to recognize the degree to which expansionism fundamentally directs the current of his poetic and political thought.[27] My entry into this debate involves resituating Whitman both biographically and ideologically in the Hispanized realm of midcentury New Orleans I have just described. The space of New Orleans heightens Whitman's already nascent sense of embodiment as a poetic strategy of erotic nationalism, and it does so in a way that brings to the fore the Spanish body left unclaimed and unremembered in the exclusively black-white rhetoric of antebellum tension. The desire to possess a subjugated body—a desire that would later be suppressed as unthinkable—gets expressed not only in response to the New Orleans scene of a slave auction that he subsequently replayed imaginatively in *Leaves of Grass*, but also in various treatments of the bodies of land within the hemisphere that the Mexican War and the filibustering efforts of the moment had rendered open and vulnerable. What I want to do here is not simply to condemn Whitman for his complicity in the rhetoric of Manifest Destiny, but rather to unveil a profound ambivalence about it that is tied to his perceptions of the subjugated, racialized body—both the enslaved black one and the conquered brown one.

Whitman, like other letrados in this study, was profoundly rooted in the public sphere of print. When he lost his job at the Democratic *Brooklyn Daily Eagle* in January 1848 because of his Free-Soil convictions and was offered a position on a new paper starting up in New Orleans, he identified principally as a journalist, halfheartedly composing his labored temperance fiction and highly imitative poetry. A young provincial, without the resources of a Longfellow or an Emerson to travel abroad and soak up influences, Whitman had had to settle for long walks with Bryant, hearing about the older poet's visits to "the cities, looks, architecture, art" of Europe, experiencing only vicariously what more privileged writers had seen firsthand.[28] The New Orleans period, as Jerome Loving underscores, was Whitman's first real experience with the world outside greater New York. It was the closest he would ever get to Paris, or to Spanish America, and also—significantly—the locus of his first direct contact with southern practices of slavery, a system he had been taught to despise but about which he knew relatively little. Not only was Whitman primed by his reading and expectations to see the city as a romantic and "foreign" site; he later embellished it as an impassioned and somehow galvanizing period in his life, writing in *November Boughs* that he had spent "several months" in New Orleans, and elsewhere extended that to "a year or two"—though, in fact, he was in the city only ninety-one days, from late February through May.[29] Moreover, as an old man Whitman famously invented a story, apparently to foil his more openly homosexual following in Britain, about a mysterious, well-born Creole woman with whom he insinuated he had had a long-time romance and several children. This unlikely story was a staple of Whitman biography for years before being discredited.[30]

What was it about New Orleans that prompted such extremes of denial and exaggeration at various points in the crafting of the mythic Whitmanian self? As generations of critics have puzzled over the central mystery of Whitman biography—how a journalist indistinguishable from many others could transform himself into one of the most astonishingly distinctive voices in the poetic tradition by the time of the first edition of *Leaves of Grass* was published in 1855—the New Orleans sojourn has seemed to promise some tantalizing clue. Yet the evidence for that correlation seems as thin as the story of the Creole mistress. What is clear is that Whitman, separated from all of his tight-knit family except his adolescent brother Thomas Jefferson (Jeff), found himself at a career crossroads, living *in* a crossroads, and newly surrounded by a very different set of racial and linguistic codes. More particularly, the assignment to New Orleans sent him into the vortex of that process of national expansion he had spent the previous two years following eagerly, as a highly partisan but distant observer of the war with Mexico. Like the Young Americans he had known in New York, Whitman had been for some time an ardent expansionist, as his editorials for the *Eagle* during 1846–47 attest: "Let our arms now be carried with a spirit which shall teach the world that, while we are not forward for a quarrel, America knows how to crush, as well as how to expand!"[31] Santa Anna, for whom he had stinging words, was a serpent to be mashed underfoot to make way for "heroic," "manly" settlement. New Orleans's central role in that "glorious" war was impossible to overlook, as Whitman would retrospectively write in 1887:

> Probably the influence most deeply pervading everything at that time through the United States, both in physical facts and in sentiment, was the Mexican War, then just ended. Following a brilliant campaign (in which our troops had march'd to the capital city, Mexico, and taken full possession) we were returning after our victory. From the situation of the country, the city of New Orleans had been our channel and *entrepot* for everything, going and returning. It had the best news and war correspondents; it had the most to say, through its leading papers, the *Picayune* and *Delta* especially, and its voice was readiest listen'd to; from it "Chapparal" had gone out, and his army and battle letters were copied everywhere, not only in the United States, but in Europe. . . . No one who has never seen the society of a city under similar circumstances can understand what a strange vivacity and *rattle* were given throughout by such a situation. I remember the crowds of soldiers, the gay young officers, going or coming, the receipt of important news, the many discussions, the returning wounded, and so on.[32]

Here, New Orleans figures as both the "opening" of the national organism, "our channel and *entrepot*," and as a locus in which common sentiments get articulated—the "voice . . . readiest listen'd to." "Going and returning," news and letters "going out," soldiers "going and coming": these insistent metaphors of circulation suggest New Orleans as the heart of a vital system of communication and language, the system of the national print body.

As Whitman reconstructs this scene, the celebratory excitement of the war also offers an opportunity to exalt the primacy of firsthand experience: "No one who has never seen . . . can understand." Yet until this journey, Whitman had himself been limited to vicarious experience. His writing about his journey to New Orleans itself—a journey that, as he was surely aware, skirted the edge of the huge territorial acquisitions that were to his mind the "brilliant" outcome of the war (even though the terms of the peace treaty had not yet been ratified by the Mexican Congress)—alternates curiously between imaginative, book-laden romanticizing and direct observation. The voyage from New York by stagecoach and steamboat, over the Alleghenies and then down the Ohio and Mississippi, took two weeks. He drew on his travel notes for subsequent effusions about the size and shape of the continent in the "Song of Myself" catalogs—on the return voyage he and Jeff traveled by a different route so they could visit Niagara Falls—and not until late in life would Whitman again travel such a distance. Out of this trip, the provincial Whitman drew the materials for his first effort at travelogue, the three-part "Excerpts from a Traveler's Note-Book." He observes the rapid circulation of ideas on the boat like the committed citizen of the print community he was: "cheap novels are in great demand, and a late newspaper is a gem almost beyond price"; in the evenings, "the two large cabin tables were sometimes surrounded by readers; and the stove by smokers and talkers" hashing over, among other things, "the late war." He also lapses into novelistic description himself, and one passage detailing a beautiful night in the Alleghenies prompts him to say that the landscape provides "first rate scenes for an *American* painter—one who, not continually straining to be merely second or third best, in *imitation*, seizes original and really picturesque occasions of this sort for his pieces."[33] Such ruminations, less overtly political than the editorials he had been accustomed to writing for the *Eagle*, fed into his growing conviction that an originary American aesthetic would have to be based on a practice of direct observation.

Nonetheless, Whitman's anxiety about his own originality was not yet to be allayed. His poetry up to this point had been thoroughly imitative: Whitman shared his era's taste for the pan-American romance, in both its Spanish and indigenous versions, and his very earliest extant poems imitate the well-circulated works by William Gilmore Simms, Longfellow, and Bayard Taylor. "The Inca's Daughter" and "The Spanish Lady," published in the *Long Island Democrat* in 1840, are both tragedies involving nobly born women who die rather than submit to sexual injustice. The former resists enslavement by conquistadores; the latter refuses to renounce her out-of-caste lover.[34] This romantic Hispanism, founded in the common perception of the primitive but eroticized tropics we saw in chapter 3, seems also to have colored Whitman's encounter with the Deep South and New Orleans. He wrote one poem during the trip,

"Midnight on the Mississippi," which was also published in the first issue of the *Crescent* under his initials. Perhaps influenced by the celebrated passages describing the heroine's river journey in *Evangeline*, the six rhymed quatrains of this poem project Gothic, otherwordly associations on the landscape: "weird-like shadows" and "River fiends, with malignant faces" seem to lurk there, "as if to clutch in fatal embraces / Him who sails their realms upon." The boat's motion creates the illusion that the trees on shore —"straight, tall giants, an army vast"—are marching past, "rank by rank." Opening out from the cliché of life as a journey, the hostile mystery of the river seems to the observer "like Death": "a murky darkness on either side / And kindred darkness all before us!"[35]

If on this journey Whitman identified with Evangeline floating down alien waters toward an uncertain fate, he carried Longfellow's romantic rendition of Latinate Catholicism in Louisiana into his general perception of the city, as well. The erotic and exotic appeal that Whitman afterward claimed to find in New Orleans attached itself to the conventional scenes and perceptions repeated by Anglo-American visitors then and since: the colorful French Market, the "delicious coffee," the elaborate dress and sensuous appeal of the Creole mulatas, and the "splendid and roomy and leisurely bar-rooms!" Letters from Jeff back home to Long Island dwell on the weather, the spectacular health that Walt was enjoying, and the surprisingly foreign customs of this overwhelmingly Catholic city and its social and religious rituals—all of which Jeff found alternately appealing and distastefully superstitious.[36] Much later, Whitman would write in "New Orleans in 1848," published in *November Boughs*:

> Sundays I sometimes went forenoons to the old Catholic
> Cathedral in the French quarter. I used to walk a good deal in
> this *arrondissement*; and I have deeply regretted since that I did
> not cultivate, while I had such a good opportunity, the chance
> of a better knowledge of French and Spanish Creole New
> Orleans people. (I have an idea that there is much and of
> importance about the Latin race contributions [*sic*] to
> American nationality in the south and southwest that will never
> be put with sympathetic understanding and tact on record.)[37]

I will return later to this claim of retrospective regret, and the silencing, even in the midst of acknowledgment, of those "Latin race contributions." In the New Orleans spring of 1848, Whitman was certainly close to them—not only the architectural forms of the past, but the geographies, languages, and voices. From a contemporary perspective, it is astonishing to see how much of each four-page issue of the *Crescent* is covered with news of Spanish America: dispatches from still-occupied Mexico City; from Querétaro, where the treaty negotiations were taking place; and from Havana, Chile, Nicaragua, and (especially) the Yucatán. From its front page to its advertisements for Spanish teachers and announcements of arrivals in port, the *Crescent* reproduced the image of New Orleans as the center of a polyglot, circum-Caribbean capital I sketched at the beginning of the chapter. The frequent complaints in its first issues about the molasses-slow pace of mail service from New York (voiced with a hint that the local post office might be corruptly delaying or redirecting mail) echo the same complaint in Jeff's letters home, suggesting that the dark passage down the Mississippi's "dense black tide" really *had* taken Whitman to a different kind of place—one very far, indeed, from New York.[38]

On the *Crescent*'s staff of five, Whitman 's principal job was that of "exchange editor," whose work consisted of "overhauling the papers rec'd by mail, and 'making up the news,' as it is called, both with pen and scissors," while a man named Da Ponte translated bits from foreign-language papers for possible selection from this archive.[39] Prominent among them is *La Patria*, which is cited quite frequently as a source during the early months of the *Crescent*. A ritual phrase such as "we are indebted to our friends at *La Patria* for this item" would introduce the latest dispatch.[40] Whitman—who, according to Loving, spent a good deal of time lounging around with other journalists in the city—could not have been ignorant of *La Patria's* presence; in fact, the paper's experiment with a bilingual edition coincides precisely with the middle of Whitman's time in the city. The following notice appears on the editorial page of the *Crescent* on 10 April:

> LA PATRIA—(OUR COUNTRY.) By an advertisement which will be found in another column, it will be seen that D. Juan Gomez has associated with him in the editorship of the Patria, Dr. Matthewson, formerly known as editor of the Vera Cruz "Genius of Liberty." The Patria will be enlarged to the medium size of the daily paper, and will be published in the future in Spanish and English. We wish that success to the enterprise which we have no doubt will attend it. We will again refer to the subject, when our columns are less crowded.

But the *Crescent*'s identification of *La Patria* as a "friend" must have been vexed, given that Gómez and Alemán were against annexation and adventurism, whereas *Crescent* editors M'Clure and Hayes took the opposite stance. Their editorials labelled Mexico a place of "anarchy and semibarbarism" populated by "animals," and denounced the crafters of the Treaty of Guadalupe-Hidalgo for having "abandon[ed] three-quarters of our conquests" rather than taking possession of all the territories south to the Sierra Madre, as well as Mexico's lucrative Gulf ports. One brief filler piece (Whitman, as the exchange editor, might have contributed this) repeats a northern editor's Thanksgiving "sermon": "Since last year at this time, we have licked one nation and fed another of about the same population. We have killed a few Mexicans, and saved the lives of ten times as many Irishmen; so there remains a handsome Thanksgiving balance in our favor."[41] Moreover, the *Crescent* agitated for a repeat in the Yucatán of recent events in northern and central Mexico. An article titled "Who Will Have Yucatán?" on 8 April urged the immediate intervention of "some adventurous Yankee" to protect the landowning Yucatecans from "a horde of unarmed, undisciplined savages, whom 2000 American rifles would drive into the Pacific." The final comment seems at first a dim-witted geographical blunder, but the writer is simply convinced that the "possessor" of the Yucatán would swiftly get a canal to the Pacific built through the Isthmus of Tehuantepec. Spain, he claims, is "dangerously seeking to reestablish monarchy upon our southern borders," while Great Britain, by setting up a puppet king in Nicaragua, is imposing "a barrier to our progress by the interposition of the Anglo-Saxon, instead of the enervated Spanish, Indian, and mixed races . . . the sovereign power of Central America will command the territory through which the proposed canal connecting the Gulf and the Pacific will pass." Whitman's metaphor of New Orleans as a "channel or *entrepot*," the swinging gate of a nation constantly shape-shifting (like the "tireless waters" in "Midnight on the Mississippi"), aptly represented a general feeling among many Democrats that control over this quadrant of the hemisphere was within their reach, and that further "acquisitions" of formerly Spanish territories were not only possible but likely during this flux in the balance of global power. Although I am not suggesting that Whitman authored this editorial, which far exceeds the anti-Mexican rhetoric he had penned for the *Eagle* (the author was almost certainly M'Clure), this hyperactive expansionism is the context against which Whitman's later regret that he had failed to record "with sympathetic understanding and tact" the "Latin race contributions to American nationality" should be positioned.

Thus we see Whitman employed at cutting and pasting, in a city unprecedentedly (for him) polyglot and multicultural, during a moment in which the present and future borders of the nation were seemingly open to daily rearrangement and speculation. It seems fitting that with the leisure afforded by his relatively light duties on the *Crescent*, and this particularly "Latin" enlargement of his prior notions about the shape of the nation and the limits of its cultural and linguistic possibilities, Whitman seems in New Orleans to have worked hard at two aesthetic practices that would later be of great importance to him: the collating of "scraps," on one hand, and the collecting of urban character types, on the other. The *Crescent* stint immersed Whitman in the constant practice of rearranging random facts and polyglot phrases into newspaper pages that "contained multitudes." His professional duty to locate interesting bits of information had also become a personal avocation: his scissoring and pasting of items from other newspapers to fill columns in the *Crescent*, as Floyd Stovall has demonstrated, amounted to a "self-directed reading program." Roughly between 1846 and 1849, he cut out items from periodicals and dissected inexpensive anthologies and atlases to rearrange into scrapbooks that, Stovall argues, are key to Whitman's development as a poet because they articulate materially the idiosyncratic combination of history, geography, current events, and future projections that come together ideologically in the first edition of *Leaves of Grass*. The manner in which he "clipped," both personally and professionally, seems just as suggestive as the ideas he may have taken from these scraps, for it rehearses some of the most salient compositional features of *Leaves of Grass*: the style of collage and juxtaposition, as well as the constant recycling and reusing of favorite images and phrases.[42]

This productive fracturing and reassemblage of language scraps finds a counterpart in a particular kind of observational consciousness— the surveying gaze of the urban flaneur who takes in a multitude of disparate impressions. The detached tone of the cosmopolitan observer, which we saw at work already in his "Traveler's Notes-Book" about the Mississippi River voyage, would be heightened and developed in the sketches Whitman published in the *Crescent*. He later recollected having enjoyed long midday walks along the levee, reminiscent of his "amblings" around Long Island, Brooklyn, and Manhattan; these similarities in tone affirm for me his authorship of "A Walk about Town, by a Pedestrian," one of the unsigned *Crescent* pieces whose attribution to Whitman has been debated.[43] In this piece, the anonymous narrator calls attention to his own directionlessness as he strolls, with no practical aim, around the city from the docks to the marketplace. The subjects who attract his attention are working people, like the "dozen stalwart sailors with bare legs, scouring the decks" of a German ship, who "seemed to be as happy as lords"; and the stevedores who strike him as "honest men, and, physically speaking, work much harder than any other class of the community."[44] He speaks sympathetically to "a poor long-shoreman lying down on a bench" who had been kicked out of his lodgings, and is struck by the eccentric appearance of a "good old man in a blue jacket and cottonade pantaloons, with a long stick of sugar cane in his hand" (this dandy, he later learns, is one of the best-known lawyers in town, but enjoys his democratically aimless daily walk as much as the narrator). He describes the colorful speech patterns of a Creole woman selling crabs, and comments on the ingenuity of competing newsboys: "These boys are 'cute' as foxes and industrious as ants," and with such qualities, "may in time be sent to Congress." At the end of the walk, the speaker goes home to "take breakfast—tea, a radish, a piece of dry toast, and an egg—read one of the morning papers, and [go] about my business." His final judgment—"Came to the conclusion that New Orleans was a great place and *no* mistake"—suggests the tone of someone new in town, rather than one of the other veteran staffers of the *Crescent*. Moreover, its sympathy with the working underside of the city as opposed to the routines of high society, its delight in the tapestry of common things, and its Jacksonian vision of the newsboy who might grow up to be a congressman all suggest Whitman's authorship.

Only one sequence in "A Walk about Town" seems out of step with the character of the compassionate, populist observer Whitman would create as his speaking persona in the the first edition of *Leaves*:

> Saw a negro throw a large stone at the head of his mule,
> because it would not pull an empty dray—wished I owned the
> negro—wouldn't treat him as he treated the mule, but make
> him a present of a cow-skin, and make him whip himself.
> (223)

Can this be the same writer who had proclaimed his hatred of slavery from his early youth—the same who would famously imagine himself giving sanctuary to a runaway slave in section 10 of "Song of Myself," who would proclaim himself the voice of "white as well as black" and build this inclusive process of identification into a model of political unification across cultures, classes, and regions? As Betsy Erkkila, Kerry Larsen, and others have underscored, the poet was throughout his life an opponent of slavery without ever freeing himself from racialist thinking.[45] Even so, this would constitute the only direct utterance on record in Whitman's work of a wish, however fleeting or arch, to *own* another human being. Phrases such as "I am the poet of slaves / and I am the poet of masters of slaves" and "a Southerner as good as a Northerner" suggest a kind of temperate identification with both poles of a binary; but "wished I owned the negro" is an utterly unthinkable phrase within the *Leaves of Grass* project as it eventually ripened into full maturity. Whitman's later poetic persona eschews possession and possessiveness of any kind in order to highlight the all-important right and responsibility to possess oneself.

It is for precisely this reason that the articulation of a forbidden desire here, in this rehearsal of certain scenes and aesthetic moves later to come in *Leaves of Grass*, is so intriguing. If one sees the *Crescent* sketches as a trying-out of various writerly voices and postures, which seems highly plausible even if we cannot definitively settle the attribution of some of them, the utterance of this phrase could be construed as an experiment in inhabiting the consciousness of a native southern white man: in the anything-goes marketplace of New Orleans, and under the anonymous guise of the *Crescent's* literary man-about-town, a curiosity about that forbidden desire to possess another may be safely indulged. Yet it is uttered between dashes—which is to say, provisionally—and ultimately not as an endorsement of the commodification of the human, but as part of a larger claim about the dignity of all flesh, both human and animal. The speaker wishes he owned the mule-driver not to have limitless power over him, but to teach "the negro" a lesson in empathy by making him whip himself and thereby feel the mule's pain. This comparison between the beast of burden and the black slave was already overdetermined, of course, by its deployment in the arsenal of slavery's defense on the grounds of the black body's "natural" animality and predisposition to physical labor (there is a particular resonance to the fact that the animal is a mule, the root of "mulato"; and that the famed "quadroon women" of New Orleans introduced the rest of the nation to the tragic mulata on stage and in fiction).

As Karen Sánchez-Eppler has argued, scenes of a racialized human body undergoing violent physical extremity and/or public degradation—such as whipping, lynching, and auctioning—appear with such frequency in the writings of white northerners that they suggest a fascination coeval to repulsion and horror. Her reading of another such moment in Whitman, the slave auction in "I Sing the Body Electric," seems particularly relevant here in that the experiential source for this section of the poem is precisely in New Orleans, where Whitman was for the first time able to witness a scene already legendary in the North: the *Crescent* not only published announcements for runaway slaves, but was located just around the corner from a building that hosted slave auctions.[46] "I Sing the Body Electric" is among other things a poem about healing, about mending the wounds of physically and mentally disturbed bodies through an erotically transcendental act of fusion between speaker and subjects. When its attention turns, in that almost antically journalistic headline, "A slave at auction!," the speaker imaginatively dismisses the auctioneer as a "sloven" who "does not half know his business" and takes over with the gavel: "Gentlemen look on this curious creature, / Whatever the bids of the bidders they cannot be high enough." From the perspective of generations of liberal critics, the poem's effort to defend and rescue the racialized body of this slave-at-auction is a radical act of solidarity, for it insists on the incorporation of every human into a biological community: "Within there runs his blood . . . the same old blood . . . the same red running blood." Yet, as Sánchez-Eppler insists, there is a paradoxically dehumanizing edge to this gaze, this invitation to "Examine these limbs, red black or white . . . they are very cunning tendon and nerve; / They shall be stript that you may see them."[47] The observer's very power to "strip" the object of his admiration in order to see the circulatory system underneath the skin, and thereby to reassure himself that black men bleed the same as white men, uncomfortably undoes the poem's claim to equality of subject and object. The erotic overtones of such "stripping" are even more disturbing in the commodifying context of the auction, a context only intensified by the characterization of New Orleans as a "fleshpot" in which sex and work could be readily bought and sold. Whitman elsewhere goes to great lengths to condemn the commodification of the body, positing instead a utopian marketplace in which all the fruits of labor are one's own, all sexual acts are "freely given," and the federal system organizes its state-bodies into a voluntary union. Of these three closely linked arenas of consensual relation, the last—the political realm—breaks down in the most obvious ways when the nation-state finds itself enforcing that pact of "Union" through a bloody war. However, the other two realms, the economic and the erotic, are haunted by the same instability: they cannot acknowledge the desire to command the bodies of others, as workers or as sexual partners, and must therefore suppress dissent. Doris Sommer follows Martí's description of Whitman's language as "a stolen kiss, a rape" to conclude, "Whitman makes real dialogue unnecessary, although, like the rapist, he demands a partner."[48]

It is from this perspective of possession, consent, and degradation that I want to return to the question of Whitman's exaggeration and eroticization of the time he spent in New Orleans in his later efforts at self-fashioning. It is generally assumed that he left the South, in late May 1848, because he could no longer tolerate being in the heart of the traffic in human commodities, though it seems as if personal disagreements with M'Clure, coupled with a desire to be reunited with his family and bring Jeff home, may have been as great a factor. I suggest, rather, that the power of the New Orleans imaginary has to do with its proximity to Latin American territory, which could be imaginatively possessed without the guilt attached to other racialized bodies. Among the sensual poems he would later organize into "Calamus" and the 1860 edition of *Leaves* are not only "I Saw in Louisiana a Live-Oak Growing" but a lyric with the title "Longings for Home." This poem (later renamed "O Magnet-South!") might be a companion piece to "Midnight on the Mississippi," which takes the homesick New Yorker down strange waters toward the unknown and seemingly toward death. In "O Magnet-South," both the direction and the valence of the journey are reversed. It is told from the perspective of the homesick, displaced southerner longing to return home and be reborn:

> O Magnet-South! O glistening perfumed South! my South!
> O quick mettle, rich blood, impulse and love! good and evil! O all dear to me!
> O dear to me my birth-things—all moving things and the trees where I was born—the grains, plants, rivers,
> Dear to me my own slow sluggish rivers where they flow,
>   distant, over flats of silvery sands or through swamps, . . .
> O pensive, faraway wandering, I return with my soul to wander their banks again . . .
> O my heart! O tender and fierce pangs, I can stand them not, I will depart.[49]

The poem turns back to the metaphor of the national landscape as a single body—a conceit Whitman had played effectively in his prose travelogue of his voyage down the arterial Mississippi—and imagines those "slow, sluggish rivers" of the Mississippi Delta circulating through the region like blood. Thus, the Whitmanian persona can voice itself as "a Southerner as good as a Northerner" (the phrase he articulates in a famous passage of "Song of Myself"); the magnetic attraction to a place, to a lover, is an "impulse" of blood longing to circulate back to the heart. Yet the insistence on the sameness of southerner and northerner requires a potentially dangerous act of imagination, for it makes the northerner complicit in the South's blood guilt—the "good and evil" that the second line strives to balance in uncertain equanimity. The "quick mettle, rich blood" the southern voice remembers, and longs for, recalls the slave-auction scene of "I Sing the Body Electric": the "cunning tendon," the "red running blood." These "longings for home," in short, are longings for an embodied place, one place synechdochically joined to another in a single national organism.

This catechrestic figure of the national land-body is fully worked out in the preface to the first edition of *Leaves of Grass*, in which a key recurring phrase envisions an "America" that encompasses the full hemisphere: "the blue breadth over the inland sea of Virginia and Maryland and the sea off Massachusetts and Maine and over Manhattan Bay and over Champlain and Erie and over Ontario and Huron and Michigan and Superior, and over the Texan and Mexican and Floridian and Cuban seas and over the seas off California and Oregon."[50] If that last phrase strikes contemporary ears as a false parallelism, it is only because Texas has been so successfully mythified as a vast land that we have suppressed its older identification with strategic access to the Gulf of Mexico: the "Texan . . . sea." The phrase neatly catalogs the march of Manifest Destiny through the 1840s and 1850s: here, the poet describes nothing less than the circum-Caribbean shipping empire of which New Orleans was the capital. The way this passage moves from "the Texan and Mexican and Floridian and Cuban seas" to "the seas off California and Oregon"— that is, from the Caribbean theater to the northern Mexican one— describes a not-yet-existent passage from one to the other that was seen as vitally necessary to the success of the expansionist project. Although Whitman did not live to see the building of the Panama Canal (or apparently take much note of the negotiations constantly going on around it), the figure of crossing between land and water draws him powerfully in "Crossing Brooklyn Ferry" and the Suez Canal of "Passage to India." The projected American canal would serve as an extension of the work done by the Mississippi—a carotid artery in the nation's circulatory system, working East to West instead of North to South. But the "new lands" of the Caribbean and the post-Mexican frontera—new limbs to be added to that body—begged another metaphor as well: they represented sources of wealth, and the proposed canal a kind of sluice through which their gold and silver were to be rinsed. Just as that early editorial in *La Patria* had sardonically observed, Mexican territory contained, in the imaginations of many, a hidden wealth of gold and jewels for the taking. This romantic Aztecs-and-conquistadores fantasy spawned not only a host of popular dime novels but a more sophisticated version of those clichés from the poet who had written "The Inca's Daughter." More than a dozen manuscript fragments dating from the 1850s indicate his fascination with the "vast national tracts" in "the new inland America." These fragments, which often have an air of the same modernist bricolage in his later poetic catalogs, take on a kind of manic lyricism of their own. One reads, "it is the new crown of the north, the mighty crown, the broad and solid democratic crown, crowning the north, full of gold and silver,—a crown of mountains / Idaho Crown of the North, new crown—the mighty serrated crown of the North the new crown of democracy, with gold and silver."[51] The oxymoronic "crown of democracy" that tumbles out of this fragmentary rush suggests that geography *is* wealth.

Earlier, I cited Whitman's retrospective 1884 memoir of the New Orleans period and his mention there of the "Latin race contributions to American nationality." The phrase does not specify what those "contributions" might be, but they are strongly hinted to be territorial, and imperially aware poems like "Facing West from California's Shores" corroborate this. So does the more leadenly jingoistic "Our Old Feuillage," with its chorus of "America always!":

> Always Florida's green peninsula! Always the priceless delta of
>   Louisiana! Always the cotton-fields of Alabama and Texas!
> Always California's golden hills and hollows—and the silver
>   mountains of New Mexico! Always soft-breathed Cuba!
> Always the vast slope drained by the Southern Sea—inseparable
>   with the slopes drained by the Eastern and Western seas.[52]

California and New Mexico, the territories "won" by the new conquistadores, are "golden" and "silver," while New Orleans's port is "priceless": again, value is linked to the key positions these places hold within the circulatory system of the hemisphere. The passage insists on linking the southern, eastern, and western seas as compass points conceived and valued through their common and presumably subordinate relation to the exemplary North. The Latin race contributions thus have to do with the reunification of the divided continents of the hemisphere into a single nation, and that process of territorial acquisition is erotic: in this poem Cuba is seductively "soft-breathed."

To be sure, there is nothing revolutionary in civic eroticism, which is observable not only in Whitman (with his "free intercourse of states") but in the works of Heredia and others described earlier in this study. However, the New Orleans context reveals a specific slippage in the logic of sexual/national consent underlying Whitmanian poetics. In New Orleans he became aware of very different kinds of racialized bodies in an immediate and daily way—from black to mulato to Creole and Spanish—and this awareness opens up erotic possibilities even as it constricts and threatens his sense of the integrity of the body politic. More importantly, however, the overlap there of black and "Latin" bodies provokes a strong ambivalence about the possession of the body. As my reading of "A Walk about Town" attempted to show, the desire to "possess" and to wield power over other bodies—a desire elsewhere taboo because of Whitman's antislavery (but not antiracist) convictions—can be expressed in the guise of a New Orleanian in ways it cannot be elsewhere. But it is an integral part of Whitman's politicized poetics that bodies (both human and national) must have the freedom to possess themselves. Thus the author of those anti-Mexican editorials in the *Brooklyn Eagle*, the staffer on the virulently antimestizo, anti-Latino *Crescent*, would confound readers looking for consistency in his political views by saying in 1864, "Mexico is the only one to whom we have ever really done wrong."[53] This represents, I suggest, not so much a change of heart but a recognition of something known all along: that the territory gained for the United States in the Mexican War was not voluntarily surrendered, that it was coerced without full consent. *La Patria* sounded this note so strongly, and in both languages, that it would have been nearly impossible for Whitman to miss.

The same sense of a long-repressed acknowledgment of guilt about possession and violation returns in "The Spanish Element in Our Nationality." Written for a civic celebration in Santa Fe in 1883, this is Whitman's final and most cited statement on the topic of *latinidad*: "To that composite American identity of the future," he writes, "Spanish character will supply some of the most needed parts." Defending Spanish culture's "grander historic retrospect" against the Black Legend, he proposes that its exaggerated cruelties are no worse than "the resume of Anglo-Norman history." In this piece, however, the older Whitman also modifies his earlier acceptance of the inevitable decline of the American Indian and other "analogous" races, contradicting the received wisdom of the 1880s that "in a few generations more [the Indians will] leave only a reminiscence, a blank." He could readily have lifted such Hispanophilic images—as well as the figure of the vanishing Indian's long past—from one of Longfellow's, Heredia's, or Bryant's authorizing gestures toward pre-Columbian civilization. Likewise, "Unnamed Lands," the poem that serves as the epigraph to this chapter, cites Latin Americanness as a mere historical trace, a tantalizing but conveniently subrogated civilization anterior to the present democracy: "What vast-built cities, what orderly republics, what pastoral tribes and nomads . . . what of liberty and slavery among them, what they thought of death and the soul." Yet Whitman does go beyond his teachers to imagine, proleptically, that Indians, mestizos, and "the Spanish stock of our southwest" will eventually reappear in the national line of vision:

> Who knows but that element, like the course of some
> subterranean river, dipping invisibly for a hundred or
> two years, is now to emerge in broadest flow and permanent
> action?[54]

Whitman's figure of the "subterranean river" of Latino linguistic and cultural presence strikingly resurrects one of his own antecedent tropes— that of the Mississippi, arterially directing the western and eastern halves of the continental body into New Orleans.

Reading *La Patria*: Hispanophone Print Culture and the Annexation Question

In an ironic but highly suggestive twist of fate, when Whitman left the *Crescent* and the Crescent City late in May 1848 to return to New York, his successor at the paper was William Walker—the same William Walker who would go on, in the following decade, to invade Baja California and Sonora with a group of filibusters, then arrange his election as president of Nicaragua before being executed by a Honduran firing squad. Sometime that year, Victoriano Alemán, cofounder of *La Patria*, argued with Walker in the street over some political difference, and the two came to blows. Walker, according to witnesses, came out ahead, leaving Alemán bruised and battered.[55] Presumably this was the end of whatever "friendship" had existed between *La Patria* and the *Crescent*, and the effort at ambassadorship with Matthewson's bilingual edition failed around the same time. But it was far from the end of *La Patria*'s efforts to consolidate a transamerican print community based in New Orleans in the language that bilingual prospectus had praised for its "native beauty, simplicity, and uniformity." To the contrary, Gómez and Alemán moved the paper out of J. L. Sollée's multilingual print offices at 137 Chartres Street and set up their own quarters in Exchange Alley with the intention of branching out into book and magazine publishing and retailing.[56]

The *Imprenta de la Patria* announced its first local production in 1848, a nicely produced engraved literary and satirical magazine, *La Risa: Enciclopedia de Extravagancias*, which shared some materials with a publication of the same name in Madrid. The editors wrote separate introductions to the first issue of the "Edición Americana." Gómez's begins with a humorous meditation on the proverb "He who runs with the wolves learns to howl," and concludes that living among the *yankis*, fondly referred to as "two-legged wolves," has taught him eccentricity:

> ¿En qué de las cuatro partes del globo se encuentra una nación mas extravagante que la gran confederación de treinta Estados con distintas leyes para cada uno, y de costumbres, usos, y abusos tan diametralmente opuestos? ¿en qué rincón del mundo pudieran hallarse reunidas más extravagancias que las que se ven amontonadas en esta ciudad de la *media-luna*? Muchos creerán tal vez que la mitad de sus habitantes son lunáticos, o que todos sean semi-lunáticos, por la simple razón de apellidarse (a causa de la curva que forma el río a su frente) la ciudad de la *media-luna*. Y quizás no falte quien se imagine que ésta es tierra de Moros . . . y si tal pensaren no van por cierto muy errados.
>
> *[In which of the four parts of the globe can one find a nation more extravagant than the great confederation of thirty States, each one with different laws and with customs, uses, and abuses so diametrically opposed? In what corner of the world could one discover more eccentricities in one place than those that pile up in this city of the* crescent moon? *Many people might believe that half of its inhabitants are lunatics, or that all are half-lunatics, for the simple reason of its being called (due to the curve that the river forms at its head) the* Crescent City. *And perhaps there will be others who imagine that this is a land of Moors . . . and if they think so, they're not so far wrong.]*[57]

Here, the heterogeneity of the various states in North America is not (as Whitman argued) a source of strength, but rather a bewildering chaos with the potential to induce madness. These jokes about the "wolves" who howl under the Louisiana moon provide great fodder for Gómez, the more ribald writer of the two; his introduction skewers the strange and "wild" customs of the Crescent City. To him, all *Luisianeses* are "Yankees"—an appellation that that the city's Creoles, Anglo-Southerners, and polyglot European immigrants might reasonably have protested. In this riff on the city's nickname Gómez is punning, of course, on the etymology of "lunatic," the association of wolves with the moon, and the crescent shape of the scimitar by which Spain and Europe symbolized Islamic "Moors" in their historic confrontations. But who are "the Moors" here? In one sense, they are the boorish, aggressive, Anglo-Americans wielding scissors or swords; but in another sense, this would seem to be an archly racist reference to the city's substantial black and mixed-race population. The jesting, dismissive categories of *moros* and *yanquis* allow Gómez to position this literary experiment within the interstices of an already marginal place. He puns on the claim that the enterprise was inspired by the *espíritu yanki* [Yankee spirit], the spirit of speculation and risk-taking, as well as the "espíritu embotellado, *alias* whisky." Alemán's own introduction follows this up with a direct swipe at "periodistas 'a lo Yanky' es decir, periodistas de tijera y engrudo, de *corta y pega*" [journalists in the Yankee style—which is to say, journalists of scissors and paste, of *cut and paste*]. This contrast between original composition and news-gathering, on one hand, and imitation or "thievery," on the other, was a recurring theme in *La Patria*'s depiction of Anglophone print culture.

Besides publishing a few issues of *La Risa*, Gómez and Alemán tried to make their office a center of Hispanophone culture. Issues of *La Patria* advertise meetings of a Sociedad Literaria Española at an address next door in Exchange Alley, and an announcement asking readers to identify themselves for a planned *Directorio de los españoles residentes en los Estados Unidos* headquartered at the paper's offices appears in the 14 June 1849 issue. Although I have found no trace of this directory, the advertisement is intriguing because it again takes "un español" to mean a Spanish speaker rather than a Spanish national, since it also asks contributors to state their native country. Gómez and Alemán occasionally published lists of letters waiting at the post office with Spanish, Italian, or Portuguese names, so apparently their outreach extended to those communities as well; in one typical issue there are sixty such names. The Librería La Patria sold books as well, and ads also appear for a different Librería Española at 141 Chartres Street. By 1849, *La Patria* had apparently established a particularly close relationship with a New York weekly, *El Correo de los Dos Mundos*, of which no copies survive.[58] As the 2 May issue states, subscribers to one could get a discount on the other, as well as a special price on "todas las publicaciones literarias que se hagan en una u otra oficina" [all the literary publications that are produced in either office]. The ad goes on to announce that the house of *El Correo de los Dos Mundos* had just published Spanish translations of Lamartine's *Confidences* and *Rafael*. The publications issuing from the Imprenta La Patria itself were eclectic: they include a translation, done locally, of a biography of "General" Tom Thumb, whose tour through New Orleans they had covered enthusiastically. Also heavily advertised in every issue of *La Unión* in 1851 (that is, after the paper's second renaming) was their translation of the labor agitator and Catholic convert Orestes Brownson's *Opiniones de un Anglo-Americano acerca de la expedición Cubana y los anexionistas* published as a twenty-page pamphlet; it was apparently later distributed in Havana and New York.[59] Translated from an article in *Brownson's Quarterly Review*, it takes direct aim at the "partidarios de las expediciones piráticas contra Cuba" [supporters of the piratical expedition against Cuba], the so-called Lopecistas, about whom I will say more momentarily. If advertisements in the paper are a fair indication, the books sold at the office were mainly novels and scientific and educational tomes from Madrid and Paris, shipped through Havana, and they were fairly expensive.

Perhaps out of frustration with the limitations Spain imposed on the free spread of print culture, and perhaps out of a deeper ideological disagreement, Gómez and Alemán openly flouted the colonial censorship policy in Cuba. Early issues of *El Hablador*, for instance, had featured a serial novelette, "Los misterios del Cerro en la temporada de 1844: Historia que parece cuento" [The Mysteries of Cerro in the Year 1844: A True Story That Seems Fictional], a roman à clef styled after Eugène Sue's outrageously popular *Mystères de Paris* and set in a neighborhood on the outskirts of Havana. Particularly revealing, in light of the rift that would later develop between the paper's editors and the Cuban separatists, is that (as a footnote explains) the story was written by a *habanero* but was not publishable in the Caribbean colonies. Thus, *El Hablador* was thumbing its nose at the censor by presenting the tale unexpurgated, and declared its hope that the story would make it to the islands.[60] Given the fact that packets from Veracruz, Mérida, and other independent cities in Spanish America frequently called in New Orleans, it is likely that books proscribed in Cuba were sold either at Librería La Patria or elsewhere in the city—perhaps at one of the other multilingual Vieux Carré print offices like Levy's or Sollée's that distributed the paper. As vehemently protective of Spanish culture and Spanish American territorial integrity as the paper's editorials were, on at least one occasion they published a poem expressing strong anti-Spanish sentiments: the anonymous "La patria," which appeared on 2 April 1846. That "homeland" is neither Spain nor Mexico (the possible patrias alluded to by the flags flanking the Stars and Stripes on the cover illustration), but Cuba. As if to encourage a connection to the title of the newspaper, the word *patria* appears repeatedly in majuscules or italics throughout the poem—as are words describing specifically Cuban fauna, like *tojosa* (a kind of Cuban dove), *sinsonte* (mockingbird), *colibrí* (a small hummingbird), *palma* (understood to be the royal palm Heredia had already enshrined as the national symbol), and *cocuyo* (a lightning bug). Some of these terms had entered Spanish from Taíno and thus signaled a move toward an indigenously Cuban literary language. "La patria" is a classic Cuban exile poem in that it identifies the homeland with birth and motherhood, and all their sacred sentimental associations; it starkly contrasts the cold northern weather to the paradisical climate of the Caribbean; and it closes with a plea to maintain "el sublime fuego / de patria y de libertad" [the sublime fire of homeland and liberty].[61]

¿Qué importa que, esclava imbécil,	[What does it matter, dumb slave,
Te aduermas libre de penas	that you fall asleep, carefree,
al ruido de las cadenas	to the sound of the chains
de tu bárbara opresión?	of your barbarous oppression?
. . .	. . .
¿Qué importa que gimas ora	What does it matter that today you cry out
si sabes, patria querida,	as long as you know, beloved country,
que ha de llegar una aurora	that someday a day will dawn
de celeste resplandor?	with celestial brilliance?
Y entonces, aunque el tirano	Then, although the tyrant
truene de rabia y de ira,	should thunder in anger and ire,
será el mundo americano	the American world will become
del viejo mundo Señor.	lord of the Old World.]

The old revolutionary analogy of republics in chains—the idea of colonial subjection of the *mundo americano* by the *Viejo Mundo*—sets up the poem's prophetic conclusion. But to utter this analogy in the context of New Orleans only deepens the inherent paradox of its inability to acknowledge racialized chattel slavery as the foundation of the very plantation economy its imagery romanticizes.[62]

Although most of the poetry published in *La Patria* is less overtly political than "La patria," the fact that the paper reprinted José de Espronceda's "El 2 de mayo," a poem that protests the "dissolute court of the monarchs," suggests its broader allegiance to the liberal spirit of European reform. *La Patria* regularly republished items from a cosmopolitan array of journals and magazines with which they had an exchange relationship (despite Alemán's insistence on the originality of their journalism, the exigencies of filling four folio pages two or three times per week made that a necessity). Some of the selections in their "Poesías" corner are attributed to newspapers in Madrid, Havana, or Mexico. One of the most common sources is *El Siglo XIX* of Mexico City, the most important Liberal Party organ of the time; it was edited at one point by Guillermo Prieto, whose strongly anti-Yankee and pro-Enlightenment views are in keeping with Gómez and Alemán's.[63] With regard to Mexico, it was as scornful of Itúrbide's failed empire as of Santa Anna's militaristic populism: one issue reprints a scabrous satirical poem titled "Contradanza de Santa Anna," attributed to the St. Augustine *Florida Herald*.[64] During the war months they printed a poem allegedly written by a Spaniard in the album of a well-known actress, Doña Isabel García Luna de Santa María, lamenting her decision to leave Madrid for a position at the Teatro Nacional in Mexico.

Isabel, ¿qué beneficio	*[Isabel, what good*
esperas de un edificio	*can you expect from a building*
que se ha quedado sin *Tejas*?	*that finds itself with no roof?*
¡Tanto va (y a sus oídos	*So much (and when you board*
cuando a aquella playa abordes,	*for that distant shore,*
lo dirán hondos gemidos)	*you'll hear heartfelt sobs)*
de los Estados discordes	*goes from those discordant states*
a los *Estados Unidos*!	*to the United States!*[65]

The "building" that finds itself with no *tejas*, the traditional roof tiles, is a reference to the loss of Texas, the uppermost "roof" of a once far-reaching territory, the Estados Unidos de México, that seemed to be caving in on its center. The author's teasing remark that the actress, too, might be "annexed" to the United States seems only half in jest. (New Orleans was on an opera circuit with Cuban cities; one issue prints three poems—one dated at New Orleans and the others a month earlier in Matanzas—in praise of "la prima donna" María Concepción Cirártegui, the "ruiseñor cubano" [Cuban nightingale].) The literary values of *La Patria*, then—like the other contemporary Spanish papers discussed in chapter 3 and unlike the English-language papers—ran more to poetry than serial fiction. Other poems include a humorous sonnet by "J. R. C." describing the lazy life of "un empleado" who never goes to the office but passes his days as a gentleman—reading the papers, smoking, and going to the theater. On the other end of the spectrum, there is also a dead-child elegy titled "Dejémosle; se ha dormido" [Let's Leave Him, He's Fallen Asleep], and a patriotic sonnet by a Mexican poetess in exile, Vicenta Irolo. However, some of the pieces in the poetry section on page four are marked "Remitido," submitted to the offices of the paper by local writers, and a whole series of more than twenty long submissions throughout much of 1849 is signed "El Observador," identified only as an "español de New Orleans." S/he penned several satirical-topical poems as well the Orientalist "El árabe."[66]

The Hispanophone literary sphere summoned into being by Gómez and Alemán thus freely mingled works from and about Mexico, Spain, and the Spanish Caribbean. Yet Cuba maintained the significant place that its proximity to New Orleans would suggest, in both the paper's literary section and its editorial page. An unsigned article on "La literatura cubana" on 13 October 1848 laments that it will not be circulated on the island despite the fact that "ni una sola idea tiene, como se verá, que respire conspiración, libertad, ni ninguno de esos fantasmas que son la pesadilla de los gobernantes de la Isla" [it doesn't have a single idea, as you will see, that breathes conspiracy, liberty, or any of the ghosts that are the nightmare of the island's governors]. Since Cuban writing "ocupa ya un lugar distinguido en la república de letras" [already occupies a distinguished place in the republic of letters], it ought to possess the same autonomy and access to public speech that other such "republics" have: "A pesar del sistema de censura que se empeña en apagar el desarrollo de las luces—sistema conocido en todo el mundo, y sobre el que no queremos hacer ninguna reflección por ser una materia demasiado importante y cuyo tratado no tendrá fin—brilla el talento de sus hijos" [Despite the system of censorship that persists in snuffing out the progress of enlightened thought—a system known throughout the world, which we don't want to reflect on further because it is too important a matter, and dealing with it here would go on forever—the talent of her sons shines brilliantly]. A condemnation of censorship emerges from this sentence, only to be locked between dashes that refuse to argue the point, effectively repressing the issue with the same force as the censor. A full-blown critique of colonial policy, or outright support of Cuban independence, would have alienated the Spanish mercantile interests (who presumably formed the base of their readership) in the city and beyond. Gómez and Alemán seemed to walk a tightrope with their stated aim of tolerating differences within the Spanish-speaking community; they insisted that their paper "sostiene las opiniones generales y no las particulares" [upholds general opinions, not individual ones]. However, there seemed to be no consensus on what those "opiniones generales" were.

It is ironic, given *La Patria*'s vigorous attempts to build a sense of solidarity with the broader imagined community of Spanish speakers and to forge connections to the Anglophone sphere of print, that the paper was eventually undone by differences over Cuba within its community—fomented by a very different kind of Hispano-Anglo alliance, the movement to annex Cuba. Many Cuban patriots, prior to the 1860s, concluded that, between the lesser of two evils—incorporation within the United States or fragile independence subjected to constant threats from foreign powers—the former was preferable. Gómez and Alemán at first seemed incredulous that after the lamentable example of Mexico anyone among their constituency could be in favor of the annexation of Cuba:

> *Sabemos positivamente* [que] hay en esta ciudad (y creemos que hay otras de la Unión) cierto *club* que se reúne en cuando para tratar de la extensión de la República, y que en ese *club* se ha hablado de la "conveniencia" de poseer la Isla de Cuba; pero si no estamos mal informados, el tal club se compone exclusivamente de AMERICANOS, y no creemos haya entre ellos un solo cubano o español: pero si todos los que proyectan la *Independencia* o la *Anexión* de la Isla de Cuba son semejantes a los de Nueva Orleans, creemos que hay poco que temer.
>
> [We know for sure *that there is in this city (and believe there are others in the Union) a certain* club *that meets occasionally to discuss the extension of the Republic, and that in this club they have spoken of the "convenience" of owning the isle of Cuba; but if we are not misinformed, this club is composed exclusively of* AMERICANS, *and we don't believe that there is among them a single Cuban or Spaniard—but if all those who are plotting the*

independence *or* annexation *of that island are like the fellows in New Orleans, the patria is safe].*[67]

The editorial goes on to imagine with glee that if the United States tries to gobble up the island of Cuba, it will give Uncle Sam terrible indigestion (a prophecy that has proven true again and again). However, by dismissing annexation as a "Yankee" scheme and refusing to leave open a space of principled opposition to Spanish rule in Cuba (a stance their own choice of literary materials would seem to support), the editors effectively excluded from participation in their public sphere many of those who should have been among the paper's greatest supporters: a group of young romantic revolutionaries who wrote patriotic poetry in the model of Espronceda, Lamartine, and Larra. Many of these writer-activists joined forces in New Orleans with the Narciso López filibusters, memorializing his "martyrdom" in *El laúd del desterrado*.

Although López, a Cuban property owner born in Venezuela, has the distinction of being the first to plant the current national flag on Cuban soil, his legacy is the subject of considerable historical controversy. López spoke of his two "liberatory" expeditions as an execution of the will of the Cuban people, but once they had landed his troops found few supporters on the island; and for most post-1959 Cuban historians, his "revolution" is hopelessly tainted by its association with U.S. slaveholding interests. Through the late 1840s, and various attempts to raise funds and men, López's political beliefs shifted with the winds: originally an abolitionist, he came to support the maintenance of slavery on the island in order to win over southern planters.[68] The two López filibusters in 1850 and 1851 increasingly pivoted less on Cuban autonomy than on adventurism (many of his "freedom fighters" were bored mercenary veterans of the Mexican War) and economic speculation; investors hoped the U.S. Treasury would pay off the Cuban bonds he sold at the same high rate as it had paid to Texas bondholders. Strongly backed by the coiner of the phrase "Manifest Destiny," John O'Sullivan, López and his allies were familiar figures in the Anglophone press, both North and South: for a brief moment his *filibusteros* were the vortex to which national debates over the sectional slavery conflict were drawn. Both expeditions were launched from New Orleans, and the *Crescent*—like the *Picayune* and the *Delta*—endorsed it with the same giddy enthusiasm they had brought to military interventions in Mexico and the Yucatán.

This forced *La Patria* into an increasingly extreme defense of the very colonial regime it was formerly willing to critique. The vitriol cited in the previous passage against "certain *clubs*" increased in intensity when they became aware that there were *cambiacasacas* [turncoats], as they called them, among the *raza española*. It is probable that *La Verdad*, the New York newspaper once edited by Villaverde and underwritten by O'Sullivan and Moses Beach, editor of the *New York Sun*, was widely distributed in New Orleans and acted as a competing Spanish-language voice to *La Patria* there.[69] Yet the paper's relations with the Anglophone newspapers were still cordial enough that Alemán's marriage to María Dolores García in St. Louis Cathedral was mentioned in all the major newspapers; the *Delta* even thanked Alemán for sending some wedding cake and champagne along with his announcement and wished the couple a "long life and happy union."[70] However, later that summer, López successfully guided his first expeditionary force (an earlier group had been prevented from leaving the country by U.S. port authorities), some five hundred men, to Cuba by way of the Yucatán. The first incursion ended within a day, and on his return to the States López returned and was arrested for violating the Neutrality Act. The trial occupied the front pages of all the New Orleans newspapers. A master of self-promotion, López bartered this arrest into public outrage and managed to raise a stronger, richer army for a second assault in 1851. His troops held a position at Las Pozas for nearly three weeks before Spanish troops captured and executed López and one of his officers, Lieutenant John Crittenden, the nephew of a U.S. senator, in August. *La Patria* changed its name in 1851, perhaps to clarify their ideological commitment to federalism, and added a new coeditor, but held firmly to its former anti-interventionist stance. When word of the executions of López and Crittenden arrived and *La Unión* declared that the filibusteros had gotten no more than the punishment they deserved, an angry mob burned down the paper's offices and bookstore, nearly killing Alemán and destroying six Spanish-owned cafés, two tobacco shops, and the office of the Spanish consulate as well.[71] The loss of *La Patria* effectively foreclosed for decades the possibility of an oppositional Latino print organ, positioned within the United States, which would be both the emblem and the material apparatus of an imagined community of Spanish speakers both in and out of the national sphere.

Songs of the Exile: The *Laúd* Poets and Quintero's Pearls

The failure of the López revolt gave anticolonialist Cubans living in exile a common point of sentimental unification—exemplified in the first exclusively Spanish-language poetry anthology to be published in the United States. It took five years to arrange the publication of *El laúd del desterrado* (1858), which showcased poems by six young separatists, Miguel Teurbe Tolón, Pedro Santacilia, José Agustín Quintero, Leopoldo Turla, Pedro Angel Castellón, and Juan Clemente Zenea, all of whom had lived in New Orleans for some period and had been involved in financing, fighting alongside, or otherwise supporting, the Lopecistas. The anthology opens with a section devoted to a seventh poet, the long-dead José María Heredia, who is referred to as "profeta de nuestra revolución y Homero de nuestra poesía." By positioning Heredia as their precursor in northern exile and as their revolutionary progenitor, the *Laúd* poets invented a politico-literary genealogy of resistance that would prove more durable than the poems themselves.[72] The anthology's editor was J. E. Hernández, one of the major forces (along with Villaverde and Betancourt) behind the Junta Revolucionaria Cubana in New York, which published *La Verdad* and *La Revolución* and increasingly militated for independence. Hernández's introduction stresses that these poems were products of both *trabajo* and *talento*, devoted not to some sanctified realm of art but to the ideological work of soliciting "una lágrima santa" [a holy tear] on behalf of the anticolonial cause. As with abolitionism— the other major sentimental discourse of the nineteenth century—this is an argument for an aesthetics of sincerity and affect, and Hernández argues that the poem's sincerity is legible in the roughness of the poems themselves: "son canciones espontáneas . . . trazadas con ligereza para los periódicos" [they are spontaneous songs . . . sketched out hastily for the periodicals] (3). "Writing for the papers" thus becomes the hallmark of the true man of patriotic feeling, who has no time for editorial revisions; he lives—to return to Heredia's phrase—in the midst of a "revolutionary whirlwind." A similar self-authentication by form would later characterize Martí's poetry as well. His claim to the persona of the *hombre sincero* is reinforced by his populist use of newspapers and easily memorized language fragments to do the work of revolutionary conversion.

El laúd del desterrado is dedicated to Miguel Teurbe Tolón, whose work dominates the anthology. Teurbe Tolón had designed the Cuban flag in New York in 1849; it flew first in New York and then in New Orleans as the Lopecista expedition sailed to Cuba. Tired of his exile, in 1857, under circumstances eerily similar to Heredia's, Teurbe Tolón had finally returned to Cuba at the behest of his mother, under a general amnesty offered by Spain in order to divide the separatist agitators (some hard-liners called those who accepted the amnesty traitors). He died there of tuberculosis. In one of the Spanish colonies that had already won their independence, Teurbe Tolón would have lived the life of a typical letrado: his early years in Matanzas were occupied with translating Lamartine and other French and English poets, and with editing various periodicals. He went into exile in the United States in 1848; during the following decade he translated Paine's *Common Sense* and Emma Willard's *History of the United States* into Spanish, taught, and published a Spanish grammar and textbook. According to Montes-Huidobro, he also edited a Spanish-language section of the New York *Herald* and composed poems in English that were published in a Boston magazine.[73] Teurbe Tolón's poetry, though in the judgment of later critics weak and unaccomplished, experiments with various styles, from the sonnet "Resolución" to the ballad-style "Himno de guerra cubano" and the Cervantine fable "La pluma y la espada: Fantasía" [The Pen and the Sword: A Fantasy].[74] Though its recourse to the didactic strains of Romanticism is sometimes formulaic, it tries to strike simple, memorable notes that will lend a folk authority to the revolutionary impulse by converting it into tradition. The works selected for inclusion in *Laúd* mine the usual exile themes: many of the censored poems he circulated in Cuba, such as "Al Pan de Matanzas," "En la muerte de Trinidad Roa," and "En una excursión por el Río San Juan," describe familiar landscapes invigorated by revolutionary desire, while the poems of his New Orleans/New York era mark the way that exile reorients temporal and spatial coordinates. His second-anniversary poetic tribute to *La Verdad* begins,

Dos veces ya del extranjero cielo	*[Twice the sun has finished its course*
Cumplió su curso el sol: dos largos años	*around this foreign sky: two long years*
La luz he visto tras el pardo velo	*I've seen the light through the dark veil*
De los climas del Norte, y nuestra Cuba	*Of the Northern climes, and our Cuba*
Aún no levanta . . .	*Still has not risen up . . .]* (39)

The reference point is Cuba, distant both in space (along the polarity of North-South coordinates) and in progressive time (the "destined" moment that has not yet arrived). Even more insistently than Heredia, Teurbe Tolón indicates that the counterweight to this threatening alienation is a set of feminine virtues. The object of desire, la patria, is hidden behind a dark veil; and the poem goes on to vilify the Spanish "Déspota" as a "Vándalo" oppressing "Cuba esclavizada" [enslaved Cuba], accusing it of sentimental outrages against womanhood such as mistreating respectable matrons and nuns.

Teurbe Tolón's "El pobre desterrado" [The Poor Exile] uses the popular ballad stanza of *octosílabos* in eight-line stanzas through eight numbered parts, the last line of each repeating, with variations, the term *desterrado*. The song is preceded by an anonymous English epigraph: "My thoughts are in my native land: / My heart is in my native place," and it begins with a description of a mythical, Edenic origin:

Allá lejos, tras los mares,	*[There, far across the seas,*
hay un suelo todo flores,	*is a land full of flowers,*
do la brisa en los palmares	*where the breeze in the palm*
	groves
suspira cantos de amores;	*sighs songs of love;*
Donde hay un cielo dorado,	*where the sky is golden,*
donde es de plata la luna,	*where the moon is silver.*
y allí se meció la cuna	*And there rocked the cradle*
de este pobre desterrado.	*of this poor exile.]* (44)

Against this paradise, the generative conflict of the poem unfolds: "el brutal brazo armado" [the brutal armored arm] of Spain ruptures his happiness, and with each stanza's refrain, the figure of "el pobre desterrado" gets elevated to heroic stature. Not unlike the wronged outlaw that is the staple of many of the *corridos* of the Texas-Mexican borderlands, this Cuban desterrado likewise adapts the traditional Spanish *romance* for social protest.[75] The "adventure" that takes place in "El pobre desterrado" is a story of flight and sanctuary akin to many corridos; but it ends with a tragic recognition that escape will not bring justice or happiness:

Mas ¡ay! el gemido ahogado	*[But oh! the suffocating moan*
de la patria en agonía	*of the homeland in agony*
viene a herir día tras día	*continues to wound, day after*
	day
¡el alma del desterrado!	*the soul of the exile!]* (46)

The audience of this mock oral poem is not, however, a collective community but rather an individual woman, to whom the pobre desterrado entrusts his story as he begs her to shed a tear over his grave. Feminized sentimentalism and folk orality thus mark two common strategies of Romantic political poetry adopted by the *Laúd del desterrado* poets; Byronic self-glorification by way of an exaggerated masculinity is another.

With "A Annie Horton," one of several of his works to feature an epigraph from Byron, Teurbe Tolón initiates what would become a popular
subgenre among this group: a carpe diem seduction poem directed
toward a beautiful, virtuous, but ignorant Anglo-American girl that
explains his higher loyalty to Cuba and her freedom. (José Agustín Quintero's best-known poem, "A Miss Lydia Robbins," is another example.)
Annie Horton is not herself the subject of the poem. Rather, her presence
triggers reminders of other absent loci of sentimental attachment: *patria*,
madre, and *hogar*, the holy trinity associated with Cuba. Both Teurbe
Tolón's poem and Quintero's end with a wish that the Yankee "virgen
tierna" [tender virgin] might treasure the memory of the poet in the
future when he lies in his tomb.

    If a similarly eroticized martyrdom runs through the anthology,
it is not without claims to genuine affect. Neither Teurbe Tolón nor
Pedro Angel Castellón lived to see *El laúd del desterrado* in print. Castellón died in poverty in New Orleans, the city where he had lived for
nearly all of his short life, working in the family provisioning business.[76]
Leopoldo Turla, too, eventually died in the city, after struggling for three
decades to make a living as a Spanish teacher, translator, and occasional
magazine contributor; he allegedly left a trunkful of manuscripts, now
lost, upon his death.[77] Son of an Anglo-American mother and an Italian
father, Turla was universally hailed as a man with a *corazón perfecto*, a
perfect heart. The Mexican politician, editor, and *poeta nacional*,
Guillermo Prieto, made Turla's funeral a central scene of his narrative of
his travels to the United States in 1877. I return to Prieto's narrative at
the close of chapter 5, which also follows the fate of Juan Clemente
Zenea, the youngest of the *Laúd* group, who—when the separatist movement turned definitively away from annexation and toward independence—would take his place as its next representative martyr.

    Pedro Santacilia and José Agustín Quintero, the remaining *Laúd*
poets, are exceptions to the other patterns of exile telos: return, alienation, or death. Both adopted, instead, new forms of activist national subjectivity—Santacilia as a Mexican civil servant, and Quintero as a
diplomat serving first the Confederacy and then the Union. The former
found his destiny one day in 1853, when he met the exiled Benito Juárez
in New Orleans. Santacilia's biographer poses this *encuentro* between
the Cuban poet and the Mexican liberal in melodramatic racial terms, as
the "enfrentamiento de 'criollo' e 'indígena de pura raza'" [meeting of
the criollo and the pure-blooded Indian]: an epic encounter of Cuban
and Mexican difference, with the elite white Santacilia adopting a dif-

ferent national cause, one bent on racial reconciliation rather than on the protection of landed property.[78] Santacilia returned to Mexico with Juárez, becoming not only an important constitutionalist (he wrote key portions of the liberal Reforma) but the president's personal secretary and son-in-law as well: he naturalized himself into Mexico's national genealogy by marrying Juárez's oldest daughter. During the French interregnum from 1864 to 1867, he lived in New York with the president's wife and daughters, supplying intelligence about Washington's slow response to the European intervention. During this time he also maintained strong ties with Cuban revolutionary clubs and juntas in New York and fostered a number of them in Mexico. Many of his works, including poetry, costumbrista sketches, and a history of Cuba, were published in New York as well.[79]

The fate of Santacilia's poem "A España" reiterates his biographical trajectory. After its publication in *Laúd*, its anticolonial message traveled as far as San Francisco—where it was reprinted in *El Nuevo Mundo*, a newspaper edited by Mexican refugees from Maximilian, as a protest against French imperialism.[80] Beginning with epigraphs that reference the downfall of empire (the famous Golden Age poem "Ruinas de Itálica," variously attributed to Caro and Rioja), the injustice of Spanish colonialism in the Caribbean (Heredia), and the corruption of the Crown (Zorrilla and Espronceda), the 180 lines of this seven-page poem address the colonial power with an aggressively intimate *tú*, retracing the history of a boy's love betrayed:

Aún era yo muy niño y me contaban	*[I was still very young and they told me*
Que fuiste grande y poderoso un tiempo,	*That you were once great and powerful,*
Que tus naves llenaban el océano,	*That your ships filled the ocean,*
Que llenaba tu nombre el universo.	*That your name filled the universe.*
. . . .	. . . .
De tu poder, España, me dijeron,	*They told me of your power, Spain,*
Y yo de Cuba en las remotas playas	*And I, from the remote beaches of Cuba*
Acariciaba cual dorado sueño,	*Embraced that golden dream,*
La esperanza feliz de ver un día	*The joyful hope of one day seeing*

| Rico en recuerdos tu fecundo suelo. | *Your fertile soil, so rich in memories.]* (74) |

The poem debunks national myth-making as fundamentally literary: the boy, like any tourist or reader of romantic travel narratives, envisions the distant land that is his object of desire through reductive images of "tus bellas mujeres, con tus bardos, / Con tus fiestas, combates y torneos" [your beautiful women, along with your bards, / Your *fiestas*, combats, and jousts]. As a young man, he approaches this desired land as a suitor. But maturity brings disenchantment: one day, "aparté los girones de su manto / Y el barro inmundo contemplé del cuerpo" [one day, I pulled off your tattered robe / And saw the filthy clay that was your body]. With this suggestive image, the romantic mantle that drapes Spain in the cloth of myth falls away before the colonial subject, and he sees it in present, contemporary time:

Transformados tus campos en desiertos,	*[Your fields gone to deserts,*
Convertidas tus fábricas en ruinas	*Your factories in ruins*
Y sin bajeles tus antiguos puertos.	*And your ancient ports lacking vessels.]* (75)

The revelation of Spain's actual "ruin" dissipates the Cuban's mystical sense of kinship with its past. Further, Spain's failure to stay on track with the progressive temporality of nation-building is seen as a kind of sexual transgression. This critique makes "A España" atypical among the exile poems of *El laúd del desterrado*, which rely on strategies of nostalgia and idealization. The poem goes on to invoke the New World's indigenous heroes, as Heredia had done in "Las sombras," and ends with the prophecy that long-suffering Cuba would eventually join the other American republics.

Santacilia's other poem in *El laúd del desterrado*, a rendering of Psalm 137 ("By the rivers of Babylon"), stands out for its simple affective power, and is the most frequently anthologized of his poems.[81] More than a translation of a translation, "Salmo 137" is considerably lengthier than the version in the Casiodoro de Reina Bible. Whereas the traditional psalm identifies the objects of desire, Zion and Jerusalem, Santacilia employs periphrastic phrases, naming these places only as "el suelo en que nacimos" and "[el] suelo que nacer le viera" [the land where we were born]; "patria adorada," and "patria querida" (80–81). While this refusal to specify Cuba universalizes the lament of the Israelites, it also suggests the exile's traumatized inability to name the lost homeland. The final synonym for Zion is even more telling: "esclava y mísera colonia" [enslaved and miserable colony]. Likewise, Santacilia represents the foreign power as enslavers: "los tiranos / Que la tierra asolaron con el hierro / Y encadenaron luego nuestras manos / Conduciéndonos crueles al destierro" [the cruel tyrants / Who ravaged the earth with their iron bands / And then chained our hands / Bringing us into exile]. This greatly expands on the Bible's simple reference to "los que allí nos habían llevado cautivos" [those who brought us here as captives]. Santacilia's "Salmo 137" is specifically indebted to Heredia (and in turn to Byronic/Lamartinian revolutionary Romanticism) for its use of the figure of the republic in chains. However, the analogy between the bereft Israelites and the exiled Cubans is if anything more unsettled and unsettling than it was before the massive violence directed against Cuban blacks and mulatos following the Escalera conspiracy.[82] The fact that the nation in which the Cubans had found sanctuary was itself embroiled in a crisis involving definition and application of racial categories on a massive scale denatured their rhetoric of liberation: exile and enslavement are not equivalent, and the "chains" of colonialism are not the same as the chains of racially based chattel slavery. As the separatist exiles living in the United States would soon see clearly, a choice to align their cause with the northern model of republican nationhood would force a decision on the question of abolition, one they were reluctant to make. Santacilia escaped the paradox by throwing in his hopes for Cuban independence with Mexico, and with the dismantling of both slavery and Indian peonage, while Quintero's overriding belief in local self-rule led him to support a movement for southern secession that he saw as parallel to the Cuban cause—even though that meant accepting the Confederate defense of slavery.

One Cuban historian traces Quintero's fall from the national canon—his patriotic poems were well known and widely memorized in Cuban schoolrooms prior to the revolution—to the very paradox of his status as "un poeta revolucionario al servicio de intereses esclavistas" [a revolutionary poet at the service of slaveholding interests].[83] Yet Quintero had been from the outset perhaps the most deeply engaged of his generation of Caribbean letrados in New England sensibilities. The son of an Englishwoman who married a wealthy Cuban tobacco-plantation owner, he was sent to Harvard as a very young man—according to his obituary, at the age of twelve; according to other sources, at fifteen. His father died suddenly, and "the family estates being much involved, he was thrown entirely upon his individual resources. Instead of returning at once to his native land, he resolved to continue his studies at Harvard, and found the means to do so by giving lessons in Spanish. Handsome, accomplished, genial, the boy-teacher was a favorite in society, and made many friends among the litterati [*sic*] of Boston and its vicinity. Those 'friends' supposedly included Emerson, Edward Everett Hale, and the internationally famous professor of Modern Languages at Harvard, Henry Wadsworth Longfellow, with whom Quintero carried on a correspondence for the following decade and a half."[84] Returning to Havana sometime in 1848, he studied law and collaborated on various reformist newspapers with Cirilio Villaverde; like other anticolonialists of that generation, he was arrested for "seditious activities" relating to the Narciso López conspiracy, tried and condemned to death for treason, and thrown into the infamous prison at Morro Castle sometime in 1850. At an undetermined point, he escaped from prison (as had Villaverde) and made his way to New Orleans, probably by 1852.[85] During these years of agitation he was also writing poems like "A Miss Lydia Robbins" and "El banquete del destierro," which would be used as templates of patriotic sentiment.

One, titled simply "Poesía" (elsewhere reprinted as "Bajo la tiranía"), invokes the language of the folk ballad in a kind of call-and-response. Each stanza of this ballad addresses an innocent-seeming question to a worker: for instance, "what are you forging, blacksmith?" The answer is, a chain with which to enslave a brother. In a similar vein, the fisherman pulling in his net is told that it will feed the tyrant's banquet table; the laborer working the hard soil for coffee and sugar cane learns that "el oro y las cosechas son de España" [the gold and the harvest belong to Spain]; and the woodcutter, removing fresh healthy trees, is told that with each he is helping create "un cadalso más y un árbol menos" [one more scaffold and one less tree]. (Quintero's sentimental identification with the uprooted tree toward the end of this poem is particularly suggestive in light of Martí's frequent use of the metaphor of "el árbol del pueblo.") Each worker is thus forced to recognize that the commodity he produces makes him an unwitting participant in a larger, virtually invisible reign of political-economic tyranny. Although the name of the *patria* is not mentioned, each of these scenes clearly recalls Cuba, positioned between the sea and the fields. The final stanza is the most disturbing, as it turns to the commodity of the human body:

[Di, ¿qué meces, mujer, en esa cuna? | *[Say, what are you rocking, woman, in that cradle?*
¡Un niño! En él mis ojos siempre clavo. | *A child! My eyes are fixed on him.*

Pese, oh madre infeliz, a tu fortuna	*Regret your luck, oh unhappy mother,*
Desvelada te encuentran sol y luna,	*Sun and moon will find you wakeful,*
Y al fin le das al déspota otro esclavo.	*And in the end you're giving the despot another slave.]*
	(67)

Montes-Huidobro correctly sees in this poem an unattributed paraphrase of the German poet Friedrich Rüeckert (149).[86] By referring pointedly to Cubans—meaning free Cubans—as "slaves" to the harsh colonial master of Spain, Quintero again invokes the troubled Romantic metaphor of the republic in chains. Yet there are hints that he may have meant the poem as a more general critique of both colonial control and racialized chattel slavery. For one thing, his family's fortune had been in tobacco rather than sugar, the industry more intensive of black labor. For another, his contact with Longfellow dates from the very same period when that writer released his *Poems on Slavery*: 1846. The other figures reported in Quintero's obituary as his "Northern friends," Emerson and Hale, were also either outright abolitionists or staunchly antislavery Whigs. It seems difficult to imagine that Quintero would have solicited the patronage of a known antislavery writer during this contentious era unless he passed what was then a serious ideological litmus test.

Moreover, Quintero maintained a correspondence with Long-fellow during the early 1850s, when he was quite possibly collaborating with Cirilo Villaverde and Manuel Antonio Marino on the bilingual, pro-annexationist *El Independiente*, of which no copies survive. On 21 June 1855, he laments: "mi fortuna ha disminuido mucho durante tres años de excitación política" [my fortune has greatly diminished over three years of political agitation], which suggests that he spent whatever remained of his father's estate on separatist activities in the States.[87] This and earlier letters are largely preoccupied with details of Quintero's process as he translated some of Longfellow's signature poems: "A Psalm of Life," "Excelsior," and "The Arrow and the Song" (he even tried his hand at *Evangeline*). Quintero apparently entrusted the translations to a Boston woman he met in New Orleans to carry to Longfellow personally. He wrote on 19 April 1855 about what, exactly, had driven him to work on those translations: his conviction that the Longfellow poems

explican con nervio y claridad las necesidades y los instintos de la época, haciendo de la poesía un órgano de la civilización, bien inteligible, poderosa y más que todo progresista e innovador.

[explain with vigor and clarity the needs and instincts of the age, making poetry an organ of civilization, highly intelligible, powerful, and above all progressive and innovative.]

The translations are destined, he says, for export to his homeland, to build manly endurance for the work of liberation that lies ahead:

> [Tengo] un objeto y una esperanza que tocan muy de cerca al bien de Cuba. Iba sido mi principal anhelo abrir a los que se dedican a las letras en aquel país algunas de las fuentes en que beben los poetas americanos, dándoles nuevos modelos; preparándoles para ese grande y gloriosa unión que espero ver realizada entre ambos pueblos en un día no lejano.
>
> *[I have an aim and a hope that touch very directly on the good of Cuba. It has been my principal desire to introduce those who dedicate themselves to letters in that country to some of the sources from which the American poets drink—giving them new models, preparing them for that grand and glorious union that I hope to see realized between both nations in a not-too-distant day.]*

The "grand and glorious union" he refers to here strongly suggests annexation. For Quintero, the reading and absorption of Longfellow's poems seem to sanctify displays of male sentimentalism—melancholy and tears—as long as that affect is directed at the higher cause of remedying one's personal loss of the homeland by fighting for its liberty. In another letter of 21 June, he says that Longfellow's works have been "para mi alma fatigada lo que es la sombra de un árbol frondoso, en un día de sol, para aquel que abrumado de cansancio desfallece a la mitad de su jornada; siente que la esperanza principia a morir en su corazón" [for my tired soul what the shade of a leafy tree is on a sunny day, for the man who is fainting with weariness in the middle of his day's work; he feels that hope is beginning to die in his heart]. Reminding Longfellow that he was "perseguido en Cuba por mi adhesión a ciertos principios" [persecuted in Cuba for my adherence to certain principles], he worries that even what seem to us innocuous sentiments like the ones in Longfellow's poems may be censored in Cuba: "mucha precaución necesitamos para librarnos de un gobierno despótico que visla cada día el secreto de la correspondencia y proscribe hasta nuestros nombres!" [we need to exercise great precautions in order to free ourselves from a despotic government that oversees the privacy of correspondence on a daily basis, and forbids even our names]. Quintero closes this letter with the news that he will shortly be accompanying Mirabeau B. Lamar to Texas hoping to find some "empleo que me dé lo suficiente para subsistir" [work that will give me enough to sustain myself].

Quintero could hardly have found a more suitable patron than Lamar, a well-read writer of sentimental verse who was deeply engaged in political activity as well. Perhaps more importantly for Quintero's intellectual and ideological formation, as president of the Republic of Texas from 1838 to 1841, Lamar had been adamantly opposed to the annexation of Texas into the Union, and had made great efforts to build ties between Texas and other Spanish-speaking states in political flux: the breakaway republic of Yucátan, for instance. He studied Spanish and was an amateur historian. One of Quintero's tasks when he moved to Lamar's estate was to translate and organize the Spanish documents in Lamar's personal collection. (Lamar was in New Orleans during the early 1850s, where he met and married the second wife of his old age, so he must have met Quintero there.)[88] Besides Lamar, Quintero met another well-known southerner, Congressman John Anthony Quitman, a veteran of the Texas Indian border wars and the siege of Monterrey who nearly accepted Narciso López's offer to head the filibuster army. Quintero's Spanish biography of Quitman was published as a pamphlet at this time, and aimed to inspire Cuban men to heroic acts. The copy he inscribed to Longfellow is still among Longfellow's papers.

Thus Quintero seems to have substituted one or more southern father figures for his earlier mentor as competing models for poetic manhood. In another letter to Longfellow, dated 26 July 1855 from Lamar's estate in Richmond, Fort Bend County, Texas, however, he expresses homesickness for the North and a wish that he could move back there if Longfellow would find him a position. This letter, unlike the previous ones, is entirely in English:

> Although I am far from you I have never been nearer to you in thought and almost in feeling, than I am now and confess sincerely it gives me great pleasure to address you a few lines.
> Since I wrote you from New Orleans my life has been an uninterrupted series of unfortunate events in which sickness has not shared the smallest part. It is now a fortnight since I left that city with the hope of making an experiment in the way

of getting into business, but this State is so thinly populated and so destitute of literary taste that I can hardly expect much from it. Besides the climate does not agree with me. I am here in the country with my good old friend Gen. Mirabeau B. Lamar many a mile away from the world.

If you can get me any employment in your state, I pray let me know it, or at least advise me on that point.

The next letter in the series, 14 June 1856, finds Quintero in San Antonio, where he switches back to Spanish to address the poet again—this time a hurried note to enclose a copy of Quintero's translations, which had appeared in the *Revista de la Habana* thanks to the intervention of his friend Rafael Mendive, whose poems Longfellow himself would later translate. He also encloses a copy of "el periódico español que se publica en esta ciudad." This would have been *El Ranchero*, the paper that Quintero founded in dialogue with *El Bejareño*, the other San Antonio paper dedicated "a los intereses de la población Méjico-tejana" and discussed in chapter 3. Although he published several of his own poems and translations in the rival paper, Quintero regularly attacks *El Bejareño* for defending "individuos particulares mas bien que principios" [particular individuals, rather than principles] and summons all of "los Méjico-tejanos que aman su raza, su sangre, sus recuerdos, sus mujeres y su clima" [the Mexican-Texans who love their race, their blood, their memories, their women, and their climate].[89] His transformation from a homesick Harvard Cuban into a spokesman for "los Méjico-tejanos" within the space of a year may seem suspect, but during that year he also traveled extensively around the border region, clerking in the Texas House of Representatives and meeting various Mexican dignitaries as well as local tejano landowners, as he helped sift through and translate Spanish land titles.[90] In this statement he argues for an even broader form of communal affiliation: that of the shared blood of *su raza*, and of shared sentimental bonds centering on women, memories, and some sort of subtropical fellow-feeling.

In the surviving issues of *El Ranchero* there is another clue to Quintero's own sentimental memories: a poem titled "A Elisa," dated from Richmond, Texas, and published 4 July 1856, about being far from one's loved one. The Elisa of the title most likely was Eliza Bournos, the daughter of an old French Creole family in New Orleans, whom Quintero married there in 1857 (They would have two daughters and two sons, named after Lamar and John Marshall, both of whom would follow in their father's careers of law, journalism, and diplomatic service.) By early 1859, however, Quintero was back in New York, where he went to edit the first experiment with a Spanish-language illustrated weekly published by the American newspaper mogul Frank Leslie: *La Ilustración Americana*.[91] Still another letter to Longfellow places him back in Austin on 2 November 1859, enclosing a copy of *El Noticioso de Nueva York*. He returned to New York in November 1860. The last of the extant letters to Longfellow (dated 21 Nov. 1860 and on stationery labeled "El Noticioso: Spanish American Journal") states,

> I last week arrived here from Texas to take charge of the editorial department of "El Noticioso." The editor has gone South "to marry a fortune," and while at the helm it is my intention to publish several translations of your beautiful poems. I will take pleasure in sending you regularly the paper.[92]

Thus Quintero seems to have maintained cordial relations with the northern literary establishment at least until the time the Civil War broke out. At this point, according to his obituary, Quintero "abandoned his situation in New York to cast in his lot with the Southern people. He took this step at great personal sacrifice, with characteristic generosity of enterprise, despite the protests and warnings of his Northern friends and employers. After enlisting in the Quitman Guards in Texas he went with that company to Virginia." There, he was transferred to the diplomatic service and made the Confederate agent in Matamoros, Brownsville, and Monterrey. Jefferson Davis's secretary of state sent him on an uncommissioned mission to solicit aid from Mexico: specifically, to do an end-run around the Union naval blockade to move matériel and to sell its cotton crop to Mexico, Europe, and South America. Quintero personally knew the caudillo Santiago Vidaurri, who controlled Nuevo León and Coahuila states, and arranged to get some 320,000 bales of cotton smuggled through "this back door." When Brownsville fell, Quintero took up permanent residence in Matamoros until the end of the war.[93]

Fernández de Castro suspects that Quintero's deeper motive for this risky diplomatic service was less to defend the Confederacy than to enlist Mexican help for the cause of Cuban independence. There were signs that, should Juárez continue to maintain his tenuous hold on power, he would help end Spanish colonial rule in the Caribbean; he had already swept the Spanish ambassador and the Guatemalan minister from their diplomatic posts in Mexico because they were thought to be "reactionary."[94] In northern Mexico, however, Quintero had a thorny ego problem to manage: Vidaurri was concerned with consolidating his own authority more than the central government's. Juárez deeply mistrusted Vidaurri and most agents of the Confederacy, who had the bad habit of making racist statements about Indians and "half-breeds" in the president's presence. Both of those parties, in turn, also made deals with the French generals supporting Maximilian when it was convenient for them to do so. Quintero, in contrast, seems to have negotiated the tricky business of the Confederate alliance with liberal enemies Vidaurri and Maximilian very skillfully—for when Guillermo Prieto, a key member of the Reforma government, came to the United States in exile during a conservative takeover in 1877, he identified Quintero as a great friend of Mexico.[95]

After the Civil War, Quintero had briefly returned to Havana, thinking to practice law, but the colonial government forebade him to do so and he returned to New Orleans in February 1866. According to a notice in the *Daily Picayune*, Quintero had first gone to Washington, D.C., to seek an official presidential pardon for his intrigues for the Confederate government: "Mr. Quintero is a native of Cuba . . . and is a gentleman of fine literary attainments."[96] Quintero seems to have quickly become one of the most prominent Spanish speakers in New Orleans: says his obituary, "after reading for some months in the office of the well known firm of Semmes and Mott he graduated in the law school of this city" and met with "a fair degree of success in the practice of the legal profession." Quintero's name appears in a "Guía Mercantil" [Business Guide] in the advertising section of *El Indicador* in 1868 as an "abogado y notario público" [lawyer and notary]. From some point in the 1860s onward, he served the U.S. government as consul for Costa Rica, a post he would hold for the rest of his life. In 1867 he was also named consul to Belgium. Despite this service to the federal government, Quintero seems to have taken a stance toward the North similar to that of New Orleans itself, which—after suffering a humiliating occupation under Benjamin Butler, known locally as "the Beast"—saw itself as oppressed by a "foreign" invader. And although he practiced law, Quintero also appealed to an authority outside the law: he authored the famous New Orleans dueling code, the *Code duello*, a document claiming that Anglo-Americans cannot understand the principles behind the duel because they "are not generally transcendental. They do not occupy a plane lifted above mundane affairs." The Code of Honor, in contrast, represents moral grounding and "true civilization" as opposed to "the foul flood of radical aggression." This is not to condone violence: "Like public war, the duello is liable to misuse. . . . Honor is the sentiment by which a high estimate is placed upon individual rights" that are not always protected by law.[97]

In the late 1860s and 1870s, Quintero became the chief editorial writer on the English-language *Picayune*—ironically, the very organ that had jingoistically led the march to Mexico. (His son Lamar, who later became the attorney for the United Fruit Company in Central America, also got his start as a journalist at the *Picayune*.) Quintero was known as a brilliant writer with a penchant for practical jokes, but he once invoked the *Code duello* on behalf of the *Picayune* itself. The paper had fallen into the hands of one Pearl Rivers, a widowed poetess in her twenties who had inherited it from her senescent husband, and some on the staff feared that a female editor would render the paper unable to continue defending its anti-Yankee stance. Newspaper legend tells Quintero's gallant response: "As knights to their ladies, so they would be to her. They would work for her, they would fight for her. José Quintero, the chief editorial writer, polished his pistols and passed out word that if anyone craved satisfaction for what the Daily Picayune said, come to him!"[98] There is a certain bathos in the ultimate transference of Quintero's affective allegiance: from the *perla de Cuba*, the home in Havana he never could return home to occupy, to the "Pearl of the *Picayune*." Over the course of four decades, Quintero shape-shifted from cosmopolitan northern man of letters, to Cuban patriot, to "Méjico-tejano," to Confederate diplomat, and finally to hereditary claimant, through his wife's well-placed family and his identification with the vestigially aristocratic Code of Honor, to a place among the Creole elites. In this vortex of exchange for Latino identities, Quintero, like Whitman's poetic persona, "contained multitudes."

5

The Deep Roots of Our America
Two New Worlds, and Their Resistors

Walt Whitman's retreat from the levees of New Orleans to the Brooklyn and Manhattan streets that were his heart's home follows a path familiar to many writers of the Anglophone Northeast: a recuperative stay in a southern clime that reinvigorates one's creative energies. Within a year, Whitman had begun the process of accumulating the ever-expanding lists, maps, and catalogs in the notebooks that would eventually get condensed into the poems of the first edition of *Leaves of Grass*. If, as Whitman critics generally assume, the three subsequent decades of revisions to *Leaves* reveal an increasingly anxious effort to consolidate national identity in the wake of the Civil War, an effort to "unread" Whitman based on the claims I made in the preceding chapter must consider the price of this consolidation on Latino and Latin American subjects and spaces. This chapter begins with another flaneur in a foreign city: Rafael Pombo, a Colombian poet, diplomat, and editor with a strongly hemispheric sensibility who, unbeknownst to Whitman, haunted the other poet's neighborhoods in New York during the latter half of the 1850s. However, unlike Whitman—and in a manner far surpassing Longfellow and Bryant, both of whom he admired and whose works he translated—Pombo made use of his scenes of urban pilgrimage to articulate a critique of antebellum expansionism and filibustering, as well as their postwar avatar: the redoubling of efforts to obtain a transatlantic canal route and to make inroads into Latin American markets. Pombo's nearly two-decade residence in New York and Washington—he would not return to live in Colombia until 1872—coincided not only with civil wars here and in his native land, but with a period of increasing sophistication in the production and distribution of English- and Spanish-language periodical networks in the Americas, into which he invested the usual hopes of the cosmopolitan letrado.

From Pombo, I turn to the backwater territory of San Francisco, examining the sectional conflict in the United States and the crisis of Mexican liberalism through the eyes of Isabel Prieto, a contributor to the Hispanophone press in California. A young dramatist and poet born in Guadalajara, Prieto accompanied her parents to California in 1865 after the French intervention. Maneuvering around gendered restrictions on women's public expression, she began publishing semianonymously in *El Nuevo Mundo*, a contentious organ directed by fellow Mexican exiles but deeply involved with local issues—notably, the ongoing tensions between the californio elites, the sudden Anglo-American majority population that had arrived after the gold rush, and other Mexican, Chilean, and Peruvian workers. After her return to Mexico and subsequent marriage, Prieto sought wider recognition by publishing in another periodical titled, similarly, *El Mundo Nuevo*. This one, in New York, initiated a new form of Hispanophone print culture. Edited, in turn, by exiled Cuban and Puerto Rican nationalists but aimed at Spanish-speaking readers spread across the hemisphere, *El Mundo Nuevo* initially established a partnership with Frank Leslie's publishing house—one of the most powerful, and profitable, engines of the nineteenth-century world of print—in a historic experiment in ethnic media niche-marketing. Pombo, and several other Hispanophone letrados who have entered this study so far, also wrote for the biweekly and its successor, *La América Ilustrada*, which together lasted from 1871 to 1875. At the height of its influence, the paper helped direct U.S. policy toward Cuba during the Ten Years' War (1868–78) by publicizing the "martyrdom" of poet Juan Clemente Zenea, who had been ambushed and imprisoned while on his way from New York to Cuba on a diplomatic peace mission. Zenea, in a transnational twist that seems too neat even for fiction, had reputedly been the secret husband of Adah Isaacs Menken—the infamous crypto-Jewish actress, partisan of Whitman, and daringly sensuous poet—during her early career in Havana.

The travels of these figures and texts from North to South and West, from cosmopolitan centers to borderland peripheries, are retraced again in the fourth and final section, which samples the three-volume travelogue and poetry anthology that the prominent Mexican liberal Guillermo Prieto composed, and sent home for serial publication, during his 1877 voyage through the United States. Prieto, a devout anti-Yankee, visited every now-familiar locus of transamerican significance: San Francisco; the Mississippi River cities and the Delta; New York City (where he stayed at Bryant's home) and Niagara Falls; and ultimately the south Texas border zone. But he was most drawn to New Orleans, where he alternately commiserated with and delighted in the company of the Cuban-born letrados José Agustín Quintero and Leopoldo Turla as they struggled to find a position in a city that was itself newly subordinated within the post-Reconstruction social and economic order. Guillermo Prieto's work, finally, articulates a common cause among Mexicans and Cubans—both within the borders of the United States and without—based on what he understood as their shared marginality and vulnerability.

The grave domestic crisis of the Civil War and its aftermath did not divert U.S. attention entirely away from the rest of the hemisphere. The period is critical, marked by the Ten Years' War in Cuba, ongoing racial tensions and violent struggles for autonomy in the Yucatán and Central America, the triumph and decline of liberalism in Mexico from Juárez's first government in 1857 through the French occupation under Maximilian (1864–67), the Guerra del Pacífico involving Chile, Peru, and Bolivia in militaristic chaos (1879–83), and the Dominican Republic's turn away from the temptation of annexation to the United States and unprecedented return to the Spanish colonial umbrella in 1868.[1] Although less political and economic energy was expended during the 1860s than during the previous two decades on aid to struggling republics in South America, on schemes to build export infrastructures or to annex islands in the Caribbean, relations with Mexico—Quintero's career suggests—became if anything more important to the warring governments in Richmond and Washington. If the 1860s and 1870s seem less eventful in terms of hemispheric relations than other periods, it is because Anglo-American influence over the Hispanophone world had shifted to the front of the borderlands. The extension of the national body Whitman had envisioned required a large-scale dismantling of existing social relations. By the time of Guillermo Prieto's transcontinental journey in 1877, Anglo dominion over both the remaining loci of indigenous resistance to settlement and the frontera territory that extended the former southern border zone overland along the Gulf of Mexico was all but complete.

Diplomatic License: Pombo in New York

In May 1855, as Whitman was busily preparing the first edition of *Leaves of Grass* for its July debut, a twenty-two-year-old poet from Bogotá—

capital of the newly reconsolidated nation of New Granada—settled in lower Manhattan, the site of Whitman's daily jaunts. Born in 1833 to an elite family that had been instrumental in the Bolivarian wars of liberation, Rafael Pombo was a typical product of his age and class. Schooled in the classic model but drawn to the already belated cause of revolutionary nationalism, he was translating Byron and mimicking the style and stature of Colombia's founding Romantic poet, José Eusebio Caro, at the age of twelve, even as he won accolades from the teachers at his military school for his translations of Horace.[2] The trip north was intended to be a brief episode in diplomatic training: Pombo had been appointed secretary of the New Granadan legation to the United States as a reward for his participation—while still in school—in the armed defense of the liberal government against a threatened military uprising. Yet, between interludes of travel and political changes in the nation he represented, this assignment-cum-exile would stretch seventeen years, and he would not return permanently to the country of his birth until a man of forty-three. Devoted to Caro's vision of a national literature that would be stylistically, as well as ideologically, original in a way that suited the new republican space, Pombo diverted his family's political ambitions for him into his pen. From his room in a Gramercy Park boardinghouse, where he joined numerous other Spanish-speaking bachelors, Pombo had a vista not only of the busiest street in the country—Lower Broadway— but of Printing-House Square, an important center of activity in the city's booming publishing industry. Shortly after his arrival, he was already translating and distributing articles in English for publication in the *New York Herald*, voicing the official Colombian perspective on such controversial issues as the overland passage through Panama and the competing interests of British and American investors in Central America.[3]

Yet Pombo was hardly prepared to allow his diplomatic responsibilities to overwhelm his poetic ambitions. Just before leaving Bogotá, he had set off a literary scandal with the publication of a long, impassioned lyric under the pseudonym of its supposedly female author, Edda. In a sphere of print culture within which the very few women to publish generally limited themselves to devotional works or harmless lyrics about nature, the carefully stylized, tormented passions expressed by Edda in this and subsequent poems brought "her" wide recognition: she was called "el Safo cristiano" [the Christian Sappho], and her work appears in anthologies of American women poets in Spanish.[4] While in New York, Pombo kept careful track of Edda's growing fame, sending four more poems home to be published under her name. Moreover, he played into the ruse publicly on more than one occasion. When the Argentine Juana Mansilla, one of the preeminent woman writers of the period, visited and expressed her admiration for Edda's verses, Pombo offered to set up a meeting with "her"—but failed to deliver.[5] What may seem a mere youthful lark—borrowing a more circumscribed, but perhaps more attention-getting, gender identity to express a passion both ethereal and physical—strikes one of Pombo's biographers as so significant that he titles the study *Edda la bogotana* [Edda of Bogotá]. The Edda poems express a woman's utter submission to the godlike figure of her beloved, but they also predict the speaker's own elevation to immortal poetic fame because of the power of the emotions she channels: one typical line reads, "Tu esclava, tu creación besa orgullosa / La mano que la inmola o la endiosea" [Your slave, your creation, proudly kisses / The hand that immolates her or enshrines her as a goddess].[6] The female speaker expresses indebtedness to the man who "created" her elevated sensibility through the fire of the flesh, seeing her relationship to him as a kind of willing slavery; yet Pombo himself is ultimately in charge of his creation. Even in New York—a place he repeatedly describes as heartless and cold—Edda provides for the young poet a name, a reputation, and per-haps most importantly an entrée into an intimate dimension of society when he otherwise had none. The intimate diary Pombo kept during his first several months in New York is full of details of his failed courtships and alternately acerbic and depressive comments on life among the yan-quis. In one passage, Pombo boasts that he melted the at first reluctant heart of a *norteamericana* named Mary Comstock by reciting Edda's verses, which provoke her to tears. Mary tells him that she thinks Edda "superior a cuanto poeta había leído, inclusos Byron, Lamartine y Moore, y agregó: en los Estados Unidos nadie, ni Longfellow, ni Bryant, ni Osborne (¡son tan fríos!) podría traducir sus versos. —Démelos, con-cluyó, mi corazón los traducirá" [superior to any poet she has read, including Byron, Lamartine, and Moore; and she added: no one in the United States, not Longfellow, Bryant, or Osborne (they're so cold!) could translate her verses. Give them to me, she concluded; My heart will translate them].[7]

On another occasion, in a conversation with the wife of his superior, General Herrán, Pombo slips into the conversation a recitation of some of his alter ego's verses. When Pombo reveals himself as the true author, she responds, "Nunca se ha expresado mejor la pasión" [Never has passion been better expressed]. Enthusiastically, Señora Herrán then translated Edda's poems herself to show to an English-speaking woman friend, who reportedly did not believe Pombo's claim to have written them: "Is there a *man* capable of such love?" the woman scoffed.[8] In the U.S. context, this role-playing allowed Pombo to affiliate freely with the female realm of sentiment, and to elevate it in opposition to what he casts as the sterile, whitened masculinity of capital accumulation. Pombo never married—a fact Héctor Orjuela attributes to his "ugliness" in order to avoid the suggestion of any "tendencias homosexuales." At the very least, Pombo's aestheticized and sentimental poetics suggests an ambivalent response to the heavy filiopietistic burdens imposed by his family and their drive to include him in the network of heterosocial reproduction.[9] In one diary entry, Pombo describes how one Rodríguez, a fellow Latin American bachelor living in his boardinghouse fell ill. Shockingly, none of the twenty or thirty women in the building seems to notice the sick man, in the way that his own mother surely would have done:

> La mujer en los Estados Unidos no es *mujer*, le falta lo que la caracteriza más y la eleva: el esmero y cuidado por el que sufre. . . . ¡Oh! vengan nuestras indias, vengan nuestras negras, vengan cualquiera de nuestras prostitutas y todas sentirán lo que yo siento. Nuestras mujeres no viven, no respiran sino para hacer algún bien, para nada son más hábiles, en nada gozan tanto; por malas que sean, en fin, son mujeres; estas *free thinkers* no son. ¡Oh *medias azules* insensibles! ¡Y los periódicos aquí se complacen en insultar a las hermanas de la caridad que hay aquí! Me invitan a celebrar el aniversario 4° de la muerte de Narciso López.
>
> —Me llaman feo dos damas—me cago en ellas.
>
> Cada dos horas de noche administro a Rodríguez unas píldoras y lo cobijo y velo. Soy hijo de mi madre. Costa Rica.
>
> *[The typical woman in the United States is not* Woman; *she lacks those qualities which characterize and elevate her most: her deep caring for those who suffer. . . . Oh! Let any of our Indian women, our black women, even any of our prostitutes come here and they would all feel as I do. Our women live and breathe only to do good: there's nothing for which they are better suited, nothing they enjoy so much; in short, as bad as they may be, they are women; these "free thinkers" are not. Oh, insensitive* blue-stockinged *women! And the papers here don't hesitate to insult the Sisters of Charity here. They've invited me to celebrate the*

fourth anniversary of the death of Narciso López.—Two women call me ugly—I shit on them. Every two hours I give Rodríguez some pills, and I stand watch and shelter him. I am my mother's son. Costa Rica.][10]

The circumstances of expatriation call forth an extraordinary blurring of gender boundaries. In the absence of suitably feminine nurses, Pombo identifies himself not only with his mother, but with an implicit hierarchy of Latin American womanhood that descends downward from the idealized holy mother through the Sisters of Charity, through Indian and African servants down to the degraded prostitute. Even the lowest of these, he says, would comprehend their own superiority in comparison to the cold norteamericanas. The hostility he expresses toward those "free thinkers" seems to reflect an anxiety about being thrust, however temporarily, into the submissive role he made Edda celebrate, or the vulnerable position he identifies with Rodríguez. In this and other passages, as well as later poems, Pombo begins to articulate a notion of redemptive, feminized Latin American morality that will take shape through opposition to the U.S. norms he identifies through categories of gender.

As this passage suggests, in Pombo's diary the private world of his poetic and sentimental ambitions is forever penetrated by the public sphere of diplomatic intrigue. The political realm is never far from his emoting consciousness, as evidenced not only by the offhand remark about his invitation to the López commemoration (presumably organized by the Revolución group of separatist Cubans in New York and perhaps attended by Quintero, who would have been in the city at this time) but also in the constant recollection of his diplomatic assignment to help settle the boundary disagreement between Colombia and Costa Rica—a dispute in which U.S. investors in various canal schemes took a keen interest. In the following pages, as Rodríguez recovers, Pombo segues from discussions of "automatic writing" into a description of a banquet in honor of the Magdalena Canal and Steamship Company. In the name of his country, Pombo receives the guests' toasts and gives a speech that—he is dismayed to learn—the English translator "dumbs down" for the Yankee audience by stripping out all of its learned classical references. The dinner, he recognizes, had nothing to do with the exchange of fine words of fraternity between nations, and everything to do with capitalizing a passage to the Pacific.

> Brindis sobre supremacia de los Estados Unidos, su misión de civilizar la América del Sur, su anexionismo. ¡Comparen al general Mosquera con *Washington*! . . . El anexionismo me

pone algo de mal humor; sin embargo, comprometido a brindar, brindé por el amor de la humanidad que hace granadinos a los norteamericanos y norteamericanos a los granadinos. . . . Oigo hablar de Nueva Granada con tanto entusiasmo que me parece que estoy en el sueño del proscrito, que el proscrito suele soñar a su patria tan bella y tan feliz a centenares de leguas de sus orillas.

[A toast to the supremacy of the United States, its mission to civilize South America, its annexationism. They compare Mosquera to Washington*! . . . Annexationism puts me in a bad mood; nonetheless, obliged to offer a toast, I saluted the love of humanity that makes New Granadians out of North Americans and North Americans out of Granadians. . . . I hear any talk from home with such enthusiasm that it seems to me I'm in the exile's dream-state—for the exile gets used to fantasizing about his beautiful, happy homeland even hundreds of leagues away from its shores.]*[11]

He concludes that the banquet was no more than "una treta de yankees para explotar al vano de Mosquera adulándolo" [a Yankee trick to exploit Mosquera's vanity by adulating him]. While Mosquera preens, in Pombo's view, New Granada is a "virgen en cadenas" [virgin in chains], vulnerable to all sorts of masculine dangers as she comes to take part in "la danza social y comercial de las naciones." The image of the feminized republic in chains—used, as we saw in previous chapters, in tandem with the fraternal rhetoric of inter-Americanism—reveals that the "civilizing mission" of U.S. capital wears a thin disguise.

Although relations between the United States and Colombia were then at a relatively high point, more pressing issues stopped the schemes of the Magdalena Canal investors short. In 1856 Pombo and the Herrán delegation went to Costa Rica, which had by then ceded the disputed territory, Bocas de Toro—a potential canal route—to Colombia, at the same time that numerous factions in Central America were struggling to reestablish autonomy against William Walker's invading army.[12] The Costa Rican government welcomed Herrán's offer of Colombian military support, and Pombo left Central America after several months with a clearer view of the shape of privately funded expansion from the United States and its increasing dangers. In two poems apparently not published in their day and recently collected by Héctor Orjuela, Pombo writes what may be the first directly anti-imperialist verse about the United States.

The biting "Diálogo entre Cortés y William Walker," dated in San José at this time, opens with Cortés's complaint that Walker is nothing but a lousy imitation of the *conquistador*—to which Walker responds, "Ya no es fácil destrozar la *indiada*" [It's not so easy to wipe out the *natives* any more], and complaining that he had been but ill instructed in empire-building by Cortés. The figure of the conquistador shrugs off Walker's quest as quixotic, and instructs him to leave him to rest in peace. In a longer ode from the same period, "A Costa Rica," Pombo characterizes the nation as "magnánimo y honrado" [magnanimous and honored], and praises it for having avenged ten years of "impune iniquidad" [unpunished iniquity]—presumably referring to the decade since the first militaristic intervention of the United States into Mexico's territory, in 1846. As in the diary entry about New Granada as a republic in chains, he imagines Costa Rica as a young woman:

> Hoy, de ti orgullosísima, te abraza
> Del Nuevo Mundo la mejor mitad.
> Tú, sola tú, de niña con tus galas
> Has tronzado del águila las alas
> Y puesto el "non plus ultra" al Gran Ladrón.

> *[Today, the better half of the New World*
> *Very proudly embraces you.*
> *You alone, a little debutante,*
> *Have smashed the eagle's wings*
> *And said* No further! *to the Great Thief.]*[13]

Costa Rica is imagined as "la más joven, la más pequeña" [the youngest and smallest] of the Latin American family of nations: "La más modesta y tímida y risueña; / Débil en todo, pero no en virtud" [The most modest and timid and retiring / Weak in everything, except in virtue]. Yet she also takes the position of an Amazon warrior, tearing off the Yankee eagle's wings. In portraying a Yankee filibuster (and by extension, the rest of the nation symbolized by that eagle) as a "great thief," this poem is a precursor of Darío's "A Roosevelt," which similarly borrows qualities of idealized, ethereal femininity from another poetic realm and drafts them into the service of an anti-imperialist message.

Just as Pombo tends toward feminized, alternately vulnerable and powerful portrayals of Latin American nationhood in these poems, so too does he locate what he sees as the soulless but seductive commercialism of the United States within gendered frames. Working outward from his tender outrage at the "free-thinking" North American women in his social orbit, who can appreciate a love poem but not nurse a strange man, he depicts North American womanhood as brassy and commercialized. "Las norteamericanas en Broadway," one of his most popular and frequently anthologized poems, was first published in the 1859 edition of José Durand's *Guía de los Estados Unidos para viajeros españoles* [Guide for Spanish Travelers to the United States]. Durand, a Guatemalan-born entrepreneur under whose name a number of Spanish imprints in New York appear, published the first edition of this guide in 1851; he apparently befriended Pombo soon after his arrival in the city and asked him to add some sections on arts and culture. Many pages of the diary detail Pombo's rambles with Durand along the wharves, through the streets, and to Blackwell's Island, where the new insane asylum drew their rapt attention. "Las norteamericanas en Broadway" continues the theme of the Latin American *viajero* leaving "el mundo tropical encantador" for the frigid realms of the North. It opens with a catalog of the many nations in the Latin American family and imagines each of them, territorially, as a vulnerable male heart in danger of losing its true sense of loyalty:

Volvernos locos tras de hacernos pérfidos	*[To make us crazy and drive us to treason*
Vuestra misión, oh americana, es:	*Is your mission, American women:*
Os anexáis el corazón suavísimas	*You annex the heart, oh so gently,*
Y en su tirano os convertís después.	*And afterward turn into its tyrant.]*[14]

The language of annexation and tyranny is threaded throughout the poem: not only would submission to the charms of the nation/woman be an act of treason against the home country, it would also set off an inevitable political sea change from benign annexation and statehood to authoritarian rule. Pombo goes on to describe a typical *hispano* exile, entering the "imperial" St. Nicholas Hotel (one of the standout hotels on Broadway and, at least according to Durand's guidebook, the chic hotel for Latin guests) full of a terrible nostalgia for the homeland that makes him sentimentally vulnerable. He is amazed by the "majestuoso ejército" [majestic army] of enchanting North American virgins who will lure him into a hopeless combat: "¡Sangre española, tú serás la pólvora / Que dando acecho al botafuego está!" [Spanish blood, you'll become the gunpowder / that sets off this firebrand's ambush!]. Comparing the blonde hair and seraphic looks of these Yankee man-killers with progressively more outrageous figurations of gems and riches, he then launches a set of metaphors that are politically suggestive as well:

Fue para estos cabellos que a
    sus náyades
Robó tan ricas perlas Panamá,

Y a sus divinas mariposas fúl-
    gidas
Sus lechos de esmeraldas
    Bogotá.

*[It was for those locks that
    Panama
Stole such rich pearls from its
    nayads;
And Bogotá took emerald beds

away from its divinely brilliant
    butterflies.]*

The image here is of a Latin American nation despoiling itself of its natural treasures—pearls, emeralds—in a desperate bid to "win" the unreachable beauty: Yankee capital, a lover who can only be bought, not won in a true affective relationship. Panama and Bogotá are scenes obviously freighted with significance, since Pombo the diplomat had spent much of the three previous years arbitrating the claims of U.S. companies against his country for losses suffered in the so-called Watermelon War of 1856, when a racially motivated riot broke out as gold-seekers, on their way to California, provoked local Panamanians. During this time, there were constant intrigues as various U.S. interests tried to foment separatist sentiments among Panamanians to encourage them to separate from Colombia.[15] Whatever other functions the poem may perform as misogynist satire, its political valence is not far beneath the surface. Each passing beauty is referred to as an "amable autócrata" [lovable autocrat]; as a whole, the "ejército fascinante" [fascinating army] marches in formation down "la imperial Broadway," in a kind of triumphal parade.

    The onslaught of capital-hungry seductresses is so difficult to resist, in fact, that the unwary Latino observer is in the same dangerous position as the boater on Lake Niagara. To end the poem, Pombo turns to that oldest of transamerican traveler's clichés—the sudden, vertiginous surprise of one's first view of Niagara. At this point the poem breaks out of its neat *endecasílabo* quatrains into six choppy, irregular lines before it resolves again into a final regular stanza—registering, in this sudden formal shift, an unexpected gravity and danger. The norteamericana, like the falls, wields the power to seduce with false surfaces—deadly surfaces:

Lindas como esos iris, risa
    falaz del Niágara;

*[Lovely as those rainbows,
    Niagara's false laugh;*

Vagas como ellos y capri- chosas;	Indeterminate, capricious like them;
Efímeras como ellos,	Ephemeral, like them;
Crueles como ese abismo de aguas y de cadáveres	Cruel as that abyss of waters and corpses,
Que eriza los cabellos . . .	That makes your hairs stand on end . . .
Y así atrayentes, vertiginosas.	Like them beckoning, dizzying.
Todo es pasión y vida bajo su frente angélica,	Beneath their angelic counte- nance, a passionate life lurks,
Como en sus altas cóleras el espantoso río.	Just like the dreadful river at the height of its anger.
¿Su corazón? Miradlo, oíd clamar sus víctimas	As for her heart? Behold—hear its victims cry out
En ese abismo oscuro . . . , sordo . . . , insaciable . . . frío . . . !	In that dark . . . silent . . . insatiable . . . frigid . . . abyss!]

In this catachrestic formulation, the false face and laughter of the woman veils the depths of her self-serving motives, just as the face of the waters hides their strong undercurrent. Pombo here takes up one of the most common literary properties about Niagara—the contrast between the rainbowed surface of the placid lake and the deadly end to which its waters lead—and uses it as an analogy for the dangers of being seduced by the cold heart of an insatiable, money-hungry woman. Maria Gowen Brooks, a few decades earlier, had worked the same metaphor to depict the temptation to destroy oneself in the name of sexual passion—sui-cide's *invitation au voyage*—but Pombo gives that temptation a specifi-cally political edge. Here, Niagara is anything but a source of sublime inspiration (or, as for Heredia, a recollection of the patria): it beckons with an invitation to collective suicide. His speaker is no mere flaneur or aesthete; he stands on the abyss of self-immolation. If Niagara and the *norteamericanas en Broadway* are alike in their deceptive seductions, nei-ther is ever satiated. No offering of emeralds and pearls—poetic or oth-erwise—will satisfy the North's voracious appetite. "He" is figured here as Spanish American, and "she" is the insatiable creation of capital and empire. In the early Edda poems, Pombo had toyed with a voice of utter submission, one he associated with a passionately feminine response to powerfully hypnotic male attention. In this mature poem, he turns the tables on the older sublime model to point out the dangers of such sub-mission.[16]

If both the streets of New York and the sublime spaces of the country are dangerously full of temptations to lose one's honor, identity, and fortune, Pombo's section of the *Guía* does suggest a space in which artistic contemplation and meditation are not sidelined by the activity of commerce: Greenwood Cemetery, another common subject of poetic odes. Greenwood, Pombo writes,

> parece mandado hacer exprofeso para los peregrinos de Nueva York. El poeta, el hijo pródigo de la religion, el ausente del bien amado, o el que como Lamartine diría "Mon coeur est plein, je veux pleurer,"—allí encuentra campo vasto y tranquilo para la estrofa, la oración, el recuerdo o la lágrima. Se maravillará de que tan cerca de Nueva York, corte imperial del dollar, exista tan romántico refugio.

> *[seems specially made for pilgrims and wanderers in New York. The poet, the prodigal son of religion, the one who is absent from what he dearly loves, or he who, like Lamartine, would say "My heart is full, I want to weep," will find here a vast and tranquil ground for a verse, a prayer, a memory, or a tear. He will marvel at the fact that such a romantic refuge can exist so close to New York, the imperial court of the dollar.]*

In opposition to the space of capital, "the imperial court of the dollar," the elegiac, sentimental space of Greenwood strikes him as a refuge for exiles and expatriates. In the diary, in his poems of the 1850s, and in his sections of Durand's *Guía*, then, Pombo registers his efforts to translate Anglo-American culture for a Latin American sensibility in a way that becomes increasingly critical of the former's construction within mechanisms of capital and empire. However, this translating role—one Martí would perform as a journalist in his dispatches for *La Nación* and other organs throughout Our America—is enabled by an originary condition of exile. Pombo's melancholic perception of his distance from all that is familiar is marshalled for political critique through two opposing pro-cesses: a rejection of what is different about the northern space (the weather, the strangely atomized family structures and social organiza-tions, the incessant drive for capital accumulation), on one hand; and a quest for literary mastery through translation and absorption, on the other. Pombo's diary records bookstore finds such as the poetry of José María Heredia, which he discovers for the first time in New York, and

James Kennedy's *Modern Poets and Poetry of Spain*—the text that did more than any other to facilitate the transmission of Cuban and Spanish poets in the Anglophone world.[17] This dialectic of critique and appreciation strongly anticipates Martí.

Such bookstore browsing would eventually lead Pombo to discover and locate a limited kinship with those very Anglo-American poets who were most receptive to Spanish American culture, that is, Bryant and Longfellow. In the 1860s, he contracted with the house of Appleton—which had been steadily developing trade with Spanish America, and came to control more of that trade than any other U.S. publisher—to produce two children's books, *Cuentos pintados* and *Cuentos morales para niños formales.* He did translations for Appleton, where Martí would labor as a translator as well. While in New York, Pombo befriended Byrant, sending him a collection of translated English poems in 1867 and rendering eleven of Bryant's poems into Spanish. Bryant published a sonnet Pombo had composed in English, "Our Madonna at Home," in the 11 March 1871 issue of the *Post.* He traveled to Boston to meet Emerson, the famous Hispanist Ticknor, and Longfellow—with whom he would keep up a correspondence for the rest of his life, translating sixteen of his poems.[18] As I outlined in chapter 3, Pombo was also instrumental in the dissemination of Carlos Morla Vicuña's *Evangelina* in the Hispanophone world (he himself had also tried his hand at translating the epic).

Pombo, like Martí, found the United States deficient in art and music but hugely promising in terms of its print culture and the democratization of access to the literary word that the cheap, vast circulation of periodicals promised. His essay for the *Guía* on "Las bellas artes en los Estados Unidos" begins with the comment that there has never been a nation as powerful as this one that has paid so little attention to the arts. Instead, the public is too preoccupied with "la constitución de un nuevo Estado, o un cambio radical en las instituciones" [the formation of some new state, or some radical change in its institutions]. Although Boston and Philadelphia (which he has not yet visited) make some claims to artistic development, New Yorkers prefer Negro shows with banjos and "el Yankee doodle" to Italian opera.[19] Far more impressive to him, as to many outside observers of the time, is the ubiquity and cheapness of printed matter in New York. He notes that there are two Spanish papers in the city, and directs the *viajero* to all the cafés where fellow Hispanophones converge, though he laments that there is not yet a mutual aid society or club for this purpose. This invites a revealing speculation about the differences between the two "razas":

Como todos saben, el espíritu de asociación es característico de este pueblo. Aquí se asocian para ayudarse y servirse mutuamente las gentes de cada profesión, nacionalidad etc., excepto los españoles: se podría inferir que en tierra extraña son insociables para objetos útiles. . . . [¿Por qué] no tengan en N. York un club, un salon de lectura, un paraje siquiera adonde ir a hojear los periódicos de 20 países que hablan su lengua y mantienen creciente comercio con la América del Norte . . . y para tomar cuenta del movimiento comercial, industrial, político y literario de su raza? . . . Si hay en el universo un punto a propósito para centralizar y difundir el cambio de ideas entre los países españoles, y aun para monopolizar su comercio literario, ese punto es Nueva York. Esto, mas que una especulación segura para los avisados que en lo futuro se aprovechan de ello, es una necesidad de los 50 millones que hablan este magnífico idioma; pero—toda la filosofía del pueblo español se encierra en una palabra: *mañana*! y toda su historia en otra: *ya es tarde!*

[As everyone knows, the spirit of joining is characteristic of this nation. Here people of every profession, nationality, etc., form mutual aid and service associations—except the Spanish: one could infer that on foreign ground, they are unsociable toward useful ends. . . . Why doesn't New York have a club, a reading room, a spot of some kind where one could go and leaf through periodicals from the twenty countries that speak the same language and maintain an ever-growing commerce with North America . . . and to take notice of the commercial, industrial, political, and literary movements of our own race? . . . If there's an appropriate point in all the world in which to centralize and disseminate the interchange of ideas among the Spanish nations, even to monopolize its literary exchange, that place is New York. This is more that just a ready speculation for the wise persons who might take advantage of it in the future; this is a necessity for the fifty million people who speak this magnificent language. But the entire philosophy of the Spanish people can be summed up in one word: tomorrow!*—and its entire history in another:* It's already too late!]*[20]

This constitutes perhaps the first call for a transnational association within U.S. space based on the shared cultural and political displacement of Latinos. The comment that New York might "monopolize" the "comercio literario" of the Hispanophone world is particularly intriguing, both because of the relative novelty of the term "monopoly" and because it would prove to be a prescient statement, as we shall see in the discussion of *El Mundo Nuevo* later in this chapter. Through his collaboration with this transnational periodical, Pombo would make a continued effort to recenter the locus of Hispanophone literary exile from Paris to New York. Yet he also registers a strong ambivalence about the models of "literary commerce" he sees in the United States: the instant community enabled by modern print technology is appealing, but commerce as a paradigm, which he sees everywhere around him in political as well as gender relations, is dehumanizing and demoralizing. He gets around this looming commodification by identifying the realm of the literary as an affective one that can bring together scattered nations and individual sensibilities into a familial relation. This is precisely the valence of Spanish American *modernismo* as practiced by Darío and especially by Martí, who would also record his promenades down the streets of New York. On one hand, the alienated, isolated dandy uses the street scene and its repulsions to retreat into an elevated realm of art. On the other, that alienation liberates the poet to express the relation of one member of the Latin American family to another tenderly, as parent to child—or elegiacally, as one lost soul wandering in the graveyard to another.[21]

Staging Gender on the California Borderlands

As Pombo's preoccupation with Central American affairs suggests, places like Nicaragua, Costa Rica, Panama, the Yucatán, and the southern reaches of Mexico were far from peripheral to the eastern imagination; rather, the securing of a sea passage and a transcontinental railway to the Pacific were major preoccupations in those metropolitan centers of political and economic power. The westward and southward vectors of U.S. expansion, as Whitman foresaw, were intimately linked. Mexico, which had suffered the greatest losses as a consequence of this continental stretch, understood its Caribbean frontier to be as vulnerable as its arid northern one. Indeed, one of the most damaging blows to Benito Juárez's liberal Reforma was the rumor that on the president's orders, Melchor Ocampo was quietly brokering a deal to sell territory in the Isthmus of Tehuantepec to the unpopular yanquis.[22] The failure of the Reforma and the civil war that followed the French occupation of Mexico led numerous liberal letrados to flee in protest or self-protection to the U.S. borderlands at the very time when the Hispanophone communal base of the former Mexican territories was quickly eroding. Historian Leonard Pitt dates the final decline of the californios to the late 1870s, the decade that saw "a hastening of both acculturation and economic deterioration" capped by the hanging of the last subversive *bandido*, the well-born but dispossessed Tiburcio Vásquez, in San José, and by Civil War–era tensions that persuaded mexicano elites to deny any possible Confederate sympathies by assimilating as much as possible. In the vast range lands of Texas, large-scale cattle drives, requiring the consolidation of massive ranches from smaller Mexican land grants, began in the 1860s and effectively redistributed political and economic power there. In the New Mexico territory, which was partitioned in half to create Arizona in 1863, a series of Indian relocations and legal maneuvers left Hispanos with some political power but with centuries-old modes of cooperation disrupted. Into all these areas, railroads would bring enormous waves of immigration, and the resulting social change, by the 1880s.[23]

The Mexican exiles who settled for a few months or years in the former province of Alta California spurred a miniboom of Spanish-language newspapers in San Francisco and Los Angeles: *La Voz de Méjico, El Indicador, La Bandera Mejicana, El Eco del Pacífico,* and particularly *El Nuevo Mundo.*[24] A biweekly founded by Guadalajaran poet and editor José María Vigil, *El Nuevo Mundo* sought common cause between recent Mexican emigrés, established californios, and the poorer Chilean, Peruvian, and Sonoran miners who were part of a bedrock service economy in the post–gold rush boomtown. Yet the paper also had sales offices in Peru, Colombia, and New York, in addition to multiple agents in five states of northern Mexico; and it contained ads for a bookstore that carried "periódicos españoles de Nueva York, Méjico, la Habana, Chile, Peru, etc.," indicating an enlarged sense of a transnational print community. The paper's prospectus, on the front page of the first issue in 1864, explains the title as a sign of their commitment to the battle for human "progress" and against monarchism:

> La América, revelada al genio de Colón para dar abrigo al pensamiento proscrito a la conciencia perseguida, no cambiará sus inmortales destinos a la voz de monarcas. . . . El mundo entero atraviesa en la actualidad una de las más tremendas y peligrosas crisis, viniendo a ser la América el gran teatro en que

se juegan los destinos de la humanidad, pues en gigantescas proporciones se debaten en ella los grandes principios de libertad y retroceso.

[America, revealed to the genius of Columbus so it could harbor the proscribed thoughts of persecuted men of conscience, will not alter its immortal destiny at the word of kings. . . . The whole world is now imperiled by a great and dangerous crisis, and America is going to be the great theater in which the destiny of humankind is acted out—for it is here that the great principles of liberty and backwardness clash on a grand scale.][25]

El Nuevo Mundo complicates Kanellos' and Martell's distinction between the "immigrant," "native," and "exile" press communities, for although founded by a prominent Mexican-in-exile, it makes both a regional and transnational case for a common cause among Americans, comparing different struggles for self-determination in the hemisphere. The paper's antimonarchical rhetoric is principally aimed at the French, but the emblematic struggle between Juárez and Maximilian and its outcome would also mark the last uses of this familiar fraternal analogy of the Monroe Doctrine.

Although staunchly republican—they carried large display ads for parades in honor of Lincoln's reelection—the paper was willing to critique even sympathetic U.S. institutions like the liberal *New York Tribune*. The 9 September 1864 issue of *El Nuevo Mundo* reprints a translated article from the New York paper criticizing Spain for its "backwardness" in continuing to tolerate slavery in Cuba and Puerto Rico. The translation is followed by a note from the editors admonishing the *Tribune* for categorizing "a toda la población hispano-americana de anarquía ingobernable, incapaz de la libertad" [the whole Spanish American population as constituting an ungovernable anarchy, incapable of liberty]. *El Nuevo Mundo* was strongly in favor of abolition and of independence for the Caribbean islands, but the editors berate *la América anglosajona* for its "inhumana preocupación de razas" [inhuman preoccupation with race]. As I mentioned in chapter 4, the paper published Pedro Santacilia's "A España," which was written specifically as a complaint against the Crown's continued possession of Cuba, in a way that invited readers to use it as inspiration for patriotic Mexican feeling. Yet the poem appears on the page next to a notice of a meeting of the Club Patriótico Chileno, organized to protect miners from the mob violence to which they were vulnerable in northern California—a placement that suggests multiple layers of protest and resistance, with the poetic text performing in different registers within the space of the periodical page.[26] Many of the poems in *El Nuevo Mundo*, as elsewhere, are identified as locally produced album poems, written in some young woman's keepsake book; others are given a specific social and temporal resonance with a dedication to a friend, or by date and place locators of the poem's composition. Thus they claim both spontaneity—the authentic voice of a nonprofessional author speaking intimately to a close circle of friends—and permanence through the medium of print.

But the most striking examples of such an oscillation between performance and permanence come in the paper's publication of occasional poems that had been read aloud at various dinners and ceremonial occasions sponsored by Mexican patriotic clubs—toasts to Mexican patriotic heroes and roasts of Maximilian and Carlota. Each poem is introduced with a description of the occasion, the speaker, and sometimes the general ambience of the reading performance and its reception. Through this venue, women's voices on political issues found their way into the public sphere as well: Luis Torres, in his invaluable study of early Spanish poetry in California, first identified *El Nuevo Mundo* as one of the territory's three best-known and significant newspapers because of its featured series on a group of women members of the pro-Juárez Zaragoza Club of Los Angeles and the Club Patriótico Mejicano of Virginia City, Nevada, whom he labels the "first Chicana poets."[27] While male writers' patriotic odes are printed in the "Variedades" section as distinct poems, the women's are swaddled in a nest of contexts: first a prose overview of the history of the Zaragoza Club, then a transcription of each speaker's statement preceding the poem, and finally the poems themselves. The poems enveloped inside these intricate boxes are presented as the sentimental, sacrificial offerings of respectably married women to their country, currently beset by extraordinary circumstances requiring them to emerge from their private spheres of influence. (Many of the husbands of las señoras seemed to belong to the corresponding men's patriotic clubs, whose rosters are also listed in the newspaper.)[28]

If Vigil devoted so much front-page space to the Zaragoza Club because he thought that San Franciscan women might follow their example, he did not seem to be successful, for no local club is mentioned. But there is an exception to the generally protective cloistering of the female writer—and particularly of the unmarried female writer—in the 6 July 1864 issue, suggesting that the exceptional circumstances of the French occupation that brought Mexican women into the public realm of the newspaper might be extended in even more subversive ways. The page again contains a poem within a set of prose contextualizations, like a pearl in a shell. Introducing the poem is a story about its composition: a newspaper in Lima, *El Comercio*, had published two misogynistic sonnets by N. P. Llona that painted "una pintura muy lisonjera de la mujer físicamente considerada" [a very flattering portrait of Woman from the physical standpoint] but insulted her other dimensions—the intellectual, the sentimental, the artistic.[29] The copy of *El Comercio* fell into the hands of a young woman, identified only as "la señorita I. A. P.," living in San Francisco; outraged, she composed a reply in kind and solicited the editor's help in airing it in public without revealing her identity. Vigil not only printed it, but offered fulsome praise of I. A. P.'s intelligence, skill, and compassion. Her poem, "a par de su inconcuso mérito literario, resalta ese sentimiento celeste, esa grandeza de pensamiento propios de la mujer" [along with its undeniable literary merit, makes that celestial sentiment, that grandeur of thought that properly belong to Woman, stand out]. This sentence is built around a dyad of feeling and thought ("sentimiento" and "pensamiento"), of heart and mind, that he takes directly from the closing lines of Llona's first sonnet:

> No halla en su mente, atónita,   *[Not one idea can be found in*
> una idea,   *her comatose mind,*
> No halla en su corazón un   *Nor a single emotion in her*
> sentimiento   *heart.]*

The sestet of Llona's second sonnet—titled "Retracción"—answers that negation directly, retracting the idea that women do not think or feel. But it answers: "¡Que *piensa* la beldad, pues . . . de palacios, joyas, telas y carruajes!" [What does my beauty *think*? Well, she thinks about palaces, jewels, rich fabrics, and carriages!]. Woman does indeed possess thoughts, but only of luxury items; and feelings, but equally suspect ones: "*Siente* . . . ¡seco egoismo, vanidad, codicia!" [She *feels* . . . dry egotism, vanity, envy!].

    I. A. P.'s rebuttal to this merry misogyny is also presented in sonnet form, and addressed "al desgraciado autor" [to the wretched author] of the two poems:

> Tú que así la mujer has con-   *[You who have conceived of*
> cebido   *woman thus*
> Y con tan negras sombras la   *And painted her in such dark*
> has pintado,   *tones,*

¿No has sido, por tu mal, jamás amado,	*Have you never been loved, poor man,*
Ni lo que es el amor has comprendido?	*Nor understood what it is to be loved?*
¿Una madre amorosa no has tenido	*Have you never had a loving mother*
Que tu sueño infantil haya arrullado,	*Who soothed your infant dreams,*
Ni el beso fraternal, puro y sagrado,	*Nor received from the lips of a sister*
Del labio de una hermana has recibido?	*A pure, sacred, fraternal kiss?*
Si de una casta esposa la ternura,	*If you had ever known the tenderness*
De una madre el afecto sobrehumano	*Of a chaste wife, the superhuman affection*
Hubieras conocido, en tu locura	*Of a mother, in your madness*
No ultrajaras con labio audaz, profano,	*You would never have profanely insulted*
A la que es el consuelo y la ventura	*She who is the consolation and the fortune*
Del niño, del adulto y del anciano.	*Of the child, adult, and elderly man.]* (emphasis mine)

Against Llona's urbane, misogynistic humor, I. A. P.'s response postulates a classic sentimental and religious notion of womanhood. If the writer had ever known the tenderness of a mother, a sister, a wife, he would not say such things. The defense relies on predictably domestic themes: woman's boundless and almost saintly tenderness, "el afecto sobrehumano," and her position in relation to others, as caretaker—in the closing line—"del niño, del adulto, y del anciano." Though it opens with a set of rhetorical questions that risk sounding tentative, the poem archly insinuates that Llona's mother might not have loved him, or that his wife was unchaste (or not well born, another connotation of *casta*). The snaky subjunctives of the last line reduce the poor *peruano* to various needy figures he once was or may yet become: a fussy baby, a helpless old man.

The most effective aspect of this poem is its very imitativeness, its careful reiteration of the structure of the original. Not only does

I. A. P. prove by her passable manipulation of the sonnet form that women have the capacity for orderly thought, she also scores nicely off Llona's formal gambit at the close of the second sonnet, where he suddenly modulates the two- and four-part verbal structures of the earlier part of the poem to unleash a devastating trio of vices: "¡egoismo, vanidad, codicia!" At this point in her poem, she lets loose with her own rhetorical trinity: "niño, adulto, anciano." The performative aspect of this duel of the genders is carefully set up in the editor's introduction, which carefully guards the señorita's modesty but also teases the audience by revealing her initials. Indeed, Vigil's introduction might be a marriage advertisement, for he underlines her status as a single woman and sighs longingly at the hint of what riches might lie within her interior sensibilities: "¡Oh la señorita I. A. P. debe encerrar un alma noble y tierna!" [Oh, surely Miss I. A. P. contains within her a noble, tender soul!]. And he gleefully imagines what Llona might think "si esta composición llega a sus manos, como esperamos" [if this composition arrives in his hands, as we hope it will]: seduced by the mysterious I. A. P., he would repent of his own poisonous ingenuity, open his eyes, and confess that he had been unjust to womankind. Thus, the context of this appearance in *El Nuevo Mundo* allows these poems to speak to each other in a transnational space that dramatizes reading and writing as dialogic, communal acts.

I. A. P. did come out of the closet, in an issue several months later, on 4 October, when *El Nuevo Mundo* published a poem under the byline of Isabel A. Prieto, this one titled "Pobre flor" and dedicated to the editor, José M. Vigil, himself. Prieto had been something of a child prodigy, fluent in four languages. She published her first poem—suggestively titled "¡No me caso!" [I Won't Marry!]—when she was sixteen and wrote several verse dramas, two of which were performed in Guadalajara after her marriage. She and her family spent the French interregnum in California (her father, Sotero Prieto, was a professor; Vigil dedicated one of his own sentimental exile poems in *El Nuevo Mundo* to him). The Prieto family returned to Mexico in 1865; shortly thereafter, Isabel married her cousin Pedro Landázuri, a diplomat, and resumed writing plays. "Al desgraciado autor de *Un tipo del siglo*" can be found in her *Obras poéticas*, but with no mention of either the place of its initial publication or the context of her "duel" with Llona.[30] Her *Obras poéticas* would eventually be edited by Vigil himself—who, after departing San Francisco, became director of the Biblioteca Nacional and a popular poet of some stature throughout Greater Mexico; he compares her to Sor Juana.[31] Vigil, as it turns out, was not the only male editor to make that comparison.

The 30 June 1872 issue of *La América Ilustrada* introduces the first of her several contributions to it with a special note from the editor. Although the pages of *La América Ilustrada* are dominated by men, Isabel Prieto de Landázuri, he says, is "la distinguida compatriota de Sor Juana Inés de la Cruz, y digna rival de la Avellaneda" [the distinguished compatriot of Sor Juana Inés de la Cruz, and a worthy rival of Gertrudis Gómez de Avellaneda]. Like her fellow mejicana María Amparo Ruíz de Burton, Prieto's works circulated first in California and then in the urban U.S. Northeast.[32]

The poem in question, "¡Oh patria mía!," is introduced as "una composición escrita en S. Francisco de California, en tiempo de la invasión francesa en Méjico" [a composition written in San Francisco, at the time of the French invasion of Mexico], published in the New York paper for the first time. "¡Oh patria mía!" is in many ways a familiar poem of exile in the cold and capital-driven North, but here the alien climate is figured through fog, rather than snow:

Era una tarde como mi alma, triste;	*[It was an afternoon sad as my soul,*
De espesa niebla el cielo se cubría,	*The sky was covered in a thick fog,*
La ciudad a lo lejos se perdía	*The city, wrapped up in its dismal wealth,*
Medio envuelto en su lúgubre caudal;	*Became lost in the distance;]*

Contemplating this somber and strange landscape, the speaker allows herself for a moment to feel the longing for home she has otherwise suppressed, and is at that instant visited by the Muse—a winged spirit who is also homesick for Mexico and announces her intention to leave California:

"Yo no puedo vivir entre estas nieblas,	*["I can't live among these fogs*
Que me sofocan en su espeso velo;	*That suffocate me in their dense veil;*
De nuestra patria el trasparente cielo	*I'm off to seek the transparent sky—*
Siempre limpio y azul voy a buscar."	*always clean and blue—of our homeland."]*

The Muse, before taking wing, promises to pass along to the exile's family at home the news that "triste y amarga tu existencia es" [your life is sad and bitter]. She promises to return when the homeland is free, and then to restore the poet's inspiration and her silenced voice:

"Olvidarás que, tímida cantora,	["Then you'll forget, shy singer,
Apenas osas levantar tu acento,	how you scarcely dare to raise your voice,
Daré a tu voz un noble atrevimiento,	I'll grant your voice a noble daring
De este triunfo, la santa majestad,	For the sacred majesty of this triumph,
Y pulsando la lira del poeta	And—strumming the lyre of the poet
Que las hazañas de valor pregona,	Which praises deeds of valor,
Dando a los héroes inmortal corona	Giving heroes an immortal crown—
El himno entonarás de LIBERTAD."	You will intone the hymn of LIBERTY."]

In the last stanza, as the speaker absorbs this hopeful promise, she watches her Muse fly away—and only weeps more bitterly.

"¡Oh patria mía!" stages the problem of gender and the propriety of public expression within the poem itself. The figure of the poet is explicitly described as a "tímida cantora," and in fact most of the poem's patriotic sentiments are ventriloquized through the voice of the Muse. Nothing in Prieto's defense of sentimental womanhood in the response to Numa Llona had allowed a place for a woman to speak on national topics: the right to celebrate arms and the man seems foreclosed to her. This self-consciousness about the poem's own place in the public sphere distinguishes it from the exile poems of the male Cuban writers examined in previous chapters. But if the speaker shies from public expression, feeling unworthy and tongue-tied, she does project the qualities of the public poet unapologetically on the feminine Muse—a kind of Winged Victory who also hints of the speaker's future fame among the ranks of epic national poets. Yet her claim to muteness is belied by the very existence of the poem. Moreover, the New York periodical's claim to bring this "distinguida señora" before the public for the first time was mistaken: The poem had in fact been published eight years previously, before Prieto's marriage, in the 16 August 1864 issue of *El Nuevo Mundo* as a local production signed simply, "Una mejicana." This appearance came after Prieto's rebuttals to Llona under the pseudonym "I. A. P.," but before the publication of the flowery lyric she allowed herself to sign— suggesting, perhaps, that the exception to norms of feminine propriety that had enabled the members of the Zaragoza Club to enter the con- joined realms of poetry and politics might not extend to her as an unmarried woman. How Prieto might have continued to negotiate the norms of gender and authorship of her day must remain a mystery; with her young children, she followed her husband on diplomatic assignment to Hamburg, Germany, where she died of breast cancer in 1876.

If the French occupation of Mexico upset the rigid gender norms through which its ideal of a national family was produced in ways that opened doors for women writers, particularly on the borderlands, some U.S. observers, despite the distraction of their own civil war, were also gripped by the drama of the two competing dynasties—the European house represented by Maximilian and Carlota, and the divided family of Juárez, whose wife and daughters took refuge in New York while he led his rebels around the country.[33] William Cullen Bryant threaded the met- aphor throughout a speech in honor of Matías Romero, one of the key members of the Reforma government and a poet whose works Bryant had translated, given at a dinner in New York in 1867. Bryant first reverts to the fraternal rhetoric of the 1820s, comparing the Union's triumph over "the tyranny of the slave-holding class" with "the gallant stand" Mexicans had made against "the imposition of a foreign yoke" and saying that their common struggle against both forms of "despotism" has cre- ated a "sure connection between the cause of Mexico and that of the United States." He then goes on to justify Juárez's order to have Maxi- milian executed (which some with a "tender regard for human nature" saw as excessive) on the grounds that Maximilian was "Napoleon's hired assassin" and therefore guilty of crimes against humanity:

> Who that knows this fact can deny that Maximilian deserved
> death as richly as the ruffian who enters your dwelling at
> midnight and shoots down the domestic who attempts its
> defense?

The national space is a home whose boundaries are sacred enough to guard to the death. Had Bryant allowed himself to figure Mexico's terri- torial integrity in the same way in 1846, he might not have abandoned his early opposition to the U.S. invasion. But on a less public occasion, in his journal, he portrays the U.S.-Mexican border as an open door, or a swinging gate, between one "house" and the next. An entry from January

1864 envisions the possibility that U.S. landowners on Mexico's northern border would become so incensed at the French that they would themselves start "a rush of our countrymen to the scene of strife, over the long frontier of northern Mexico . . . as steadily as the stream of the Rio Grande toward the ocean." This interesting reverse migration over the Rio Grande imagines a case of U.S. "domestics," as it were, loyally defending the property rights of the absent homeowner—Juárez. He goes on to speculate that, to increase the possibility of such allied aid, the liberals would try to "prolong their war until ours is over," which might result in a southward rush of former Union *and* Confederate soldiers, possessed of many common interests in Mexico, to defend them—"and thus it may happen that the American loyalist and the American rebel will fight side by side in the war for Mexican independence."[34] This did not, of course, happen, but it is a fascinating fantasy vision of a reconciliation of the U.S. national family within a foreign—but neighborly— space.

Brave *Mundo Nuevo*: The Marketing of Transnational Spanish Culture

While Bryant continued to direct liberal sentiments at the helm of the New York *Evening Post*, José Agustín Quintero, as I suggested in the previous chapter, entered into an alliance with the Frank Leslie organization, one of the contenders for monopoly on the American literary marketplace. From 1854, when the hugely popular *Illustrated News* was established, through the next three decades, Leslie's family of periodicals was rivaled only by the house of Harper Brothers; at various points in its history the publishing house launched successful newspapers in German and in Spanish.[35] No copies of Leslie's *Ilustración Americana*, listed in Quintero's obituary as one of his editing projects, survive; but there is a tantalizing clue about how he may have come into the project. Miriam Florence Follin, later to take over ownership of the entire organization as Mrs. Frank Leslie, worked at the print offices of *El Noticioso* in New York at the same time as Quintero, between 1859 and 1860. A fascinating transnational performer in her own right, Follin had traveled to Peru and California in her youth and accompanied her former husband, an archaeologist with a stake in the Honduras Railway Company, to Mexico and Central America. It was in fact her knowledge of Spanish that attracted Leslie to invite her to write for his paper in the first place. When she and her new employer began carrying on a public affair and were then married, she moved more aggressively to enter the Spanish-language market, and thus one of the most significant Hispanophone papers of the time was born and funded.[36]

Longer lasting than its namesake in San Francisco, the illustrated biweekly *El Mundo Nuevo/La América Ilustrada*, published in New York between 1871 and 1875, reiterates and goes beyond *La Patria*'s efforts to build a transnational audience. Initially redacted in the Leslie offices on Pearl Street, where it presumably drew on the resources of his hundreds of employees, the magazine shared the priority the Leslie organization placed on eye-catching illustrations but edged away from its tendency toward sensationalism. For unknown reasons, the tie to Leslie was severed a year after its formation, but as *La América Ilustrada* it continued to thrive.[37] Like *Harper's*, the *Atlantic*, or the *Century*, *El Mundo Nuevo/La América Ilustrada* turned culture into a marketable commodity for a designated segment of the middle-class readership. *El Mundo Nuevo* encouraged its readers to align themselves along multiple lines of affiliation: as residents or citizens of the United States who took pride in their cultural Hispanism, or as members of a far-flung transnational community of progressive, elite Spanish Americans—with the political valence of that term left deliberately vague. The midwife of *El Mundo Nuevo*'s birth in April 1871 was Enrique Piñeyro, who, like so many other Cuban letrados of his generation, took refuge in the United States after the beginning of the Ten Years' War in 1868. There he was an active figure in the Antillean proindependence organization, the Junta Central Republicana de Cuba y Puerto Rico, and took over the editorship of its organ, *La Revolución de Cuba*. As they had done with Heredia, the Spanish colonial administration sentenced him to death in absentia for his seditious activities. The *Revolución* circle, which included Cirilo Villaverde, the Puerto Rican Eugenio María de Hostos, and other key intellectual figures of independence and emancipation, were increasingly divided between factions who supported the more interventionist Quesada and those who supported a slower and more diplomatic course. According to Salvador Bueno, with the founding of *El Mundo Nuevo* Piñeyro attempted to mollify both of the major groups, though he was himself affiliated with the latter; Hostos himself would edit *La América Ilustrada* at a later point.[38]

But Piñeyro's aspirations for the illustrated weekly extended beyond the partisan concerns of building community among the independentistas. Although a broadly progressive political stance is discernible in its news coverage, *El Mundo Nuevo* was structured as a semi-monthly "illustrated encyclopedia" that digested important international and local news. It also devoted a good deal of space to belletristic essays, serialized novels, descriptive and scientific engravings, poetry and at one point even fashion plates in sixteen lavish folio pages per issue. Piñeyro's inaugural editorial promises "un periódico esencialmente artístico y literario, original y americano" [an essentially artistic and literary publication, original and American], and those two terminal adjectives—familiar from decades of literary manifestos since Bello—drive the journal's selection of subject matter: "viajes, noticias literarias, novelas, bien traducidas o bien originales," "de interés general o americano" [travels, literary news, and novels, well translated or powerfully original . . . having general or American interest]. This high-minded cultural project was clearly linked to an ideology of modernization and positivism. Piñeyro derides the sketchy reproductions of lesser-quality publications, saying that *El Mundo Nuevo*'s larger-format engravings, available to them through the resources with the behemoth Leslie organization, will be "inferiores a ninguno . . . en los periódicos del mundo viejo" [inferior to none in the journals of the Old World]. For, he says, the more detailed the engraving, the greater the reader's capacity to grasp the rapid and complex movement of modern life. Here Piñeyro adopts the rhetoric of entrepreneurial yanqui editors like Leslie himself, grounding the postindependence call for textual novelty in the claim to America's mastery of advanced print technologies and mechanisms of production and distribution superior even to those of Paris.[39] Appearing in the premiere issue between a Pombo translation and a traveler's letter from Niagara, an introductory message from the editor asks,

> Varias son las publicaciones de esta especie que la Europa envia en castellano a la América, y todas hasta ahora han obtenido siempre cercido número de lectores. Los Estados Unidos están más cerca, ofrecen recursos cuantiosos para este género de empresas, ¿no es tiempo ya de que aparezca un periódico, de grandes proporciones, que esté respecto de los eeuu, en la misma relación que otros periódicos respecto de Europa?
>
> *[There are many publications of this type that Europe sends to America, even in Spanish, and all, up until this point, have attracted an ever-larger number of readers. The United States is closer: it offers bountiful resources for this type of enterprise. Isn't it time that such a publication came on the scene—a publication*

on a grand scale, which would stand in the same relation to the
United States as other periodicals do to Europe?]

On one hand, this comment reduces New York to a mere funnel for the movement of Spanish culture across national boundaries; but on the other, the rhetorical "¿no es tiempo . . . ?" assumes a preference among readers for a local, "American" product. Piñeyro's argument is supple, for it allows readers to form an allegiance to *El Mundo Nuevo* either because of or despite its editorial origins in the United States.

The nameplate of the journal's front page featured a turning globe overwritten by the words "Norteamérica" and "Sudamérica" and surrounded by a feminine muselike figure, preserving an integrated América as an inspirational ideal if not a political reality. If, as Pombo had predicted, the most commercial city in "Norteamérica" should happen, for reasons of technology and convenience, to offer the largest hub for extending *El Mundo Nuevo*'s print community to the rest of the hemisphere, that fact does not threaten to relocate the emotional center of the reader's political affections for his *patria*. Indeed, the New York location promises to tone down what would otherwise be the more powerful allegiances to specific national homelands, for in Nueva York, Spanish speakers have more in common than they might elsewhere. Allegiance to Americanness, this illustration suggests, is a blanket sentiment, one that admits of smaller subsets within: on occasion the editorial voice also addresses itself to a very specific group such as "nuestros lectores mexicanos" [our Mexican readers]. A regular column profiled leaders and folkloric customs (in an early example of this ethnoregional aesthetic) of different Latin American nations. In stressing the essential linguistic and geographical identity of the paper's readership, Piñeyro reiterates a fundamental tenet of Latin American intellectuals since Bello and Bolívar, that all are members of the same family with strong affective and genealogical ties. Yet he updates that independence-era claim by stressing the power of print to keep this family together under the pressures of modernity—a note that Martí's editorial and oratorical activism would sound again some years later.

Stymied by the fact of the independence movements' failure to achieve universal civil stability across the southern continent and to define what, exactly, "los países de habla española" did have in common, the paper echoes the melancholy tone commonly sounded in the northern press during Reconstruction—the rhetoric of common grief. For instance, a report on Colombian revolutionary hero José Antonio Páez's reception in Peru (he had recently toured the United States) ends with the moral that "los padecimientos comunes de todo ese continente" [the sufferings of that continent as a whole] have made the general "un compatriota de todos los americanos que hablan el español" [a compatriot of all those who speak Spanish]. Political affiliation is brought about, in other words, by linguistic affiliation: Piñeyro—like Victoriano Alemán and Eusebio Gómez, the similarly ambitious editors of La Patria before him—defines El Mundo Nuevo's constituency in the broadest terms possible, writing in a New Year's statement that it will work "al progreso y bienestar inmediato de todos los países americanos donde se habla esta hermosa lengua castellana" [toward the progress and immediate well-being of all the American nations in which this beautiful Spanish language is spoken]. In a paternal tone, Piñeyro promotes, even dictates, the terms of his readership's common cause. One editorial encourages informative submissions from diplomatic legations while warning that it will censor contributions that could be perceived as insulting to other Spanish-speaking nations, or that would "mantener abiertas llagas deplorables" [keep open disgraceful wounds] of territorial and diplomatic disagreements. El Mundo Nuevo seeks to be "campo neutral de expansión y mútuo conocimiento" [a neutral ground of expansion and mutual understanding], a goal it advances by downplaying national differences on the scene of the page.[40]

A list of locations of sales agents for La América Ilustrada in 1872 suggests that its print community was, indeed, broad: Mexico City, Panama City, Veracruz, San Salvador, Guatemala City, Aspinwall, Bogotá, Cartagena, Puerto Cabello, Guayra, Caracas, Valencia, Maracaibo, Pará, Rio de Janeiro, Montevideo, Buenos Aires, Valparaíso, Cuba, and Puerto Rico. However, its U.S. sales network was just as impressive. Piñeyro initially had sales agents in Boston, New York, and Texas, but under its second editor, Juan de Armas, the paper contracted with a powerful distributor, the American News Company, to cater to its U.S. readership. Apparently, it was widely noticed across continents: a double-column spread on 30 June 1872 issue of La América Ilustrada offers no fewer than eighteen blurbs praising the new publication, ranging from well-established journals like the Lima Heraldo and El Siglo XIX and the Diario Oficial—Mexico's two major cultural organs—to the curiosity of the Burlington Hawk-Eye in faraway Iowa, which claims that El Mundo Nuevo is for Spanish Americans what "Harper's Weekly is for the United States." Notices from the Boston Post, the New York Tribune, the Washington Chronicle, the Springfield Republican and the San Francisco News Letter attest to the paper's circulation to Spanish speakers and bilingual Anglos around the nation, while the testimonials from Brazil (there was apparently also a Portuguese-language edition) and Santo Domingo suggest its impressive reach across the hemisphere.

Although the editors did not go so far as to introduce an English-language section to facilitate bilingualism, as Alemán and Gómez had in *La Patria*, there was a consistent block of English text on the back of each sixteen-page folio issue. Among the ads for sarsaparilla and boardinghouses is an in-house promotion directed at English speakers, claiming, "The circulation of this Newspaper extends throughout the world wherever the Spanish language is spoken. Its duration and punctuality is [*sic*] secured by the capital which the editors and publishers command and the reliable connections they have formed in all foreign parts. No better means, than the columns of this paper, is offered to advertisers desirous of making known their business in Spanish countries." Typical advertisements featured images of U.S.-manufactured items for export to Latin America (water turbines, bank notes, and Gatling guns); Latin American items for import to the United States (discounted Cuban tobacco); and goods and services of interest solely to Spanish speakers living in the United States (books and bilingual lawyers). The United States, implicitly, is included in the loose definition of an American place where Spanish is spoken; thus, the imagined readership of the journal makes ample room among its many constitutive identities for that new subject, the cosmopolitan, the Latino. Although the target subjects of each of these marketing ventures may be distinct, they indicate that U.S. investment in Latin America, especially in new technologies, was flourishing, and that a new market of potentially wealthy Spanish speakers was emerging. Thus, the paper produced transnational affiliation and bilingual bicultural fluency not just as a political ideal but as a commodity.

In contrast to the advertisements for Latin American investment on its back pages, the journal's front matter treats cultural issues with almost reverent seriousness. This focus remained consistent throughout the terms of the various editors. Juan Manuel Mestre joined as coeditor in 1872 and the editorial offices moved to a different location, eventually merging with *La América Ilustrada* and no longer appearing under the Frank Leslie logo but as "a J. C. Rodrigues publication," with editorial offices in the New York Times building. Both editors solicited original and translated work from every U.S.-based *letrado* they could find. Pombo and Quintero contributed articles, poems, and translations. Longfellow and Bryant appeared on various covers of *La América*

Ilustrada, as did Santacilia. Various reviews of Morla's translation of *Evangelina* appeared here, as did two different translations of Poe's "Raven."[41] While most of the paper's discussions of U.S. culture stress the fraternal ties that this rather tight network of translations and homages would suggest, at least one unsigned piece, titled "La moralidad pública en los Estados Unidos"[Public Morality in the United States], anticipates Martí and Rodó in the way it defines Latin Americanness through its spiritual opposition to the economically dictated values of the United States. Commenting on an accompanying engraving of a crowded Wall Street scene in which wealthy bankers pass beggars on the sidewalks, the writer concludes, "En los Estados Unidos no hay todavía más que la riqueza, la riqueza enorme pero áspera y aislada" [There is still nothing besides wealth in the United States, a wealth that is enormous, but bitter and isolated]. Anticipating the tone of many populist writers of the Gilded Age, he blames the poverty visible on New York streets on the immoral capital accumulation of *los Vanderbilts*—that family being, presumably, a particularly apt target because of the patriarch's investment in Central American ventures. With this condemnation comes outrage that Latin Catholic mores are so poorly understood in the United States: "en general los magistrados y empleados del país del Dollar nada tienen que enseñar sino más bien mucho que aprender en punto a la moralidad de los de cualquier país en que se hable nuestra lengua" [When it comes to morality, the judges and civil servants in the land of the Dollar have nothing to teach—and much to learn—from those of any country in which our language is spoken].[42]

Martí would go on to complicate the basic binary structure of *El Mundo Nuevo*—the two Americas, antagonistic yet inextricably bound to each other—and supply it with its missing components: racial consciousness, in the form of an insistence on the mestizo identity of Our America, and political consciousness in the form of a critique of economic imperialism. Yet *El Mundo Nuevo/La América Ilustrada*, whose initial number in 1871 predates Martí's arrival in New York by nine years, brings together in its pages many of the essential components of his foundational thought, anticipating Martí's vision of *Nuestra América* as a linguistically based print community. In its five-year lifespan, *El Mundo Nuevo* acted out grand ambitions to become one of the premier cultural organs of the Spanish-speaking world.[43] This is not to suggest that *El Mundo Nuevo*'s critique of capitalism was as extensive or thoughtful as Martí's. Rather, the editors adopted what would increasingly become a standby topic of urban U.S. journalists at the turn of the century—the spectacle of wealth without values—and defined Spanish American identity against it in moralizing terms rooted, albeit vaguely, in Catholic communitarianism. This strategy of contrast is not without its contradictions: some issues of *El Mundo Nuevo* manifest an apparently uncritical enthusiasm for railroads, for the violent resolution of the "Indian problem" in the western territories, and other hallmarks of Yankee "progress." The journal's conscious marketing strategy, which touts its privileged access to Latin American resources and buyers on the advertising pages, suggests a paradoxical relationship to the dominance of U.S. capital that this article decries.[44]

This paradox is evident in one of *El Mundo Nuevo*'s most pointedly political moments, when it publicized the case of the much admired poet Juan Clemente Zenea y Fornaris, who was imprisoned and eventually executed in Cuba for his proindependence activities. The outrage that the editors expressed both verbally and visually on the front page sits uneasily with the advertisements from sugar and tobacco merchants—the very forces who were pressuring the U.S. government not to intervene in Spanish colonial affairs—on the back page. Zenea, who remains one of the more controversial figures of the independence period, had been the youngest of the poets whose work was collected in *El laúd del desterrado* some fifteen years before, and had lived for some time in New York. After the failure of the López revolt, he stayed on in New Orleans, affiliating himself with a club called El Orden de la Joven Cuba [Young Cuba, patterned after the European revolutionary clubs of the 1848 moment] and working on such Spanish newspapers as *El Correo de Luisiana*, *El Independiente*, and *Faro de Cuba*, registering his outrage against the punitive measures that the Spanish colonial administration tried to take against Cubans living abroad (outrageous taxes and surveillance). Zenea was condemned to death in absentia in 1853, but was allowed to return under amnesty the following year and lived in Havana until 1865. There, he led a life not unlike the one Longfellow pursued at Harvard, teaching languages, contributing to and founding various literary and cultural journals, and writing romantic poems. Had Longfellow resided in Cuba under the worsening conditions of the colony in the later part of the century, he too might have changed his mind about divorcing poetry from politics. Frustrated by the glacial pace of reform, Zenea went to New York with his wife and daughter on a business venture that bankrupted him, then took refuge in Mexico, as had Heredia had before him; Pedro Santacilia, his former collaborator among the Lopecistas, found him journalistic work.[45] Zenea was, in fact, working on a study of Heredia, along with a tract on the need for revolution in Cuba, when the

Grito de Yara began the Ten Years' War in 1868, and he hurriedly abandoned his work in Mexico and left, again, for New York. He briefly took over the editorship of *La Revolución* but left it and became involved in an unfortunate diplomatic intrigue regarding a peace offer to end the hostilities in Cuba. The revolutionaries on the island under Carlos Manuel de Céspedes thought he was a traitor, a Trojan horse paid off by the Spanish. Aboard the ship on which he was to return from this unsuccessful mission, he was taken prisoner by Spanish troops, despite the safe-conduct letter he carried from the Spanish minister to the United States. Zenea was held in prison outside Havana for eight months, during which he composed numerous patriotic and sentimental poems.[46]

Under Piñeyro, Zenea's political ally in the more conservative faction of independentistas, *El Mundo Nuevo* was instrumental in protesting the poet's imprisonment and execution in August 1871, and published the prison poems serially under the title *Diario de un mártir* [A Martyr's Diary]. Their publication is spread out over several issues, each adding a new melodramatic detail: the poems were written in pencil because Zenea was deprived of a pen; undescribed tortures turned his black hair to pure white; he cut off a lock of bloodied hair to smuggle out to his daughter, Piedad, who also smuggled out the poems on her person. Again, the dramatic context in which these poems are presented emphasizes the performance of their creation and distribution; the serial publication seems intended to build a suspense that would keep the Zenea affair in the public eye even after his execution. U.S. readers indoctrinated in the Hispanophilia of Longfellow and Bryant are given guideposts by which to understand Zenea's travails: his situation is compared to the tragedy of Plácido, whose final poems composed in prison after the Matanzas slave uprising of La Escalera had been similarly thrust before the international public to provoke their sentimental outrage. But even more provocative is the poem titled "Infelicia," which (as the editor reminds us) is the title of the posthumous collection of sensual poems by the notorious actress and artiste Adah Isaacs Menken, to whom Zenea may have been secretly married as a seventeen-year-old in Havana.

The nature of the relationship between Menken and Zenea is so heavily romanticized as to be nearly indistinguishable from fiction. Menken was herself a masterful self-promoter after the model of Whitman, of whom she was an early and ardent supporter and whose intimate style of free verse she imitates in her posthumously published collection, *Infelicia*. To foster her public image as a romantic outsider, she encouraged rumors of a noble Creole background (even hinting that she was of mixed race) and played on her assumed Judaism: she is so strongly identified with the religion to which she converted on marrying first husband, Alexander Menken, that she is regularly included in anthologies of Jewish women writers. She made much of her fluency in multiple languages, including Spanish, which she learned as a girl when her family relocated from New Orleans to a plantation outside Matanzas, and called herself "Dolores" onstage. This fluency would serve her well when she did her California acting tour in 1863, playing Spanish characters to the delight of californio theatregoers. (Her affected Cubanness recalls the less public, but similarly self-fashioning, career of María del Occidente.) In her memoirs, Menken writes that, while on her first tour of Havana as a budding theatrical sensation, she was rescued from the unwanted attentions of the island's capitán-general by his handsome seventeen-year-old nephew, "the Count Juan Clemente Zenea" (he was no such thing), whom she met openly and unchaperoned at night on the plaza, a scandal that delighted the Havana press. She adds that they were afterward secretly married, enjoying a blissful interlude until they were separated by their angry parents, never to see each other again. Although Menken shaves four years off her birthdate, making herself out to be a twelve-year-old acting sensation, the chronology of Zenea's life would place their affair or marriage sometime in 1849.[47] The version of their youthful relationship recounted in Zenea's verse—looking only at the most obvious poems in his "Martyr's Diary" sequence, those titled "Infelicia" and "A. M."—suggests a somewhat different story.

"A. M." describes the adolescent lovers, like a Cuban Paolo and Francesca, beginning their affair while learning the other's language, declaiming lines from *Romeo and Juliet*. It also recounts the resulting public scandal similar to that described in Menken's autobiography. In Zenea's poem, however, "A. M." begs him to allow her full erotic submission—to be to him "como esclavo al dueño" [as the slave is to the master]. The themes of slavery and captivity recur again in "Infelicia: Escrita en un calabozo del Castillo de la Cabaña" [Infelicia: Written in a Jail Cell in La Cabaña Fortress].[48] Here the speaker recalls in detail a sensual night, long ago, when he and Infelicia pledged their eternal love: "un gran naufragio en las mundanas olas" [a great shipwreck on the waves of the ordinary]. On that night, Infelicia realized that other women had been "dueño de mi corazón" [master of my heart] before her; in helpless abandonment, she offered her virginity. Given the magnitude of that gift, the speaker concludes that if it were at all possible, she would appear in La Cabaña to rescue him:

Con sangre de tus venas   *[With the blood of your own*
                                 veins

Contenta y generosa com- prarías La libertad de tu primer amante.	*You'd gladly, generously pur- chase The liberty of your first lover.]*

Both Menken's memoir and Zenea's poem imitate a Byronic scenario of hyperbolic freedom and sacrifice (Menken's most famous stage role had been the underclothed heroine in an adaptation of Byron's *Mazeppa*), but each tells a differently self-serving version of that story. Menken's makes her a fairly passive actress in the drama of her affair, suggesting that her more cosmopolitan and widely traveled upbringing created a spiritual kinship between her and "Count" Zenea that made him willing to sacrifice family and reputation to possess her. Zenea's "Infelicia" not only imagines the balance of power falling in the opposite corner—it is he, not she, who dictates the terms of their relationship—but it summons the remembered scene of her sexual self-sacrifice to help make sense of his own impending civic sacrifice. Menken herself had died a pauper in Paris just a few years earlier, in 1868, prompting a sudden renewal of interest in her poetry and her career in the very same New York press that had long grown tired of her. *El Mundo Nuevo*'s decision to display for public scrutiny the bodies of the transnational lovers thus seems a strategy for publicizing the Cuban cause in national-sentimental terms that also appeal to the sensationalist bent of New York journalism. Summoning Menken's ghost to express her presumed sympathy for Zenea and the cause of a free Cuba is perhaps meant to stir a desired response of mourning and outrage among Anglo-American readers. When Piñeyro's editorial house published the first edition of Zenea's complete poems in 1874, his "Infelicia" was given pride of place, at the end of the book, as if to capitalize on the near coincidence of their untimely deaths.

Most Faithful Fidel: Guillermo Prieto's Reconstruction Travelogue

As editor of some of its most influential newspapers and literary journals, Guillermo Prieto was a colossal figure in nineteenth-century Mexican intellectual and political life—the popular favorite for the title of *poeta nacional*. Like Heredia and Pombo, his sense of national identity was importantly shaped around and against certain cosmopolitan and sublime spaces in the United States, but his attitude toward Mexico's perceived adversary was far sharper and more caustic than even Pombo's. Prieto, a self-made letrado from humble origins, was barely thirty when the conflict erupted in Texas, and his house in Mexico City was sacked by Scott's occupying forces in 1847. In a series of topical poems, distributed in broadside during those years, he vociferously denounced both the gringos and the defeatists who signed the Treaty of Guadalupe-Hidalgo in the Mexican Congress, of which he was then a member. Prieto was outspoken in identifying U.S. policy as imperialist through a series of pointed comparisons to corrupt Rome. Throughout his extraordinary literary production—two dozen books of poetry, a detailed history of the American invasion, folkloric studies, political and juridical treatises, and many volumes of memoirs—he was an influential cultural nationalist, an advocate of the "Mexicanization of letters" who sought to "dehispanicize" the language with strong doses of local and regional idioms.[49]

However, only ten years after the *invasión yanqui*, as he referred to it, Prieto had to enter the belly of the beast himself. In late 1857, after the tender liberal regime established by the Plan de Ayutla and at the beginning of what became known as the Wars of the Reform, several members of Juárez's cabinet, Prieto among them, accompanied their president to New Orleans, his former haunt in exile just a few years previous, to seek financial and military support. Known by the joking code name of La Familia Enferma [The Sick Family] to emphasize the wholeheartedness of their devotion to the cause, they found kinship with the Cuban independentistas of the *Laúd del desterrado* group, notably Quintero and Santacilia. It was a brief and successful trip, in stark contrast to the one Prieto would make two decades later. In 1877, five years after Juárez's death and after Prieto's final resignation from government service, he was again pushed into taking a nine-month sojourn *al norte* while the party's current political troubles cooled. Disillusioned, sick at heart, and mourning the unachieved promise of Juarezian liberalism, the sixty-year-old Prieto amused himself on this unwanted voyage by writing the three-volume, thousand-page *Viaje a los Estados Unidos por "Fidel"* (his journalistic nickname), which was published serially in Mexico. The *Viaje* contains a chaotic mixture of genres and rhetorical styles, containing sociological and political observations, soul-searching musings, slightly off-color jokes, gossip, and notes about machines and industry (he was particularly interested in new printing technologies), punctuated throughout by a massive accumulation of lyrics. On this trip he seemed to produce poems like a machine, and nearly every chapter ends with stanzas composed late at night or in the early hours of the morning in a kind of logorrheic delirium. Many of the poems are surrounded by a discussion of the context that prompted him to write them as well as a description of the opinions of his fellow travelers as he recited them—as if to bring about an effect of spontaneity and readerly participation in the text as a whole.

Like *El laúd del desterrado,* Prieto's *Viaje* is structured elegiacally, poised between recollections of the hopeful 1857 journey and this crushing moment of return. After a miserable sea voyage and a month in San Francisco (where he hates the "barbaric" food, the bad hotels, and the beggars in the streets), Prieto and his entourage take trains and coaches to St. Louis, a part of the journey he skips over quickly as uninteresting. The real goal is New Orleans, where the group would make its longest stop, and which he identifies with his lost Mexico. Waking the first morning in the St. Charles Hotel, he writes, "Fue como el cambio de una decoración teatral, gozábamos las delicias de un clima templado, y como que nos sorprendía la vegetación de nuestro país" [it was like the changing of a stage backdrop; we enjoyed the delights of a temperate climate, and the vegetation of our own country suprised us]. "Our own country," he says, without resorting to simile. He leaves the city immediately on a pilgrimage to see the Gulf of Mexico, to see "*algo* de Méjico, por Dios; que ya estaba sudando *wiskey* hace tres días" [to see *something* of Mexico, for God's sake: I'd been sweating whiskey for three days].[50] But he registers his first real joy on being reunited with Quintero, now an editor at the *Picayune* and the acknowledged head of an informally constituted Hispanophone literary community that gathered at his home (Prieto calls it "mi casa de Orleans"). In the worst throes of a dual nostalgia—mourning both his lost youth and his lost *presidente*—Prieto writes, "En aquel abrazo con que confundía nuestras almas, sentía la patria, la familia y la sociedad de cuanto más ama mi corazón" [In that soul-confounding embrace, I felt homeland, family, and the company of those my heart holds most dear].

> Los primeros tragos entre Pepe (porque así llamamos a
> Quintero en familia) y yo, desataron esa conversación deliciosa,
> con una interrupción a cada palabra . . . de los versos a los
> viajes, de éstos a las recetas de cocina, y salta a las muchachas,
> y se caracolea entre juicios literarios, paseos, crónica
> escandalosa y altas cuestiones sociales; conversaciones a pierna
> suelta, sin pies ni cabeza, sin ortografía conocida.

[The first swigs Pepe and I took together (because that's what we call Quintero among family) unloosed a wonderful conversation, with an interruption at every word . . . from poetry to traveling, and from that to recipes, and then it jumps to women, and winds around among literary opinions, walks, scandalous news and serious social questions; one-legged conversations, footless and headless, with no known way to write them down.] (2:51–52)

To some extent, Prieto paints himself as an orphan purely as a rhetorical gesture: far from being estranged from his family, he had actually brought his son along with him, and his wife had died some years earlier. But taking on the role of the utterly bereft exile is crucial to the aim of this travelogue, which is to resanctify Mexican nationality by saturating himself and his readers with the extended absence of it. He comes to terms with the trauma of the failure of Mexican liberalism through a series of suggestive identifications with different American versions of the *familia enferma*—notably, the figuratively orphaned family of former Lopecistas. Recording the activities of Quintero and his circle with great interest, he readily identifies the Cuban exiles with the local French Creole aristocracy in particular and the Confederacy in general, picking a fight with Pierre Soulé about slavery and debating the reasons for the failure of the López revolt. His continual remarks about the familiarity of the scenes and conversations he witnesses there surely originate, in part, by the fact that Reconstruction New Orleans, like the Mexico City of the 1850s, felt a strong sense of communal outrage and identification because it had recently been occupied by Yankee troops they perceived as disrespectful to their culture. The decline of the Creoles spurs him into an inventory of the relations between various ethnic groups in the city. Of Mexicans, he writes, "El yankee a su vez ve al mexicano como a un mono que pudiera explotar, después de haberse apoderado del árbol en que se guarece" [The Yankee, for his part, sees the Mexican as a monkey he can exploit, after he expropriates the tree in which the monkey sits]. This perception, he muses, may have much to do with the near-total lack of accurate information in English about Mexicans (2:132).

Prieto made it a point of pride to learn as little English as possible on his trip, so that when a Cuban Orleanian offered to give lessons to him and some of his compatriots, he jokes about what poor students they make: "nosotros habíamos resuelto aprender el escabrosa idioma de Milton y Shakespeare sin estudiar palabra y sin fijar en nada la atención"

[We'd resolved to learn the scabrous tongue of Milton and Shakespeare without studying a single word and without paying the least bit of attention] (2:124). But Quintero succeeds in convincing him to read some *literatura norteamericana,* and he duly records Quintero's preferences and judgments for his own future reference, calling his friend the only man in the United States "de raza latina" who can make sense of the yanquis to him (2:165). Moreover, he soon has further reason to pick up a little English: at Quintero's *tertulias,* he extends his social sphere beyond the local Cuban community to include a female poet associated with the *Picayune* (then owned by fellow poet "Pearl Rivers," née Eliza Nicholson, to whom Quintero had gallantly pledged his honor). Mary Ashley Townsend, a native New Orleanian married to a prominent physician, had spent some time in Mexico; after meeting Prieto and his group, she published a series of poems dedicated to the exiled liberal "family" in the newspaper under her openly known pseudonym, Xarifa. She begins to make "frecuentes visitas" to Prieto to help him master English, and his head seems to spin (2:163).[51]

Flirtations aside, New Orleans provokes one of the most poignant scenes in the *Viaje,* occasioned by the death and funeral of Leopoldo Turla. One of the original *Laúd* poets, Turla was well known to the international Cuban exile community at large: he corresponded with both Cirilo Villaverde and his wife Amelia. Barely supporting himself by piecing together translating and tutoring jobs, Turla, unlike Quintero, was a failure at integrating himself into the postbellum city order. He died, like many intellectual exiles then and since, a pauper.[52] Prieto crashed Turla's funeral, slipping in with an apparently uncharacteristic silence. It was, he remarks,

> entierro humildísimo, acompañado de unos cuantos cubanos
> que llevaban en sus semblantes el lóbrego duelo del emigrado,
> como si tuvieran que lamentar la más triste de las orfandades,
> la orfandad de la tumba . . . aquella soledad, aquel silencio,
> aquel poeta que soltaba de sus garras la miseria para entregarlo
> a la muerte en suelo extraño, me hicieron hondísima impresión
> . . . un estado de tristeza imposible de describir.
>
> *[a very simple burial, attended by a few Cubans who wore on*
> *their faces the lugubrious mourning of the emigrant, as if they*
> *were there to mourn the saddest of all orphanhoods, the*
> *orphanhood of the tomb . . . that solitude, that silence, that poet*
> *who cast off the rags of his poverty to give himself up to death on*

foreign soil, made a very profound impression on me . . . a state of sadness impossible to describe.

The otherwise incorrigibly energetic Prieto then tells us that after Turla's funeral, night after night he would leave his companions and sit for hours on end by the statue of Henry Clay—who was, among other things, the architect of a lost cause to pay serious attention to the fate of republicanism in Latin America:

> Allá, en la oscuridad más completa, sangrando mi corazón de amargura por circunstancias las más acerbas de mi vida, produje una serie de composiciones . . . que nos los hace preciosos el amor, la gratitud, el peligro o la muerte.
>
> *[There, in the fullest darkness, with my heart bleeding bitterly from being in the most difficult circumstances of my life, I produced a series of poetic compositions . . . which make life, gratitude, danger, or death alike precious to us.]* (2:171)

Writing as sublimation is hardly a new concept. But Prieto's use of it here suggests an acknowledgment that exile warps one's relationship to time: an exile never knows whether he or she might return. Without that grasp of even an immediate futurity, Prieto senses, Turla had suffered from what would become a quintessentially Cuban condition—the inability to be fully in place in the present moment because the desire points toward a future elsewhere. As a would-be architect of the Mexican future, Prieto seems to fear that this loss of time will affect him as well. However, the act of poetic composition itself—he stresses repeatedly that it is the activity, more than the object of the finished poem, that matters to him—helps make sense of the confusing present.

As the entourage marches up the Mississippi and toward New York, after many tearful goodbyes, Prieto repeats a similar scene of temporal dislocation at Greenwood Cemetery, the place that had prompted Pombo to name it the most aesthetically pure location in the United States and the natural gathering place for exiles of Latin sensibility:

> Yo he sentido mi polvo mezclado a esta tierra, he visto mi tumba como una usurpación; el hielo de la extranjería de la muerte ha llevado el frío a mis huesos; y advenedizo de la misma nada, a mí tornaba mi duelo como el polvo que se lanza contra el viento y ciega nuestros ojos. . . . Sentía mi corazón enfermo, mi salida del Cementerio era como una exhumación.

Creía, en mi alucinación de muerte, que había visto hecho cadáver el Parque Central.

[I have felt my dust mingled with this earth, I have seen my tomb like a usurpation; the ice of the foreign land of death has brought a chill to my very bones. And arising from this same nothingness, my mourning hit me like the dust that is kicked up in the wind and blinds us. . . . My heart felt sick; my departure from the cemetery was like being exhumed. I believed, in my hallucination of death, that Central Park itself had become a cadaver.] (3:36)

Yet from this point on, Prieto turns the funereal note into a metaphor of political and spiritual regeneration. In one hilarious but pointed scene, he goes to Dr. Jordan's Museum of Anatomy and spooks himself nearly to death imagining that he sees the ghosts of Mexican independence heroes; it turns out that he has walked into a set of wax figures of Washington and his generals that had been forgotten and stuffed into a corner. It is difficult for him to resist finding an allegory here, either to the mummification of revolutionary principles in this capital-driven and newly centralized nation, or to his own continual birth and rebirth. "Quiero darme cuenta a mí solo de las causas de la prosperidad de este pueblo; quiero estudiar afanoso el secreto de su desarrollo sorprendente, para formar conciencia, y después de purificado mi criterio, llevar a mi país la buena nueva de su propia regeneración" [I want to find out for myself the causes of the prosperity of these people; I want to dedicate myself to studying the secret of their amazing development, to form an understanding; and after I've winnowed down the causes, to take back to my country the good news of its own rebirth], he writes with new determination (3:49).

Three final encounters in New York give further shape to this resolution. The first is a trip to Niagara, which Prieto describes in alternately humorous and awed tones. The entourage spends the fourth of May contemplating various views of the lake and falls, inspiring more of the poems that gush out of him generously. The end of his second poem on the subject, however, swerves away from the usual invocation of Niagara as a reminder of the transience of all things human. Instead, he chastises the falls themselves for their *vanitas vanitatum*:

¿A qué nuestra vanidad,   [To what end does our vanity,
Mirando en tí al iris bello,   Admiring your lovely rainbow,
Lo interpreta como el sello   Interpret it as a sign
De la augusta eternidad?   Of lofty eternity?

¡Morirá tu majestad	*Your majesty will perish*
Del tiempo al fatal vaivén,	*In the fluctuations of time,*
Y te hundirá su desdén	*Your contempt will fall down*
En los abismos profundos,	*Into the deep abyss,*
Con el polvo de otros mundos	*With the dust of other worlds*
Y con mi polvo también!	*And with my dust as well!]*

(3:312)

He signs the poem with the date: it is three in the morning on the fifth of May, the day of one of the Reforma's great military victories. The writing of the poem seems to compensate for the missing presence of Juárez, whom Prieto remembers always as a kind of lost father.

The second compensation comes in the form of a visit to Bryant, whom Prieto had met during the yanqui poet's earlier two-month trip to Mexico. Bryant not only arranges for Prieto to get tours of the city's publishing houses; he invites him to stay at his home. Prieto praises Bryant fulsomely, making particular note that he is "muy distante de las ideas del *destino manifiesto*, de la usurpación y la violencia." Bryant listens tolerantly to the lyrics Prieto has penned on his trip to Niagara a few weeks earlier and arranges to get a sheaf of recent Spanish-language newspapers for him to read on the train, satisfying Prieto's continual longing for printed matter, on one hand, and a live audience, on the other (3:492). However, he is obliged to note that despite Bryant's respect for Mexico, he is somewhat lacking in concrete ideas about it. The "poeta de ambas Américas," he believes, has yet to appear, unless it is Quintero, who had turned most of his compositional energies toward translation.

The third and final event, a meeting with the young Venezuelan expatriates Jacinto Gutiérrez Coll and Juan Antonio Pérez Bonalde in Delmonico's, is ultimately more satisfying, for the two men respond profoundly to Prieto's new theme of exile as a form of necessary death leading to regeneration. At their insistence (he says), Prieto unrolls the sheaf of manuscripts he carries with him and reads the poems he has been writing—on his knees, with a pencil, on his wallet, wherever:

> Olvidé el café y las conveniencias todas; leía como si no tuviera auditorio; leía como quien tiene la conciencia de que por primera vez se le comprende. Era la lectura cansada; pero yo seguía, sin considerar que del mismo Homero habrían fastidiado dos horas de versos. Pero a los literatos y los conocidos no existían; eran los confidentes; eran los amigos; era el viejo marino que contaba sus naufragios a los que solo

conocían del mar los esplendores y las brisas. Insensiblemente nos veíamos el espíritu: patria inspiraba; la raza reclamaba sus fuerzos; las auras de los primeros años replegaban el ala, para besar nuestras frentes enamoradas con el canto de nuestros recuerdos.

El café había quedado medio solitario cuando acabé de leer, en medio de testimonios de generosa estimación, que nunca olvidaré.

[I forgot about the café and all material concerns; I read as if I didn't have an audience; I read like someone with a sudden awareness that for the first time he is truly understood. The reading was exhausting, but I went on, without considering that people would have tired of hearing verses from Homer himself after two hours. But they no longer seemed like literary folk or like acquaintances; they were confidantes, they were friends, and I was the ancient mariner speaking about shipwrecks to those whose knowledge of the sea is limited to splendid vistas and gentle winds. Unconsciously, we recognized the same spirit in each other: the homeland inspired us, la raza laid claim to its powers; the gentle breezes of those first years folded back a wing to kiss our foreheads, in love with the song of our memories.

The café was half empty by the time I finished reading, to the sound of generous praise which I shall never forget.]
(3:183)

What does Prieto mean by *la raza*, and what kinship does he claim to Pérez Bonalde and Gutiérrez Coll, whom he has never met before? The homeland he shares with them is imaginary, discursive; it is the as yet unarticulated community of *Nuestra América*.

The Future's Past
Latino Ghosts in the U.S. Canon

> Each epoch not only dreams the next, but also, in dreaming, strives toward the moment of waking.
>
> —Benjamin, "Paris, Capital of the Nineteenth Century"

The twists and turns that political and cultural relations between the Americas took in the final two decades of the nineteenth century would require another book to elaborate. One might easily, if overgenerally, locate the beginning of the era of a frankly neocolonial and imperialist turn to U.S. policy in Latin America in 1880, the year in which the navy was charged to "take necessary steps to secure adequate coaling stations and harbors for the use of the naval forces of the United States at proper points on the Atlantic and Pacific coasts of Central America and of the American Isthmus."[1] But we might trace this shift through other cultural markers as well: 1880, for instance, is the year in which José Martí arrived for the first time in New York, to write for the Hispanophile Charles Dana's New York *Sun*. Although his stay was brief, he would return the following year to begin the rest of his nearly lifelong exile. It is also the year in which Juan Antonio Pérez Bonalde, the young Venezuelan poet and perfume-seller who had silently listened to Guillermo Prieto playing ancient mariner in a coffeehouse in New York, first published his Niagara ode—a poem that Martí would identify as the herald of a new literary spirit in America.[2] And it was the year in which the elderly Henry Wadsworth Longfellow received two communications from different liminal points on the transamerican frontera—a rural rancho in California, and a poet's study in Caracas. The first came from the figurehead of the californios:

Muy señor mío de mi respeto.

Le viviría yo muy agradecido lo restante de mi vida (que no es mucho pues ya paso de los 70) si me honrará U. con la poesía compuesta después de la lamentable muerte de mi muy estimado amigo, Bayard Taylor—"Dead he lay among his books." Estoy persuadido que no me negaría U. mi súplica, si supiera en cuanto apreciaría yo las líneas autógrafas del mejor poeta americano, escritas por el mejor de mis amigos.

Suplicándole me dispense la libertad que me tomo, me suscribo de U. atto. y obicuente servidor, M. G. Vallejo.

[I would be grateful to you for the rest of my days (which won't be many, since I'm already over 70) if you would honor me with the poem you composed after the sad death of my very dear friend, Bayard Taylor—"Dead he lay among his books." I am convinced that you would not deny my request if you knew how much I would appreciate these lines from the pen of the best of all American poets, written for the best of all my friends. Begging your forgiveness for taking the liberty of making this request, I sign myself your attentive and obedient servant, M. G. Vallejo.][3]

It is not known whether Longfellow obliged and sent the poem—or if he even recognized the name of Mariano Vallejo, once the head of the most powerful family in California and the living embodiment of a history that was soon to be lost for several generations.[4] But in the elegy to which Vallejo refers, the poet had integrated a subtle acknowledgment of Taylor's connection to the Spanish-speaking West into this description of the poet's dead body laid out in his study:

> As the statues in the gloom,
> Watch o'er Maximilian's tomb,
> So those volumes from their shelves,
> Watched him, silent as themselves.[5]

The analogy suggested in these lines is both uncanny and cryptic. The word "themselves" has a dual referent, to both the books on the shelves and the statues watching Maximilian. The "statues in the gloom," whatever their identity, testify to the failure of Maximilian's efforts to transform himself into an emperor and a Mexican; likewise, the spirits of the writers entombed in Taylor's books await him with a similar message of transiency. Within these lines, we witness the process of the live poetic word becoming stilled and silent. Vallejo's letter, written in the politest style of a Spanish that had ceased to be the language of power in California, seems to echo this loss, this encroaching entombment, with its reference to his advanced age. Yet at the same time, Vallejo's very motive for writing seems to be to disrupt the ossification of literary language: the published poem was widely available, as were all of Longfellow's works, but he wants a copy in the poet's own hand—a live performance, as it were, of the affective ties that linked the national poet, through Taylor's dead body, to the dispossessed letrado himself.

The same themes resonate through the second letter Longfellow received, this one from Rafael Pombo, with whom he had had a fairly extensive correspondence about various translation projects each had embarked on. This is their last recorded exchange. Intermingling English and Spanish, Pombo writes, "I dreamed of you three times":

> [Fue] un sueño perfectamente continuo en tres actos, cosa rara. El sueño fue que yo estaba en casa de Ud., que hablé con sus hijas en castellano, y que cuando Ud. llegó y me saludó, me dijo: "You look very much like a jeweller."—Y en efecto, soy amigo de montar en castellano diamantes extranjeros.

> *[It was a perfectly continuous dream in three acts—a strange thing. I dreamed that I was at your house, that I spoke to your daughters in Spanish, and that when you arrived and greeted me, you said, "You look very much like a jeweler." And, in effect, I've befriended the process of mounting foreign diamonds into Spanish settings.]*[6]

The dreaming Pombo seems to redeem Longfellow's daughters from the model of the monstruous acquisitive women in "Las norteamericanas en Broadway" by making them speak Spanish. Moreover, the dream recalls the metaphor of gem-mining in that same early poem, which had envisioned Latin American countries despoiling their precious stones, their natural patrimony, to trade for dubious Yankee favors. In the older Pombo's subconscious reworking of that metaphor, it is he who takes the raw materials of other people's diamonds and decides how to process them—as if to reverse the direction of the translative economy as well as the political one. The irony of both letters is that the fate described in Longfellow's "To Bayard Taylor" eventually befell every one of the figures I have described as ambassadors of a transamerican culture: their enshrinement as founders of national literatures transformed most of them, literally, into statues in parks and libraries. Their work—once the object of performative declamations in countless schoolrooms throughout the hemisphere—goes virtually unread and, perhaps more importantly given its original performative overtones, unvoiced. In that sense, they share a final destiny with the often anonymous writers in borderlands periodicals of the nineteenth century, who themselves survive only in scraps and echoes.

To acknowledge the pathos of their disappearance is not to endorse the writings of either group uncritically. In emphasizing the often paradoxical ideological vectors of these poetic expressions, I have tried to see the writers in this study not as models of a resistant subjectivity but as historically situated speakers. It seems important to reiterate in closing that the Hispanophone writers of the nineteenth century do not share the class and racial affiliations of most present-day Latinos. They shared a possessive investment in whiteness, in certain definitions of cultural literacy, and in a masculinist model of nationhood; thus the texts they produced do not always contest, resist, or interevene in the power of institutions and forms of knowledge in ways that contemporary readers, attuned to inequalities of race, gender, and class, might desire. As I stated in the preface, my emphasis here on communities of print is not intended to diminish the significance of other, primarily oral forms of expression among Hispanophone and indigenous populations. The importance of periodical-based literary culture is simply that it accommodates different stages along the orality-literacy continuum by speaking to a range of readerly abilities and needs on the same page. Because the language of print is less divided by dialect and regional usage than is oral culture, it helps establish the conditions of possibility for a transnational body of Latino writing—understood both as a body of work and as a set of textual practices involving reading, writing, performing, editing, collecting.

The attempt to recover poetry, editorials, and other materials from the obscurity of history suggests a fundamental faith in the mythic unity of the Archive, yet assembling this archive into a narrative is itself an ideological act. The task of "recovery" takes for granted the existence of a distinctively Latino tradition, pressing the divergent historical experiences and contemporary circumstances of different constituencies into a continuous narrative of common linguistic and social struggles. The fragmentary and episodic nature of this study does not provide a stable point of origin for Latino writing. Indeed, it reveals the limits of this act of archival unification, for it shows how deeply rooted are the major identity paradigms of different Latino groups, who suffer from differential access to political, economic, and cultural power at the present moment.

As far back as the 1830s, one can see a nascent Caribbean sense of its colonial relationship to the United States, and the Cuban exile's obsession with the tantalizing closeness of the island as a sensual object of desire that cannot be reached. Meanwhile, the Mexican-Chicano sense of self begins to shape itself, with the annexation of Texas, primarily through the figure of betrayal and territorial contestation. Yet bi- or tricultural writers like Heredia, Santacilia, and even Guillermo Prieto disrupt that division between *cubano* and Chicano genealogies, as they identify with the experience of emigrés of both countries from within the United States. Editors of these Spanish-language print organs, aware that they were addressing far-flung readers from New York to California through the common practice of newspaper exchange, began to address a broader constituency, constructing new coalitions across traditional divisions between their nations of origin. This print community of writers, editors, and readers practiced a form of affiliation by assent rather than descent, identifying with each other through the bond of language and a common condition: the fact that they were regarded by the Anglo-American world with an admixture of desire and suspicion. Besides this nascent consciousness of externality, we can see other points of common ground as well: a valorization of Spanish-language cultural artifacts and ritual forms; a sense of moral values based loosely in Catholic tradition that are understood to oppose an individualistic profit motive associated with the Anglo-American sphere; and a tendency to define their suffering as a political subject in strongly affective (even hyperbolically sentimental) terms, through direct contrast to some aspect of the U.S. landscape.

Editors and writers on the borderlands may have been presciently aware of the ways that language could be enlisted in other forms of political and social exclusion, but we must be careful not to see the assertion of Spanish and its bilingual hybrids as legitimate literary languages of the U.S. solely as a historical problem, when it is very much a contemporary one. A venture into the past such as this one must raise the question of its presumed and implicit relevance to the present moment. Literary histories, whether assembled around national or ethnic communities, are always implicitly if not explicitly reflections of the most pressing needs and exigencies of the time in which they are written, and in that sense interventionist. For instance, F. O. Matthiessen's conclusion in 1940 that the founders of the "American" literary tradition had in common a powerful nonconformity and resistance to authority suited his interbellum democratic socialism.[7] The Recovering the U.S. Hispanic Literary Heritage (RUSHLH) project, like related archival work such as the

Schomburg project on African American writers, the Nineteenth-Century American Women Writers Web, or the Languages of What Is Now the United States project, aim to patch a perceived hole in the historical fabric, a missing piece of the Archive, in order to lay the groundwork for the invention of a new, more usable past. That effort is itself driven by the implicit teleology of the idea of "tradition," which attempts to impose a continuity onto past, present, and future. The profuse repetition of the demographic projection that Latinos will constitute a new "majority minority" in the near future suggests that the state, too, has an interest in supporting the construction of a usable Latino past. We might see that interest benignly, as an effort at inclusion coming out of the civil rights movement, or more ominously, as a proactive effort to make productive citizens out of a group it has historically feared would prove dangerously inassimilable.

This national investment in the making of Latino tradition points out a fundamental ambiguity in the RUSHLH project's title: "literary heritage" can refer either to Hispanics as a group or to the United States in general. Revision of the U.S. literary canon, as practiced by the multiculturalism of the late 1980s, aims to accommodate Latino cultural memory through an additive process, by juxtaposing (for instance) Mariano Vallejo with Melville to acknowledge that they jointly inhabited a continent and, eventually, a country. The recent flurry of interest in Martí indicates that U.S. literary study is rediscovering a wheel that Latin American criticism has long taken for granted: the significance of transnational perspectives on culture and politics.[8] In turning toward the Archive for a wholesale revision of hemispheric literary culture rather than simply the construction of a Latino past, I have tried to bring together regional and transnational perspectives—at the expense (but not the wholesale exclusion) of the national. Even more deeply, I have tried to suggest that, like Toni Morrison's vision of a spectral African American presence in even the "whitest" of canonical texts, the "other America" was always present as a repressed national memory. Continental expansion and U.S. designs on the rest of the hemisphere are central to the very definition of its nationhood throughout the nineteenth century. Although historicist literary criticism has begun to link the great works of the "American Renaissance" to conflicts over sectionalism, slavery, and gender, the role of Cuba and Santo Domingo in the slavery question, of the invasion of Mexico in the debate over state's rights, or of racism against mestizos and anti-Catholic nativism in the shaping of fundamental paradigms of American identity remains underexamined. These events launched a deep uncertainty over whether the United States would ever be able to assimilate a Spanish-speaking population to itself under the same terms by which it assimilated others, and this uncertainty has continued to inform acts of language and politics through the present moment. Ultimately, the challenge posed by the changing demographics of the United States, I would argue, is not to integrate Latinos to an existing national tradition, but to reshape that tradition in a way that recognizes the continuous life of Latinos within and around it.

Preface

1. This list of course leaves out Brazilian and other non-Spanish nations in the Greater Caribbean, including Surinam and Guyana, for the simple reason that I am limited here to bilingual contexts of Spanish and English; neither have I done any work on the indigenous languages also represented within this list of countries. I regret both gaps, and refer readers to other sources whenever possible.

2. R. Sánchez, *Telling Identities*, 304.

3. Oboler, *Ethnic Labels*, 171. Throughout this book, I use the terms "Latino" or "Latina" in preference to "Hispanic," which has assimilationist rather than pluralist connotations—the roots of which Oboler lays out clearly.

Chapter I
"Alone with the Terrible Hurricane":
The Occluded History of Transamerican Literature

1. Heredia, *Niágara*, 135. The translation attributed to Bryant renders this section as follows: "A whirling ocean that fills the wall / Of the crystal heaven, and buries all. / And I, cut off from the world, remain / Alone with the terrible hurricane."

2. S. Brau in Amy, *Musa bilingüe*, 6–7. The Spanish version precedes the English, but there is—perhaps appropriately—no indication of which is the original language of Brau's manifesto.

3. The prolific amount of recent criticism on the role of print culture in the making of modern national identities originates in Anderson, *Imagined Communities*. Also powerfully influential are Bhabha, *Location of Culture*, and Sommer, *Foundational Fictions*.

4. The RUSHLH project, under the direction of Nicolás Kanellos and funded by a ten-year, $20 million grant from the Ford Foundation (among other sources), represents a greater public investment than the similar Schomburg project to recover works by nineteenth-century African-American writers. In the initial stages of the project, its sense of the community for whom this tradition is being recovered is left deliberately broad, and the relationship between the subcategories of

"Hispanic" populations it so carefully balances has not been articulated by the project itself. Most editions to emerge to date from the RUSHLH series claim their place in the "U.S. Hispanic heritage" on the basis of a more specific ethnic affiliation (e.g., the local tejano customs described by Jovita González; the Afro-Puerto Rican activism of Jesús Colón; or the complaints against the disenfranchisement of Mexican-American citizenship and property rights articulated by María Amparo Ruíz de Burton). However, none of these community-within-a-nation models adequately accounts for a text like *El laúd del desterrado*, a collection of patriotic poems by Cuban-born writers (including Heredia, but mainly comprising a younger generation) originally published in New York in 1858. The so-called *Laúd* group, which I discuss in chapter 4, plays an important role in Cuban literary history but, as editor Matías Montes-Huidobro acknowledges, in no sense understood themselves as marginalized U.S. subjects at that time. More obviously than the other works in the series but not uniquely, *El laúd del desterrado* requires a transnational critical frame to make its presence in the series meaningful.

5. The modern discipline of Latin American literature originated in consciously transnational paradigms and in this respect has much to teach its U.S. counterpart, which consistently ignores comparative studies to pursue the white whale of the national character. I recognize that "Latin America" is a fictive disciplinary construct and use it here guardedly, making regional distinctions explicit whenever possible. On the unstable nature of the discipline of Latin American literature, see Mignolo, "Posoccidentalismo," and González Echevarría, *Myth and Archive*, 53–55. On the ideological compromises of the discipline of U.S. literary study, see Reising, *Unusable Past*. Some exemplary comparative studies of nineteenth-century U.S. literature include Chai, *Romantic Foundations*; L. J. Reynolds, *European Revolutions*, and Weisbuch, *Atlantic Double-Cross*.

6. I am indebted to a number of critical predecessors in U.S. studies who have questioned this conflation of the United States and America, particularly Vera Kutzinski and José David Saldívar. See also Hortense Spillers's "Introduction" to *Comparative American Identities*, the collections by Pérez Firmat and Chevigny and Laguardia, and Porter, "What We Know That We Don't Know." For a forceful argument against the monolingual bias in U.S. literary study, see Lauter, *Canons and Contexts*, and Sollors, *Multilingual America*.

7. My approach thus echoes recent work in diasporic and postcolonial studies, but these links should be taken provisionally. I have deliberately avoided using the terms "hybrid" and "subaltern" to avoid the dubious anachronism of projecting postmodern consciousness onto nineteenth-century subjects in divergently modern spaces. However, I hope this study will suggest some potential disturbances to contemporary notions of identity. Critics such as Arjun Appadurai and Néstor García Canclini, for instance, base their notion of a fluid diasporic identity on the material conditions of the media age: the near-spontaneity of communications and travel, as contrasted with "premodern" conditions in the developing world. This study will implicitly contest Appadurai's claim that a *collec-*

tive transnational imagination, a "community of sentiment," is made possible only with the advent of the mass media in the later twentieth century.

8. Johannsen, *Halls*, 248. On the ironic influence of the antiexpansionist Prescott's *History* on enthusiasm for the war in the United States, see more generally 243–50.

9. Kanellos and Martell, *Periodicals*, 5–7. This is the definitive reference work at the moment. The most extensive scholarship on the literary efforts of local borderlands periodicals has been done with reference to New Mexico. See Meyer, *Speaking for Themselves*; Meléndez, *So All Is Not Lost*; and Gonzales-Berry, *Pasó por aquí*.

10. As Bourdieu has described the field of cultural production: "A number of the practices and representations of artists and writers . . . can only be explained in reference to the field of power, inside of which the literary (etc.) field is itself in a dominated position. The field of power is the space of relations of force between agents or between institutions having in common the possession of the capital necessary to occupy the dominant positions in different fields (notably economic or cultural). It is the site of struggles between holders of different powers (or kinds of capital) which . . . have at stake the transformation or conservation of the relative value of different kinds of capital, which itself determines, at any moment, the forces liable to be engaged in these struggles" (*Rules of Art*, 215). For a schematic example of how these competing kinds of power are expressed as specific literary genres in nineteenth-century France, see pp. 122 and 124.

11. For the U.S. case, see in particular Shields, *Civil Tongues*; Warner, *Letters of the Republic*. Franco Moretti's recent work on the spread of the novel across nineteenth-century Europe has usefully complicated nationalistic models of print culture and its relationship to forms of power. Moretti argues that England and France competed for "cultural hegemony" in the rest of Europe by centralizing the production of novelistic models in their capital cities, thereby "depriv[ing] most of Europe of all creative autonomy" (*Atlas*, 186). His history of the spread of these models across Europe produces a striking theory of formal imitation in literature as an index of inequalities in the world market and political systems: "latecomers don't follow the same road of their predecessors, only later: they follow a different, and *narrower*, road. They are *constrained* to it by the success of the products from the core: a veritable 'development of underdevelopment' in the literary field" (191). An "atlas" of the spread of poetic forms might provide a useful counterexample, since the channels of poetry's publication and distribution, as I argue here, are more fluid and less controlled than those of the novel—a genre strongly associated with the rise of the nation-state. Lacking the extensive data that Moretti summons from Europe for the case of the Americas, I cannot make this case with anything like the same kind of rigor; however, I share his concern with mapping the relationship between the consecration of literary genres and other methods of hierarchization: "Forms are the abstract of social relationships: so, formal analysis is in its own modest way an analysis of power" (66).

12. Lewis Hanke's 1964 collection of essays includes contributions from the most important comparative historians of this era: Arthur Whitaker, José de Onís, and Silvio Zavala. More recent efforts in this vein include Lester Langley's important series of transamerican histories. It is important to point out that most of the enthusiasm for "comparative" historical and cultural studies of América has originated in the United States, and that many Latin American scholars are skeptical about this move as a kind of intellectual imperialism.

13. Quijano and Wallerstein, "Americanity as a Concept," 551. In part 2 of this short essay, they take up the historical question of the different developmental trajectories of North and South America after the era of independence, citing "differences in the way power was constituted" under the English and Spanish empires (552).

14. One exception is de Onís, *The United States as Seen by Spanish American Writers*, with its attention to the increasingly estranged diplomatic relations between the United States and Latin America. Comparative works that attend to common tropes with little or no regard of disparities of power include those of Fitz and MacAdam. Besides the works mentioned in n. 6, more socially situated comparative studies include Lois Parkinson Zamora's two books, Richard Morse's *New World Soundings*, and José Ballón's *Lecturas norteamericanas de José Martí*.

15. Spillers, "Introduction," 9.

16. I have relied particularly on the critical historicism exemplified by Limón, *American Encounters*; Foley, *White Scourge*; Weber, *Spanish Frontier*; Pitt, *Decline of the Californios*; Montejano, *Anglos and Mexicans*; Haas, *Conquests and Historical Identities*. Both Saldívar and Mignolo, in *Local Histories/Global Designs*, in somewhat different ways, have adopted Anzaldúa's term as a way to represent and validate subjugated forms of knowledge.

17. Many of the classic texts of American Studies pivot around the three historical events I have just mentioned: R. W. B. Lewis's *American Adam*; Henry Nash Smith's *Virgin Land* and Leo Marx's *Machine in the Garden*; and Alan Trachtenberg's *Incorporation of America*.

18. See the essays in Kaplan and Pease, *Cultures of United States Imperialism*, particularly Kaplan's introduction.

19. See W. A. Williams, *Empire*, 73ff. for a detailed itinerary of such interventions during the century.

20. Pike, *United States and Latin America*. See also Coerver and Hall, *Tangled Destinies*, and J. J. Johnson, *Caricature*. On these transatlantic canal plans, see Parks, *Colombia*, 181–82, and in general McCullough, *Path*.

21. The degree to which such claims to autonomy may be valid is, of course, a longstanding debate in which Marxist theory is particularly invested. In that tradition, Bourdieu follows Barthes in arguing that the intellectual "is constituted as such by intervening in the political field in the name of autonomy and of the specific values of a field of cultural production" (*Rules of Art*, 129). The category of the independent intellectual arises precisely at the moment true autonomy has become impossible.

22. See Rama, *Lettered City*. Ramos, *Desencuentros*, concretizes this thesis. For a somewhat different take on the links between the colonial bureaucracy and nineteenth-century narrative, see González Echevarría, *Myth and Archive*.

23. The phrase comes from Brodhead, *Cultures of Letters*. There is a growing body of work on the social functions of authorship in the antebellum period in the tradition of Charvat. See Newbury, *Figuring Authorship*; Railton, *Authorship and Audience*; Rowland, *Literature and the Marketplace*; Simpson, *Man of Letters*. I have also found useful Gross, *Rise and Fall of the Man of Letters*, on the British scene. However, few of these studies look at lesser-known Men of Letters; rather, they take already consecrated writers and examine their (usually negative) responses to the marketplace. I am interested here in seeing how these popular and publicly known figures were imitated and mirrored by other cultural arbiters on the local level.

24. On the poet as secular priest, see Rubin, *Middlebrow Culture*, 14; J. M. Gutiérrez, *América poética*, viii; Griswold, *Poets and Poetry*, vi.

25. To cite just one instance, one of Emerson's early journal entries about the American cultural scene calls Bryant's poems "chaste, faultless, beautiful, but uncharacterized. . . . They are all *feminine* or receptive and not masculine or creative" (*Journals*, 5:195). On the feminization and decline of the Man of Letters, see Cox, "What Need"; Fletcher, "Whitman and Longfellow"; Haralson, "Mars"; Pattee, *Feminine Fifties*.

26. See Pratt, *Imperial Eyes*, 6–11, and on the Americas, 111–200.

27. In "Ideologies of Lyric," Jeffreys makes a useful distinction between reading for ideological content in lyric and reading for the "ideological expectations of a lyric text"—meaning its position within a social field of production. He recalls Adorno's identification of lyric as an antibourgeois reaction against reification, in the mode of Baudelaire. Other recent critics to explore the ideological conditions of Romantic lyric include Magnuson, *Reading Public Romanticism*, and Janowitz, "Class," whose essay on Chartist poetry of the early nineteenth century resuscitates "the idea of poetry as intervention instead of meditation." This social poetry, Janowitz argues, "asserts itself *as* action, while explicitly claiming and analytically revealing an equally Romantic inheritance" (247–48).

28. Although the definition and function of "lyric" has shifted significantly over time, I assume here the kind of vulgar definition that dominates discourse after Romanticism: that lyric is primarily an exploration of individual subjectivity. On the history of the shaping of this definition, see Lindley, *Lyric*, 49–83; and in general, W. R. Johnson, *Idea*; Welsh, *Roots*.

29. Greene, *Unrequited Conquests*, 4, 2. "Interpretation ought to consider alternatives to the individualist conception of personhood . . . as horizons of the lyric poem" and look at tropes for readings of "lyric's position in relation to events" and "the poem as a medium of social process" (3).

30. Jeffreys argues: "Lyric became the dominant form of poetry only as poetry's authority was reduced to the cramped margins of culture. The rise of the bourgeois-beloved novel to economic and academic dominance displaced poetry's most authoritative narrative form, the patriarchal epic, from the pseudo-Aristotelian

poetic trinity of lyric, epic, and drama. Poetry was pushed into a lyric ghetto because prose fiction became the presumptive vehicle for narrative literature, not because the rhetoric of lyric conquered all of poetry" ("Ideologies of Lyric," 200).

31. See Levine, *Highbrow/Lowbrow.* Nye, *Muse,* has a very useful chapter on the role of popular poetry in the United States; see 88–137. He writes: "The position of the poet in early nineteenth-century society was more elevated and secure than at any other period in American history. People read poetry for amusement, exhortation, and edification; the poet had a place in society which he knew and the public acknowledged" (100). On the novel and its market dominance, see n. 11.

32. Zboray, *Fictive People,* xvi. Although Zboray takes a more or less celebratory view of literacy as a feature that bound individuals together in a sense of national community, other scholars have highlighted the damage that certain kinds of literacy campaigns inflicted on speakers of nondominant languages and on principally oral cultures. See Ohmann, *Politics* and "Literacy"; H. J. Graff, *Labyrinths,* 340–65. For the particular resonance of this issue among indigenous groups, see Lienhard, *Voz;* Vizenor, *Manners.* I am also aware that the term "literacy" itself is deeply conflictual and elides important differences of degree and kind (alphabetic vs. nonalphabetic, hegemonic vs. dominated language, etc.); see opening chapters of Graff's works.

33. See Zboray, *Fictive People,* 233 n. 15, for a problematization of census literacy statistics; he reports that aggregate female literacy was probably less than 50 percent. Census data were not taken for African Americans, who were largely prohibited from acquiring literacy, or for American Indians unincorporated into the state structure. H. J. Graff, *Legacies,* 343–45 gives a more useful breakdown by state, showing the considerable regional differences in literacy—although, again, the missing presence of slaves is elided in the tables. Moreover, census figures are misleading, for instance, with regard to the frontera zone in the southern United States, where individuals who could read and write in Spanish but not in English were identified as illiterate.

34. On the history of Latin American literacy campaigns, see Archer and Costello, *Literacy and Power.* Mexico statistics are from Alvarez, *Enciclopedia.* City size is from Fornet, *Libro,* 74. The other large cities were New York and Philadelphia. My colleague Juan Poblete's forthcoming work, and the current research of other scholars, will greatly expand our knowledge of the history of the book in nineteenth-century Latin America.

35. O'Keeffe, *Visible Song,* 13–14. See, in general, Ong, *Orality;* Stock, *Listening.*

36. Roach, *Cities,* 10, 29.

37. On reading practices in the antebellum period, see Hedrick, "Parlor Literature"; Zboray, *Fictive People,* and the articles collected in Davidson, *Reading;* Hobbs, *Women;* Machor, *Readers.* There is a larger body of work for the colonial and early republican period on the performative aspects of reading, and the locales—coffeehouses, salons, clubs and colleges—where public reading took place. See the work of David Shields.

38. To redefine the varieties of poetry cultures and their penetration into different areas in America is a daunting task. A more fully informed study might measure, among other things, the publication and sales records of books of poetry by individual authors as well as anthologies; the way such figures compare to the production of works in other literary genres; and changes in such preferences over the course of the century. Records of libraries' purchases and lending records would help reconstruct a set of readerly interests. Such a comprehensive survey for the entire hemisphere is beyond my reach here; indeed, it might qualify as its own impossible archival fiction. I have settled instead for a broad-ranging, inclusive effort to locate any of those forms of evidence, and to deploy them in a way that acknowledges their incompleteness, referring whenever possible to more complete studies of the conditions of reading and writing. In general, however, I would like to bring the same open-endedness to the study of printed texts as Roach does to ritual and theater: as iterable acts that, nonetheless, "cannot happen the same way twice" (*Cities*, 5).

39. There has recently been a tremendous critical interest in the question of conventionality in nineteenth-century fiction, most of it with regard to sentimental novels primarily written by women. Not only does such work make "stock" characters and plots newly interesting; it validates the work of nonprofessional—and in many cases, distinctly disadvantaged—writers by investigating the social contexts of their urge to publish. To date, however, very little of this attention has been focused on poetry. One exception is Bennett's *Nineteenth-Century American Women Poets*, 1998, an anthology selected and annotated with readerly communities considered foremost. Another is Loeffelholz, "Who Killed Lucretia Davidson?" Loeffelholz reads through conventional lyric moves to conclude that poetry, "especially poetry by women, was an important staging ground in the early nineteenth-century United States for one of the classic antinomies of bourgeois thought: the dichotomy between head and heart, education and untutored spontaneity. And this antinomy, in its turn, is key to poetry's role in fashioning and reflecting the cultural work of the 'disciplinary-tutelary complex' which forged both terms of the antinomy into a paradoxically spontaneous and literate discipline" (274).

40. This term inevitably invokes Houston Baker's influential discussion of a "vernacular theory" arising from the specific local practices and traditions of African Americans; see *Blues*. More recently, Thomas McLaughlin, *Street Smart*, has adopted Baker's formulation to encompass "the practices of those who lack cultural power and who speak a critical language grounded in local concerns, not the language spoken by academic knowledge-elites" (5–6), founding this idea on Foucault's notion of subjugated knowledges. My usage here tries to avoid romanticizing vernacular practices as purely indigenous to the community in which they are used, in order to account for their selective incorporation of "mainstream" language as well.

41. Cited in S. I. Williams, *Background*, 2:138.

42. Richard, "Latin American Problematic," 455. On imitation and the American originality fetish, see esp. Riddel, *Purloined Letters*; Spengemann, *Mirror*; González Echevarría, *Voice*; and O'Gorman, *Invention*. The trope of origins is also at

the heart of some of the most influential essays about American identity by non-academic writers such as Octavio Paz, William Carlos Williams, and Alfonso Reyes.

43. This point is obviously indebted to Stuart Hall's argument for the agency of recipients or consumers of popular culture forms. While "popular culture" is more often associated with the forms of mass reproduction of the twentieth century, Hall's definition of the term as denoting a process rather than a source is very useful in this context. The study of popular culture, he says, "looks, in any particular period, at those forms and activities which have their roots in the social and material conditions of particular classes; which have been embodied in popular traditions and practices. . . . But it goes on to insist that what is essential . . . is the relations which define 'popular culture' in a continuing tension (relationship, influence and antagonism) to the dominant culture. It is a conception of culture which is polarized around this cultural dialectic. It treats the domain of cultural forms and activities as a constantly changing field. Then it looks at the relations which constantly structure this field into dominant and subordinate formations" ("Notes," 462).

Chapter 2
The Chain of American Circumstance: From Niagara to Cuba to Panama

1. See esp. McKinsey, *Niagara Falls*. McKinsey explores many of the hundreds of nineteenth-century works about Niagara listed in Dow, *Anthology*. There is an enormous bibliography on the American nature cult in early literary works; for a fine summary and extension of this critical tradition, see Jehlen, *American Incarnation*. On the idea of the American sublime in general, I have found most useful Wilson, *American Sublime*; Arensberg, *American Sublime*; and Horwitz, *Law of Nature*, chap. 1.

2. On painters' journeys to South America, see Manthorne, *Tropical Renaissance*. On the uses of Niagara as an international peace symbol, see McGreevy, *Imagining Niagara*, 66–67. The list of distinguished foreign visitors in the antebellum period who wrote about their Niagara voyages includes Charles Dickens, Frances Trollope, and Fredrika Bremer. On the many nuances of the "pilgrimage" to the falls, see McKinsey, *Niagara Falls*, 86–125.

3. Both quotes from Slicer, "Visitors," 310, 313. Of the rest of Dow's poetic inventory (*Anthology*, 693–846), those most frequently referred to during the nineteenth century are John G. Brainard's short 1826 ode and Joseph Rodman Drake's "To the Heroes of Niagara," posthumously published in 1835. Indescribability was a standard sublime convention (see McKinsey, *Niagara Falls*, 41–42; Horwitz, *Law of Nature*, 34–35), but the other important factor in the United States' "failure" to produce a great Niagara ode was that the completion of the Erie Canal in 1825 made the approach so easy and so common that the reverential mode was usurped and eventually replaced by the satiric or skeptical (see McKinsey, *Niagara Falls*, 30–36, 124–25).

Niagara's centrality as a reference point for discussions about national literature is best demonstrated by Longfellow's *Kavanagh* (1849), a fine antebellum satire in which the ridiculed Young American, Hathaway, wants to name his new magazine "The Niagara" despite moderate Churchill's caution that an American will not "necessarily write better poems than another, because he lives nearer Niagara" (366).

4. McGreevy traces the dominance of the death cult at Niagara back to the 1830s and concludes that "visitors regarded Niagara not only as a symbol of death but also as a stage on which to act out individual responses to death" (*Imagining Niagara*, 42; see in general 41–70). On the relation of the "negative sublime," repression, and the fear of death, see Weiskel, *Romantic Sublime*.

5. Brooks, *Idomen*, 194. Interestingly, McKinsey corroborates that early naturalists were fascinated with documenting animal "suicides" at the falls; see *Niagara Falls*, 26–27.

6. The reference comes in V. W. Brooks's chapter on Longfellow: "There was not a poet in New England, except perhaps Maria Gowan [*sic*] Brooks, who could have written a stanza of the translation with which the Cambridge professor had shown his mettle [the *Coplas de Manrique*]. . . . Mrs. Brooks, who had lived in Boston, although she had, decidedly, not been read there, had written with this bell-like depth of tone." His paragraph discussing the merits of *Zóphiël* concludes, "Her notes were an armory of exotic learning. Her fancy, like a Cuban jungle, rioted with Byron and Thomas Moore. But Mrs. Brooks possessed an energy that triumphed over all these fripperies . . . [her poems] had a glow and movement that made it one of the best of a short-lived school, on either side of the ocean" (*Flowering*, 161–62). Perhaps the analogy between the two writers came to Brooks the critic from Longfellow's flattering citation of "those tender, melancholy lines of María del Occidente" in his *Kavanagh* (387). Longfellow owned a copy of *Zóphiël* and placed it on his 1847 reading list.

7. This is a composite of information shared by the major biographical sources on Brooks. The earliest is Griswold, "Sketches," and his introductions to her chapters in *Poets and Poetry* and *Female Poets*. A later investigator is Gustafson, "Maria del Occidente," whose research is the basis for Groves, "Maria Gowen Brooks," and Mabbott, "Maria del Occidente." Mabbott's collection of Brooks-related material is now in the Manuscripts Collection of the New York Public Library.

8. Griswold, "Sketches," 548. The first known critical reference to Brooks is in Kettell, *Specimens*, which says "the study of many languages, a residence where the Spanish is almost exclusively spoken . . . and a struggle to shake off the feebleness, attached by common consent and confirmed by submissive habit, to the minds of women, all conspired to give an unusual energy to the efforts of her muse" (76). Griswold calls Brooks "the only American poet of her sex whose mind is thoroughly educated. . . . Learning, brilliant imagination, and masculine boldness of thought and diction, are characteristics of her works" (*Female Poets*, 150). Aside from the republications of "Niagara" mentioned earlier and the Griswold

anthologies, her poems can also be found in Griswold's *Poetry of Love* (1844); Frances Osgood's *Floral Offering* for 1847 and other gift books; Sampson Law's *Poets of the West* (1859); Caroline May's *American Female Poets* (1849); Longfellow's *Poems of Places* (1879); and Bryant and Wilson's *Family Library of Poetry and Song* (1880).

9. Letter to Rufus Griswold, 12 December 1843, Maria Brooks Collection, New York Public Library. The previous citation is from Gustafson, "Maria del Occidente," xvi. Brooks, like Poe and Whitman, was never above self-promotion: she takes direct aim at the tepid reception of her masterwork in the United States in the preface to the second American edition of 1834, which is included in Gustafson's edition. "No poetical work ever written in the New World has received greater praise in Europe than the Oriental story, or poem, now presented," and as proof she cites Southey's inclusion of her "Disappointment" lyric in "The Doctor" (xlix). "Mr Southey and others think it will take a permanent place among such English works as are thought worth preserving: if that should be the case, it will probably owe its preservation to the nature and treatment of its subject, or, in other words, to its originality" (xlx). Americans, she complains, are too concerned with "utility" to nurture the fine arts.

10. On travel writings about Cuba, see the annotated bibliography by Louis Pérez in Dimock, *Impressions*. Mabbott's annotations to his Brooks collection (see n. 7) indicate that the Boston Public Library has a partial manuscript of a poem about "Leonor, the lover of Columbus," her lost final epic (which she had first committed to memory, then written down—a strange compositional practice she claimed to always follow). However, "Leonor" is written in a different hand than the Brooks letters, casting its authenticity in doubt.

11. Mabbott, a Poe scholar, believes that Poe read Brooks's work ("Maria del Occidente," 422). On Poe in Latin America, see Englekirk, *Edgar Allen Poe*. On Latin American Romantic poetry in general, see Carilla, *Romanticism*; Lazo, *Romanticism*.

12. José María Heredia y Heredia (1803–39) is not to be confused with his cousin, the French Parnassian José María de Heredia (1842–1905).

13. Bryant, *Letters*, 1:227–28, 8 December 1826.

14. See Orjuela, *Revaloración*, for a complete history of the debate over Bryant's authorship of the translation. Orjuela concludes that Thatcher Taylor Payne was the unnamed collaborator. According to Dow (*Anthology*, 703–5), the translation appeared in Barnham's *Descriptions of Niagara*; Johnson's *Niagara: Its History, Incidents, and Poetry*; and Bryant and Wilson's *Family Library of Poetry and Song*. I have also located it in Longfellow's *Poems of Places* (1879) and *The American Common-Place Book of Poetry* (1831). The Houghton Library at Harvard owns an undated broadside of the translation, which looks to me like a product of the late nineteenth century and reprints the poem along with a brief biography of Heredia and the comment "All other efforts to picture the American continent appear tame and insignificant when compared to the inspired words of this Spanish exile."

15. See Bryant, *Letters*, 1:248.

16. The major biographical sources from which I draw are S. T. Williams, *Background*, 2:122–51; C. S. Johnson, *Politics*; Godwin, *Biography*; and C. H. Brown, *Bryant*.

17. See María del Carmen Ruiz Castañeda's introduction to Heredia, *Minerva*; Augier, *De la Sangre*; Chacón y Calvo, *Estudios*; Vitier, *Crítica*, 283–89; and Montes-Huidobro, *Laúd*, 7–22. On Heredia's contributions to U.S. print culture, see Cortina, "History," 50–51. On Cubans in the United States prior to 1868, see Poyo, "With All, and for the Good of All," 1–19.

18. During this period, U.S. economic interests in Latin America in general were less extensive than those of Britain; they had not yet solidified into the more overtly colonial relations of corporate control over local governing bodies that would be firmly in place by the end of the century. See Bulmer-Thomas, *Economic History*, 35–37. Much of the English-language travel literature on Cuba prior to 1860 is obsessed with the island's potential for fantastic agricultural yields, which suggests an obvious influence of the word on the world. But Colás, "Of Creole Symptoms," makes the argument that such foundational Latin American poems as Andrés Bello's 1826 "Silvas americanas" were also complicit in such economic colonialization (see 386–88).

The first hydroenergy project was proposed for Niagara in 1876 (McKinsey, *Niagara Falls*, 256); generation began in 1895.

19. See Horsman, *Race and Manifest Destiny*; Florescano, *Memory, Myth, and Time*; Maddox, *Removals*.

20. *Bosquejo ligerísimo de la revolución de México* by Rocafuerte y Bejarano, 1822. Anáhuac is the Nahuatl name for the central valley of Mexico.

21. Heredia, *Niágara*, 58–59. All subsequent citations from Heredia's poetry and travel narratives are from this edition, with references given in the text.

22. Heredia's *Poesías* were reprinted several times in New York: by Roe, Lockwood in 1853 and 1862, and by Ponce de León in 1875, as well as in the anthology *Joyas de la poesía española*, ed. Javier Vingut (New York, 1855). Translations of Heredia's poems were published in James Kennedy, *Poets of Spain and Spanish America* (Havana, 1844). According to Chacón y Calvo, *Estudios*, Heredia lived at 88 Maiden Lane, in a Frenchman's home. On the early Hispanophone community in New York, see Poyo, "With All, and for the Good of All," chap. 1; on exile print culture outside Cuba, see Fornet, *Libra*, 174–79. On Varela's importance, see Luis Leal's introduction to *Jicoténcal*, xiii–xv.

23. Major biographical sources include Chacón y Calvo, *Estudios*; Augier's introduction to *Niágara*; and Vitier, *Poetas cubanos*. On Heredia's supposed treachery, his reception in Cuba, and the resuscitation of his reputation by Martí, see also Martínez, *Domingo del Monte*, 215–17. Prefacing the second edition of his collected poems (Toluca, 1832), he had written: "El torbellino revolucionario me ha hecho recorrer en poco tiempo una vasta carrera, y con más o menos fortuna he sido abogado, soldado, viajero, profesor de lenguas, diplomático, historiador y poeta a

los 25 años. Todos mis escritos tienen que resentirse de la rara volubilidad de mi suerte. La nueva generación gozará días más serenos" [The whirlwind of revolution has made me travel a vast range of careers in a short period of time, and by the age of twenty-five I had been a lawyer, soldier, traveler, professor of languages, diplomat, historian, and poet, with greater or lesser luck. All my writings consequently suffer from the strange volubility of my fortunes. The new generation will enjoy calmer days] (qtd. in Chacón y Calvo, *Estudios*, 70).

24. Thus the scene of poetic composition resembles that of Brooks's poem. In his "Carta de Niágara," which was eventually published in a leading Cuban periodical, Heredia writes the following about what prompted the poem's composition: "Yo no sé que analogía tiene aquel espectáculo solitario y agreste con mis sentimientos. Me parecía ver en aquel torrente la imagen de mis pasiones y de las borrascas de mi vida . . . ¡Oh! ¿Cuándo acabará la novela de mi vida, para que empiece su realidad? Allí escribí apresuradamente los versos" [I don't know what analogy that lonely, bitter spectacle has with my feelings. I seemed to see in that torrent the image of my passions, and all the false starts of my life. . . . Ah! When will the novel of my life end, so that its reality can begin? There I hastily wrote the poem] (253).

25. In the "Carta de Niágara," he makes this link between the experience of a Caribbean hurricane and Niagara even more explicit: "El dios que se mira en el mar y habla en medio de las tempestades puso también su mano en los desiertos de Norteamérica y el Niágara, grande y sublime como los truenos, y el océano, dejó una huella profunda de su omnipotencia" [The god who can be seen in the ocean, who speaks in the midst of storms, also left a deep trace of his omnipotent hand on the deserts of North America and Niagara—as grand and sublime as the thunder and the ocean] (253). See McVay, "Sublime Aesthetic," on Heredia's reading of Burke and Blair, his interest in Ossian, and the "sublimity of moral conduct" in "Niágara."

26. Augier speculates that this coalescence of the erotic and the spatial took root when Heredia had to leave his first love on a brief trip to Mexico at the age of fifteen: "la circunstancia de haber sido en Cuba donde Heredia despertó las sensaciones del amor . . . fue estímulo decisivo para moldear su emoción patriótica" [the circumstance that it was in Cuba where Heredia first awoke to the feeling of love . . . was a decisive influence in shaping his patriotic emotion] (*De la sangre*, 25). But as a consequence Heredia's love lyrics are abstract, devolving into a kind of "panteísmo patriótico" (27). Also see Vitier, *Crítica*, 284: "El Eros poético era ya indiscernible del Eros político." Vitier's meditation on the erotic feeling of "las palmas, ¡ay! las palmas deliciosas" in this poem (287) is very convincing.

27. In his Niagara letter, Heredia mentions his excitement at walking near the edge (253), and recounts a story about an Indian who was sucked into the rapids (254–45), showing that he was no less affected by Niagara's death cult than Brooks. Also, in his "Carta sobre los Estados Unidos" (1824), he says that he was in such despair at leaving Cuba that he briefly considered suicide (*Revisiones*, 249).

28. Heredia, *Revisiones*, 249–50.

29. Heredia, *Discurso*, 26. On his publications during this period, see González, *Ensayos*, 65–69; Orjuela, *Imagen*, 71–75.

30. On Byron, see Heredia, *Revisiones*, 111. For Heredia's review of the miscellany *El aguinaldo* (Philadelphia: Carey, Lea and Carey, 1829), see *Revisiones*, 156–57. The Carey franchise was one of the major publishers in the United States. Heredia praises the engravings and the transamerican content of the work, which included a poetic dialogue between Washington and Cortés. He also reviews his friend del Monte's edition of the works of Nicasio Gallego, a Spanish poet and popularizer of Ossian (whom Heredia had also translated); the edition was dedicated to Heredia.

31. James Kennedy published an English translation of some of Heredia's poems in Havana in 1844. Javier Vingut, a Cuban who taught Spanish at New York University, brought out *Joyas de la poesía española*, which featured several Heredia poems, at his own expense in that city in 1855. His wife, Gertrudis Vingut, translated the book as *Selections from the Best Spanish Poets* (New York, 1856), and included the translation attributed to Bryant. For the poem's other nineteenth-century appearances, see n. 22.

32. Bryant, *Letters*, 1:227. The unsigned translation originally appeared as "Niagara, from the Spanish of José María Heredia," *United States Review and Literary Gazette*, January 1827, 283–86. Orjuela, *Revaloración*, rehearses a long-standing bibliographical argument over the translation's source and concludes that the unacknowledged collaborator on "Niagara" was Thatcher Taylor Payne.

33. See Charvat, *Origins*, 14, 60, on the rejection of Byronism in the United States, and in general 3–22 on the development of antebellum poetic taste and the critical alliance with bourgeois morality.

34. See Lozada, "Catastrofismo," who points out that Heredia's trip to the falls was preceded by a visit to the Philadelphia Museum of Natural History, and that his trip was in part prompted by his interest in the geological-theological problem of catastrophism.

35. Heredia, *Revisiones*, 168.

36. Wilson, a very sympathetic reader of Bryant, calls this a "commonplace convention of transport" and concludes that it is "a rather picturesque poem trying to be sublime" (*American Sublime*, 128–29). On the importance of Bryant as literary critic and his familiarity with British and German aesthetic theory, see *American Sublime*, 120–23 and Ferguson, "William Cullen Bryant."

37. Bryant, *Poetical Works*, 130–33.

38. Baxter, "Dilemma," 17. Weinstein, "Bryant," and C. H. Brown, *Bryant*, 317–23, speak to the conflict between Bryant's editorial policies and the nostalgia of his poetry. A less critical summary and sampling of his editorials for the *Post* is in Bryant, *Power*. Other treatments of Bryant and Manifest Destiny can be found in Newlin, "*The Prairie*," and Zanger, "Premature Elegy."

39. The theory, which one can see at work in Jefferson's *Notes on the State of Virginia* as well, was popularized by Barton's 1798 *New Views of the Origin of the*

Tribes and Nations of America, which proposed that the Mound Builders were "further advanced in civilization than the greater number of nations north of the empire of Mexico" (qtd. in Miller, "Nationalism," 229). See also Ostrowski, "I Stand," 300–302 on the theory of cyclical history.

40. This is not to deny the existence of a good number of earlier Indianist poems. Lydia Sigourney wrote many, including "The Cherokee Mother," "Indian Names," and "The Indian's Welcome to the Pilgrim Fathers." But although Sigourney's work partakes of the same kind of nostalgic sentimentality evident in this section of "The Prairies," its violence is not so explicit, and indeed the vivid detail of the scene is uncharacteristic of Bryant's other works as well.

41. Maddox, *Removals*, esp. 5–17, 29–38; H. Carr, *Inventing*, esp. 22–50, 60–68; and in general Deloria, *Playing Indian*, and Pearce, *Savagism*.

42. "The Hurricane. Written in the West Indies," *Talisman*, New York, 1828, 114.

43. The strong ambivalence I see in these closing lines runs counter to prevailing critical opinion on Bryant, which views him primarily as a celebrant of unity and domestic order despite his frequent explorations of the elegiac mode. See, e.g., Pearce, *Continuity*, 206–10; Duffey, *Poetry*, 6–15, 43–60; Gelpi, *Tenth Muse*, 2–4, 63–67.

44. On the fascination with the Spanish American past as early as Freneau and Barlow, see Wertheimer, *Imagined Empires*. Besides several general histories of South America, English translations of Clavijero's *History of Mexico* were published in 1806 and 1817, and Thomas Francis Gordon's *History of Mexico* was published the same year as "The Prairies." See S. T. Williams, *Background*, 1:157–60 for a complete inventory of such works before Prescott. Bryant was also acquainted with the early Mayanist John L. Stephens, whose *Incidents of Travel in Central America, Chiapas, and Yucatan* created a sensation on its publication in 1841 (*Background*, 2:131), as well as with Prescott and Ticknor (2:123, 324).

On the complicity of Romantic archeological and historical views of Aztec and Mayan civilization with the discourse of "right conquest" surrounding the U.S. war on Mexico, see Johannsen, *Halls*, 154–60, 241–69, and Ernest, "Reading."

45. See Lewis, *American Adam*. He speaks of Bryant's pursuit of a "rarified and beautiful blank" (88) in the prairie.

46. Bryant, "Jicoténcal," *United States Review and Literary Gazette*, February 1827, 336–46 (hereafter cited parenthetically in text). The first edition of *Jicoténcal* was published anonymously by Guillermo Staveley in two volumes, and has recently been republished with an introduction by Luis Leal in which he offers compelling evidence that the author was Félix Varela (xviii–ixix). Heredia has been discussed as one of the possible authors (xxv), and the two were certainly close: Varela reviewed Heredia's poetry and helped publicize his work in Cuba and among U.S. exiles (xxxi). Leal notes that Bryant's was the only review of *Jicoténcal* published in English *or* Spanish during the nineteenth century (xix). See also Castillo-Feliú's introduction to the recent English translation.

47. In addition, Bryant endows the Tlascalans with the same nobility that the Mound Builders possess: "it seems like an anecdote of Grecian or Roman greatness of mind, to read that this officer [Jicoténcal] sent provisions to the famishing troops of Cortés, and waited until they had refreshed themselves before he would give them battle" (339).

48. For a summary of Bryant's supportive editorials on the South American republics, see C. T. Williams, *Background*, 2:328. Mexico, as I discuss in chapter 4, was a glaring exception to this generosity. To get a sense of the current of national prejudice against Spanish America that Bryant fought, his biographer and son-in-law's words are revealing: "Even for the less imposing revolts of the South Americans against the Spanish yoke, he uttered many a friendly word, defending the character and conduct of such chiefs as Bolívar" (Godwin, *Biography*, 1:261). See also Pike, *United States and Latin America*, 40–85.

49. On the history of the doctrine, see in general E. R. May, *Making*; Merk, *Monroe Doctrine*; and especially Perkins's three-volume study, which demonstrates how little importance was initially attached to Monroe's statement among Latin Americans (*Monroe Doctrine, 1823–26*, 156–57, 198–200). He calls 1826–41 a period of "quiescence" during which interhemispheric relations were not particularly friendly, but the document was not interpreted in the United States as a free license for interventionism and expansionism, either. Polk's direct reference to it in relation to U.S. interests in Texas, in December 1845, marked that change (Perkins, *Monroe Doctrine, 1826–1867*, 87–89). The citation of the doctrine itself is from Ammon, *James Monroe*, 488.

50. Bulmer-Thomas, *Economic History*, gives the three-year average of export values circa 1850 as about US$24 million for Mexico versus $26 million for Cuba; the disparity widened by 1870 ($21 million vs. $67 million) and 1890 ($50 million vs. $90 million), leveling out to a similar figure only in 1912. These figures also give some sense of the tremendous dominance of Cuban export products within the hemispheric market despite its relatively small size and population. Only Brazil had higher export values through the rest of the century, with Chile and Colombia following Mexico (433).

51. For del Monte's critical influence, see Martínez, *Domingo del Monte*, 145–46. "Las sombras" was published in the *Gaceta de México*, 23 October 1825, just after Heredia's arrival in Mexico.

52. The Chagres (or Chagre) is the major river in Panama. Its invocation here implies that the American empire of the past stretched from North to Central America—poetic license, perhaps, but also a utopian projection. In one of Heredia's later excursions, he ascended the Nevado de Toluca, a 15,000-foot mountain in the Sierra Madre; at one point in his beautiful letter on this excursion (published in 1832) he writes, "Dos días forman época en mis recuerdos por haberse asociado a grandes misterios y prodigios de la naturaleza. En el último subí al Nevado de Toluca; el anterior me vio inmóvil, atónito, al pie de la gran catarata del Niágara" [Two days make up a single event in my memory as being associated with the grand

mysteries and wonders of nature. In the latter, I climbed the Nevado of Toluca; the former saw me immobile and dumbstruck, at the foot of the great cataract of Niagara] (*Revisiones*, 261).

53. To cite only two of the best-known examples: in "Proyecto," a poem of Cuban liberation, he refers to "la esclava tierra" [the land that is enslaved]; in "A Emilia," he writes, "De mi patria / bajo el hermoso desnublado cielo / no pude resolverme a ser esclavo, / ni consentir que todo en la Naturaleza / fuese noble y feliz menos el hombre" [Beneath the beautiful cloudless sky / of my country, / I couldn't resign myself to being a slave, / nor allow that everything in Nature / should be noble and happy except mankind] (*Niágara*, 61, 57).

54. Fliegelman traces Jefferson's thinking about the colonial power "reducing us to slavery" and calls this "a sentiment that everywhere accompanies the Revolutionary insistence on self-determination." He also observes, "The metaphorization of slavery in Revolutionary discourse as any constraint on the private will had the rhetorical consequence of trivializing the literal reality of chattel slavery at the same time that it permitted a new kind of sympathetic identification with blacks as, ironically, another oppressed people" (*Declaring Independence*, 141–42).

55. See Sundquist, *Nations*, 31–35, 135–43, 182–87, 199–221.

56. "In 1823, when a band of Cuban conspirators descended on Washington looking for assistance, Adams had shunted them aside, observing later that Cuba better served the U.S. as a weak vassal in the Spanish Empire until the day arrived when it would fall into America's outstretched hands. Clay still professed his old commitment to the revolutionary tradition, but his views were moderating noticeably as the framer of American foreign policy" (Langley, *America*, 50). Neither of the two U.S. representatives ever made it to Panama; one died of fever on the way and the other was too worried about meeting the same fate to continue. See also Schoultz, *Beneath the United States*, 12–13; Stansifer, *United States–Central American Relations*, 25–33.

57. Heredia, *Revisiones*, 135–36. Note the original uses the intimate form of address.

58. Cited in Augier, "Heredia," 742. Augier caustically remarks, "Parecía olvidar que las riquezas del norte tenían un origen igual que las de Cuba" [he seemed to forget that the riches of the North had the same origin as those of Cuba]. This is something of an oversimplification, but the point is well taken.

On U.S. racial fears about "Latins," see Horsman, *Race and Manifest Destiny*, 231–35, 280–86; Johannsen, *Halls*, 22–24; Schoultz, *Beneath the United States*, 3–58.

59. See Reed, *Guerra de Castas*, 128–29. Eduardo Galeano's poetic history of Latin America describes this event in a way that perfectly summarizes the paradox of many of the revolutionary generation of poets whose livelihoods depended, directly or indirectly, on the racialized exploitation of labor. In "Poeta en crisis," he depicts the Spanish poet José Zorrilla, whose works inspired many of the poets in this study, mourning his lost investment in just such a scheme to export Mayan

slaves to work the sugar plantations in Cuba (*Memoria de fuego*, 224–25). Thanks to Gloria Chacón for bringing this to my attention.

60. On the rise of the *azucarero* class, see Ortiz, *Cuban Counterpoint*, 1950–71, and Kutzinski, *Sugar's Secrets*, 93–95, 228–30, and in general on sugar's permeation in Cuban literary culture. On Horace's career, see Mabbott, 419–20, and Gustafson, "Maria del Occidente," ix–xiv. On Brooks's contact with Ticknor, see Mabbott, "Maria del Occidente," 422. Although she was literally insulated from Anglo-American literary culture in Cuba, Brooks did travel to the United States, Canada, England, and France on several occasions during her twenty-two years of residence there, and according to Griswold, *Female Poets*, entertained and held salons.

61. See Instituto de Literatura y Lingüistica (Academia de Ciencias de Cuba), *Perfil*, 190–98. According to Fornet, there were 670 periodicals published in Cuba between 1800 and 1868; 59 percent of them were in Havana (*Libre*, 27). Matanzas was the second most important publishing center. The first Cuban poetry anthology was published there in 1833, and it was also the home of the important paper *La Aurora*. Brooks portrays Cuban criollos and their passion for letters positively in *Idomen*. There is no reason she would not have read *La Moda*, which besides being an important source of veiled progressive statements published her favorite authors—Chateaubriand, Scott, Byron.

62. To cite just a few further examples: "Despondency . . . will as surely pass away, if they can only bear it awhile, as that flowers and verdure will spring from those sods of Canada, which are seen crushed and hidden with snow-drifts; or that night and clouds must give place to those heavens of gold and azure which show, in bold relief, the mamey and palm-tree of Cuba" (Brooks, *Idomen*, xii). Idomen, who dresses all in white in both countries, prepares for her suicide by removing her white linen "of Cuba" and putting on a white robe "just washed by a laundress of Canada" (146). The "timid doe" of Canada and the "delicate dove of Cuba" will both "brave danger in defense of her young" (170). The hero Ethelwald's hand "was white as the petals of the magnolia of Florida, and warm and soft as down beneath the wing of the ptarmigan of Canada" (81).

63. In the original editions, the notes were jumbled on the same page as the poetic text. Gustafson's 1879 edition assails this as too distracting and exiles the notes to the back—losing, in the process, much of the dynamism I at least find in *Zóphiël*. Caroline May, who disapproved of the eroticism of *Zóphiël*, even wrote: "The Notes to this poem are full of curious information, and more interesting than the poem itself" (*American Female Poets*, 58).

64. Brooks, *Zóphiël*, 206–7. All references to this poem and its notes, given subsequently in the text, are to the 1879 Gustafson edition. Gustafson does not, however, reprint the interesting preface to the first edition of 1825 (which contains only Canto One), which I cite as *Zóphiël: A Poem* to avoid confusion.

65. *Idomen*, likewise, engages those aspects of New World civilization to which Anglo-Americans were most likely to respond sympathetically. Dalcour gives

Idomen a copy of Marmontel's *Les Incas*; she later is enthralled by a play on the same theme (145). She also imagines that her lover looks like a white "warrior of Potosí" (81).

66. See especially Groves, "Maria Gowen Brooks," who discusses Brooks's destabilization of gender roles, and Bennett, *Poets*, 23–24. Her work is also included in the recent nineteenth-century poetry anthology by Janet Gray, *She Wields a Pen*.

67. Brooks, *Zóphiël: A Poem*, 18, 8. Subsequent references to this preface given in the text. Again, it is intriguing to speculate on whether Brooks might have personally known any of the well-placed women writers who began to publish in Cuba during the period. She surely knew of the island's most famous literary citizen, Gertrudis Gómez de Avellaneda, but Avellaneda was living abroad at the time. Luisa Campuzano's work in progress on Cuban women writers such as Luisa Pérez de Zambrona, Mercedes Valdés Mendoza, and the Condesa de Merlin has begun to explore their lost lives; see also her "Muchachas de la Habana."

68. Bennett, who otherwise praises Brooks's ingenuity and feminist consciousness, takes her to task for rendering the slavery theme abstract in *Zóphiël*: "To my knowledge, the fact that her romantic pleasure in this lushness was dependent on slave labor did not bother her. Indeed, despite slavery having been notorious in Cuba for its brutality, she takes no notice of it anywhere in her printed texts. Brooks's lack of political awareness sets her strikingly apart from every other major woman poet of the first half of the century" (*Poets*, 23). The difficulty in securing copies of Brooks's work (*Idomen* has never been republished, although Gustafson apparently had plans to do so) makes Bennett's oversight of the 1825 preface, and of her pro-Indian poem "The Oration," understandable.

69. To drive this point home, the later Preface lectures readers on Latin American history, pointing out that Las Casas himself had begun the importation of Africans into America in order to save the Indians: "The natives of Cuba, as well as the gentle and highly civilized Peruvian, wept, repined, and perished" under plantation conditions (xv); but Africans supposedly thrived on them. The dolphin of "Niagara" appears again in a far more ominous context to prove this assertion: "A dolphin cannot endure the air; and an eagle must die in the limpid waves of the Bahamas" (xiv).

70. Letter to Robert Southey, 23 October 1837, Maria Brooks Collection of the New York Public Library Manuscript Division. I cite from Mabbott's typescript of "The Oration" in that collection. Brooks mentions in a footnote to the poetic "Invocation" to the 1825 edition of *Zóphiël* that it "was intended to precede a series of poems entitled Occidental Eclogues; which work the writer has never found opportunity to finish." The note glosses references to Indian life and America's "bright native streams," and mentions the "dark-bosomed maid that makes the wild her home" (*Zóphiël: A Poem*, 18). *Judith, Esther, and Other Poems* includes a number of then-fashionable Indian-themed poems as well.

71. See, for instance, scenes on pp. 33, 40, 42–43, 63, 67, 202, 211–13.

72. A note to the "Stanzas to Niagara" makes a point of saying that the scene witnessed by Idomen and her guide has changed since their visit: "Since the falls have become a fashionable resort, wild animals, of course, have most of them deserted the place" (233). Brooks recommends Chateaubriand's description of Niagara while it was "untouched by any hand save that of Nature" (234).

73. Letter to Rufus Griswold, 24 July 1844. Griswold reprints part of the letter along with the poem in *Female Poets*, 80–81. Curiously, he makes minor changes to her original words.

74. See Paquette, *Sugar*, 209–66; Kutzinski, *Sugar's Secrets*, 81–100; and Stimson, *Cuba's Romantic Poet*, 72–84.

75. Griswold, *Female Poets*, 86.

Chapter 3
Tasks of the Translator: Imitative Literature, the Catholic South, and the Invasion of Mexico

1. "The Poetry of Spanish America," *North American Review* 142 (January 1849): 129–60. The essay is unsigned, but Hurlbert's authorship is confirmed because he includes a revised version of the piece in *Gan-Eden* (Boston: J. P. Jewett, 1854). The translations contained in the unsigned article were, however, frequently misattributed to Bryant (see, e.g., Stimson, *Orígenes*, 68). Page citations are hereafter given parenthetically in text.

2. "The vapors partly mantling the hull, through which the far matin light from her cabin streamed equivocally . . . [the ship] showed not unlike a Lima intriguante's one sinister eye peering across the Plaza from the Indian loop-hole of her dusk *saya-y-manta*. It might have been a deception of the vapors" (Melville, *Billy Budd and Other Stories*, 162).

3. Franchot's overarching argument is that "anti-Catholicism operated as an imaginative category of discourse through which antebellum American writers . . . indirectly voiced the tensions and limitations of mainstream Protestant culture" (*Roads*, xvii). See especially her chapter on the "attraction of repulsion," 197–220, and on responses to Mariolatry, 143ff.

4. Harold Dijon's 1890 article on Sor Juana in the *Catholic World* mentions earlier tributes to her in that publication in April 1871, suggesting that she (and, by extension, the presence of a Latin American literary culture) was known at least to U.S. Catholics.

5. See, in general, Dumond, *Machete*. I comment further on U.S. responses to the Yucatán revolts in chap. 4.

6. Hurlbert is rather protective and modest about his translations because, according to him, the originals "are very spirited, but so intensely Spanish American in feeling and expression, that we dread to submit them in an English dress to American eyes." Here again, he feminizes Latin American "modesty" in a protective, if patriarchal, manner. His English sources on Plácido, which provide further evi-

dence of the poet's North American following, include William Wurdemann, who lent Hurlbert his "large and very complete collection of the pieces published by him [Plácido] in the Matanzas Aurora" (151). Wurdemann, a Philadelphia doctor, had recently written his *Notes on Cuba* (1844), in which he mentions a pilgrimage to María del Occidente's home, so he obviously had a good deal of interest in Cuban and Cubanist writing.

Hurlbert also thanks "an anonymous writer in the New York Tribune" for a translation of "Hymn to Liberty." On Plácido in the United States, see chap. 2, no. 74.

7. Pike, *United States and Latin America*, gives numerous examples that demonstrate the anxious U.S. tendency to render the other America less threatening by feminizing it; see esp. xiv, 5–30, 44–60. The political cartoons in J. J. Johnson, *Caricature*, are also very convincing in this regard. The work of Antonia Castañeda gives more localized detail about how this operates on the borderlands; see esp. "Political Economy." On the Latin American analogue of feminization and nation-building, see Sommer, *Foundational Fictions*, and Masiello, *Between Civilization and Barbarism*.

8. I am not suggesting that this Mexico/Cuba split appears in Hurlbert's essay; he does not devote sufficient space to Mexico and Central America to make this a fair judgment. I will, however, return to the idea of differential stereotyping of the Latino/a body, which continues to inform disparate treatments of the major Latino groups in the United States. Anne Norton makes a similar argument about the northern depiction of the "conquered" southern states following the U.S. Civil War, showing the range of forms that such feminization takes—from courtship and submission, to penetration and "deserved" rape. See *Alternative Americas*, esp. 164–99.

9. Amy Kaplan coins the phrase "manifest domesticity" to link this national effort to the feminine sphere, arguing that "the concept of female influence at the heart of the sentimental ethos is underwritten by and abets the imperial expansion of the nation" ("Manifest Domesticity," 599). See also, in general, the psychologizing approach of Merk, *Monroe Doctrine*.

10. On Translation Studies as a central tool in decolonization, see Bassnett, *Translation Studies*. On Anzaldúa as an exemplary figure for translation/transculturation, see Saldívar, *Dialectics*, 83–85, and Alarcón, "Traddutora, Traditora."

11. See Charvat, *Profession*, and Haralson, "Mars," on Longfellow's popularity among different classes of readers.

12. Long, *Pioneers*, 163.

13. S. T. Williams, *Background*, 2:153–79, 335–36. Longfellow was ever concerned to maintain the hard-won linguistic facility of his youth. When he entertained Domingo Faustino Sarmiento on his first American tour in 1847, the future Argentine president gushed to a friend, "He speaks Spanish better than you or I" (Sarmiento, *Travels*, 54).

14. L. A. Sánchez, *Historia*, 340–43; de Onís, *United States*, 100, 157–58; Engelkirk, "Notes," 295. Engelkirk, *Bibliografía*, 51–52, gives a good sense of where Longfellow's works were published in Latin America, and of who his translators were. The selections under "Enrique Wadsworth Longfellow" in the *Antología de poetas americanas* (n.a., 1941), 344–56, suggest which of his poems were particularly compelling (the early short lyrics). Most of the translators can be found as primary authors elsewhere in the volume. In Rafael Pombo's *Traducciones poéticas*, pp. 44–61 are devoted to Longfellow, who is the major presence in the volume after Shakespeare and Byron.

15. See Barnstone, *Poetics*, 108–13.

16. See Alonso, *Castellano*; Morse, *New World Soundings*, chap. 1.

17. Rama, *Lettered City*, 21. Rama describes this as a change from a closed cultural economy (during the colonial period, he says, "the producers and consumers of this literature were largely the same individuals, and their verses moved in a closed circuit that originated in viceregal power" [18]) to a limited market system. González Echevarría, *Myth and Archive*, likewise sees nineteenth-century literature as emerging from the colonial bureaucratic hierarchy, although he stresses the letrados' dependence on previous forms like historical *crónicas* and does not mention poetry. See also, in general, Zea, *Pensamiento*.

18. See Carilla, *Romanticismo*, 1:67–95 on the French, 114–48 on French translations of German, and 176–77 and 197–203 on the general fear of French linguistic interference.

19. Ibid., 1:115.

20. Next to the developing Whitman myth, Longfellow has to be portrayed as pathetically unaware of the creative genesis going on around him, representing all that was conventional and hidebound in Cambridge. Matthiessen deals the death-blow to the "plaster bust" of Longfellow's reputation by reinventing him, in the 1950 *Oxford Book of American Poetry*, as a simple balladeer (Fletcher, "Whitman and Longfellow," 133–34). The mirror of this *other* American literary history would seem to confirm Angus Fletcher's recent insinuation that the elevation of Whitman's reputation that culminated in *American Renaissance* required an equal and deliberate denigration of the other "good gray poet."

21. Venuti, *Invisibility*, 7; see also 88–118. Venuti is foremost among a group of translation theorists influenced by poststructuralism (especially de Man's reading of Benjamin's "Task of the Translator" and Derrida's "Des tours de Babel") who are attempting to rid translation of its centuries-old stigma as an inferior, second-order form of expression. See also Steiner, *After Babel*, 236–78, and Barnstone, *Poetics*, 83–107.

Rama, *Lettered City*, describes the apex of letrado authority as a "situation of diglossia" that "exhibited a sharp and habitual distinction between two separate kinds of language"—one public, baroque, manneristic, bureaucratic and the other "the informal speech of everyday life" (31). Thus, in some sense, the letrados were always translators, moving "back and forth between the two lexical codes," so that you have *costumbrista* writers of the late century providing actual glosses alongside their texts. Rama traces the gradual confluence of these two "languages" to suggest that truly original writing comes about when letrado translation ceases, when the "explanatory metalanguage" is absorbed "into the work's narrative language." In another influential essay, he labels this process *transculturación*, following Fernando Ortíz.

22. Venuti, *Invisibility*, 20; emphasis mine.

23. Ibid., 68–74. Schleiermacher's 1813 lecture *Uber die verschiedenen Methoden des Ubersetzens* is now considered one of the cornerstones of modern translation theory. According to Berman, *Experience*, translation was one of the foundation stones of modern German culture. It "rested on a chauvinistic condescension toward foreign cultures, a sense of their ultimate inferiority to German-language culture, but also on an antichauvinistic respect for their differences, a sense that German-language culture is inferior and therefore must attend to them if it is to develop" (99). Although Venuti does not discuss this crucial period of literary nationalism in the Americas, the paradox of national chauvinism coexisting with national inferiority anxieties during the first century of the republics is visible perhaps more powerfully than in Germany or France. See Pym, *Chronology*, for an outline history of Spanish and Spanish American translators, with an emphasis on their work as a political action.

24. Venuti, *Invisibility*, 119–20, 123.

25. See Hatfield, *New Light*. Longfellow's Germanism was, in fact, a sore point to his harshest critic, Edgar Allan Poe, who complained that both the poet and the nation were too moralistic. In his review of Longfellow's *Ballads* (1842), Poe writes: "Of the translations we scarcely think it necessary to speak at all. We regret that our poet will persist in busying himself about such matters. *His* time might be better employed in original conception" (*Essays and Reviews*, 692). Of course, Poe himself is an interesting figure in the as-yet-unwritten history of antebellum translation, not because he practiced it much but because of the deep, underlying fears of plagiarism and secondariness that prompted his excessive defenses of his own originality and his accusations of plagiarism by Longfellow. In the context of this discussion, what is perhaps most pertinent is that Poe was an early champion of the theory of the translator's invisibility: criticizing a "too literal" translation of Sue's *Mystères de Paris*, he writes in 1846, "The phraseology of every nation has a taint of *drollery* about it in the ears of every other nation speaking a different tongue. Now, to convey the true spirit of an author, this taint should be corrected in translation. We should pride ourselves less upon literality and more upon dexterity at paraphrase. Is it not clear that, by such dexterity, *a translation may be made to convey to a foreigner a juster conception of an original than could the original itself?*" (*Marginalia*, 127). Riddel, *Purloined Letters*, makes Poe's anxiety about the status of original and translation the center of his argument that American literature and criticism, in general, is plagued by an impossible desire to avoid repetition and assert its originality at all costs.

26. See Wagenknecht, *Mrs. Longfellow*, for an argument that Fanny was the unnamed collaborator on much of Longfellow's work. On the coincidence of this sentimental event with Longfellow's increasing popularity, and on women's access to the "masculine" work of anthologizing and working in literary criticism, see my "Feeling for the Fireside."

27. Longfellow, *Letters*, 1:551, 23 November 1843. This letter begins by expressing an anxiety about the sense that he has not produced much original work since his marriage: "A dozen poems on slavery, written at sea, and a translation of sixteen Cantos of Dante is all I have accomplished in that way." But his statement that doing translation work makes him feel "lazy" is contradicted by the great attention he pays later in the letter to the importance of making translations available to the general reading public; he apologizes for not having published more translations of Freiligrath's work and praises the other's translations of both his work and Bryant's. In light of the association I traced in chapter 2 between Niagara and rambunctious nationalism, which Longfellow critiques in *Kavanagh*, the final line of the letter is amusing: "I must go now and bathe in 'gods great waterfall' Niagara!" (552). Freiligrath, ironically, became one of the first international champions of the socialist element in Whitman's work.

28. See, in general, Spencer, *Quest*, and Ruland, *Native Muse*.

29. Carey and Hart was one of a number of publishing houses spun out of the great dynasty founded by Matthew Carey; another, Lea and Carey, published Spanish works as well. See Tebbel, *History*, 373–74. The *Poems of Places* volume on the Americas includes poems by Maria Gowen Brooks as well as Bryant and Heredia.

30. Longfellow, *Kavanagh*, 369. When the gung-ho Hathaway produces his idea for "a great national drama, to be set in New Mexico," Churchill wonders skeptically, "it does not strike me as particularly national," to which Hathaway responds, "Prospective, you see!" Churchill is humoring his excesses; he says, "I perceive you fish with a heavy sinker,—down, far down in the future, among posterity, as it were" (370–71). Compare this proleptic vision with Whitman's New Mexico speech, described in chap. 4.

31. Longfellow, *Life*, 3:94–95. This is cited as a letter to John Neal dated 2 August 1867.

32. Qd. in Haralson and Hollander, *Encyclopedia*, 269.

33. This is not to say, of course, that they were the first. As I argued previously, many U.S. poets of the antebellum period saw translating from the modern languages as a kind of apprenticeship for their own creative evolution. Charles Timothy Brooks was better known as the translator of Schiller and *Faust I* (1856) than for his own poetry, and Emerson translated Dante's *Vita nuova*. Interestingly, a good number of the early female poets included translations in their collections: Maria White Lowell translated from the German; Elizabeth Ellett, from French and Spanish; Anne Lynch, from French and later Italian and German; Eliza Lee Follen, from French and German. Jane Johnston Schoolcraft, an Ojibwa woman and senti-

mental poet, was an essential translator who enabled her husband's influential "renditions" of Native folklife and culture. Unlike in Latin America, however, the translation of poetry was not considered serious literary work for an ambitious poet by the end of the nineteenth century, if the near absence of translations from anthologies at that period is any indication. Griswold's vintage anthology of women poets, and Bennett's modern one, do include some of these translations.

34. Longfellow, *Life*, 3:370. Venuti is also careful to point out that Schleiermacher's statement is "shaky grounds for an ethics of translation" (*Invisibility*, 111). He himself lays out such a postcolonial ethos in *Scandals*.

35. Beatty, *Bayard Taylor*, 275–76.

36. As Beatty comments, Taylor "liked writing from behind the curtain" (Ibid., 58)—perhaps we should more accurately say the *veil?*—of an other culture. As a young man, he might have been the model for Longfellow's character Hathaway: he was a close associate of the engine behind Young America, Evert A. Duyckinck, and in an 1847 letter he enlisted Duyckinck's help in researching a projected poem on the "Aborigines of America," north and south: "Prescott's 'conquest of Mexico' furnishes, perhaps, one of the best statements concerning the Aztecs, which exists in *our* language but there may be many interesting works in the Spanish, on the subject. I should be obliged for any information of this character, which you may be able to give. There are many fields yet untouched in the fast-spreading domain of American literature" (Wermuth, *Letters*, 64).

37. Simon, *Gender*, esp. 1–38. Her analysis begins with the Renaissance translator Jean Florio's equation of "defective" translations with "reputed females," claiming that "the femininity of translation is a persistent historical trope, 'Woman' and 'translator' have been relegated to the same position of discursive inferiority" (1). See also Chamberlain, "Gender."

38. Besides Horsman, *Race and Manifest Destiny*, and Johannsen, *Halls*, see Vázquez, *Mexicanos y norteamericanos*; Brack, *Mexico*; Eisenhower, *So Far from God*.

39. "Spoilers" editorial quoted in C. H. Brown, *Bryant*, 317; subsequent quotations from Weinstein, "Bryant," 19, 21. Weinstein judges Bryant's position on Mexico as shamefully out of keeping with his otherwise left-liberal political sympathies. Bryant reputedly said to a Mexican ambassador some decades later that it had been "a war in which I take no pride" (C. H. Brown, *Bryant*, 496).

40. Although James Russell Lowell's *Biglow Papers* is probably the best-remembered literary statement against the war, William Lloyd Garrison, Orestes Brownson, and Whittier were its most high-profile opponents. Whittier's journal and letters describe several antiwar protests in New England throughout 1846 and 1847; see esp. Whittier, *Letters*, 2:69–71. Thoreau, of course, made his principled stance on "resistance to civil government" in part as a protest against the war: "this people must cease to hold slaves, and to make war on Mexico, though it cost them their existence as a people . . . [we must] do justice to the slave and to Mexico, cost what it may" (*Writings*, 4:362).

41. Johannsen, *Halls*, 216–17. Longfellow also includes the work in *Poems of Places*, vol. 30.

42. Whittier, *Works*, 36.

43. Ibid., 308–9.

44. Longfellow, *Life* 1:76ff. For a good summary of Longfellow's political sympathies during the late 1840s and 1850s, see Ferguson, "Longfellow's Political Fears."

45. Qd. in Cameron, *Longfellow*, 23. As one critic qualified, "it is an epic, however, whose heroism is . . . the heroism of virtue and endurance, or religion and love, not the heroism of brutality" (43). The luckless Acadian bride demonstrates utter vulnerability to the emotions that fill her as well as self-containment in the face of those feelings—just like the youth in "Excelsior!" and the subtitular Young Man of "A Psalm of Life," two of Longfellow's similarly successful attempts to transgress gendered spheres of behavior.

46. The ideological purposes to which the *Evangeline* myth has been put in French Canada are laid out exhaustively by Taylor, "Poetry," and, more controversially, by Chevalier, *Semiotics*, who claims that the poem has an ambivalent political message, suspicious of armed resistance but also critical of assimilation of the conquered. Chevalier sees this as the basis of pre-1960 Quebecois political thought. For a good summary of pop-cultural versions of the story in the United States—which peaked around 1920, the date of the silent film version—see Hawthorne and Dana, "Origins," 201–2 and Brasseaux, *In Search of Evangeline*.

47. Longfellow, *Works*, 62. Subsequent quotations from this edition, cited parenthetically in text.

48. See Eisenhower, *So Far from God*, 65–67.

49. Franchot, describing *Evangeline* as "America's most popular nineteenth-century example of Catholicism as Protestant romance" (*Roads*, 203), argues that Longfellow's gravitation toward Spanish and Italian themes is typical of his culture's ambivalent association of Catholicism with the splendid corruption of the Old World past. Reading Evangeline's journey through the wilds as a version of the American tourist's fetishistic pilgrimage to holy sites in Europe, Franchot suggests that Longfellow projects his own "New England sense of exile from an unrecoverable Catholic community" onto his heroine (205).

50. Engelkirk, "Notes," 301; L. A. Sánchez, *Historia*, 1:340. After Morla Vicuña's translation, which was published in Spain, Colombia, and Chile in separate editions, came others: by J. T. Medina (Santiago de Chile, 1874), Vicente de Arana (Bogotá, 1882), Juan de Izaguirre (Mexico, 1885), and Rafael Merchán (Bogotá, 1909). Engelkirk, *Bibliografía*, lists twenty editions prior to 1915 (51). For Pombo's correspondence with Longfellow, see Engelkirk, "Epistolario."

51. Morla Vicuña, *Evangelina*, xi–xii. All page citations from Morla's preface and translation are hereafter given parenthetically in text.

52. "Evangelina, romance de la Acadia," *El Mundo Nuevo*, 10 December 1871. Even secular liberal writers in Latin America at the time were heavily indebted to Chateaubriand. As they saw it, he had invented a literary past for the New World. He was beloved of conservatives, in contrast, because (in *La génie du christianisme*) he identified the progressive design of future history with the Catholic nations of the Americas, which bore a special responsibility to see to it that the pagan world

would surrender ecstatically—like the feminized warrior-convert Atala—to that design (see Carilla, *Romanticismo,* 1:87–89; Sommer, *Foundational Fictions,* 24–25).

53. Brodhead, *Cultures of Letters,* 13–47, has influentially linked this cliché of the sentimental novel—education in self-control—to emergent institutions of social control in the 1840s and 1850s.

54. Julian describes the reading as a moment of silent communion between them, as both were mysteriously moved: "My father listened silently and intently, and, as I read the last verses, a feeling came upon me that *there was something in the occasion more memorable than I had thought of,* so that I could hardly conclude without a falling of the voice." Nathaniel murmured, "I like that" (Hawthorne, *Hawthorne and His Wife,* 2:335; emphasis mine). Their shared emotion simply indicates the trained response of even the most sophisticated antebellum readers to the conventions of devotional discourse. For an account of the "passing" of the Evangeline story from Hawthorne to Longfellow, and for excerpts from Hawthorne's enthusiastic review of *Evangeline,* see Hawthorne and Dana, "Origins," 171–74, 199–200.

55. The number of Irish and German Catholic immigrants in Louisiana increased greatly in the 1840s and 1850s, adding to the longstanding population of Acadians, Creoles, and *gens libres de couleur.* Ahlstrom, *Religious History,* 540–54.

56. Although controversial, the most influential broad history of Mexicanos/Chicanos remains Acuña, *Occupied America,* who has insisted on the paradigm of Chicanos as a colonized people. See also McWilliams and Meier, *North from Mexico;* Griswold del Castillo, *Treaty;* Robinson, *Journeys;* and the essays in Weber, *Foreigners.* More regional sources include Montejano, *Anglos and Mexicans;* Pitt, *Decline of the Californios;* Haas, *Conquests and Historical Indentities;* Monroy, *Strangers;* Rosenbaum, *Resistance.*

57. In general, see Chabrán and Chabrán, "Press"; Kanellos, "Study"; and Leal, "Press." As Kanellos puts it, "newspapers have functioned as purveyors of education, high culture, and entertainment. During the nineteenth century and the first half of the twentieth, they became the principal publishers of literature . . . as a function of cultural preservation and elevating the level of education of the community" ("Study," 108). On the New Mexico press, see Meyer, *Speaking for Themselves,* and Meléndez, *So All Is Not Lost,* as well as many of the essays in Gonzales-Berry, *Pasó por aquí.* On the racial composition of settlers to northern Mexico, see Weber, *Spanish Frontier.*

58. See Chabrán and Chabrán, "Press," 364–65; Reilly, "War Press."

59. *El Bejareño* 7 February 1855.

60. *El Bejareño* 29 March 1856.

61. Pitt, *Decline of the Californios;* Monroy, *Strangers,* 219–22; and Griswold del Castillo, *Barrio,* 125–27, have studied the politics of *El Clamor Público* in some detail. It may have been named after a well-known publication in Madrid that published in the 1840s and 1850s; the Cuban Rafael de Mendive worked for that paper before being exiled to the United States in the 1870s, where he translated and was translated by Longfellow.

62. *El Clamor Público*, 18 September 1855. This article is attributed to *La Crónica*, and although there was a Spanish paper of that name the following decade in Los Angeles, I cannot find any evidence that there was another *Crónica* at that time in the United States. It may have been a Mexican paper.

63. *El Clamor Público*, 25 September 1855.

64. On Vallejo's risky love of books, see R. Sánchez, *Telling Identities*, 118–19; on his post-1848 protests against the racialization of language and his defense of Spanish, see 298–302. On Escobar, see Meyer, *Speaking for Themselves*, 59–97.

65. The reference is to Weber, "'Scarce More Than Apes.'" On racial stereotyping of Latin Americans, see chap. 2, n. 58.

66. Torres, *World*. See also Leal, "Truth-Telling Tongues."

67. *El Clamor Público*, 19 June 1855.

68. *El Clamor Público*, 28 August 1855. On the dispossession of the californios, see Griswold del Castillo, *Barrio*, 105–15, R. Sánchez, *Telling Identities*, 272–85, Monroy, *Strangers*, 203–5 and 228–32.

69. *El Clamor Público*, 12 July 1856.

70. *El Clamor Público*, 23 August 1856. The Hugo preface argues that readers need to consume what a writer produces in order to give that writing any meaning—a democratic empowerment of the reading audience that resonates with Ramírez's local editorial philosophy.

71. *El Clamor Público*, 7 August 1855.

72. *El Clamor Público*, 25 September 1855.

73. The periodical titles and locations are given at the beginning of the Works Cited. The partial inventory of poets in issues I was able to examine is as follows. Mexican: Salvador Díaz Mirón, Federico Escobedo, Enrique González Martínez, Juan de Dios Peza, Guillermo Prieto, Isabel Prieto, Emilio Rabasa, José Rosas Moreno, Luis G. Urbina, José María Vigil. Spanish: Vital Aza, Federico Balart, Gustavo Adolfo Bécquer, Eusebio Blasco, Ramón de Campoamor, José Echegaray, Gabriel García Tassara. Cuban: Julián del Casal, Gertrudis Gómez de Avellaneda, Rafael María Mendive, Enrique Piñeyro, José Agustín Quintero, Pedro Santacilia. New Granadan/Colombian: José Caicedo Rojas, Miguel Antonio Caro, Gregorio Gutiérrez González, Rafael Pombo. Venezuelan: Abigaíl Lozano, Juan Antonio Pérez Bonalde. Argentine: Esteban Echeverría, Rafael Obligado. Guatemalan/Salvadoran: José Batres. Chilean: Augusto Ferrán. Peruvian: Numa Pompilio Llona.

Chapter 4
The Mouth of a New Empire:
New Orleans in the Transamerican Print Trade

1. See Sommer, "Supplying Demand," and Santí, "Accidental Tourist," on "second-order appropriations" of Whitman in Latin America. Allen and Folsom, *Walt Whitman*, reprints translations of several key statements by writers like Martí and Borges about Whitman on 71–127, along with an introductory essay by Fernando Alegría. In Erkkila and Grossman, *Breaking Bounds*, Jorge Salessi and José Quiroga argue for an unrepressed reading of the homoerotic Whitman in the Latin

American tradition; see also Sylvia Molloy's essay in the same volume, which discusses Martí's sense of familial affiliation with Whitman as homoerotic.

2. On antebellum Creole society in general, see Tinker, *Creole City*; Reinders, *End of an Era*; Holditch, *In Old New Orleans*. On race in particular, see Domínguez, *White by Definition*, and Hirsch and Logsdon, *Creole New Orleans*. Jeran Johnson's article in Hirsch and Logsdon, *Creole New Orleans*, and Bell, *Revolution*, 40–46, describe the impact of refugees from Santo Domingo on the Creole population and their intermarriage with *gens libres de couleur*. Bell details the participation of free persons of color in the Mexican wars of independence on 49–63.

3. Ryan, *Civic Wars*, 22–23. In both New York and New Orleans in 1850, more than 40 percent of the population was foreign-born, which ranks them among the most diverse U.S. cities at the time.

4. Roach, *Cities*, 179.

5. For meditations on trans-Caribbean slavery, see Curtin, *Rise and Fall*; Gilroy, *Black Atlantic*; Paquette, *Sugar*.

6. J. S. Kendall, "Some Distinguished Hispano-Orleanians," 15.

7. Hamnett, *Juárez*, 51–53.

8. See C. H. Brown, *Agents of Manifest Destiny*, chap. 4 on Soulé and 13–14 on Slidell.

9. MacCurdy, *History*, claims that there were a dozen Spanish periodicals in the city between 1840 and 1851, the period of greatest Spanish immigration and filibustering activity (20). In the course of this investigation I found references to other periodicals not included in MacCurdy's definitive bibliography. In *La Patria*, 18 March 1849, there is a lengthy review of Spanish papers in the city preceding that publication. According to this article, there was a short-lived 1828 newspaper titled *El Español*; another called *El Misisipí* published by Ramón Soler for several months between 1834 and 1835; a *Fénix* that published a few issues in 1843; and one "señor Cocco" gathered subscribers to a publication called *La Avispa* and invested in a press, but subscribers never received copies. "Vingut" (perhaps the Cuban Javier Vingut, who later taught languages at New York University from 1848 to 1857) produced *La Indiana* for a few months, and "el señor Quintana Warnes" published *El Padilla* for more than six months in 1845.

10. Carbonell y Rivero, *Poesía*, 151.

11. Reilly, "War Press." The Democratic *Delta*, the middle-of-the-road *Crescent*, for which Whitman wrote, and the *Commercial Times* were, whatever their other editorial positions, so strongly hawkish that they were collectively called the War Press of New Orleans. On Kendall, see Copeland, *Kendall of the Picayune*. His history of the war was copiously and beautifully illustrated with lithographs by the German Karl Nebel (who had last been to Mexico a decade before); see G. W. Kendall, *War*. There is a recurring advertisement in *La Unión* throughout 1851 for a "Historia Ilustrada de la Guerra entre los EEUU y Méjico" for sale at the Librería La Patria, but I cannot determine whether this was an actual translation of Kendall's text, an original history written in Spanish, or simply a Spanish ad for the English book.

12. Reilly, "War Press," 90–91; Reilly, "Voice of Dissent." In the latter article especially, Reilly has done a remarkable job of retracing the responses of English-language newspapers to the existence of *La Patria*. Although this work is invaluable, it is based on readings of only a few copies of the newspaper itself. Apparently Reilly did not have access to the holdings of the Historic New Orleans Collection, which has on microfilm *El Hablador* for 1846; the entire runs of *La Patria* for 1846 and 1848; and the whole of *La Unión* from 3 January 1851 to 20 August 1851, just before the editorial offices were attacked and burned by a mob. While we are still lacking the crucial years 1847 and 1850 (there are stray copies from 1847 at the American Antiquarian Society, which I have not seen, and one at the Louisiana State Museum and Archives, which I have), it remains for a historian of journalism to return to this greater archive of primary sources and make another effort to write a more complete history than Reilly's.

13. Reilly, "Voice of Dissent," 333.

14. See Cohen, *Directory*. Only three of the others were English. The French bilingual paper *L'Abeille/The Bee* was an important presence up to the Civil War.

15. Qtd. in Reilly, "Voice of Dissent," 327.

16. *El Hablador*, 1 January 1846. See also 11 January 1846.

17. The article on 18 March 1849 giving an overview of the history of Spanish papers in New Orleans (see n. 9) ends with an endorsement of "la importancia de sostener en esta ciudad un periódico español . . . sostener con decoro y energía los intereses de aquellos que se ven aislados,—puede decirse—en un pais extraño" [the importance of maintaining a Spanish newspaper in this city . . . to uphold, with dignity and energy, the interests of those who find themselves isolated, one might say, in a strange country].

18. *La Patria*, 3 September 1846.

19. *La Patria*, 9 April 1846.

20. Reilly, "Voice of Dissent," 332–36.

21. *La Patria*, 10 December 1846.

22. *La Patria*, 4 June 1846.

23. *La Patria*, 4 June 1846. Merk, *Monroe Doctrine*, and Johannsen, *Halls*, interpret the broad psychological reasons for the Mexican War within the terms of romantic adventurism.

24. *La Patria*, 14 November 1848.

25. *La Patria*, 18 May 1849.

26. *La Patria*, 19 September 1849

27. For an overview of the Latin American debate, see the sources cited in n. 1. Grunzweig, "Noble Ethics," traces some of the defensiveness among Whitman's partisans in the international Left with regard to the accusations made by González de la Garza and others about his imperialism. Of his editorials in the *Eagle*, he writes, "the pieces quoted are journalistic and have little in common with his later poetry" (154). He concludes, "Whitman himself had been unable to differentiate between progressive internationalism and what would later be called imperialism" (157), dis-

tinguishing between "expansionist" and "imperialistic" rhetoric on the basis of proximity. Mexico was a neighboring territory; therefore, the invasion was not an imperial act. One wonders why Cuba, only seventy miles from U.S. territory, would not also be counted as a "neighboring" country. Grunzweig still seems under the sway of the Monroe Doctrine's language of proximity.

28. Whitman, *Poetry and Prose*, 1201; Krieg, *Chronology*, 17–18.

29. Loving, *Walt Whitman*, 114. "New Orleans in 1848," in Whitman, *Poetry and Prose*, 1199–1204.

30. The myth of the Creole woman comes from a letter to John Addington Symonds, and was fostered by Horace Traubel's recollection that a "grandson" had once come to visit Whitman. Allen, *Solitary Singer*, 91–98 gives a good overview of the eventual discrediting of the story, which was helped by the proof in Holloway, *Uncollected Poetry and Prose*, 1:xlvii–lii that the original gender of the lover referred to in "Once I Pass'd through a Populous City" was male before being changed to female for inclusion in the 1860 *Leaves*; this now argues for New Orleans as an origin point for Whitman's recognition of his queerness. Most early biographers through Rubin, *Historic Whitman*, thus place a strong emphasis on the New Orleans period. This can still be seen in J. Kaplan, *Walt Whitman*, and Allen, *Solitary Singer*. The more recent trend among biographers, however, is to downplay it as relatively insignificant: see, e.g., D. S. Reynolds, *Whitman's America*; Loving, *Walt Whitman*. Greenspan, in his painstaking reconstruction of the early work, typifies this shift: "it seems to me extremely unlikely that the young man who returned to his family in Brooklyn that May . . . came back a radically changed man. . . . Nor does his writing during these months, the place which would most likely register any sudden change of sensibility, reveal major changes" (*Whitman and the American Reader*, 63–64). I am not arguing for any "major changes" in Whitman's literary output during 1848 but looking for the seeds of his discursive claim on "universal citizenship" as it specifically pertains to the South and to "Spanishness."

31. Qtd. in Brasher, *Whitman as Editor*, 88. These editorials (some of the most virulent were suppressed by Brasher) are the source of González de la Garza's claim in *Walt Whitman* that Whitman's writings for the *Eagle* created the conditions of possibility for anti-Mexican racism among Anglos—a phenomenon that surely went deeper than Whitman.

32. Whitman, *Poetry and Prose*, 1200. "Chapparal" was John H. Peoples, a veteran correspondent for the *Delta* who had been stolen away by the *Crescent* (Reilly, "War Press," 89).

33. Holloway, *Uncollected Poetry and Prose*, 1:188, 190, and 186.

34. Whitman, *Early Poems*, 6–7, 10–11.

35. Ibid., 42–43. Whitman later rewrote this poem for inclusion in *Collect*, and I agree with Brasher that the highly didactic revision—which enjoins the "helmsman" to be "steady" and omits the Gothic details of the original altogether— is inferior to the original. On Whitman's strong affection for Longfellow and *Evangeline*, see Price, *Whitman and Tradition*, 56–61, 82–83. Whitman's line "shapes of

mist and phantoms dim" recalls the last line of *Evangeline* ("here in the dusk, in the darkness deep and dim"). This affection makes Stovall, *Foreground*, shake his head at Whitman's reading habits, commenting that there is "no way to account for" his love for *Evangeline* except to conclude that "there was a residue of conservatism in his nature that he never lost" (282). Bryant provided a model of a poet who was also engaged with the world, and with politics. Longfellow's life would have been more difficult for Whitman to emulate, but if, as I have argued, the former was something of a populist intellectual, then this also helps account for Whitman's indebtedness to him.

36. No letters from Whitman during this period survive. However, he seems to have guided some of Jeff's, which are accordingly reproduced in Whitman, *Correspondence*, 1:27–36.

37. Whitman, *Poetry and Prose*, 1201.

38. Some short filler pieces in the *Crescent* that spring seem quite likely to have come from the hand of Whitman: the notes that "the vegetation hereabouts is as far advanced as it is in the latitude of New York by May," and the appreciation of that wonderful "acceleration" of blossom-time in the South. See the 7 March 1848 issue, p. 2, and 28 March's "Nights of New Orleans."

39. Loving, *Walt Whitman*, 115.

40. See esp. the 7 March, 15 March, 20 March, 10 April, 14 April, 5 May, 13 May, and 19 May issues.

41. The first two quotes are from the lead editorial on 11 March 1848. The "Thanksgiving sermon" appeared on 16 March 1848. Although most of the *Crescent*'s articles on Mexicans reveal a similar racism, a strong desire for Mexico is also evident. A small item on p. 4 of the 16 March issue uses statistics about Spain's financial management of its North American and Caribbean colonies during the 1810s to prove that Mexico had the greatest natural resources among them, and that "Louisiana . . . [and] the fertile isles of Cuba and Porto Rico . . . were thus dependent on the surplus wealth of Mexico."

42. Stovall, *Foreground*, 140–47.

43. There is some controversy over the authorship of the pieces from the *Crescent* that Holloway, in *Uncollected Poetry and Prose*, identified as Whitman's, and that White included in his 1969 bibliography of Whitman's journalism. Loving, *Walt Whitman*, argues that many of these sketches, such as "Miss Dusky Grisette," are not his (120–21). I am inclined to be more generous: "Habitants of Hotels" references the latest habits and customs in New York, suggesting that the author had recently been there. "Hero Presidents," with its disappointment that the war hero Zachary Taylor, who is described arriving at a theater in New Orleans, turned out to be a Whig, fits with Whitman's other writings on the subject. "University Studies" is highly Emersonian, even lifting phrases from "The American Scholar," which also seems in keeping with Whitman's preferences. Loving's argument that the disputed sketches do not always resonate with Whitmanian style is legitimate, but it also seems plausible that he was experimenting, like any writer, with different

voices and generic registers. Thus I am treating "A Walk about Town," for which I find the evidence of both style and content compelling, as Whitman's work, though the attribution can never be final. ("Habitants of Hotels" is also interesting to think about as a production of Whitman's observations: it describes a kind of rough who "generally live[s] in the West, or South America, or Mexico.") Finally, in issues of the Cre:cent that immediately postdate Whitman's departure for New York, such sketches disappear altogether.

On flâneurisme as characteristic of Whitman's style, see esp. Brand, Spectator, 156–70, who discusses Whitman's love of "panoramic and spectatorial" walks in New York, which are visible in all his descriptions of the city. Brand sees this trend starting around 1846.

44. Holloway, Uncollected Poetry and Prose, 1:234. Page citations are hereafter given parenthetically in text.

45. On Whitman and race, see esp. Beach, Politics, chap. 2; Erkkila, Whitman; Klammer, Whitman, Slavery; Sánchez-Eppler, Touching Liberty; Larson, Whitman's Drama; Thomas, Lunar Light; and D. S. Reynolds, Whitman's America.

46. Loving, Walt Whitman, 119.

47. Sánchez-Eppler, "'To Stand Between,'" is most critical of Whitman's claim to be "the poet of slaves and of the masters of slaves," arguing that his weak effort to overcome racial divisions through binaries such as body/soul "must remain contingent upon the very divisions it claims to heal" (924).

48. Sommer, Proceed with Caution, 52.

49. Whitman, Poetry and Prose, 584–85. I reprint here the 1892 version.

50. Ibid., 7. This portion of the prose preface would be reworked into the later poem "By Blue Ontario's Shore."

51. Fragment, dated 1863; Whitman, Notebooks, 1965. "Is not the America West side of the Mississippi destined to preponderate over the East side?" he asks rhetorically in one fragment (1943). A talk with Eliza Farnham, author of an 1856 book on California life, prompted an enthusiastic note about how "every thing seems to be generated and grow on a larger scale. . . . Humanity is also freer and grander . . . life seems more intense and determined . . . the tulé grass—the cañon the ranch—the adobé hut—the gulch—the vaquero—" (Notebooks, 1949). See also the fragments on pp. 1947–48, 1963.

52. Whitman, Poetry and Prose, 318.

53. Cited in Shively, "Mexican War," 428.

54. Whitman, Poetry and Prose, 1146–48, quotation on 1147.

55. Reilly, "Voice of Dissent," 337.

56. See Jumonville, Bibliography. Although most extant Spanish imprints from New Orleans date from the period of Spanish governance, evidence of an antebellum market for such books has survived. A few works about Texas and Mexico were published in Spanish by Benjamin Levy in the 1830s; and J. L. Sollée reprinted Spanish classics in the late 1840s and sold various pamphlets, as well as a translation of the Louisiana constitution. Some business and governmental contracts

appear in the 1850s and 1860s as well. An edition of the poetry of Gabriel de la Concepción Valdés, "Plácido," held by the Biblioteca Nacional José Martí in Havana bears a New Orleans 1847 imprint but no publisher. It may be a reprint of the 1845 Lockwood and Son New York edition.

57. *La Risa*, 1848, p. 1.

58. Kanellos and Martell do not list a New York paper of this name during the period, although there was a weekly paper in 1874. The name *El Correo de los Dos Mundos* echoes that of a very influential French-Spanish newspaper published in Paris.

59. Both the edition at the Bancroft Library and the one at the Biblioteca Nacional in Havana are dated New York, 1852, well after Gómez and Alemán's paper had folded, and the title is somewhat different: *España y los Estados Unidos: Las expediciones piráticas de ciudadanos americanos contra la isla de Cuba y las relaciones entre los Estados Unidos y España que de aquellas han resultado.* I have not yet been able to locate a copy of the edition advertised in *La Unión* to compare the two, but given the well-developed connections between Spanish print communities in New Orleans and New York it seems highly unlikely that they would be different translations.

60. *El Hablador*, 1 January 1846. On colonial censorship see Fornet, *Libro*, 28–35.

61. I have not yet been able to identify this poem as the work of any known Cuban writer. Although it strongly resembles to the works of the later *Laúd del desterrado* group, it cannot be found among their works. Heredia also had a poem titled "La patria," on which this may be partially modeled, although its language is less pointedly "Cubanized." Gómez de Avellaneda's "Al partir!," which begins "Perla del mar . . . hermosa Cuba!" is also a classic of the genre.

62. See Poyo, "With All, and for the Good of All," 1–19; Foner, *History*, 11–29. A similar logic of compromise informed liberal sentiment about slavery. Most, like del Monte, found the institution distasteful but felt that abolition would bring civil chaos or a Haitian-style race war. On the contradictions of Cuban liberalism prior to the Ten Years' War, see in general Martínez, *Domingo del Monte*.

63. Prieto's elegy, "A Escobedo: Un Recuerdo," was first published in the 17 February 1844 *Diario del Gobierno de la República Mexicana* in New Orleans. His observations of the city and its Cuban exile community are discussed in chapter 5.

64. *La Patria*, 15 September 1848.

65. *La Patria*, 5 July 1846.

66. *La Patria*, 28 May 1846; 8 December 1848; 20 August 1848; 11 April 1849.

67. "Los enemigos de la patria," *La Patria*, 18 October 1846.

68. In general, see Chaffin, *Glory*; he reviews the historiography on 1–10. Foner, *History*, 41–66, concurs with most post-revolutionary Cuban historians in labeling López unsympathetically as a tool of southern slaveholding interests. Chaffin presents him as a charismatic opportunist with a genuine desire for Cuban self-rule but who lacked the ability to perceive the severe ideological rifts within his

own coalition. De la Cova, "Filibusters and Freemasons," details a number of trans-national connections in the northern as well as southern states.

69. Merk, *Monroe Doctrine*, presents *La Verdad* as a sham mouthpiece for O'Sullivan and Beach, excluding the Cuban contribution almost entirely. Rodrigo Lazo, in "The Cuban Newspapers of New York" (unpublished MS), powerfully contradicts that assertion.

70. New Orleans *Delta*, 30 April 1850. Announcements appear on the same date in the *Picayune* and the *Commercial Bulletin*.

71. Reilly, "Voice of Dissent," 325–26. The next Spanish paper in New Orleans, *El Pelayo*, appeared in September 1851 under the editorship of E. San Just (perhaps a pseudonym?). On a smaller scale than *La Patria* and *La Unión* and without their literary ambitions, surviving issues of *El Pelayo* contain ads for the remainder of the inventory of the Librería La Patria and list Gómez as a sales agent for various books and subscriptions. An anti-López poem titled "Invasión de la Vuelta-Abajo" appears in the 15 November 1851 issue; the last extant issue was published in December 1851.

72. In his critical introduction to the new edition of *Laúd*, Matías Montes-Huidobro makes this general point. All subsequent citations of the poems are from this edition and are hereafter given parenthetically in the text.

73. Ibid., 134–36; Carbonell, *Poetas; Enciclopedia de Cuba.*

74. For examples of such negative dismissals of the Laúd Poets, see Instituto de Literatura y Lingüística, *Perfil*, 318.

75. See especially the work of Américo Paredes and María Herrera-Sobek, who have in different ways made powerful arguments for the centrality of the corrido and its heroic figures to Chicano/a poetics. There is an extensive bibliography on this topic that I can only touch on here except to suggest its interesting parallels with the Cuban poets' gesture toward the folk form.

76. Montes-Huidobro, *Laúd*, 159–62.

77. According to J. S. Kendall, who reports on the missing trunk, Turla married a New Orleanian and is buried in St. Vincent de Paul cemetery ("Some Distinguished Hispano-Orleanians," 50). There is a poem dedicated to him in the *Diario del Gobierno de la República Mexicana*, New Orleans, 10 January 1844.

78. Jorge Carrión, introduction to Santacilia, *Pedro Santacilia*, xiv.

79. In various catalogs I have found, among a small sampling of Santacilia's considerable work, *Lecciones orales sobre la historia de Cuba* (New Orleans, 1859); a collection of poetry, *El arpa del proscripto* [The Outlaw's Harp], with its imitative title (New York: L. Hansen, 1864; also J. Durand, 1864); *El papa en el s. XIX*, 2d ed. (New Orleans: Imprenta de Sherman, Wharton, y co., 1855); and *La clava del indio: Leyenda cubana* (Mexico, 1862; also New Orleans: Imprenta L. E. de Cristo, 1859). The last edition sounds as though it may be a false imprint ("ley de Cristo"?). Fornet remarks that Cuban imprints sometimes listed New Orleans as their place of publication to escape scrutiny.

80. *El Nuevo Mundo*, 2 April 1866.

81. Instituto de Literatura y Lingüistica, *Perfil*, 317–18. See also Chacón y Calvo, *Cien mejores poetas*, 177–78.

82. Teurbe Tolón had used a similar passage referring to the Babylonian captivity from Isaiah as an epigraph for his "Cantar de los cubanos," written in New York, in 1850; it appears on pp. 35–36 of *Laúd*. Of course, this particular use of biblical typology was very important to early African American writing as well.

83. Fernández de Castro, *Ensayos cubanos*, 121.

84. "Joseph A. Quintero," New Orleans *Daily Picayune*, 8 September 1885. The obituary's version would place him in the Boston/Cambridge area from roughly 1842 to 1848. However, Harvard University has no record of Quintero's enrollment there. See also Dabney, *100 Great Years*, 247.

85. Quintero's death certificate says he was a "resident of this city 34 years," which if accurate would put his return around 1851–52. Succession Document 17, 140, Civil District Court of New Orleans.

86. The Rüeckert poem appears in Longfellow's *Poets and Poetry of Europe*, 343–44, as "The Patriot's Lament." Quintero did know German, but if he was so well acquainted with Longfellow it is also likely that he adapted, or knew, the English translation of the poem. In any case, his adaptation is substantially different: he changes Rüeckert's fruit orchard to Cuban coffee and sugar; he includes a fisherman rather than a hunter of stags; and most interestingly, he excludes both Rüeckert's stanza about the poet who writes songs to combat tyranny—as well as the final three stanzas, which give a moral and an invocation.

87. This and the other letters between Quintero and Longfellow are in the possession of the Houghton Library Longfellow Collection [bMS Am 1340.2 (5694), (4569), (4456)], and are published by permission of the Houghton Library, Harvard University.

88. "Lamar, Mirabeau," *Handbook of Texas Online*.

89. *El Ranchero*, 19 July 1856.

90. "Quintero, José Agustín," *Handbook of Texas Online*.

91. Under the general editorship of George Squires, another paper by this name would be published from 1866 to 1870. *El Mundo Nuevo/La América Ilustrada*, the important illustrated weekly edited by Enrique Piñeyro and later by Eugenio María de Hostos, was also initially funded by Leslie.

92. There are no surviving copies of this paper. Kanellos and Martell list a paper running from 1836 to 1859, *Noticioso de ambos mundos: Dedicado a las artes, comercio, agricultura, política y bellas artes*. Quintero's letter suggests that this journal, if it is indeed the same, lasted at least a year longer.

93. Mahoney, *Mexico and the Confederacy*, 58–65. See also the obituary referenced in n. 84 and Montes-Huidobro, *Laúd*, 146–52, which draws heavily from Carbonell, *Poetas*.

94. Fernández de Castro, *Ensayos cubanos*, 127–31.

95. Mahoney, *Mexico and the Confederacy*, 63.

96. New Orleans *Picayune*, 2 February 1866.

97. Quintero, *Code of Honor*, 18.

98. Dabney, *100 Great Years*, 247–48, 266. When Quintero died in 1885, of cirrhosis of the liver, he left no estate except a claim against the U.S. government for $700 for "services rendered," probably in his consulships. His obituary stated that his health had been failing for "over a year," and closes with praise of his "eventful and romantic career." "In New Orleans no man was more widely known or more generally beloved. We who knew and loved him most of all cannot yet realize that he has indeed gone forever beyond the reach of earthly companionship, but we know that in the days to come many a word in kindness spoken, many a gentle, unobtrusive deed of charity, will recall to us 'the touch of a vanished hand and the sound of a voice that is still,' to keep his memory fadeless and precious to our hearts." Somewhat curiously for a lawyer and a consul/diplomat, he died intestate. The appraiser went to the house and affirmed that he saw "no property and being unable to point out any," underscored that Quintero was essentially a pauper. However, Lamar did get the claim from the U.S. government a year later, with interest. See n. 85.

Chapter 5
The Deep Roots of Our America: Two New Worlds, and Their Resistors

1. See Schoultz, *Beneath The United States*, chaps. 4–5. Discussing the debate in the United States over whether to accept the Dominican Republic's 1866–70 offer to annex itself to the nation, he writes, "Buried with the Dominican annexation treaty was the process of expansion through absorption" (83).

2. For this period in Pombo's biography I have relied on Miramon, *Angustia*; Romero, *Pombo*; and especially Orjuela, *Edda*, chap. 2, as well as Orjuela's introductions to his critical editions of Pombo's works.

3. Orjuela, *Edda*, 23–27. Pombo's journals during the period indicate that he was reading the poems of Plácido for the first time, in the James Kennedy edition (87–89).

4. Orjuela's claim that Pombo's verses in the Edda disguise inspired a generation of women poets who would follow (*Edda*, 131) is perhaps overstated, given that there were several women writing at the time. See the *Poetisas americanas* anthology edited by Cortés, and Campuzano, *Mujeres*.

5. Edda's identity seems to have remained a secret while Pombo was in the United States. He reports getting a Bogotá newspaper in the mail and noting, with satisfaction, "Edda es hoy una reputación allá, dice 'El Tiempo' que 'su estro es profundo como el de Byron'" [Edda is now a woman with a reputation there; *El Tiempo* says that "her poetic inspiration is as deep as Byron's"] (Romero, *Pombo*, 103). The rarified term *estro* is itself interesting in this context, since it refers to feminine estrus.

6. Cortés, *Poetisas*, 57.

7. Cited in Romero, *Pombo*, 160–61.

8. Ibid., 59.

9. See Orjuela, *Edda*, 53. However, Orjuela also records another of Pombo's claims that would seem to work against rigid notions of gender: "Todos sabemos, o sentimos que hay sexos en las almas, no siempre coincidentes con los respectivos cuerpos" [We all know or sense that souls are sexed in ways that do not always coincide with their respective bodies] and (more outrageously) "el amor humano es mujer siempre que ama de veras" [human love is always feminine when it loves truly] (53). Rafael Maya writes: "era un alma dúplex. Sentía el amor por activa y por pasiva, con alma de hombre y con alma de mujer" [he was a dual personality. He experienced love both actively and passively, with the soul of a man and of a woman] (cited in *Edda*, 52). Maya argues that Pombo took on the Edda persona because he saw artistry as principally feminine and "passive" in nature.

10. Cited in Romero, *Pombo*, 59–60.

11. Ibid., 64. Mosquera, a general who rose to power during the national wars of liberation, later became an archenemy of Pombo's liberal family and party. After the conservatives gained control in 1856, Mosquera led a successful revolt (1860–62) that resulted in a federalist United States of Colombia. He served as its provisional president until 1864. Domineering, unscrupulous, and violently emotional, he was feared and mistrusted even by his adherents. Relations between the United States and Colombia were fairly good during the Mosquera era, apparently because of his willingness to work with the Magdalena Company and its U.S. investors. See Parks, *Colombia*, 164, and Randall, *Colombia*, 26–30.

12. See Guillén, *Costa Rica*, 154ff.

13. Pombo, *Poesía inédita*, 1:138–40.

14. Pombo, *Antología*, 29–34.

15. See Conniff, *Panama*, 19–21, on the Bidlock-Mallorino Treaty of 1848, which promised U.S. aid to Panamanians if they declared independence from Colombia; and 38–39 on the Watermelon War.

16. Five years later, Pombo composed a long poem entirely about Niagara would be frequently republished. But here he begins from the viewpoint of one who has already "seen" the falls through Heredia's eyes, seeking to reaffirm the sublime terror that restores the observer to home and self. However, a few stanzas of due homage, of repeating the shopworn praise for Niagara "enorme, augusto," give way to a caustic observation of the ways in which the falls have been domesticated by "el activo / cíclope anglosajón, probando al mundo / que es digno amo de ti . . . te da su abrazo atlético de hierro / Esto que el hombre (insecto de un instante / Y atolondrado por su instante) llama / La civilización" [the busy / Anglo-Saxon cyclops, proving to the world / that he's a worthy master for you . . . giving you his iron athlete's embrace / This is what Man (an insect that lives only an instant / And heedless of his moment) calls / Civilization] (*Antología*, 65). The poem is thus transformed into a vicious critique of the shortsighted "Anglo-Saxon" efforts to seduce Niagara's wildness with the iron embrace of an athlete. Pombo reverses the seducing roles—here, the brawny athlete gets associated with the North, and the wild, feminized Niagara of Heredia's imagining with the beloved patria—in order to

reject pan-American union. This version ends with a bored scoff at Niagara's commodified sublimity: "te pago tu olvido con olvido" [I repay your forgetfulness with forgetting].

17. Romero, *Pombo*, vii–viii; Orjuela, *Edda*, 51–53.

18. See Overton, *Portrait of a Publisher*, 33–36, for information on the publisher's marketing strategies in Latin America. This in-house history reports that Appleton's entered the Spanish-language market in the 1840s, and by the mid-1860s was publishing nearly fifty Spanish books a year for both the domestic and export markets. Pombo's children's books appeared in 1867 and 1869, respectively.

19. Durand, *Guía*, 154, 158. Pombo may well have contributed to the *Guía*'s section on Niagara Falls, too, which makes a long, curious detour of comparing the falls unfavorably to Tequendama, in Colombia—mentioning Heredia's famous poem on the former, but citing José Joaquín Ortíz's similar ode to Tequendama (168–69). Yet Pombo also rises to the defense of the United States, citing Church's monumental paintings and noting that Philadelphia, Boston, and New Orleans have perhaps greater claim to being the "Athens of the U.S." than does New York (155).

20. Ibid., 148. Note the pun on *mañana* and *tarde*, which mean "morning" and "afternoon" as well as "tomorrow" and "late."

21. There is an ample bibliography on Martí's political use of affective metaphors and on his exile in New York in general. I have been particularly influenced by Ramos, *Desencuentros*.

22. On the Ocampo treaty's misrecognition in Mexico, see Ysunza Ozeta, *Juárez*. Throughout his struggles to consolidate a government against the conservative opposition and then during the French occupation, Juárez's relative friendliness to the United States was personally expedient but politically devastating. While his wife and children suffered a spartan exile in New York, his efforts to raise loans were stonewalled and the treaty his government negotiated, which would have given the United States perpetual rights to the Tehuantepec canal–access route and the northern railway lines they coveted, created a terrible backlash at home. See also Fuentes Mares, *Juárez y los Estados Unidos*, and Villegas Revueltas, *Liberalismo moderado*.

23. Pitt, *Decline of the Californios*, 229ff. He discusses the second generation of dispossessed californios as plagued by "alienation and assimilation," despite the fact that the Spanish-surnamed population of Los Angeles, for instance, was still 25 percent of the city's census in 1880 (249–76). He describes the years of the French occupation as bringing about something of a renaissance among the californios, helping them shake off their "political apathy," in part because easterners were suspicious that the West harbored "Copperhead" Confederate sympathizers (230, 234). On the even swifter pace of the loss of Hispanophone control in Texas, see Montejano, *Anglos and Mexicans*. He writes that after 1866 there was only "token" tejano political representation in San Antonio (40), and tejanos suffered great losses of land through confiscation, coercion, and new forms of mercantile competition that arose in the border region and disadvantaged Mexico landowners (50–54). The

building boom of 1875–85 coincided with the Anglos' nearly complete domination of the cattle industry by the 1870s (70).

24. See Goff, "Spanish-Language Newspapers," 64–65, for a discussion of *El Eco del Pacífico*. This coalescence of the native and exile press seems not to have occurred in New Mexico; Meléndez's history spends only a paragraph on the decades 1860–80 because there was very little press activity before the railroad came to New Mexico in 1879 and Urbano Chacón began to found his series of newspapers (*So All Is Not Lost*, 24).

25. *El Nuevo Mundo*, 4 November 1864.

26. See for instance, *El Nuevo Mundo*, 2 April 1866.

27. Torres, *World*, 278–301 and 472–76. The other major papers he cites are *El Clamor Público* of Los Angeles and Santa Barbara's *La Gaceta*, published between 1879 and 1881. He identifies the most original poets among the californios as the pseudonymous Dantés [Dante] of *La Gaceta* and El Cura de Tamajona of *El Nuevo Mundo*, whose slangy punning in three languages in "Ze Yankee Dul" [The Yankee Doodle] makes it perhaps the first published poem in *caló*, or Chicano slang. On Dantés, see Torres, 433–37 and 438–41. On El Cura de Tamajona, and his satire "El cura aprendiendo inglés," an innovative example of bilingual punning and play, see 455–59 and 469–72, and Torres, "Bilingualism as Satire."

28. See especially the 17 March, 29 March, 31 March, and 21 July 1865 issues of *El Nuevo Mundo*, where the elaboration of the Zaragoza Club activities spills over nearly every page. Jean Franco, in *Plotting Women*, 92–101, remarks on the noticeable absence of visible women writers in Mexico during the period of nation formation. Whereas Cuban women like Gómez de Avellaneda, the Condesa de Merlin, and Luisa Pérez de Zambrona, as well as Argentine women like Eduarda Mansilla, took a relatively active role in the public sphere, Mexican women were, according to Franco, "slow to challenge the domestication of women" (93).

29. Numa Pompilio Llona, in addition to having a minor poetic career, had been an editor of *El Comercio*, the most important paper in Lima (Sáinz de Robles, *Ensayo*, 698).

30. On Prieto's biography, see De Maria's introduction to *Un lirio*, 20–24; Sáinz de Robles, *Ensayo*, 936; Suárez Radillo, "Isabel Prieto," 99.

31. See Vigil's introduction to Prieto, *Obras poéticas*, cxii–cxvi. Although one of her dramatic works, *Un lirio entre zarzas* [A Lily among Blackberries], was reissued in a facsimile edition in 1964, only one short critical article on her work has appeared in several decades. Franco mentions Vigil's support of Prieto as the exception to this general period of silence among Mexican women writers, but notes correctly that Vigil works strenuously to portray her as an exemplary mother and "ángel del hogar" [angel of the home]—which was, in fact, the title of one of her plays (*Plotting Women*, 95).

32. On Ruíz de Burton, see Sánchez and Pita's introductions to *Who Would Have Thought It?* and *The Squatter and the Don*; on her various affiliations see esp. Aranda, "Contradictory Impulses."

33. Guillermo Prieto's travel diary of his voyage to the United States likewise pivots around a sentimental vision of the national family, as I discuss in the final section of this chapter. See Ridley, *Maximilian and Juárez*, 243–45 on the general perception of the Mexican delegation and the female members of the Juárez family in the United States. Mahoney, *Mexico and the Confederacy*, describes in detail the Confederate resettlements in Mexico after the Civil War and their vexed relationship to Juárez.

34. The citation from the Romero speech is in Bryant, *Prose Writings*, 2:238–39; the journal entry from 1864 immediately follows. Bryant's account of his trip to Mexico by way of Cuba in 1872 may be found in the same volume, 148–200; his meeting with Juárez, coupled with some views on "the restlessness of the mixed race in Mexico," is on 168–70. For Bryant's views against Cuban annexation, see his *Power for Sanity*, 50, 313, 334–35.

35. J. Brown, "Reconstructing Representation," 7. See also Gambee, *Frank Leslie*.

36. Stern's *Purple Passage* tells Follin's story, which is striking for its parallels with that of Adah Isaacs Menken, which I discuss later in the chapter. Born in New Orleans in 1836—a fact she would later embroider, suggesting a mixed-race ancestry (6)—Follin traveled to South America and California as a young woman as the supposed younger sister of Lola Montez, the famously scandalous actress (19). She would later return to California and have an affair with Joaquin Miller, as did Menken. Follin's time at *El Noticioso* led to a visit to Havana in late 1860, which Quintero could well have facilitated (30–31). Both her father and her first (or second) husband Ephraim Squier had business interests in Central America, and she was fascinated with all things Latin American and Spanish. Her first published article was about the Venezuelan patriot José Antonio Páez's 1850 visit to New York (13). In 1884 Follin was awarded the Order of the Bust of Bolívar from the Venezuelan government.

37. By 1871, circulation of *Frank Leslie's Illustrated Newspaper* had slipped from a Civil War height of 100,000, but its constellation of allied publications (such as *Frank Leslie's Lady's Magazine, Once a Week,* and a well-established German-language weekly, *Frank Leslie's Illustrierte Zeitung*), at Follin's initiative, produced a healthy profit. *El Mundo Nuevo, A Frank Leslie Newspaper*, mimicked the English-language flagship paper in format, size, subscription structure, and, eventually, price. Though the initial subscription was offered at a rather high $4.50 per year, the editors apologized, "Quisieramos que pudiesen venderse las publicaciones impresas en castellano al mismo ínfimo precio a que se venden en los EEUU los periódicos ingleses, y antes de mucho tiempo tal vez allá lleguemos" [We'd like to be able to sell publications in Spanish at the same ridiculously low price at which they sell English papers in the United States—and perhaps before long, we'll get there] (10 February 1872).

38. Bueno, introduction to *Prosas*, ix. See in general Poyo, *"With All, and for the Good of All"*; and Pérez, *Cuba*, on exile culture in the United States prior to the 1895 revolution.

39. *El Mundo Nuevo,* 25 May 1871.

40. *El Mundo Nuevo,* 10 January 1872; 25 June 1871.

41. See, for instance, Quintero's "Hoy y mañana, paráfrasis del ingles" in the 25 January 1871 issue.

42. *El Mundo Nuevo,* 10 May 1872.

43. The idea that print communities enable political affiliations during this crucial period is hardly new. In their 1876 study of *La Revista Ilustrada,* Chamberlin and Schulman credited that New York publication with the feat of bringing a truly pan-Hispanic literary modernism into being—an argument that, ironically, makes New York the yanqui center of the most significant aesthetic and social movement since independence. Because of its easy transatlantic access, its substantial local Hispanophone readership, its powerful production and distribution mechanisms, and its innovative print technologies, New York was an obvious location in which to launch a cultural project on that scale. But *La Revista Ilustrada* began publishing in 1886—fifteen years after the first number of *El Mundo Nuevo* appeared.

44. On the transatlantic railroad, see for instance the 10 March 1872 issue. At the same time, however, the journal also launched a series of Greeley-style exposés of overcrowded prisons and homelessness; see 25 February 1872.

45. This biographical information is summarized from Carbonell, *Poetas,* 14ff.

46. On the debate over Zenea and his decision to make this voyage, which was widely interpreted as an abandonment of the revolutionary cause, see Vitier, *Rescate.* His strongest defender is Piñeyro, *Vida.*

47. The major biographical source on Menken is Lesser, *Enchanting Rebel,* which gives a critical overview of all previous conflicting sources on key issues such as her parentage and actual age; this edition also reprints Menken's own "Notes of My Life" of 1868. According to this obviously fictionalized autobiography, she was known as Dolores Adios in Cuba and dominated the Havana stage as well as the hearts of the many handsome Cubans who wooed her. Paul Lewis, however, reads the diary somewhat more skeptically and concludes that while in Cuba she supplemented her stage income as a prostitute (*Queen of the Plaza,* 37–49). Carbonell, *Poetas,* perhaps with greater access to Havana materials, contends that Menken was a very significant force in Zenea's young life: at her side, he "perfeccionó sus conocimientos en las lenguas inglesa y francesa" [perfected his knowledge of English and French], which would help him teach to make a living (1–8).

48. Coincidentally, or not, when the poem first appeared in the 10 January 1872 number of *El Mundo Nuevo,* it was placed adjacent to an antislavery short story, "La venganza de Falalá," which details how a noble slave outwits his master and repays the torments by playing the innocent. He is martyred, but vengeance comes from an outside source.

49. See in general McLean, *Vida.*

50. Prieto, *Viaje,* 1:614, 619. Page citations are hereafter given parenthetically in text.

51. On Townsend, see Prieto, *Viaje,* 2:88–93, 213–15. A notice on the *Pica-yune*'s front page on 22 April 1877 next to Townsend's poem "To the Exiles" notes

that "The only two American writers who have been made members of the Liceo Hidalgo, the most distinguished literary society in the city of Mexico, are William Cullen Bryant and Mary Ashley Townsend." This poem and her other Mexicanist writing can be found in Townsend, *Down the Bayou*, 85–86.

52. Carbonell, *Poetas*. Turla is also mentioned in J. S. Kendall, "Distinguished Hispano-Orleanians," which claims Martí stayed with Turla in New Orleans. This is not possible, however, since Martí came to the United States in 1880.

Coda
The Future's Past: Latino Ghosts in the U.S. Canon

1. Cited in Schoultz, *Beneath the United States*, 87. Schoultz adds that, because of the perceived racial "alienness" of Latin Americans articulated so powerfully during and since the Mexican War, "officials in Washington were confronted for the first time with a tension between the nation's long-standing commitment to self-determination, on the one hand, and the widespread desire to use the nation's new power for commercial expansion, on the other. The management of this tension became a central issue of public discussion in the 1890s and 1900s, and *the* central issue of U.S.-Latin American relations" (89). The Pan-American Congress, forerunner of the Organization of American States, formed in 1889; Martí would correctly observe that the balance of power in this group bears no resemblance to the fraternal vision articulated by Bolívar or Clay. Another landmark occurs in 1890, year of the founding of the United Fruit Company, an icon of neocolonial economic relations between the United States and Latin America.

2. On Pérez Bonalde, see my article "*El gran poeta* Longfellow," 414–19.

3. Letter from Mariano Vallejo dated 9 January 1880, published by permission of the Longfellow Collection, Houghton Library, Harvard University [bMS Am 1340.2 (5694), (4569), (4456)].

4. On Vallejo's significance, see Padilla, *My History*, chap. 3; R. Sánchez, *Telling Identities*.

5. Longfellow, *Works*, 3:236.

6. Letter from Rafael Pombo dated 18 October 1880, published by permission of the Longfellow Collection, Houghton Library, Harvard University [bMS Am 1340.2 (5694), (4569), (4456)].

7. The very existence of the RUSHLH project protests the damaging misperception that Latinos possess no cultural memory of the United States. The title of Roberto Suro's 1998 book, *Strangers among Us: How Latino Immigration Is Transforming America*, is symptomatic of that assumption: the "us" of the title makes Latinos perpetual newcomers, strangers in Babylon. On Matthiessen, see esp. Pease, "Negative Interpellations."

8. See, e.g., Belnap and Fernández, *José Martí's "Our America."*

WORKS CITED

Newspapers

La América Ilustrada, New York
El Bejareño, San Antonio
El Clamor Público, Los Angeles
The Crescent, New Orleans
Diario del Gobierno de la República Mexicana, Mexico City–New Orleans
La Gaceta, Santa Barbara
El Hablador, New Orleans
El Indicador, New Orleans
El Mundo Nuevo, New York
El Nuevo Mundo, San Francisco
La Patria, New Orleans
El Ranchero, San Antonio
La Risa, New Orleans
La Unión, New Orleans

Books and Journal Articles

Acuña, Rodolfo. *Occupied America: A History of Chicanos*. New York: Harper and Row, 1988.

Ahlstrom, Sidney E. *A Religious History of the American People*. New Haven: Yale University Press, 1972.

Alarcón, Norma. "Traddutora, Traditora: A Paradigmatic Figure of Chicana Feminism." In *Dangerous Liaisons: Gender, Nation, and Postcolonial Perspectives*, edited by Anne McClintock, 278–99. Minneapolis: University of Minnesota Press, 1997.

Allen, Gay Wilson. *The Solitary Singer: A Critical Biography of Walt Whitman*. Rev. ed. New York: New York University Press, 1967.

Allen, Gay Wilson and Ed. Folsom, eds. *Walt Whitman and the World*. Iowa City: University of Iowa Press, 1995.

Alonso, Amado. *Castellano, español, idioma nacional*. 2d ed. Buenos Aires: Losada, 1943.

Alvarez, José Rogelio, ed. *Enciclopedia de México*. Mexico City: Enciclopedia de México, 1998.

Ammon, Harry. *James Monroe: The Quest for National Identity*. New York: McGraw-Hill, 1971.

Amy, Francis J., ed. *Musa bilingüe: Being a Collection of Translations, Principally from the Standard Anglo-American Poets, into Spanish; and Spanish, Cuban, and Porto Rican Poets, into English, with the Original Text Opposite, and Biographical Notes; Especially Intended for the Use of Students*. San Juan: El Boletín Mercantil, 1903.

Anderson, Benedict R. O. G. *Imagined Communities: Reflections on the Origin and Spread of Nationalism*. Rev. and extended ed. London: Verso, 1991.

Antología de poetas americanos. Buenos Aires: Santiago Rueda, 1941.

Appadurai, Arjun. *Modernity at Large: Cultural Dimensions of Globalization*. Minneapolis: University of Minnesota Press, 1996.

Aranda, José F., Jr. "Contradictory Impulses: María Amparo Ruíz de Burton, Resistance Theory, and the Politics of Chicano/a Studies." *American Literature* 70, no. 3 (1998): 551–79.

Archer, David, and Patrick Costello. *Literacy and Power: The Latin American Battleground*. London: Earthscan, 1990.

Arensberg, Mary. *The American Sublime*. Albany: State University of New York Press, 1986.

Augier, Angel. *De la sangre en la letra*. Havana: Unión de Escritores y Artistas de Cuba, 1977.

———. "José María Heredia: Novela y realidad de América Latina." *Revista Iberoamericana* 56, no. 152–53 (1990): 733–46.

Baker, Houston A. *Blues, Ideology, and Afro-American Literature: A Vernacular Theory*. Chicago: University of Chicago Press, 1987.

Ballón, José C. *Lecturas norteamericanas de José Martí: Emerson y el socialismo contemporáneo, 1880–1887*. Mexico City: Universidad Nacional Autónoma de México, 1995.

Barnstone, Willis. *The Poetics of Translation: History, Theory, Practice*. New Haven: Yale University Press, 1993.

Bassnett, Susan. *Translation Studies*. London: Methuen, 1980.

Baxter, David J. "The Dilemma of Progress: Bryant's Continental Vision." In *William Cullen Bryant and His America*, edited by Stanley Brodwin and Michael D'Innocenzo, 3–25. New York: AMS Press, 1983.

Beach, Christopher. *The Politics of Distinction: Whitman and the Discourses of Nineteenth-Century America*. Athens: University of Georgia Press, 1996.

Beatty, Richmond Croom. *Bayard Taylor: Laureate of the Gilded Age*. Norman: University of Oklahoma Press, 1936.

Bell, Caryn Cossé. *Revolution, Romanticism, and the Afro-Creole Protest Tradition in Louisiana, 1718–1868*. Baton Rouge: Louisiana State University Press, 1997.

Belnap, Jeffrey, and Raúl Fernández, eds. *José Martí's "Our America": From National to Hemispheric Cultural Studies.* Durham: Duke University Press, 1998.

Bennett, Paula. *Nineteenth-Century American Women Poets: An Anthology.* Malden, Mass.: Blackwell Publishers, 1998.

Berman, Antoine. *The Experience of the Foreign: Culture and Translation in Romantic Germany.* Albany: State University of New York Press, 1992.

Bhabha, Homi K. *The Location of Culture.* London: Routledge, 1994.

Bigelow, John. *William Cullen Bryant.* New York: Chelsea House, 1980.

Bourdieu, Pierre. *The Rules of Art: Genesis and Structure of the Literary Field.* Cambridge: Polity Press, 1996.

Brack, Gene M. *Mexico Views Manifest Destiny, 1821–1846: An Essay on the Origins of the Mexican War.* Albuquerque: University of New Mexico Press, 1975.

Brand, Dana. *The Spectator and the City in Nineteenth-Century American Literature.* Cambridge: Cambridge University Press, 1991.

Brasher, Thomas L. *Whitman as Editor of the Brooklyn Daily Eagle.* Detroit: Wayne State University Press, 1970.

Brasseaux, Carl A. *In Search of Evangeline: Birth and Evolution of the Evangeline Myth.* Thibodaux, La.: Blue Heron Press, 1988.

Brito, Aristeo. *El diablo en Texas/The Devil in Texas.* Translated by David William Foster. Tempe, Ariz.: Bilingual Press, 1990.

Brodhead, Richard H. *Cultures of Letters: Scenes of Reading and Writing in Nineteenth-Century America.* Chicago: University of Chicago Press, 1993.

Brodwin, Stanley, and Michael D'Innocenzo, eds. *William Cullen Bryant and His America.* New York: AMS Press, 1983.

Brooks, Maria Gowen (María del Occidente). *Idomen; or, The Vale of Yumuri.* New York: Samuel Colman, 1843.

———. *Zóphiël: A Poem.* Boston: J. H. A. Frost, 1825.

———. *Zóphiël; or, The Bride of Seven.* Edited by Zadel Barnes Gustafson. New York: Lee and Shepard, 1879.

Brooks, Van Wyck. *The Flowering of New England.* New York: E. P. Dutton and Company, 1936.

Brown, Charles Henry. *Agents of Manifest Destiny: The Lives and Times of the Filibusters.* Chapel Hill: University of North Carolina Press, 1980.

———. *William Cullen Bryant.* New York: Scribner, 1971.

Brown, Joshua. "Reconstructing Representation: Social Types, Readers, and the Pictorial Press, 1865–1877." *Radical History Review* 66, no. 5 (1996): 5–38.

Bryant, William Cullen. "Jicotencal." *United States Review and Literary Gazette,* February 1827, 336–46.

———. *Letters of a Traveller; or, Notes of Things Seen in Europe and America.* New York: G. P. Putnam, 1850.

———. *The Poetical Works of William Cullen Bryant.* New York: D. Appleton, 1880.

———. *Power for Sanity: Selected Editorials of William Cullen Bryant, 1829–1861.* New York: Fordham University Press, 1994.

————. *Prose Writings*. Edited by Parke Godwin. New York: Russell and Russell, 1964.

————. *The Letters of William Cullen Bryant*. Edited by William Cullen Bryant II and Thomas G. Voss. 6 vols. New York: Fordham University Press, 1975.

Bryant, William Cullen, and James Grant Wilson. *The Family Library of Poetry and Song, Being Choice Selections from the Best Poets, Including Translations*. New York: Fords Howard and Hulbert, 1880.

Buell, Lawrence. *New England Literary Culture from Revolution through Renaissance*. Cambridge: Cambridge University Press, 1986.

Bueno, Salvador, ed. *Prosas de Enrique Piñeyro*. Havana: Letras Cubanas, 1980.

Bulmer-Thomas, Victor. *The Economic History of Latin America since Independence*. New York: Cambridge University Press, 1994.

Bushnell, David, and Neill Macauley. *The Emergence of Latin America in the Nineteenth Century*. New York: Oxford University Press, 1988.

Cameron, Kenneth Walter. *Longfellow among His Contemporaries*. Hartford: Transcendental Books, 1978.

Campuzano, Luisa. "'Las muchachas de la Habana no tienen temor de Dios.'" *Revista Canadiense de Estudios Hispánicos* 16, no. 2 (1992): 307–18.

Campuzano, Luisa, ed. *Mujeres latinoamericanas: Historia y cultura, siglos XVI al XIX*. Havana: Casa de las Américas, 1997.

Carbonell, José. *Leopoldo Turla: Su poesía y su actuación revolucionaria*. Havana: Siglo XX, 1926.

————. *Pedro Santacilia: Su vida y sus versos discurso pronunciado en la inauguración del curso académia Dr. Jose Manuel Carbonell*. Havana: Siglo XX, 1924.

————. *La poesía revolucionaria en Cuba*. Official ed. Havana: Siglo XX, 1928.

————. *Los poetas de "El laúd del desterrado": Quintero, Teurbe Tolón, Santacilia, Turla, Castellón, Zenea*. Havana: Avisador Comercial, 1930.

Carilla, Emilio. *El romanticismo en la América hispánica*. 3d ed. 2 vols. Madrid: Gredos, 1975.

Carr, Albert H. Z. *The World and William Walker*. Westport, Conn.: Greenwood Press, 1975.

Carr, Helen. *Inventing the American Primitive: Politics, Gender, and the Representation of Native American Literary Traditions, 1789–1936*. New York: New York University Press, 1996.

Carter, Boyd G. *Historia de la literatura hispanoamericana a través de sus revistas*, Vol. 5 of *Historia literaria de Hispanoamérica*. Mexico City: De Andrea, 1968.

Castañeda, Antonia. "The Political Economy of Nineteenth-Century Stereotypes of Californianas." In *Between Borders: Essays on Mexicana/Chicana History*, edited by Adelaida R. del Castillo, 213–36. Encino, Calif.: Floricanto Press, 1990.

Castillo-Feliú, Guillermo. Introduction to *Xicoténcatl: An Anonymous Historical*

Novel about the Events Leading Up to the Conquest of the Aztec Empire. Austin: University of Texas Press, 1999.

Chabrán, Rafael, and Richard Chabrán. "The Spanish-Language and Latino Press in the United States: Newspapers and Periodicals." In *Handbook of Hispanic Cultures in the United States: Literature and Art*, edited by Francisco Lomelí, 360–84. Houston: Arte Público Press, 1993.

Chacón y Calvo, José Maria. *Los cien mejores poetas cubanos*. Madrid: Reus, 1922.

———. *Estudios heredianos*. Havana: Letras Cubanas, 1980.

Chaffin, Tom. *Fatal Glory: Narciso López and the First Clandestine U.S. War against Cuba*. Charlottesville: University of Virginia Press, 1996.

Chai, Leon. *The Romantic Foundations of the American Renaissance*. Ithaca: Cornell University Press, 1987.

Chamberlain, Lori. "Gender and the Metaphorics of Translation." In *Rethinking Translation: Discourse, Subjectivity, Identity*, edited by Lawrence Venuti, 57–74. London: Routledge, 1992.

Chamberlin, Vernon-A., and Iván Schulman. *La Revista Ilustrada de Nueva York: History, Anthology, and Index of Literary Selections*. Columbia: University of Missouri Press, 1976.

Charvat, William. *The Origins of American Critical Thought, 1810–1835*. New York: Russell and Russell, 1968.

———. *The Profession of Authorship in America, 1800–1870: The Papers of William Charvat*. Columbus: Ohio State University Press, 1968.

Chevalier, Jacques M. *Semiotics, Romanticism, and the Scriptures*. Berlin: Mouton de Gruyter, 1990.

Chevigny, Bell Gale, and Gari Laguardia. *Reinventing the Americas: Comparative Studies of Literature of the United States and Spanish America*. New York: Cambridge University Press, 1986.

Coerver, Don M., and Linda B. Hall. *Tangled Destinies: Latin America and the United States*. Albuquerque: University of New Mexico Press, 1999.

Cohen, H. *Cohen's New Orleans Directory, Including Jefferson City, Carrollton, Gretna, Algiers, and McDonough, for 1850*. Microform. New Orleans: Printed at the Office of the Picayune, 1850.

Colás, Santiago. "Of Creole Symptoms, Cuban Fantasies, and Other Latin American Postcolonial Ideologies." *PMLA* 110, no. 3 (1995): 382–95.

Conniff, Michael L. *Panama and the United States: The Forced Alliance*. Athens: University of Georgia Press, 1992.

Copeland, Fayette. *Kendall of the Picayune*. Norman: University of Oklahoma Press, 1943.

Córdova, María Gayón, ed. *La ocupación yanqui de la ciudad de México, 1847–1848*. Mexico City: Consejo Nacional para la Cultura y las Artes, 1997.

Cortés, José Domingo, ed. *Poetisas americanas: Ramillete poético del bello sexo hispano-americano*. Paris: A. Bouret, 1875.

Cortina, Rodolfo. "History and Development of Cuban American Literature: A Survey." In *Handbook of Hispanic Cultures in the United States: Literature and Art*, edited by Francisco Lomelí, 40–61. Houston: Arte Público Press, 1993.

Cox, F. Brett. "'What Need, Then, for Poetry?': The Genteel Tradition and the Continuity of American Literature." *New England Quarterly* 57, no. 2 (1994): 212–33.

Curtin, Philip D. *The Rise and Fall of the Plantation Complex: Essays in Atlantic History*. Cambridge: Cambridge University Press, 1990.

Dabney, Thomas Ewing. *100 Great Years: The Story of the Times-Picayune*. Baton Rouge: Louisiana State University Press, 1944.

Dauber, Kenneth. *The Idea of Authorship in America: Democratic Poetics from Franklin to Melville*. Madison: University of Wisconsin Press, 1990.

Davidson, Cathy N. *Reading in America: Literature and Social History*. Baltimore: Johns Hopkins University Press, 1989.

de la Cova, Antonio. "Filibusters and Freemasons: The Sworn Obligation." *Journal of the Early Republic* 17, no. 1 (1997): 95–120.

de Onís, José. *The United States as Seen by Spanish American Writers, 1776–1890*. 2d ed. New York: Gordian Press, 1975.

de Voto, Bernard Augustine. *The Year of Decision, 1846*. Boston: Little, Brown and Company, 1943.

del Castillo, Adelaida R. *Between Borders: Essays on Mexicana-Chicana History*, Encino, Calif.: Floricanto Press, 1990.

del Valle, Francisco Gonzalez, ed. *Poesías de Heredia traducidas a otros idiomas*. Havana: Molina y Compañia, 1940.

Deloria, Philip Joseph. *Playing Indian*. New Haven: Yale University Press, 1998.

Dijon, Harold. "Some Notes on Mexican Poets and Poetry." *Catholic World* 52, no. 308: 236–48.

Dimock, Joseph Judson. *Impressions of Cuba in the Nineteenth Century: The Travel Diary of Joseph J. Dimock*. Edited by Louis A. Pérez. Wilmington, Del.: Scholarly Resources, 1998.

Domínguez, Virginia R. *White by Definition: Social Classification in Creole Louisiana*. New Brunswick, N.J.: Rutgers University Press, 1986.

Dow, Charles Mason. *Anthology and Bibliography of Niagara Falls*. Vol. 2. Albany: State of New York, 1921.

Duffey, Bernard. *Poetry in America: Expression and Its Values in the Times of Bryant, Whitman, and Pound*. Durham: Duke University Press, 1978.

Dumond, Don E. *The Machete and the Cross: Campesino Rebellion in Yucatan*. Lincoln: University of Nebraska Press, 1997.

Durand, José, ed. *Guía de los Estados Unidos para viajeros españoles*. 3d ed. New York: F. J. Vingut, 1859.

Eisenhower, John S. D. *So Far from God: The U.S. War with Mexico, 1846–1848*. New York: Doubleday, 1989.

Emerson, Ralph Waldo. *Journals and Miscellaneous Notebooks*. Edited by William H. Gilman. 16 vols. Cambridge: Harvard University Press, 1960–82.

Enciclopedia de Cuba. Vol. 1, *Poesia.* San Juan: Clásicos Cubanos, 1973.

Engelkirk, John Eugene. *Bibliografía de obras norteamericanas en traducción española.* Mexico City: 1944.

———. *Edgar Allan Poe in Hispanic Literature.* New York: Russell and Russell, 1972.

———. "El epistolario Longfellow-Pombo." *Thesaurus* 10 (1954): 16–17.

———. "Notes on Longfellow in Spanish America." *Hispania* 36 (1942): 295–308.

Erkkila, Betsy. *Whitman the Political Poet.* New York: Oxford University Press, 1989.

Erkkila, Betsy, and Jay Grossman. *Breaking Bounds: Whitman and American Cultural Studies.* New York: Oxford University Press, 1996.

Ernest, John. "Reading the Romantic Past: William H. Prescott's *History of the Conquest of Mexico.*" *American Literary History* 5, no. 2 (1993): 231–49.

Evans, Clement A., ed. *Confederate Military History.* Vol. 13 (Louisiana). Wilmington, N.C.: Broadfoot Publishing, 1988.

Ferguson, Robert A. "Longfellow's Political Fears: Civic Authority and the Role of the Artist in 'Hiawatha' and 'Miles Standish'." *American Literature* 50, no. 2 (1978): 187–214.

———. "William Cullen Bryant: The Creative Context of the Poet." *New England Quarterly* 52 (1980): 431–63 (1980).

Fernández de Castro, José Antonio. *Ensayos cubanos de historia y de crítica.* Havana: Jesús Montero, 1943.

Fitz, Earl E. *Rediscovering the New World: Inter-American Literature in a Comparative Context.* Iowa City: University of Iowa Press, 1991.

Fletcher, Angus. "Whitman and Longfellow: Two Types of the American Poet." *Raritan* 10, no. 1 (1991): 131–45.

Fliegelman, Jay. *Declaring Independence: Jefferson, Natural Language, and the Culture of Performance.* Stanford: Stanford University Press, 1993.

Florescano, Enrique. *Memory, Myth, and Time in Mexico: From the Aztecs to Independence.* Austin: University of Texas Press, 1994.

Foley, Neil. *The White Scourge: Mexicans, Blacks, and Poor Whites in Texas Cotton Culture.* Berkeley: University of California Press, 1997.

Foner, Philip S. *A History of Cuba and Its Relations with the United States.* New York: International Publishers, 1962.

Fornet, Alfonso. *El libro en Cuba: Siglos XVIII y XIX.* Havana: Letras Cubanas, 1994.

Franchot, Jenny. *Roads to Rome: The Antebellum Protestant Encounter with Catholicism.* Berkeley: University of California Press, 1994.

Franco, Jean. *Plotting Women: Gender and Representation in Mexico.* New York: Columbia University Press, 1989.

Fuentes Mares, José. *Juárez y los Estados Unidos.* Mexico City: Jus, 1972.

———. *Juárez, los Estados Unidos y Europa.* Barcelona: Grijalbo, 1983.

Galeano, Eduardo. *Memoria de fuego.* Vol. 2, *Las caras y las máscaras.* Mexico City: Siglo XXI, 1984.

Gambee, Budd Leslie, Jr. *Frank Leslie and His Illustrated Newspaper, 1855–1860.* Ann Arbor: University of Michigan Department of Library Science, 1964.

García Canclini, Néstor. *Culturas híbridas: Estrategias para entrar y salir de la modernidad.* Mexico City: Grijalbo, 1990.

Gelpi, Albert. *The Tenth Muse: The Psyche of the American Poet.* 2d ed. Cambridge: Cambridge University Press, 1991.

Gilroy, Paul. *The Black Atlantic: Modernity and Double Consciousness.* Cambridge: Harvard University Press, 1993.

Godwin, Parke. *A Biography of William Cullen Bryant.* 2 vols. New York: Appleton, 1883.

Goff, Victoria. "Spanish-Language Newspapers in California." In *Outsiders in 19th-Century Press History: Multicultural Perspectives,* edited by Frankie Hutton and Barbara Straus Read, 55–70. Bowling Green: Popular Press, 1995.

Gonzales-Berry, Erlinda. *Pasó por aquí: Critical Essays on the New Mexican Literary Tradition, 1542–1988.* Albuquerque: University of New Mexico Press, 1989.

González, Manuel Pedro. *Ensayos críticos.* Caracas: Universidad Central de Venezuela, 1963.

González de la Garza, Mauricio. *Walt Whitman: Racista, imperialista, antimexicano.* Mexico City: Colección Málaga, 1971.

González Echevarría, Roberto. "Latin American and Comparative Literatures." In *Poetics of the Americas: Race, Founding, and Textuality,* edited by Bainard Cowan and Jefferson Humphries, 47–62. Baton Rouge: Louisana State University Press, 1997.

———. *Myth and Archive: A Theory of Latin American Narrative.* Cambridge: Cambridge University Press, 1990.

———. *The Voice of the Masters: Writing and Authority in Modern Latin American Literature.* Austin: University of Texas Press, 1988.

Graff, Gerald. "American Criticism Left and Right." In *Ideology and Classic American Literature,* edited by Sacvan Bercovitch and Myra Jehlen, 91–124. Cambridge: Cambridge University Press, 1986.

Graff, Harvey J. *The Labyrinths of Literacy: Reflections on Literacy Past and Present.* Rev. and expanded ed. Pittsburgh: University of Pittsburgh Press, 1995.

———. *The Legacies of Literacy: Continuities and Contradictions in Western Culture and Society.* Bloomington: Indiana University Press, 1991.

Gray, Edward G. *New World Babel: Languages and Nations in Early America.* Princeton: Princeton University Press, 1999.

Gray, Janet, ed. *She Wields a Pen: American Women Poets of the Nineteenth Century.* Iowa City: University of Iowa Press, 1997.

Green, Ernest S., and H. Von Lowenfels, eds. *Mexican and South American Poems.* San Diego: Dodge and Burbeck, 1892.

Greene, Roland. *Unrequited Conquests: Love and Empire in the Colonial Americas.* Chicago: University of Chicago Press, 1999.

Greenspan, Ezra. *Walt Whitman and the American Reader.* Cambridge: Cambridge University Press, 1990.

Griswold, Rufus Wilmot. "Biographical Sketches of Living American Poets and Novelists, No. VI: Maria Brooks (Maria del Occidente)." *Southern Literary Messenger* 5, no. 8 (1839): 541–48.

Griswold, Rufus Wilmot, ed. *The Female Poets of America*. Rev. ed. Philadelphia: Carey and Hart, 1879.

———. *The Poets and Poetry of America*. Philadelphia: Carey and Hart, 1842.

Griswold del Castillo, Richard. *The Los Angeles Barrio, 1850–1890: A Social History*. Berkeley: University of California Press, 1979.

———. *The Treaty of Guadalupe Hidalgo: A Legacy of Conflict*. Norman: University of Oklahoma Press, 1990.

Gross, John J. *The Rise and Fall of the Man of Letters: A Study of the Idiosyncratic and the Humane in Modern Literature*. New York: Macmillan, 1969.

Groves, Jeffrey D. "Maria Gowen Brooks." *Legacy* 12, no. 1 (1995): 38–45.

Gruesz, Kirsten Silva. "Feeling for the Fireside." In *Sentimental Men: Masculinity and the Politics of Affect in American Culture*, edited by Mary Chapman and Glenn Hendler, 43–63. Berkeley: University of California Press, 1999.

———. "*El gran poeta* Longfellow and a Psalm of Exile." *American Literary History* 10, no. 3 (1998): 395–427.

Grunzweig, Walter. "Noble Ethics and Loving Aggressiveness: The Imperialist Walt Whitman." In *An American Empire: Expansionist Cultures and Policies, 1881–1917*, edited by Serge Ricard, 151–66. Aix-en-Provence: Université de Provence, 1990.

Guillén, Diana. *Costa Rica*. Mexico City: Alianza Editorial Mexicana, 1988.

Gustafson, Zadel Barnes. "Maria del Occidente." In *Zóphiël; or, The Bride of Seven, by Maria del Occidente*, edited by Zadel Barnes Gustafson. New York: Lee and Shepard, 1879.

Gutiérrez, J. M., ed. *América poética: Colección escogida de composiciones en verso, escritas por americanos en el presente siglo*. Valparaíso: Impr. del Mercurio, 1846.

Gutiérrez, Ramón A., and Genaro M. Padilla. *Recovering the U.S. Hispanic Literary Heritage*. Houston: Arte Público Press, 1993.

Gutiérrez-Jones, Carl. *Rethinking the Borderlands: Between Chicano Culture and Legal Discourse*. Berkeley: University of California Press, 1995.

Haas, Lisbeth. *Conquests and Historical Identities in California, 1769–1936*. Berkeley: University of California Press, 1995.

Hall, Stuart. "Notes on Deconstructing the Popular." In *Cultural Theory and Popular Culture: A Reader*, edited by John Storey, 455–66. New York: Harvester/Wheatsheaf, 1993.

Hamnett, Brian R. *Juárez*. London: Longman, 1994.

Hanke, Lewis, ed. *Do the Americas Have a Common History? A Critique of the Bolton Theory*. New York: Alfred A. Knopf, 1964.

Haralson, Eric. "Mars in Petticoats: Longfellow and Sentimental Masculinity." *Nineteenth-Century Literature* 51, no. 6 (1996): 327–55.

Haralson, Eric L., and John Hollander. *Encyclopedia of American Poetry*. Chicago: Fitzroy Dearborn, 1998.

Hatfield, James Taft. *New Light on Longfellow, with Special Reference to His Relations to Germany*. New York: Houghton Mifflin Company, 1933.

Hawthorne, Julian. *Hawthorne and His Wife: A Biography*. 2 vols. Boston: James Osgood, 1884.

Hawthorne, Manning, Henry Wadsworth Longfellow and Dana. "The Origins of Longfellow's *Evangeline*." *Papers of the Bibliographical Society of America* 41 (1947): 165–203.

Hedrick, Joan D. "Parlor Literature: Harriet Beecher Stowe and the Question of 'Great Women Artists'." *Signs* 17, no. 2 (1992): 275–303.

Heredia, José Maria. *Discurso pronunciado . . . por Daniel Webster*. New York: Librería Wilder y Campbell, 1825.

———. *Minerva: Periódico literario*. Mexico City: Universidad Nacional Autónoma de México, 1972.

———. *Niágara y otros textos: Poesía y prosa selectas*. Edited by Angel Augier Caracas: Ayacucho, 1990.

———. *Revisiones literarias*. Havana: Publicaciones del Ministerio de Educación; Dirección de Cultura, 1947.

Herrera-Sobek, María. *Northward Bound: The Mexican Immigrant Experience in Ballad and Song*. Bloomington: Indiana University Press, 1993.

Hirsch, Arnold R., and Joseph Logsdon. *Creole New Orleans: Race and Americanization*. Baton Rouge: Louisiana State University Press, 1992.

Hobbs, Catherine, ed. *Nineteenth-Century Women Learn to Write*. Charlottesville: University of Virginia Press, 1995.

Holditch, W. Kenneth. *In Old New Orleans*. Jackson: University Press of Mississippi, 1983.

Holloway, Emory, ed. *The Uncollected Poetry and Prose of Walt Whitman*. 2 vols. Garden City, N.Y.: Doubleday, Page and Company, 1921.

Horsman, Reginald. *Race and Manifest Destiny: The Origins of American Racial Anglo-Saxonism*. Cambridge: Harvard University Press, 1981.

Horwitz, Howard. *By the Law of Nature: Form and Value in 19th Century America*. Oxford: Oxford University Press, 1991.

Hurlbert, William Henry. *Gan-Eden: or, Pictures of Cuba*. Boston: John P. Jewett and Company, 1854.

Instituto de Literatura y Lingüística (Academia de Ciencias de Cuba). *Perfil histórico de las letras cubanas: Desde los orígenes hasta 1898*. Havana: Letras Cubanas, 1983.

Janowitz, Anne. "Class and Literature: The Case of Romantic Chartism." In *Rethinking Class: Literary Studies and Social Formations*, edited by Wai-Chee Dimock and Michael Gilmore 239–66. New York: Columbia University Press, 1994.

Jeffreys, Mark. "Ideologies of Lyric: A Problem of Genre in Contemporary Anglophone Poetics." *PMLA* 110, no. 2 (1995): 196–205.

Jehlen, Myra. *American Incarnation: The Individual, the Nation, and the Continent.* Cambridge: Harvard University Press, 1986.

Johannsen, Robert Walter. *To the Halls of the Montezumas: The Mexican War in the American Imagination.* New York: Oxford University Press, 1985.

Johnson, Curtiss S. *Politics and a Belly-Full: The Journalistic Career of William Cullen Bryant, Civil War Editor of the New York Evening Post.* Westport, Conn.: Greenwood Press, 1974.

Johnson, John J. *Latin America in Caricature.* Austin: University of Texas Press, 1980.

Johnson, W. R. *The Idea of Lyric: Lyric Modes in Ancient and Modern Poetry.* Berkeley: University of California Press, 1982.

Jumonville, Florence M. *Bibliography of New Orleans Imprints, 1764–1864.* New Orleans: Historic New Orleans Collection, 1989.

Kanellos, Nicolás. "A Socio-Historic Study of Hispanic Newspapers in the United States." In *Recovering the U.S. Hispanic Literary Heritage,* edited by Ramón A. Gutiérrez and Genaro M. Padilla, 107–28. Houston: Arte Público Press, 1993.

Kanellos, Nicolás and Helvetia Martell. *Hispanic Periodicals in the United States, Origins to 1960: A Brief History and Comprehensive Bibliography.* Houston: Arte Público Press, 2000.

Kaplan, Amy. "Manifest Domesticity." *American Literature* 70, no. 3 (1998): 581–606.

Kaplan, Amy, and Donald E. Pease. *Cultures of United States Imperialism.* Durham: Duke University Press, 1993.

Kaplan, Justin. *Walt Whitman: A Life.* New York: Bantam Books, 1980.

Kendall, George Wilkins. *The War between the United States and Mexico Illustrated, Embracing Pictorial Drawings of All the Principal Conflicts.* New York: Appleton, 1851.

Kendall, John Smith. "Some Distinguished Hispano-Orleanians." *Louisiana Historical Quarterly* 18 (1935): 40–55.

Kettell, Samuel, ed. *Specimens of American Poetry* 1829. Reprint, New York: Benjamin Blom, 1967.

Klammer, Martin. *Whitman, Slavery, and the Emergence of Leaves of Grass.* University Park: Pennsylvania State University Press, 1995.

Krieg, Joann P. *A Whitman Chronology.* Iowa City: University of Iowa Press, 1998.

Krupat, Arnold. *Ethnocriticism: Ethnography, History, Literature.* Berkeley: University of California Press, 1992.

Kutzinski, Vera M. *Against the American Grain: Myth and History in William Carlos Williams, Jay Wright, and Nicolás Guillén.* Baltimore: Johns Hopkins University Press, 1987.

———. "Commentary: American Literary History as Spatial Practice." *American Literary History* 4, no. 3 (1992): 550–57.

———. *Sugar's Secrets: Race and the Erotics of Cuban Nationalism.* Charlottesville: University Press of Virginia, 1993.

LaFeber, Walter. *The Panama Canal: The Crisis in Historical Perspective.* Updated ed. New York: Oxford University Press, 1989.

"Lamar, Mirabeau Buonaparte." *The Handbook of Texas Online.* http://www. tsha.utexas.edu/handbook/online/articles/view/LL/fla15.html [Accessed Nov 30 19:36:42 US/Central 2000].

Langley, Lester D. *America and the Americas: The United States in the Western Hemisphere.* Athens: University of Georgia Press, 1989.

———. *The Americas in the Age of Revolution, 1750–1850.* New Haven: Yale University Press, 1996.

Larson, Kerry C. *Whitman's Drama of Consensus.* Chicago: University of Chicago Press, 1988.

Lauter, Paul. *Canons and Contexts.* New York: Oxford University Press, 1991.

Lazo, Raimundo. *El romanticismo: Fijación sicológico de su concepto.* Mexico: Porrúa, 1971.

Leal, Luis. "The Spanish-Language Press: Function and Use." *Americas Review* 17, no. 3 (1989): 157–62.

———. "Truth-Telling Tongues: Early Chicano Poetry." In *Recovering the U.S. Hispanic Literary Heritage*, edited by Ramón A. Gutiérrez and Genaro M. Padilla, 91–105. Houston: Arte Público Press, 1993.

Lefevere, André, ed. *Translation, History, Culture: A Sourcebook.* London: Routledge, 1992.

Lesser, Alan. *Enchanting Rebel: The Secret of Adah Isaacs Menken.* New York: Beechurst Press, 1947.

Levine, Lawrence W. *Highbrow/Lowbrow: The Emergence of Cultural Hierarchy in America.* Cambridge: Harvard University Press, 1988.

Lewis, Paul. *Queen of the Plaza: A Biography of Adah Isaacs Menken.* New York: Funk and Wagnalls, 1964.

Lewis, R. W. B. *The American Adam: Innocence, Tragedy, and Tradition in the Nineteenth Century.* Chicago: University of Chicago Press, 1955.

Lienhard, Martín. *La voz y su huella: Escritura y conflicto étnico-social en América Latina, 1492–1988.* Hanover, N.H.: Ediciones del Norte, 1991.

Limón, José Eduardo. *American Encounters: Greater Mexico, the United States, and the Erotics of Culture.* Boston: Beacon Press, 1998.

Lindley, David. *Lyric.* New York: Methuen, 1985.

Llanes Abeijón, Manuel, Mayra Rodríguez Pérez, and Eugenio Pérez Ramírez. "La traducción martiana de un poema de Longfellow." *Islas* 79 (1984): 15–26.

Loeffelholz, Mary. "Who Killed Lucretia Davidson? or, Poetry in the Domestic-Tutelary Complex." *Yale Journal of Criticism* 10, no. 2 (1997): 271–93.

Long, Orie William. *Literary Pioneers: Early American Explorers of European Culture.* Cambridge: Harvard University Press, 1935.

Longfellow, Henry Wadsworth. *Kavanagh.* Boston: Tickner and Fields, 1849.

———. *Letters of Henry Wadsworth Longfellow.* Edited by Andrew Hilen, 6 vols. Cambridge: Harvard University Press, 1966–82.

———. *The Poets and Poetry of Europe.* Philadelphia: Porter and Coates, 1871.

Longfellow, Samuel, ed. *Life of Henry Wadsworth Longfellow, with Extracts from His Journals and Correspondence.* 3 vols. Boston: Houghton, 1886.

———. *Works of Henry Wadsworth Longfellow.* 14 vols. Boston: Houghton, 1886.

Lopez, Debbie L. "Maria Gowen Brooks (Maria Del Occidente) (1794–1845)." In *Nineteenth-Century American Women Writers: A Bio-Bibliographical Critical Sourcebook,* 15–18, Westport, Conn.: Greenwood Press, 1997.

Loving, Jerome. *Walt Whitman: The Song of Himself.* Berkeley: University of California Press, 1999.

Lozada, Alfredo. "El catastrofismo y el tiempo indefinido: Ecos del debate geológico en la poesía de Heredia." *La Chispa* (1983): 159–69.

Mabbott, Thomas Olive. "Maria del Occidente." *American Collector* 2 (1926): 415–24.

MacAdam, Alfred J. *Textual Confrontations: Comparative Readings in Latin American Literature.* Chicago: University of Chicago Press, 1987.

MacCurdy, Raymond R. *A History and Bibliography of Spanish-Language Newspapers and Magazines in Louisiana, 1808–1949.* Albuquerque: University of New Mexico Press, 1951.

Machor, James L. *Readers in History: Nineteenth-Century American Literature and the Contexts of Response.* Baltimore: Johns Hopkins University Press, 1993.

MacLachlan, Colin M., and William H. Beezley. *El Gran Pueblo: A History of Greater Mexico, 1821–1911.* Vol. 1. Princeton: Prentice Hall, 1994.

Maddox, Lucy. *Removals: Nineteenth-Century American Literature and the Politics of Indian Affairs.* New York: Oxford University Press, 1991.

Magnuson, Paul. *Reading Public Romanticism.* Princeton: Princeton University Press, 1998.

Mahoney, Harry Thayer. *Mexico and the Confederacy, 1860–1867.* San Francisco: Austin and Winfield, 1998.

Manthorne, Katherine. *Tropical Renaissance: North American Artists Exploring Latin America, 1839–1879.* Washington, D.C.: Smithsonian Institution Press, 1989.

Martí, José. *Obras completas.* 31 vols. Havana: Ed. Nacional de Cuba, 1963–65.

Martínez, Urbano. *Domingo del Monte y su tiempo.* Havana: Unión de Escritores y Artistas de Cuba, 1997.

Marx, Leo. *The Machine in the Garden: Technology and the Pastoral Ideal in America.* London: Oxford University Press, 1967.

Masiello, Francine. *Between Civilization and Barbarism: Women, Nation, and Literary Culture in Modern Argentina.* Lincoln: University of Nebraska Press, 1992.

May, Caroline, ed. *The American Female Poets.* Philadelphia: Lindsay and Blakiston, 1849.

May, Ernest R. *The Making of the Monroe Doctrine.* Cambridge: Harvard University Press, 1992.

May, Robert E. "Young American Males and Filibustering in an Age of Manifest Destiny: The United States Army as a Cultural Mirror." *Journal of American History* 78, no. 3 (1991): 857–86.

McCullough, David G. *The Path between the Seas: The Creation of the Panama Canal, 1870–1914.* New York: Simon and Schuster, 1977.

McGreevy, Patrick V. *Imagining Niagara: The Meaning and Making of Niagara Falls.* Amherst: University of Massachusetts Press, 1994.

McKinsey, Elizabeth. *Niagara Falls: Icon of the American Sublime.* New York: Cambridge University Press, 1985.

McLaughlin, Thomas. *Street Smarts and Critical Theory: Listening to the Vernacular.* Madison: University of Wisconsin Press, 1996.

McLean, Malcolm Dallas. *Vida y obra de Guillermo Prieto.* Mexico City: El Colegio de México, 1960.

McVay, Ted E., Jr. "The Sublime Aesthetic in the Poetry of José María Heredia." *Dieciocho* 17, no. 1 (1994): 33–41.

McWilliams, Carey, and Matt S. Meier. *North from Mexico: The Spanish-Speaking People of the United States.* New York: Greenwood Press, 1990.

Medina, José Ramón, ed. *Biografía de Juan Antonio Pérez Bonalde.* Caracas: Fundación Eugenio Mendoza, 1983.

Meisel Lanner, Roberto. *Tres titanes de la literatura colombiana.* Barranquilla, Colombia: Ediciones Gobernación del Atlántico, 1996.

Meléndez, A. Gabriel. *So All Is Not Lost: The Poetics of Print in Neuvomexicano Communities, 1834–1958.* Albuquerque: University of New Mexico Press, 1997.

Melville, Herman. *Billy Budd and Other Stories.* New York: Viking Penguin, 1986.

Menken, Adah Isaacs. *Infelicia.* New York: n.p., 1868.

Merk, Frederick. *The Monroe Doctrine and American Expansionism, 1843–1849.* New York: Knopf, 1966.

Meyer, Doris. *Speaking for Themselves: Neomexicano Cultural Identity and the Spanish-Language Press, 1880–1920.* Albuquerque: University of New Mexico Press, 1996.

Mignolo, Walter D. *The Darker Side of the Renaissance: Literacy, Territoriality, and Colonization.* Ann Arbor: University of Michigan Press, 1995.

———. *Local Histories/Global Designs: Coloniality, Subaltern Knowledges, and Border Thinking.* Princeton: Princeton University Press, 2000.

———. "Posoccidentalismo: Las epistemologías fronterizas y el dilema de los estudios (latinoamericanos) de área." *Revista Iberoamericana* 62, no. 176–77 (1996): 679–96.

Miller, Ralph N. "Nationalism in Bryant's 'The Prairies'." *American Literature* 21 (1950): 227–32.

Mintz, Sidney W. *Sweetness and Power.* New York: Penguin Books, 1985.

Miramon, Alberto. *La angustia creadora en Núñez y Pombo.* Bogotá: Caro y Cuervo, 1975.

Molloy, Sylvia. "His America, Our America: José Martí Reads Whitman." In *Breaking Bounds: Whitman and American Cultural Studies,* edited by Betsy Erkkila and Jay Grossman, 83–91. New York: Oxford University Press, 1996.

Monroy, Douglas. *Thrown among Strangers: The Making of Mexican California in Frontier California.* Berkeley: University of California Press, 1990.

Montejano, David. *Anglos and Mexicans in the Making of Texas, 1836–1986.* Austin: University of Texas Press, 1987.

Montes-Huidobro, Matías. *El laúd del desterrado.* Houston: Arte Público Press, 1995.

Moretti, Franco. *Atlas of the European Novel, 1800–1900.* London: Verso, 1998.

Morla Vicuña, Carlos, ed. *Evangelina, Romance de le Acadia / Henry Wadsworth Longfellow.* New York: Eduardo O. Jenkins, 1871.

Morse, Richard. *New World Soundings: Culture and Ideology in the Americas.* Baltimore: Johns Hopkins University Press, 1989.

Moylan, Michele, and Lane Stiles, eds. *Reading Books: Essays on the Material Text and Literature in America.* Amherst: University of Massachusetts Press, 1997.

Mueller-Vollmer, Kurt, and Michael Irmscher, eds. *Translating Literatures, Translating Cultures: New Vistas and Approaches in Literary Studies.* Stanford: Stanford University Press, 1998.

Newbury, Michael. *Figuring Authorship in Antebellum America.* Stanford: Stanford University Press, 1997.

Newlin, Paul A. "*The Prairie* and 'The Prairies': Cooper's and Bryant's Views of Manifest Destiny." In *William Cullen Bryant and His America*, edited by Stanley Brodwin and Michael D'Innocenzo. New York: AMS Press, 1983.

Nolan, James. *Poet-Chief: The Native American Poetics of Walt Whitman and Pablo Neruda.* Albuquerque: University of New Mexico Press, 1994.

Norton, Anne. *Alternative Americas: A Reading of Antebellum Political Culture.* Chicago: University of Chicago Press, 1986.

Nye, Russel Blaine. *The Unembarrassed Muse: The Popular Arts in America.* New York: Dial Press, 1970.

O'Gorman, Edmundo. *The Invention of America: An Inquiry into the Historical Nature of the New World and the Meaning of Its History.* Westport, Conn.: Greenwood Press, 1972.

O'Keeffe, Katherine O. Brien. *Visible Song: Transitional Literacy in Old English Verse.* Cambridge: University Press, 1990.

Oboler, Suzanne. *Ethnic Labels, Latino Lives.* Minneapolis: University of Minnesota Press, 1995.

Ohmann, Richard M. "Literacy, Technology, and Monopoly Capital." *College English* 47, no. 7 (1985): 675–89.

———. *Making and Selling Culture.* Hanover, N.H.: University Press of New England, 1996.

———. *Politics of Letters.* Middletown, Conn.: Wesleyan University Press, 1987.

Ohmann, Richard M., and Wallace Douglas. *English in America: A Radical View of the Profession, with a New Introduction.* Middletown, Conn.: Wesleyan University Press, 1996.

Olliff, Donathon C. *Reforma Mexico and the United States: A Search for Alternatives to Annexation, 1854–1861.* Birmingham: University of Alabama Press, 1981.

Ong, Walter J. *Orality and Literacy: The Technologizing of the Word.* London: Routledge, 1991.

Orjuela, Héctor H. *Edda la bogotana: Biografía de Rafael Pombo.* Bogotá: Kelly, 1997.

———. *Imagen de los Estados Unidos en la poesía de Hispanoamérica.* Mexico: Universidad Nacional Autónoma de México Instituto de Investigaciones Filológicas, 1980.

———. *Revaloración de una vieja polémica literaria: William Cullen Bryant y la oda "Niagara" de José María Heredia.* Bogotá: Caro y Cuervo, 1964.

Ortiz, Fernando. *Cuban Counterpoint: Tobacco and Sugar.* Translated by Harriet de Onís. Durham: Duke University Press, 1995.

Ostrowski, Carl. ""I Stand Upon Their Ashes in Thy Beam": The Indian Question and William Cullen Bryant's Literary Removals." *American Transcendental Quarterly* 9, no. 4 (1995): 299–312.

Otero, Gustavo. *La cultura y el periodismo en América Latina.* Quito: Liebmann, 1953.

Overton, Grant. *Portrait of a Publisher: The First Hundred Years of the House of Appleton.* New York: Appleton, 1925.

Owsley, Frank Lawrence, and Gene A. Smith. *Filibusters and Expansionists: Jeffersonian Manifest Destiny, 1800–1821.* Tuscaloosa: University of Alabama Press, 1997.

Pacheco, José. "Crónica del 47." Edited by Andrés Reséndez. Mexico City: Clío, 1997.

Padilla, Genaro, ed. *My History, Not Yours: The Formation of Mexican American Autobiography.* Madison: University of Wisconsin Press, 1993.

Padrón Toro, Antonio. *Juan Antonio Pérez Bonalde: Un hombre de hoy.* Caracas: n.p., 1979.

Paquette, Robert L. *Sugar Is Made with Blood: The Conspiracy of La Escalera and the Conflict between Empires over Slavery in Cuba.* Middletown, Conn.: Wesleyan University Press, 1988.

Paredes, Américo. *"With His Pistol in His Hand": A Border Ballad and Its Hero.* Austin: University of Texas Press, 1958.

Parker, Andrew. *Nationalisms and Sexualities.* New York: Routledge, 1992.

Parks, E. Taylor. *Colombia and the United States, 1765–1934.* Durham: Duke University Press, 1935.

Pattee Fred Lewis. *The Feminine Fifties.* Port Washington, N.Y.: Kennikat Press, 1966.

Pearce, Roy Harvey. *The Continuity of American Poetry.* Princeton: Princeton University Press, 1961.

———. *Savagism and Civilization: A Study of the Indian and the American Mind.* Berkeley: University of California Press, 1988.

Pease, Donald E. "Negative Interpellations: From Oklahoma City to the Trilling-Matthiessen Transmission." *Boundary 2* 23, no. 1 (1996): 1–33.

Pérez, Louis A. *Cuba: Between Reform and Revolution*. New York: Oxford University Press, 1988.

Pérez Bonalde, Juan Antonio. "Vuelta a la patria." In *Antología de la moderna poesía venezolana*, edited by Otto D'Sola, 3–13. Caracas: Monte Avila, 1984.

Pérez Firmat, Gustavo. *The Cuban Condition: Translation and Identity in Modern Cuban Literature*. Cambridge: Cambridge University Press, 1989.

Pérez Firmat, Gustavo, ed. *Do the Americas Have a Common Literature?* Durham: Duke University Press, 1990.

Perkins, Dexter. *The Monroe Doctrine, 1823–1826*. Gloucester, Mass.: P. Smith, 1965.

———. *The Monroe Doctrine, 1826–1867*. Gloucester, Mass.: P. Smith, 1965.

———. *The Monroe Doctrine, 1867–1907*. Gloucester, Mass.: P. Smith, 1966.

Pickard, John B., ed. *The Letters of John Greenleaf Whittier*. Cambridge: Belknap Press, 1975.

Pike, Fredrick B. *The United States and Latin America: Myths and Stereotypes of Civilization and Nature*. Austin: University of Texas Press, 1992.

Piñeyro, Enrique. *Bosquejos, retratos, recuerdos: Obra póstuma*. Havana: Consejo Nacional de Cultura, 1964.

Piñeyro, Enrique, ed. *Vida y escritos de Juan Clemente Zenea*. Havana: Consejo Nacional de Cultura, 1964.

Pitt, Leonard. *The Decline of the Californios: A Social History of the Spanish-Speaking Californians, 1846–1890*. Berkeley: University of California Press, 1971.

Poe, Edgar Allan. *Essays and Reviews*. Edited by G. R. Thompson. New York: Library of America, 1984.

———. *Marginalia*. Edited by John Carl Miller. Charlottesville: University Press of Virginia, 1981.

Pombo, Rafael. *Antología poética*. Edited by Hector Orjuela. Bogotá: La Candelaria, 1975.

———. *Poesía inédita y olvidada*. Edited by Héctor Orjuela. 2 vols. Bogotá: Caro y Cuervo, 1970.

———. *Traducciones poéticas*. Edited by Antonio Gómez Restrepo. Bogotá: Imprenta Nacional, 1917.

Porter, Carolyn. "What We Know That We Don't Know: Remapping American Literary Studies." *American Literary History* 6, no. 3 (1994): 467–526.

Portuondo, José Antonio. *Capítulos de literatura cubana*. Havana: Letras Cubanas, 1981.

Poyo, Gerald E. *"With All, and for the Good of All": The Emergence of Popular Nationalism in the Cuban Communities of the United States, 1848–1898*. Durham: Duke University Press, 1989.

Pratt, Mary Louise. *Imperial Eyes: Travel Writing and Transculturation*. London: Routledge, 1992.

Price, Kenneth. *Whitman and Tradition: The Poet in His Century.* New Haven: Yale University Press, 1990.

Prieto, Guillermo. *Viaje a los Estados Unidos, por Fidel.* 3 vols. Mexico City: Dublan y Chávez, 1877–78.

Prieto de Landázuri, Isabel. *Obras poéticas.* Edited by J. M. Vigil. Mexico City: Imprenta I. Paz, 1883.

———. *Un lirio entre zarzas.* Edited by Armando de María y Campos. Mexico City: Instituto Nacional de Bellas Artes, 1964.

Pym, Anthony. *Attempt at a Chronology of Hispanic Translation History: Nineteenth Century* [World Wide Web]. 1998 [cited 1999]. Available from http://www.fut.es/~apym/19.html.

Quijano, Aníbal, and Immanuel Wallerstein. "Americanity as a Concept, or the Americas in the Modern World-System." *International Social Science Journal* 44, no. 4 (1992): 549–57.

Quintero, J. A. *The Code of Honor: Its Rationale and Uses by the Tests of Common Sense and Good Morals.* 2d ed. New Orleans: A. Brand, 1883.

"Quintero, José Agustín." *The Handbook of Texas Online.* tp://www.tsha.utexas.edu/handbook/online/articles/view/QQ/fqu5.html [Accessed Nov 30 19:36:42 US/Central 2000].

Railton, Stephen. *Authorship and Audience: Literary Performance in the American Renaissance.* Princeton: Princeton University Press, 1991.

Rama, Angel. *La ciudad letrada.* Hanover, N.H.: Ediciones del Norte, 1984.

———. *The Lettered City.* Translated by John Charles Chasteen. Durham: Duke University Press, 1996.

Ramos, Julio. *Desencuentros de la modernidad en América Latina: Literatura y política en el siglo XIX.* Mexico: Fondo de Cultura Económica, 1989.

———. *Paradojas de la letra.* Caracas: eXcultura, 1996.

Randall, Stephen J. *Colombia and the United States: Hegemony and Interdependence.* Athens: University of Georgia Press, 1992.

Read, Thomas Buchanan, ed. *The Female Poets of America.* 6th ed. Philadelphia: E. H. Butler, 1855.

Reed, Nelson. *The Guerra de Castas in Yucatán.* Stanford: Stanford University Press, 1964.

Reilly, Tom. "A Spanish-Language Voice of Dissent in Antebellum New Orleans." *Louisiana History* 23, no. 4 (1982): 325–39.

———. "The War Press of New Orleans." *Journalism History* 13, no. 3–4 (1986): 86–95.

Reinders, Robert C. *End of an Era: New Orleans, 1850–1860.* New Orleans: Pelican, 1964.

Reising, Russell J. *The Unusable Past: Theory and the Study of U.S. Literature.* New York: Methuen, 1986.

Reynolds, David S. *Walt Whitman's America: A Cultural Biography.* New York: Alfred A. Knopf, 1995.

Reynolds, Larry J. *European Revolutions and the American Literary Renaissance.* New Haven: Yale University Press, 1988.

Richard, Nelly. "The Latin American Problematic of Theoretical-Cultural Transference: Postmodern Appropriations and Counterappropriations." *South Atlantic Quarterly* 92, no. 3 (1993): 453–60.

Riddel, Joseph N. *Purloined Letters: Originality and Repetition in American Literature.* Baton Rouge: Louisiana State University Press, 1995.

Ridley, Jasper Godwin. *Maximilian and Juárez.* New York: Ticknor and Fields, 1992.

Roach, Joseph R. *Cities of the Dead: Circum-Atlantic Performance.* New York: Columbia University Press, 1996.

Robinson, Cecil. *Mexico and the Hispanic Southwest in American Literature.* Tucson: University of Arizona Press, 1977.

————. *No Short Journeys: The Interplay of Cultures in the History and Literature of the Borderlands.* Tucson: University of Arizona Press, 1992.

Robinson, Cecil, ed. *The View from Chapultepec: Mexican Writers on the Mexican-American War.* Tucson: University of Arizona Press, 1989.

Romero, Mario Guzman. *Rafael Pombo en Nueva York.* Bogotá: Kelly, 1983.

Rosenbaum, Robert J. *Mexicano Resistance in the Southwest.* Dallas: Southern Methodist University Press, 1998.

Rowe, John Carlos. *At Emerson's Tomb: The Politics of Classic American Literature.* New York: Columbia University Press, 1997.

Rowland, William G., Jr. *Literature and the Marketplace: Romantic Writers and Their Audiences in Great Britain and the United States.* Lincoln: University of Nebraska Press, 1996.

Rubin, Joan Shelley. *The Making of Middlebrow Culture.* Chapel Hill: University of North Carolina Press, 1992.

Rubin, Joseph Jay. *The Historic Whitman.* University Park: Pennsylvania State University Press, 1973.

Ruiz de Burton, María Amparo. *The Squatter and the Don.* Edited by Rosaura Sánchez and Beatrice Pita. Houston: Arte Público Press, 1992.

————. *Who Would Have Thought It?* Edited by Rosaura Sánchez and Beatrice Pita. Houston: Arte Público Press, 1995.

Ruland, Richard, ed. *The Native Muse.* New York: E. P. Dutton and Company, 1976.

Ryan, Mary P. *Civic Wars: Democracy and Public Life in the American City during the Nineteenth Century.* Berkeley: University of California Press, 1997.

Sáinz de Robles, Federico Carlos. *Ensayo de un diccionario de la literatura.* 3d ed. Madrid: Aguilar, 1965.

Saldívar, José David. *Border Matters: Remapping American Cultural Studies.* Berkeley: University of California Press, 1997.

————. *The Dialectics of Our America: Genealogy, Cultural Critique, and Literary History.* Durham: Duke University Press, 1991.

Salessi, Jorge, and José Quiroga. "Errata sobra la erótica, or, the Elision of Whitman's Body." In *Breaking Bounds: Whitman and American Cultural*

Studies, edited by Betsy Erkkila and Jay Grossman, 123–32. New York: Oxford University Press, 1996.

Sánchez, Luis Alberto. *Historia comparada de las literaturas americanas.* 4 vols. Buenos Aires: Losada, 1973–76.

Sánchez, Rosaura. *Telling Identities: The California Testimonios.* Minneapolis: University of Minnesota Press, 1995.

Sánchez-Eppler, Karen. "'To Stand Between': A Political Perspective on Whitman's Poetics of Merger and Embodiment." *English Literary History* 56, no. 4 (1989): 923–49.

———. *Touching Liberty: Abolition, Feminism, and the Politics of the Body.* Berkeley: University of California Press, 1993.

Santacilia, Pedro. *Pedro Santacilia: El hombre y su obra.* Edited by Boris Rosen Jelomer 2 vols. Mexico City: Centro de Investigación Científica Jorge L. Tamayo, 1983.

Santí, Enrico Mario. "The Accidental Tourist: Walt Whitman in Latin America." In *Do the Americas Have a Common Literature?*, edited by Gustavo Pérez Firmat, 156–76. Durham: Duke University Press, 1990.

Sarmiento, Domingo Faustino. *Travels in the United States in 1947.* Translated by Michael Aaron Rockland. Princeton: Princeton University Press, 1970.

Schoonover, John. *Dollars over Dominion: The Triumph of Liberalism in Mexican–United States Relations, 1861–1867.* Baton Rouge: Louisiana State University Press, 1978.

Schoultz, Lars. *Beneath the United States: A History of U.S. Policy toward Latin America.* Cambridge: Harvard University Press, 1998.

Seeyle, John. "Attic Shape: Dusting Off Evangeline." *Virginia Quarterly Review* 60, no. 1 (1984): 21–44.

Shields, David S. *Civil Tongues and Polite Letters in British America.* Chapel Hill: University of North Carolina Press, 1997.

———. *Oracles of Empire: Poetry, Politics, and Commerce in British America, 1690–1750.* Chicago: University of Chicago Press, 1990.

Shively, Charles. "Mexican War." In *Walt Whitman: An Encyclopedia*, edited by J. R. LeMaster and Donald D. Kummings, 427–28. New York: Garland Publishing, 1998.

Shurbutt, T. Ray, ed. *United States–Latin American Relations, 1800–1850: The Formative Generations.* Tuscaloosa: University of Alabama Press, 1991.

Simon, Sherry. *Gender in Translation: Cultural Identity and the Politics of Transmission.* New York: Routledge, 1996.

Simpson, Lewis P. *The Man of Letters in New England and the South: Essays on the History of the Literary Vocation in America.* Baton Rouge: Louisiana State University Press, 1973.

Slicer, T. R. "Famous Visitors at Niagara Falls." In *The Niagara Book*, edited by W. D. Howells, Mark Twain, Nathaniel T. Shaler et al., 15–25. New York: Doubleday, Page and Company, 1901.

Sollors, Werner. *Multilingual America: Transnationalism, Ethnicity, and the Languages of American Literature*. New York: New York University Press, 1998.

Sommer, Doris. *Foundational Fictions: The National Romances of Latin America*. Berkeley: University of California Press, 1991.

———. *Proceed with Caution, When Engaged by Minority Writing in the Americas*. Cambridge: Harvard University Press, 1999.

———. "Supplying Demand: Walt Whitman as the Liberal Self." In *Reinventing the Americas: Comparative Studies of Literature of the United States and Spanish America*, edited by Bell Gale Chevigny and Gari Laguardia, 68–91. Cambridge: Cambridge University Press, 1986.

Spencer, Benjamin Townley. *The Quest for Nationality: An American Literary Campaign*. Syracuse, N.Y.: Syracuse University Press, 1957.

Spengemann, William C. *A Mirror for Americanists: Reflections on the Idea of American Literature*. Hanover, N.H.: University Press of New England, 1989.

Spillers, Hortense J. "Introduction: Who Cuts the Border? Some Readings on 'America'." In *Comparative American Identities: Race, Sex, and Nationality in the Modern Text*, edited by Hortense J. Spillers, 1–25. New York: Routledge, 1991.

Spillers, Hortense J., ed. *Comparative American Identities: Race, Sex, and Nationality in the Modern Text*. New York: Routledge, 1991.

Stansifer, Charles L. "United States–Central American Relations, 1824–1850." In *United States–Latin American Relations, 1800–1850: The Formative Generations*, edited by T. Ray Shurbutt, 25–46. Tuscaloosa: University of Alabama Press, 1991.

Steiner, George. *After Babel: Aspects of Language and Translation*. London: Oxford University Press, 1975.

Stephan, Beatriz González. "La historiografía literaria del liberalismo hispánico." In *La historiografía literaria del liberalismo hispanico*, 10–11, 32–37, 56–59. Havana: Casa de las Américas, 1987.

Stern, Madeleine B. *Purple Passage: The Life of Mrs. Frank Leslie*. Norman: University of Oklahoma Press, 1953.

Stimson, Frederick S. *Cuba's Romantic Poet: The Story of Plácido*. Chapel Hill: University of North Carolina Press, 1964.

———. *Orígenes del hispanismo norteamericano*. Mexico City: Ediciones de Andrea, 1961.

Stock, Brian. *Listening for the Text: On the Uses of the Past*. Philadelphia: University of Pennsylvania Press, 1996.

Stovall, Floyd. *The Foreground of Leaves of Grass*. Charlottesville: University Press of Virginia, 1974.

Suárez Radillo, Carlos Miguel. "Isabel Prieto de Landázuri: Una dramaturga romántica." *Cuadernos Hispanoamericanos* 548 (1996): 99–107.

Sundquist, Eric J. "Exploration and Empire." In *The Cambridge History of American Literature*, vol. 2, edited by Sacvan Bercovitch, 125–32. Cambridge: Cambridge University Press, 1995.

———. *To Wake the Nations: Race in the Making of American Literature.* Cambridge: Harvard University Press, 1993.

Suro, Roberto. *Strangers among Us: How Latino Immigration is Transforming America.* New York: Alfred A. Knopf, 1998.

Taylor, M. Brook. "The Poetry and Prose of History: 'Evangeline' and the Historians of Nova Scotia." *Journal of Canadian Studies* 23, no. 1–2 (1988): 46–67.

Tebbel, John William. *A History of Book Publishing in the United States.* New York: R. R. Bowker, 1972.

Thomas, Amy M. "Literature in Newsprint: Antebellum Family Newspapers and the Uses of Reading." In *Reading Books: Essays on the Material Text and Literature in America,* edited by Michele Moylan and Lane Stiles, 101–16. Amherst: University of Massachusetts Press, 1997.

Thomas, M. Wynn. *The Lunar Light of Whitman's Poetry.* Cambridge: Harvard University Press, 1987.

Thompson, G. R., ed. *Edgar Allen Poe: Essays and Reviews.* New York: Literary Classics of the United States, 1984.

Thoreau, Henry David. *Writings.* 20 vols. Boston: Houghton, Mifflin, 1906.

Tinker, Edward Larocque. *Creole City: Its Past and Its People.* New York: Longmans Green, 1953.

Torres, Luis A. "Bilingualism as Satire in Nineteenth Century Chicano Poetry." In *Another Tongue: Nation and Ethnicity in the Linguistic Borderlands,* edited by Alfred Arteaga, 247–62. Durham: Duke University Press, 1994.

———. *The World of Early Chicano Poetry: California Poetry, 1855–1881.* Encino, Calif.: Floricanto Press, 1994.

Townsend, Mary Ashley. *Down the Bayou.* Philadelphia: Lippincott, 1892.

Tucker, Robert W., and David C. Hendrickson. *Empire of Liberty: The Statecraft of Thomas Jefferson.* New York: Oxford University Press, 1990.

Varela, Félix. *Jicoténcatl.* Edited and introduction by Luis Leal. Houston: Arte Público Press, 1995.

Vázquez, Josefina Zoraida. *Mexicanos y norteamericanos ante la guerra del 47.* Mexico: Atenco, 1977.

Venuti, Lawrence. *The Scandals of Translation: Towards an Ethics of Difference.* London: Routledge, 1998.

———. *The Translator's Invisibility: A History of Translation.* London: Routledge, 1995.

Villegas Revueltas, Silvestre. *El liberalismo moderado en México, 1852–1864.* Mexico City: UNAM, 1997.

Vitier, Cintio. *Crítica cubana.* Havana: Letras Cubanas, 1988.

———. *Poetas cubanos del siglo XIX: Semblanzas.* Havana: Unión, 1969.

———. *Rescate de Zenea.* Havana: Unión, 1987.

Vizenor, Gerald Robert. *Manifest Manners: Postindian Warriors of Survivance.* Hanover, N.H.: Wesleyan University Press, 1994.

Wagenknecht, Edward, ed. *Mrs. Longfellow: Selected Letters and Journals.* New York: Longmans and Green, 1956.

Walker, Cheryl, ed. *American Women Poets of the Nineteenth Century: An Anthology.* New Brunswick: Rutgers University Press, 1992.

Wallerstein, Immanuel Maurice. *Historical Capitalism; With Capitalist Civilization.* London: Verso, 1995.

———. *The Modern World-System: Capitalist Agriculture and the Origins of the European World-Economy in the Sixteenth Century.* New York: Academic Press, 1976.

Walsh, Thomas, ed. *Hispanic Anthology.* New York: Kraus Reprint Company, 1969.

Warner, Michael. *The Letters of the Republic: Publication and the Public Sphere in Eighteenth-Century America.* Cambridge: Harvard University Press, 1990.

Weber, David J. "'Scarce More Than Apes': Historical Roots of Anglo-American Sterotypes of Mexicans in the Border Region." In *New Spain's Far Northern Frontier: Essays on Spain in the American West, 1540–1821,* edited by David J. Weber, 295–307. Dallas: Southern Methodist University Press, 1988.

———. *The Spanish Frontier in North America.* New Haven: Yale University Press, 1992.

Weber, David J., ed. *Foreigners in Their Native Land: Historical Roots of the Mexican Americans.* Albuquerque: University of New Mexico Press, 1973.

Weinstein, Bernard. "Bryant, Annexation, and the Mexican War." *Emerson Society Quarterly* 63 (1971): 19–24.

Weisbuch, Robert. *Atlantic Double-Cross: American Literature and British Influence in the Age of Emerson.* Chicago: University of Chicago Press, 1986.

Weiskel, Thomas. *The Romantic Sublime: Studies in the Structure and Psychology of Transcendence.* Baltimore: Johns Hopkins University Press, 1986.

Welsh, Andrew. *Roots of Lyric: Primitive Poetry and Modern Poetics.* Princeton: Princeton University Press, 1978.

Wermuth, Paul C., ed. *Selected Letters of Bayard Taylor.* Lewisburg, Pa.: Bucknell University Press, 1997.

Wertheimer, Eric. *Imagined Empires: Incas, Aztecs, and the New World of American Literature, 1771–1876.* New York: Cambridge University Press, 1999.

White, William. *Walt Whitman's Journalism: A Bibliography.* Detroit: Wayne State University Press, 1969.

Whitman, Walt. *The Correspondence.* Edited by Edwin Haviland Miller. 6 vols. New York: New York University Press, 1961–77.

———. *The Early Poems and the Fiction.* Edited by Thomas L. Brasher. New York: New York University Press, 1963.

———. *Notebooks and Uncollected Prose Manuscripts.* Edited by Edward F. Grier. Vol. 6. New York: New York University Press, 1984.

———. *Poetry and Prose.* Edited by Justin Kaplan. New York: Library of America, 1982.

Whittier, John Greenleaf. *The Complete Poetical Works of John Greenleaf Whittier.* New York: Houghton, Mifflin and Company, 1894.

———. *Letters of John Greenleaf Whittier.* Edited by John B. Pickard. 3 vols. Cambridge: Harvard University Press, 1975.

Williams, Stanley T. *The Spanish Background of American Literature.* 2 vols. New York: Archon Books, 1968.

Williams, William Appleman. *Empire as a Way of Life: An Essay on the Causes and Character of America's Present Predicament.* New York: Oxford University Press, 1980.

Wilson, Rob. *American Sublime: The Genealogy of a Poetic Genre.* Madison: University of Wisconsin Press, 1991.

Ysunza Ozeta, Salvador. *Juárez y el tratado McLane-Ocampo.* Mexico City: Sociedad Mexicana de Geografiá y Estadística, 1964.

Zamora, Lois Parkinson. "The Usable Past: The Idea of History in Modern U.S. and Latin American Fiction." In *Do the Americas Have a Common Literature?,* edited by Gustavo Pérez Firmat, 7–41. Durham: Duke University Press, 1990.

———. *The Usable Past: The Imagination of History in Recent Fiction of the Americas.* Cambridge: Cambridge University Press, 1997.

———. *Writing the Apocalypse: Historical Vision in Contemporary U.S. and Latin American Fiction.* Cambridge: Cambridge University Press, 1989.

Zanger, Jules. "The Premature Elegy: Bryant's 'The Prairies' as Political Poem." In *Interface: Essays on History, Myth, and Art in American Literature,* edited by Daniel Royot, 13–20. Montpellier, France: Publications de La Recherche, 1985.

Zboray, Ronald J. *A Fictive People: Antebellum Economic Development and the American Reading Public.* New York: Oxford University Press, 1993.

Zea, Leopoldo. *El pensamiento latinoamericano.* Mexico: Pormaca, 1965.

Zweig, Paul. *Walt Whitman: The Making of the Poet.* New York: Basic Books, 1984.

Where names of nations, regions, or states have changed during or since the nineteenth century, references are classified according to current usage. Periodicals are arranged by title first, city second. *Passim* indicates scattered references to a term across a range of pages.

authorship (*cont.*)

217n. 23; vernacular, 25–29, 105, 142. *See also* letrado; print culture

Aztec civilization: interest of transamerican writers in, 51–52, 56–8, 74; relationship to Toltecs and Tlascalans, 52; wealth of, 134. *See also* indigenous peoples in the Americas; Mexico

Babylonian captivity, analogues to, 64–65, 151–52

Baker, Houston, 219n. 40

ballad form, 21–22, 24, 88, 147. *See also* poetry

Barton, Benjamin Smith, 50, 52

Baxter, David, 49

Bejareño, El (San Antonio), xv, 101, 157

Bello, Andrés: and American language, 5, 12, 79; call for Americanist poetry, xiii, 188, 223n. 18; as transnational subject, 15, 189

Benjamin, Walter, 109, 205, 233n. 21

Bennett, Paula B., 219n. 39, 230n. 68, 236n. 33

Berman, Antoine, 82

Betancourt, Salvador Cisneros, 146

bilingualism, 44, 104–7, 118–19, 126, 191, 209, 251n. 27. *See also* English language; language; Spanish language; translation

Bolívar, Simón, 39, 58–60 *passim*, 189, 227n. 48

Bolivia, 163

Bolton, Herbert, 8–9

book trade. *See* print culture

borderlands: Latinos identified with, 10, 209–11; relation to national center, 10, 20, 76, 103; representations of, 148, 185–86; as theoretical concept, 6, 9–10. *See also* entries for names of nations and states

Borges, Jorge Luis, xvi

Bourdieu, Pierre, 7, 216n. 21

Brau, Professor S., 2–4 *passim*

Brazil, 79, 191, 213n. 1, 227n. 50

Britain: as colonial power in North America, 94; interest in Nicaragua, 127

Brito, Aristeo, ix

Brodhead, Richard H., 217n. 23, 238n. 53

Brooks, Maria Gowen ("María del Occidente"), xiii, 14, 38, 172; biography of, 33–35, 61–62; and Cuba, 62–70 *passim*, 232n. 6; and Longfellow, 33; and Poe, 32, 35; views on race, 66–70; views on women, 64–65, 68

—"Beatriz," 35, 38

—*Idomen*, 32, 34–35, 62–68

—*Judith, Esther and Other Poems*, 33, 64

—"Ode to the Departed," 69–70

—"Oration, The," 66

—"Stanzas to Niagara," 31–33, 35, 43, 62

—*Zóphiël*, 34–35, 62–64, 67–68

Brooks, Van Wyck, 33

Brownson, Orestes, 137, 236n. 40

Bryant, William Cullen, 20, 70, 102, 119, 214n.4; biography of, 36–37; interest in Spanish language and cultures, 36–37, 52–55, 194; Latin American reputation, 2, 19, 191; poetry of characterized as feminine, 217n. 25; political views, 49, 61, 87–88, 185–86, 252n. 34; and Pombo, 161, 174; and Prieto, Guillermo, 203; reviews *Jicoténcal*, 52–55, 58–59, 71; and Spanish American revolutions, 53–55; translation of Homer, 85; translations of Heredia, xiii, 1, 36, 45–47, 51, 75, 213n. 1; as translator, 27, 53, 165, 231n. 1; travels to Latin America, 18, 35, 185–86; views on race, 252n. 34; and Whitman, 122

—"Prairies, The," xiii, 38, 48–52, 54, 56, 87

—"Story of the Island of Cuba," 36

Bueno, Salvador, 187

Butler, Benjamin, 159

Byron, George Gordon Lord: invoked, 119, 149, 165; translations of works in Americas, 27, 80, 105–6, 164; vogue of Byronic sensibility, 4, 35, 44, 148, 152, 196

California: *californio* identity, 104, 177, 205–7; Gold Rush in, 102, 134, 162, 177; Mexican exiles in, 177–82; poetry about, 89;

print culture in, 100–106, 162, 177–82; race relations in, 102–6; travelers to, 16, 186, 195, 198, 244n. 51; U.S. attempt to purchase from Mexico, 87

Campbell, George, 44

Campuzano, Luisa, 230n. 67

Canada: climate represented, 34–35, 62, 229n. 62; possible U.S. annexation of, 117. *See also* Acadian Removals (1755)

canon, literary: formation of, 16, 21–22, 80–81, 103, 207–8; and nationalist ideology, 25, 90–91. *See also* cultural capital

capitalism, critiques of, 166, 192–93, 202, 209. *See also* transamerican relations, economic

captivity narratives, 104, 195–96. *See also* Babylonian captivity, analogues to; slavery

Carey and Hart Publishers, 83, 225n. 30

Caribbean region: climate represented, 33, 35; and transamerican geography, 47, 110–11, 132–33; U.S. expansion into, 49, 161, 167–68, 176–77. *See also* entries for names of individual countries

Carilla, Emilio, 80–81

Caro, José Eusebio, 79, 164

Caro, Miguel Antonio, 79, 81

Carpio, Manuel, 31

Cass, Lewis, 117

Castellón, Pedro Angel, 146, 149

Caste Wars. *See* Yucatán region

Catholicism: defense of, 166–67, 192–93, 209; in *Evangeline*, 94–100, 125; and immigration anxieties, 99, 101; represented by Protestant writers, 73, 98, 125; as unifying force, 94–95, 99, 209

Catlin, George, 31

Central America: archaeological interest in, 226n. 44; filibustering, 11, 111, 205; as site of transoceanic canal, 11, 127, 164, 176, 186, 205; U.S. economic interests in, 252n. 36, 254n. 1. *See also* entries for names of individual countries

Cervantes, Miguel de: canonical status, 78, 147; as icon of linguistic purity, 101, 102, 106, 107

Céspedes, Carlos Manuel de, 194

Chagres River (Panama), 59

Chateaubriand, François-René de, 96, 231n. 72

Chicanos. *See* Latinos in the United States; Mexicans in the United States

Child, Lydia Maria, 66, 88

Chile: general history of, 15, 126, 163; economy of, 227n. 50; literacy rates in, 22

Chileans in the United States, 177–78

Choluteca pyramid (Mexico), 56–57

Church, Frederick, 31

cities: and center/periphery model, 16–17; growth of in Americas, 10–11; rise of urban subject, 128–29, 161, 176, 244n. 43. *See also* entries for names of individual cities

civilizationism. *See* empires, rise and fall of; indigenous peoples in the Americas

Clamor Público, El (Los Angeles), xiv, 101–7

class, social: and access to authorship, xvi, 215n. 10; and bias in Spanish borderlands, 102–3; and political agency of dispossessed, 25–29. *See also* capitalism, critiques of

classicism. *See* Greco-Roman civilization

Clay, Henry, 60, 201

Clifford, James, 13–14

code-switching. *See* bilingualism

Colás, Santiago, 223n. 18

Colombia: civil wars in, 161–62; and Costa Rican border dispute, 167–68; economy of, 227n. 50; independence of, 189; national literary canon of, 79, 164; and Panama Congress, 60; and transoceanic canal, 12, 18, 38, 167–68, 171. *See also* Panama

Colombians in the U.S., 161–76

colonialism: center/periphery model, 28; defining, 76–77; in Latin America, 28, 140–41, 151; and Latinos, 77–78, 117, 209; United States compared to Europe, 8–9, 76, 127, 205. *See also* imperialism; transamerican relations

Columbus, Christopher, as iconic figure, 38, 64, 85, 177–85

comparative literature, methodologies of, 4, 9, 13, 21, 77, 216n. 12

Confederate States of America, supporters of, 111, 157–59, 163, 177, 186, 250n. 23

conquest of America. *See* Spain

convention and cliché. *See* imitation; originality

Cooper, James Fenimore, 15

corrido form, 148. *See also* ballad form; orality

Cortés, Hernán, 52–54, 169

cosmopolitanism: on borderlands, 105, 191; as literary value, 14–15, 19–20; vs. nativism, 83–87; and translation, xiv, 19, 27, 78. *See also* nationalism; transnationalism

Costa Rica, 159, 166–69, 176

Creoles: defined in Latin America, 68; in New Orleans society, 109, 111, 125, 135, 157, 194, 199

Crescent (New Orleans), 120–22, 125–30 *passim*, 135–36

Cuba: annexation to United States discussed, xv, 1, 61, 111, 117, 139, 143–46, 154–56; climate represented, 63–68; economy of, 62, 227n. 50; Escalera Revolt (1844), 58, 62, 69–70, 152, 194; general history of, 46; national literary canon of, 4, 17, 47–48, 140, 142–43; print culture in, 62, 75, 139–40, 142–43, 246n. 79; slavery in, 57, 62, 69–70, 178; Ten Years' War (1868–78), 46, 163, 187, 194; U.S. interest in, 35, 74–75, 105, 134–35; War of Independence (1895–98), 76, 193–96

Cubans in the United States, 111–12, 209; independence movement among, 167, 187, 193–94, 223n. 22; and López revolt, 139–40, 196, 199–201

Cubí y Soler, Mariano, 36, 53

cultural capital: 7, 77, 79, 215n. 10. *See also* popular culture

cultural production, field of: autonomy and, 216n. 21; defined, 7; within transamerican sphere, 13, 20–25. *See also* print culture

Dana, Charles, 205

Dana, Richard Henry, 14, 35

Dante Alighieri: American imitators, 16, 251n. 27; translations of in Americas, 27, 78, 85, 235n. 33

Darío, Rubén: and anti-imperialism, 13, 169; and *modernismo*, 80, 176

DeBow's Review (New Orleans), 1

de la Concepción Valdes, Gabriel ("Plácido"): death of, 62, 69–70; editions of works of, 245n. 56; U.S. reputation of, 75, 231nn. 6–7; and Villaverde, 111; Zenea compared to, 194

de la Cruz, Sor Juana Inés, 71, 73, 106, 182–83

del Monte, Domingo, 39–40, 57, 62, 223n. 23, 225n. 30, 245n. 62

Delta (New Orleans), 113, 120, 123, 145

Democratic Party, 117, 127

de Onís, José, 216nn. 12, 14

Diario del Gobierno de la República Mexicana, 112, 245n. 63

Dickinson, Emily, 14, 81

domesticity, cult of. *See* women

Dominican Republic: annexation discussed, 163; geography of, 110; as refugee destination, 47, 95; U.S. intervention in, 11

Dryden, John, 82

Durand, José, 170, 173–76

Duyckinck, Evert A., 86

Eagle (Brooklyn, New York), 121, 124, 135, 241n. 27

"Edda." *See* Pombo, Rafael

editors and editing. *See* entries for names of individual persons and publications; periodicals; print culture

elegy form, 21. *See also* poetry

Ellett, Elizabeth, 34, 235n. 33

Emerson, Ralph Waldo: as critic of poetry, 217n. 25; and Latin America, 154, 174; and Whitman, 5, 122, 235n. 33, 243n. 43

empires, rise and fall of: and Britain, 94, 97; in precolumbian Americas, 51, 53–54, 99–100, 169; and Spain, 150–51, 169. *See also* Greco-Roman civilization; history; imperialism

English language: characterized by Spanish speakers, 44, 99–100, 118–20; learning of, 199–200. *See also* bilingualism; language; translation

epic form, 21, 90–92, 99. *See also* poetry
Ercilla, Alonso de, 106
Erkkila, Betsy, 130
Escalera Revolt. *See* Cuba
Escobar, José, 102
Espronceda, José de, 78, 141, 144, 150
Europe compared to Americas. *See* Americanist ideology, claims of
exile, as literary theme, 39–48 *passim*, 90–94, 104, 140, 145–52 *passim*, 160, 178, 183–84, 197, 201, 209
expansionism, U.S.: Caribbean compared to Western, 161, 167–68, 176–77; critiques from Anglo-American sources, 84, 87–90, 161, 215n. 8; critiques from Latin American sources, 113–20; ethics of debated, 76, 99, 121; and *Evangeline*, 92–94, 99; Latino ambivalence toward, 193; and "The Prairies," 48–51; and westward movement, 8–9, 11, 37, 76, 87–90, 121, 133. *See also* Free Soil Party; imperialism; Mexican War; Monroe Doctrine; transamerican relations; Young America movement

family, metaphors of: Latin Americans as children of same mother, 60, 176; Mexico as sick family, 185–86, 197, 199; Western hemisphere as fraternal republics in Monroe Doctrine, 55, 102, 178. *See also* sentimentalism
female poets. *See* women
Fernández de Castro, José Antonio, 158
Fields, Mrs. James T., 85–86
filibusters, xiv, 11, 111; motives for, 144, 156; Pombo's critique of, 161, 169. *See also* Central America; López, Narciso; Walker, William
Fletcher, Angus, 233n. 20
Fliegelman, Jay, 228n. 54
folk literature. *See* orality; Romanticism, literary
Follin, Miriam Florence, 186–87. *See also* Leslie, Frank, Publishers
Franchot, Jenny, 73, 237n. 49
Free Soil Party, 61, 88, 117, 121

Freiligrath, Ferdinand, 83–84
French culture: and Latin American writers, 79–80; in Louisiana, 108–10, 112
frontier. *See* borderlands
Fuller, Margaret, 33

Gaceta, La (Santa Barbara, California), 16
Galeano, Eduardo, 228–29n. 59
García Luna de Santa María, Isabel, 141–42
Garrison, William Lloyd, 88
geography: and Americanist ideology, 30–31, 37, 96, 99, 227n. 52, 250n. 19; argument for transamerican, 7–12; representations of North/South difference, 30–38 *passim*, 48–49, 61, 89, 133; Whitman and, 128, 133–36. *See also* borderlands; expansionism, U.S.; imperialism; transamerican relations
German culture, transamerican interest in, 80, 82, 84–86, 225n. 36
Gilroy, Paul, 9
globalization theory, 5–6, 80
Goethe, Johann Wolfgang von, 84–86 *passim*
Gómez, Eusebio Juan, 113–20 *passim*, 126–27, 137–45 *passim*, 190–91
Gómez de Avellaneda, Gertrudis, 17, 20, 31, 105, 183, 230n. 67, 245n. 61
Gómez Farías, Valentín, 110
González, José Elías, 101
González de la Garza, Mauricio, 121, 242n. 31
González Echevarría, Roberto, 214n. 5, 217n. 22, 233n. 17
Greco-Roman civilization: compared to European colonizers, 40, 197; compared to precolumbian Americas, 49–50, 52, 58, 227n. 47; and translation practice, 79
Greeley, Horace, 102, 253n. 44
Greene, Roland, 21
Greenspan, Ezra, 242n. 30
Greenwood Cemetery (Brooklyn, New York), 173, 201–2
Griswold, Rufus Wilmot: as anthologist, 17, 24, 69, 236n. 33; and Brooks, 32, 34, 69; and Longfellow, 83

Grunzweig, Walter, 241–42n. 27
Guadalupe-Hidalgo, Treaty of, ix, 11, 74,
    100, 126–27, 197. *See also* Mexican War
Guido y Spano, Carlos, 79
Gustafson, Zadel Barnes, 34, 229nn. 63–64,
    230n. 68
Gutiérrez, J. M., 17, 24
Gutiérrez Coll, Jacinto, 203–4

Habermas, Jürgen, 7
Hablador, El (New Orleans), 113
Haiti, 47, 59, 109
Hale, Edward Everett, 154
Hall, Stuart, 220n. 43
Harte, Bret, 14
Havana, Cuba: as center of print culture,
    126; compared to New Orleans, 100–111;
    landmarks, 38, 64, 194
Hawthorne, Nathaniel, 85, 90, 97
Hegel, Georg Wilhelm Friedrich, 53
Heine, Heinrich, 19, 27, 106
hemispheric relations. *See* transamerican
    relations
Herald (New York), 147, 164
Heredia y Heredia, José María, 20, 38, 70,
    74, 91, 115, 140, 172–73, 187, 196, 209,
    245n. 61; biography of, 37, 39–40, 44, 57;
    as exemplary exile poet, 146, 150, 152,
    193; as journalist, xiii, 37, 112; and Mex-
    ico, 56–61; and Poe, 43; as translator, 44;
    U.S. reputation of, 1–5, 8–9, 51, 75;
    views on race, 60; views on United States,
    43–44, 60–61
— "A Emilia," 39–40, 228n. 53
— "Al huracán," 1–5, 8–9, 51, 75
— "Carta de Niágara," 224nn. 24, 25, 27
— "Carta sobre los Estados Unidos,"
    224n. 27
— "En un teocalli de Cholula," 38, 56–57
— "Las sombras," 38, 57–58, 151
— "Niágara," xiii, 35–36, 40–48, 54, 56, 75
— "Oda a los habitantes de Anáhuac," 57
— "Proyecto," 228n. 53
— "Vuelta al Sur," 40
Hernández, J. E., 146
Hernández, José (*Martín Fierro*), 26, 81

heroism: attributed to indigenous leaders,
    52–55, 57–58; attributed to military
    leaders of American revolutions, 53–54,
    202
Herrán, Pedro Alcantara, 165, 168
Hispanophilia in United States, xiv, 27, 119,
    136, 174, 194, 205. *See also* entries for
    names of individuals
history: case for common hemispheric, 8–9,
    95–96, 210; cyclical theory of, 51; as
    poetic theme, 38–39, 49–55, 136; pro-
    phetic use of, 135–36, 237–38n. 52. *See
    also* empires, rise and fall of; nationalism;
    transamerican relations
Homer: Heredia compared to, 146; transla-
    tions of, 82, 85–86, 91
Honduras, 136, 186
Hostos, Eugenio María de, 187, 247n. 91
Houghton Mifflin Publishing Co., 83
Howe, Julia Ward, 35
Hugo, Victor, 27, 80, 105, 106
Humboldt, Alexander von, 85
Hurlbert, William Henry, 71–75, 87, 89,
    119

"I. A. P." *See* Prieto de Landázuri, Isabel
identity formation, 214–15n. 7. *See also*
    Latinos in the United States; nationalism;
    transamerican relations
imitation: as form of agency, xiii, 25–29;
    and journalistic practice, 138; in Latino
    writing, 103–4, 181–82; and literary con-
    vention, 24–25; and secondariness, 20;
    and translation, 27, 81–82. *See also*
    authorship; originality
immigration in United States, 101, 109, 178,
    185–86, 238n. 55. *See also* Cubans in the
    United States; Latinos in the United
    States; Mexicans in the United States
imperialism: Anglo-American critiques of,
    12, 192; applicability to U.S. case debated,
    11–12, 205; Latin American/Latino cri-
    tiques of, 12–13, 112, 168–71 *passim*,
    192–93, 197, 216n. 12; in nineteenth-
    century world, 18–19, 117–20, 133–34.
    See also empires; transamerican relations

Incan civilization, 51–52, 58. *See also* indigenous peoples in the Americas

independence movements. *See* revolutions in the Americas

indigenous peoples in the Americas: in Caribbean, 52; civilized status debated, 50–51, 66, 136; languages and place names, 57, 140; and literacy/orality, 18, 102, 218n. 32; and nationalist ideology, 38–39, 48–52, 56–58, 236n. 36; as popular literary theme, 50, 57, 66, 235–36n. 33; and racial categories, 53, 117; U.S. policies toward, 51, 61, 66, 177, 193; as "vanishing" culture, 49–51, 92, 135–36. *See also* Aztec civilization; empires, rise and fall of; Incan civilization; Mayan peoples; racial mixing

influence, literary. *See* originality

intellectuals, 7, 216n. 21. *See also* authorship; letrado

inter-americanism. *See* transamerican relations

interventions, military. *See* Monroe Doctrine; transamerican relations

Iris, El (Mexico City), 37, 47–48

Irolo, Vicenta, 142

Irving, Washington, 62, 78

Itúrbide, Agustín de, 12, 110, 141

Jackson, Andrew, 10

Janowitz, Anne, 217n. 27

Jefferson, Thomas, 30, 37, 91, 228n. 54

Jeffreys, Mark, 217nn. 27, 30

Jicoténcal (anon.), 38, 71; authorship of, 52; Bryant's review of, 52–55

Johanssen, Robert K., 90

Júarez, Benito: family of, 149–50, 185–86; as iconic figure, 197, 203; and Maximilian, 176–79, 185–86; in New Orleans, 110–11; and U.S. Civil War, 158–59, 163. *See also* Mexico

Kanellos, Nicolás, 6, 178, 213–14n. 4, 238n. 57, 245n. 58, 247n. 92

Kaplan, Amy, 216n. 18, 232n. 9

Kearney, Stephen, 119

Kendall, George Wilkins, 112

Kennedy, James, 174, 223n. 22, 225n. 31

Know-Nothing Party, 101

Lamar, Mirabeau S., 156–57, 160

Lamartine, Alphonse, 80, 106, 137, 144, 147, 173

language: American particularities of, 48, 77; English and Spanish contrasted, 79, 99–100, 118–20, 167–68; learning of, 2–3, 44, 79, 100–101; and social power, xvi, 2, 22–25, 77, 100–107, 120, 207, 215n. 11; as source of collective identity, 113–14, 208–9. *See also* bilingualism; English language; Spanish language

Larsen, Kerry, 130

Latin America, problem of defining, 215n. 5. *See also* entries for names of individual countries; transamerican relations

Latinos in the United States: defined, x, 6, 160, 213n.3; diversity of, x–xi, 210, 214n. 4; emergence as group in nineteenth century, 3–5, 114–15, 135–36, 145, 174–76, 191–92, 208–11; external factors shaping identity of, xi–xii, 13, 209; marginality of, xii, 13, 210–11; racialization of, xi, 210; relation of to collective past, x, 4, 13, 136, 208–11

Latino writing: defined, xiii; distinctiveness of, 208–9; history represented in, ix–x, 210; and literacy/orality, 148, 208; and U.S. literary canon, 10, 209–20

Laúd del desterrado, El, xiv, 111, 144, 146–52, 193, 197, 214n.4, 245n. 61

Leslie, Frank, Publishers, xv, 158, 162, 186–88. *See also* Follin, Miriam Florence

Letrado: decline of in twentieth century, 207–8; defined in relation to state, 16–17, 80–81; in peripheries of nation, 101–7; role of poetry in training, 79–80. *See also* authorship; intellectuals; print culture

Levine, Lawrence, 22

Limón, José, 10

Lincoln, Abraham, 178

literacy: on borderlands, 20, 26–29, 102–3, 208; and conquest of Americas, 18–19; rates in nineteenth-century Americas, 22–23; state investment in, 13, 103; transitional, 23–25; varied skills comprising, 6–7. *See also* language; orality; print culture

literary history, ideology of, xi–xii, 10–11, 108–11. *See also* archival research; canon, literary

literary societies, 24, 138, 174–76

Llona, Numa Pompilio, 180–82, 184

Loeffelholz, Mary, 219n. 39

Longfellow, Frances Appleton, 83

Longfellow, Henry Wadsworth, xiv, xv, 15, 19, 20, 119, 165, 193; as anthologist, 80, 82–84, 222n. 14; biography of, 78, 82–83; and Brooks, 33; canonical status, 77, 81, 97; interest in Spanish language and culture, 78–79, 194; and Poe, 234n. 25; and Pombo, 79, 94, 161, 174, 207–8, 233n. 14; popularity of across social class, 78, 80; and Quintero, 153–58; relations with publishers, 83–84; and religion, 94–100; and sentimentalism, 97–98; translation of *Coplas de Manrique*, 78, 85, 221n. 6; translation of *Divine Comedy*, 78, 85; as translator, 80–87, 106, 165, 238n. 61; and Vallejo, 205–7; views on Mexican War, 17–18, 71, 99; views on slavery, 90, 154; and Whitman, 122, 124, 125, 235n. 30; works of translated into Spanish, 79–82, 87, 90–94, 106, 111, 154, 191–92, 207–8

—*Evangeline*, 82, 87–99, 111

—*Kavanagh*, 84, 221nn. 3, 6, 235n. 27, 236n. 36

—"Psalm of Life, A," 81, 237n. 45

—"To Bayard Taylor," 206–7

López, Narciso: critiques of, 246n. 71; filibustering activity of, 111, 139, 143–44, 153, 156, 193, 199; as iconic figure, xv, 145–46, 166–67. *See also* Cuba; expansionism, U.S.

Los Angeles, California, 179, 177

Louisiana, 91–93, 109. *See also* New Orleans

Loving, Jerome, 122, 126, 243n. 43

Lynch (Botta), Anne, 34, 235n. 33

lyric form: ideological readings of, 6, 21–22; and individualism, 21, 24; and reading skills, 26. *See also* poetry

Maddox, Lucy, 51

Magdalena Canal and Steamship Company, 167–68

Manifest Destiny: and Bryant, 49; as slogan, 11, 72, 87, 144; and Whitman, 109, 121, 133. *See also* expansionism, U.S.; Mexican War; O'Sullivan, John

Man of Letters. *See* letrado

Mansilla Gorriti, Juana, 165

"María del Occidente." *See* Brooks, Maria Gowen

markets. *See* capitalism; transamerican relations, economic

Martell, Helvetia, 6, 178, 245n. 58, 247n. 92

Martí, José: Americanist literary themes of, 31, 36, 58, 153, 176, 205; and Heredia, 223n. 23; and Longfellow, 179; and originality, 20, 80; and print culture, 173, 189; as transamerican theorist, xv, 5, 58, 176, 192, 204, 210; and U.S. exile, 174, 176, 192–93, 205, 210, 254n. 52; and Whitman, 121, 240n. 1. *See also* Cuba

Matanzas, Cuba: as center of print culture, 62, 69–70, 231–32n. 6; political conditions in, 69–70

Matthewson, Dr., 118–19, 126, 136

Matthiessen, F. O., 209, 233n. 20

Maximilian, Emperor of Mexico, 178–79, 185–86, 206–7

May, Caroline, 229n. 63

Maya, Rafael, 249n. 9

Mayan peoples, 60, 117, 226n. 44. *See also* indigenous peoples in the Americas

Mejía, José Antonio, 110

Meléndez, Gabriel, 251n. 24

Melville, Herman, 72, 89, 210

memorization, 23–24

memory, collective: and performance, 23; role of in establishing national identity, 10, 210–11; and suppression of racial difference, 38–39, 67–68, 210. *See also* nationalism; print culture

Mendive, Rafael, 78, 157, 238n. 61

Menken, Adah Isaacs, xv, 162, 194–96, 252n. 36

Mestizaje. *See* racial mixing

Mestre, Juan Manuel, 191

Mexicans in the United States: 10, 14, 100–101, 104–7, 177–86 *passim*, 209. *See also* borderlands; Latinos in the United States

Mexican War (1846–48): Anglo-American critiques of, 17–18, 71, 75–76, 87–90, 99, 135; Anglo-American support of, 122–23; battles, 87–88, 197; consequences for Mexicans in borderlands, ix–x, 14, 100–101, 104–7; journalistic coverage of, 101, 112–17, 123; Latin American/Latino critiques of, 115–17, 197; as pivotal moment in transamerican relations, xiv, 1, 11–12, 61, 74–76, 93, 135, 169; veterans of engaged in filibustering, 144. *See also* expansionism, U.S.; Guadalupe-Hidalgo, Treaty of

Mexico: Anglo-American representations of, 49, 199; and Cuba, 40, 60, 112, 149–50, 152, 163; economy of, 227n. 50; French occupation under Maximilian, xv, 2, 150, 159, 162–63, 178–79, 185–86; geography of, 31, 127, 176–77; historiographic tradition, 52; independence and Santa Anna dictatorship, 38, 57, 110–11; Liberal *Reforma* and civil wars, 110–11, 141–42, 162–63, 176–77, 182, 197; literacy rates in, 22–23; national literary canon of, 197–99; print culture in, 37, 112, 141; and U.S. Civil War, 158–59, 185

Mexico, Gulf of, 49, 110, 127, 133–36, 198. *See also* geography

Mignolo, Walter, 10, 18, 214n. 5, 216n. 16

Milanés, José Jacinto, 74–75 *passim*

Miller, Ralph, 50

Miralla, José Antonio, 40

Misisipí, El (Louisiana), 111, 240n. 9

Mississippi River, 7–8, 124–25, 127, 132–33. *See also* New Orleans

Mitre, Bartolomé, 79

modernism, literary: in Latin America, 35, 80, 176, 253n. 43; and popular culture, 22; rejection of letrado, 18, 80–82; and sentimentalism, 97; and U.S. imperialism, 11

Monroe Doctrine, 11–12, 38, 54–56; later interpretations of, 59–61, 242n. 27; Latin American response to, 60–61; and Mexican War, 76, 93. *See also* transamerican relations

Montes-Huidobro, Matías, 214n. 4, 246n. 72

Moore, Thomas, 44, 106, 166

Moretti, Franco, 22, 215n. 11

Morla Vicuña, Carlos, 94–100 *passim*, 174, 192

Morrison, Toni, 210

Mosquera, Tomás Cipriano de, 167–68

Mundo Nuevo, El (New York), xv, 162; ambivalence toward U.S. culture, 191–93; and Cuban politics, 193–96; publishing history of, 186–89; reviews *Evangeline*, 96–100; transamerican reach of, 188–90. *See also América Ilustrada*

nationalism: and borders, 10; and cultural nativism vs. cosmopolitanism, 83–87; and institutions of historical memory, 10–11, 72, 210–11; and literary canon, 25, 90–91; and public sphere of print, 7, 15–16; vs. Latin Americanism, 43. *See also* revolutions in the Americas; transamerican relations

Native Americans. *See* indigenous peoples in the Americas

nativism. *See* Americanist ideology, claims of natural history and Americanist ideology, 30–33. *See also* geography

Neruda, Pablo, 15, 42, 80, 121

New England region: climate represented, 43–44; inhabitants characterized, 68, 94, 152–54

Newman, Francis, 82

New Mexico: annexation of, 87, 90, 119; *neomexicano* identity, 177; print culture in, 100, 102, 215n. 9, 251n. 24; Whitman on, 135, 235n. 27

New Orleans: as Caribbean city, 132–33; Catholic influence in, 125; compared to New York City, 109, 111, 139–40, 245n. 59; and Cuba, 109, 142, 195; diversity of population, 137–38; during Mexican War, 112–13, 123, 133; during U.S. Civil War and Reconstruction, 159–60, 199; exoticized by Northerners, 131; French influence in, 108–11 passim; importance in transamerican trade, xiv, 110, 133–34, 142, 195; Latin Americans in, 109–11; print culture in, 71, 111–20, 136–44, 193; slavery in, 129–32 passim

newspapers. See periodicals

New World. See transamerican relations

New York City: Cuban separatists in, 146–48, 201–4; diversity of population, 10; print culture in, 158, 164, 186–95; travelers' reports of, 170, 173–76, 201–4

Ngugi wa Thiong'o, 23

Niagara Falls: and American sublime, xiii, 30–48 passim, 58; death-cult at, 32–33, 224n. 27; poems to, 31, 36, 171–73, 202–3, 205, 220n. 3, 249–50n. 16; travelers to, 124, 163, 188, 250n. 19

Nicaragua, 12, 126–27, 136, 176

Nicholson, Eliza ("Pearl Rivers"), 160, 200

North American Review, 16, 71

Norton, Anne, 232n. 8

Noticioso, El (New York), 158, 186

Nuevo Mundo, El (San Francisco), xv, 1–2, 150, 162, 177–82

Nye, Russell, 218n. 31

Oboler, Suzanne, xi

Ocampo, Melchor, 111, 176–77

ode form, 21. See also poetry

Ong, Walter, 23

orality: and folk traditions, 21, 23; in Latino culture, 148, 208. See also language; literacy

Orientalism, 64–65, 72, 104, 142, 222n. 9

originality: as Americanist ideology, 28, 77, 80, 86–87, 188; and colonialism, 28–29, 232n. 10; and gender, 87; Romantic fetish of, 26–27; sacred valence of, 80; vs. trans-

lation, xiv, 3, 100. See also cultural capital; imitation

Orjuela, Hector, 166, 168, 222n. 14, 248n. 4, 249n. 9

Osgood, Frances Sargent, 34

O'Sullivan, John, 48, 117, 144–45

Paine, Thomas, 147

Panama: geography represented, 14; as site of transoceanic canal, 6, 12, 127, 164, 176; "Watermelon War" in, 171. See also Colombia

Panama Congress (1826), 59–61

Pan-Americanist movement, 2, 254n. 1. See also transamerican relations

Patria, La (New Orleans), 112–20, 126, 136–45, 187, 190–91

Payne, Thatcher Taylor, 222n. 14

Pelayo, El (New Orleans), 246n. 71

Pérez Bonalde, Juan Antonio, 31, 79, 203–5

performance: in orality/literacy continuum, 23–25, 28–29, 110; and poetic experience, 179–82, 194, 198, 203–4, 206–8

periodicals: bilingualism in, 101–7 passim, 112, 118, 126, 136–37, 147, 186, 191; borrowing from exchanged papers, 101, 105, 113–14, 120, 126, 128, 138; circulation among multiple readers, 23; circulation within transamerican sphere, 6, 78, 105, 113–15, 157, 162, 177, 182–84, 187, 190–91; and democratic ideology, 121–22; ephemerality of, ix–x, xvi, 208; literary content of, xii–xiii, 6, 21–25, 142, 146, 178–79; Spanish-language published in the United States, ix–xii, 5–6, 77–78, 101–7, 112–20, 136–45. See also entries for place names and periodical titles; print culture

Peru: history of, 163, 190, 229–30n. 65, 230n. 68; print culture in, 177, 180–82

Peruvians in the United States, 162, 177

Peza, Juan de Dios, 79

Picayune (New Orleans), 112–13, 120, 123, 159–60, 198, 200

Pike, Fredrick, 12

Piñeyro, Enrique, 187–90, 196

Pitt, Leonard, 177

"Plácido." *See* de la Concepción Valdes, Gabriel

Poe, Edgar Allen: compared to Brooks, 32, 35; compared to Heredia, 43; influence in Latin America, 35, 79, 192; and Longfellow, 234n. 25

poetry: and criticism, 23–24; and nationalism, 6, 154–55, 201; in periodicals, xii–xiii, 6, 21–25, 146, 178–79; relative prestige of forms, 21–22, 79–80, 100, 103, 215n. 11; shifting tastes and values in, 25, 80–81, 225n. 33. *See also* ballad form; canon, literary; epic form; lyric form; ode form; performance; translation

Polk, James K., 12, 93, 113, 227n. 49

Pombo, Rafael, xiv, xv; and Bryant, 161, 174; diary-keeping, 165–68; as diplomat, 18–19, 163–64; and "Edda" pseudonym, 164–67, 172; and Heredia, 173; and Longfellow, 79, 94, 161, 174, 207–8, 233n. 14; and *El Mundo Nuevo*, 188, 191; and sexuality, 166–67; as translator, 79, 94, 161, 164, 174, 207–8, 233n. 14; views of United States, 163–68, 170–76, 196

—"A Costa Rica," 169

—"Diálogo entre Cortés y William Walker," 169

—"Las norteamericanas en Broadway," 170–73

—"Niágara," 31, 249–50n. 16

popular culture, 79–80, 103, 213n. 31, 215n. 11, 220n. 43. *See also* canon, literary

Post (New York), 174, 186

postcolonial theory, 214n. 7. *See also* colonialism; imperialism; race

Pratt, Mary Louise, 14, 18–19

Prescott, William Hickling, 5, 51, 90, 236n. 36

Prieto, Guillermo, xv, 14; and Bryant, 203; and exile, 201–2; poetic works of, 31, 197, 202–3; political views of, 199; and print culture, 141; and Quintero, 198–200; sentimentalization of national family, 197, 252n. 33; travel writings of, 149, 162–63, 196–204

Prieto de Landázuri, Isabel ("I. A. P."), xv, 162; biography of, 182–83; reputation, 184–85

—"Al desgraciado autor de *Un tipo del siglo*," 179–82

—"O patria mía," 182–83

print culture: in California, 100–106, 162, 177–82; and censorship, 139–40; in Cuba, 62, 75, 139–40, 142–43, 246n. 79; and democratic ideology, 146, 187; of literary history, xii, 4, 20–25, 77–78, 208–9; in Mexico, 37, 112, 141; in New Mexico, 100, 102, 215n. 9, 251n. 24; in New Orleans, 71, 111–20, 136–44, 193; in New York, 158, 164, 173–76, 186–95, 203; Spanish-language in the United States (general), 100, 178, 187–89, 190–91, 209–11; and technological innovations, 188, 197; in Texas, 100–101, 157–58; in the United States (general), 7–8, 16, 83–84, 174, 189. *See also* authorship; periodicals

Protestantism, representations of by Catholics, 95–98

public sphere, 7, 18, 167. *See also* authorship; print culture

publishing. *See* print culture

Puerto Rico, literary canon of, 105, 214n. 4; separatist movement in, 60, 187; U.S. annexation of, 2–3, 110, 178

Quintero, José Agustín, xiv–xv, 14, 146; biography of, 152–53; and Cuban separatism, 152–54; death of, 160; diplomatic service to Confederacy, 149, 152, 157–59; diplomatic service to the United States, 149, 159; as journalist, 156–57, 186; and Longfellow, 153–58; in New Orleans, 153, 159–60, 197–200; and Prieto, Guillermo, 163, 167, 198–200; as translator, 154–55; views on slavery, 154

—"A Miss Lydia Robbins," 149, 153

—"Poesía," 153–54

Quijano, Aníbal, 8

Quitman, John Anthony, 156, 158

race: and access to authorship, xvi; contrasts between Anglo- and Latin American views, 75, 167, 174–75, 178; erotics of racialized body, 65–67, 129–32, 157; in Mexico, 149–50; political consequences of, 60–61, 127, 208. *See also* Africans in the Americas; indigenous peoples in the Americas; Latinos in the United States; racial mixing

racial mixing: negative views of, 127, 135, 149, 159; positive views of, 136, 192

railroads, 176–77, 193

Rama, Angel, 16, 79–80, 233n. 17, 233–34n. 21

Ramírez, Francisco P., 101–7 *passim*

Ranchero, El (San Antonio), xiv, 101, 157–58

Read, Benjamin, 32

reading, varied definitions of, 6, 23–25. *See also* literacy; performance

Recovering the U.S. Hispanic Literary Heritage project, xi, 4, 106, 209–10, 213–14n. 4

Reforma. See Júarez, Benito; Mexico

Reilly, Tom, 101

representation: of ambassadors to nations, 15–16; of editors to readers, 16, 19; and taint of secondariness, 20

Revolución, La (New York City), 112, 167, 187, 194

revolutions in the Americas: compared to past historical struggles, 57–58; in Cuba, 140–41; in Haiti, 58; justness of defended, 55; metaphor of colonial condition as slavery, xiii, 55, 58–61, 75, 140–41, 151–54 *passim*, 185–86; in Santo Domingo, 58, 240n. 2; Spanish American contrasted to U.S., 53–56, 72–73, 75–76, 95, 102, 202, 216n. 13, 227n. 48. *See also* Britain; colonialism; nationalism; Romanticism, literary; Spain

Richard, Nelly, 28

Riddel, Joseph, 234n. 25

Rioja, Francisco de, 106, 150

Risa, La (New Orleans), 137–38

Riva Palacio, Vicente, 31

"Rivers, Pearl." *See* Nicholson, Eliza

Róa Bárcena, José María, 79

Roach, Joseph, 9, 23, 110, 219n. 38

Rodó, José Enrique (*Ariel*), 13, 80, 192

Romanticism, literary: interest in folk and indigenous themes, 15, 21–22, 24, 147, 236n. 36; and national identity, 15, 19; and revolutionary ideology, 15, 44, 147–48, 152. *See also* sublime, romantic

Romero, Matías, 185

Rousseau, Jean-Jacques, 44, 65, 67

Rüeckert, Friedrich, 154

Ruíz de Burton, María Amparo, 14, 183, 214n. 4

Ryan, Mary P., 10

Salazar, Mercedes, 14

Saldívar, José David, 10, 216n. 16

Sánchez, Luis, 9

Sánchez, Rosaura, xi, 245n. 4

Sánchez-Eppler, Karen, 130–31, 244n. 47

San Francisco, California, 177–84, 198

Santa Anna, Antonio López de, 40, 93, 110, 116, 123, 141

Santacilia, Pedro, xiv, 111, 146, 193, 197, 209; biography of, 149–50
—"A España," 150–51, 178
—"Salmo 137," 151–52

Sarmiento, Domingo Faustino, 5, 79

Schleiermacher, Friedrich, 81–82, 84, 106

Scott, Winfield, 5, 115, 197

sentimentalism: as critique of capitalism, 181–82; in *Evangeline*, 90–91, 99; and masculinity, xiv, 75, 148, 155; and Mexican War, 88–89, 99, 232n. 9; as poetic mode, 165–67; as political tactic, 111, 145, 148–49, 157, 170–72, 194–96; and regulation of subjectivity, 96–98, 219n. 39; and translation, 87. *See also* women

Siglo XIX (Mexico City), 141, 190

Sigourney, Lydia, 31, 32, 34, 41, 66, 226n. 40

Simms, William Gilmore, 124

Simon, Sherry, 87

slavery: as contradiction in democratic ideology, 38–39, 59–61, 121, 128–32, 154; economics of, 3, 8, 11, 57, 141, 144–45,

210; of indigenous peoples, 56–57, 60; used as metaphor for colonial condition, xiii, 55, 58–61, 75, 140–41, 151–54 *passim*, 185–86; used as metaphor for wifehood, 64–68, 165, 195–96; and Western expansion, 61, 76. *See also* abolitionism

Slidell, John, 87, 111

Smith, Elizabeth Oakes, 34

socialism, 80

Sommer, Doris, 132

Soulé, Pierre, 111, 199

Southey, Robert, 34, 66

Spain: conquest of Americas, 18, 52, 58, 169; Cuban policy, 148, 178; depicted by former colonies, 17, 76, 139–40, 150–51, 127; economic policy of in Caribbean, 37–38; 143–44, 193, 243n. 41; liberal reforms of Cortes, 12, 141. *See also* revolutions in the Americas

Spanish-American War (1898). *See* Cuba, War of Independence

Spanish language: defended by native speakers, 106–7, 114, 175–76, 209; as unifying force across Americas, 113, 137, 188–90, 192. *See also* bilingualism; language; print culture

Spillers, Hortense, 9

Squier, Ephraim, 252n. 36

stereotypes of Anglo-Americans, Latin American, xii; as aggressive, 137–38, 249–50n. 16; as capital accumulators, 166, 192–93; as cold, 165–67; as unoriginal, 138; as unspiritual, 159–60

stereotypes of Latin Americans, Anglo-American, xi–xiii; as exotic, 71–72, 125; as feminine, 88–89, 107, 125; as ignorant, 101–3, 117, 127; as racially inferior, 12, 14, 51, 59–60, 199, 243n. 41; as violent, 74–75, 127, 178

Stovall, Floyd, 128, 243n. 35

Stowe, Harriet Beecher (*Uncle Tom's Cabin*), 15, 91, 96

sublime, romantic: and Americanist ideology, 30–32, 37–39, 48; and commodification, 37, 172–73; conventions of, 41–43; and landscape, 56, 63–

64, 89; and repression, 38–39. *See also* Romanticism, literary

Sun (New York City), 145, 205

Sundquist, Eric, 59

Tacón, Miguel, 40, 62

Talisman, The (New York), 52

Taylor, Bayard, 85–86, 90, 124, 206–7

Taylor, Zachary, 76, 115, 117, 243n. 43

Tehúantepec, Isthmus of, 127, 176–77. *See also* Mexico, geography of; transoceanic canal

Telégrafo, El (New Orleans), 112

Ten Years' War. *See* Cuba

Teurbe Tolón, Miguel, xiv, 111, 146–49

Texas: annexation of, 11, 61, 156–57; independence and Republic of, 110, 144, 156; and Mexican War, 76, 93, 112, 141, 227n. 48; print culture in, 100–101, 157–58; *tejano* identity in, 10, 101, 157, 160, 214n. 4, 250n. 23; in transamerican geography, xiv, 141

Thoreau, Henry David, 88

Ticknor, George, 62, 174

Ticknor and Fields Publishers, 83

Tlascalan peoples, 52

Torres, Luis, 103, 179

Townsend, Mary Ashley ("Xarifa"), 200

transamerican relations: anticolonialism as shared value, 54–55, 102, 216n. 13; during U.S. Civil War, 157–60; economic, 9, 12, 37, 110, 161, 163, 167–68, 191, 243n. 41; literary contacts and exchanges, xiii, 4–5, 13–19, 47, 71–75, 105–6, 174–76, 225n. 30; and print culture, 6, 78, 105, 113–15, 157, 162, 177, 182–84, 187, 190–91; shifts in balance of geopolitical power over nineteenth century, 3, 12–13, 72–73, 76, 87–88, 112, 117, 205, 210–11. *See also* colonialism; expansionism; filibusters; geography; imperialism; Mexican War; Monroe Doctrine; Panama Congress; revolutions in the Americas; stereotypes; transoceanic canal

translation: of Bible, 151; on borderlands, 104–7, 139; and cosmopolitanism, xiv, 19, translation (*cont.*)

27, 78; feminized, 87; figured in literary works, 91, 100, 207; oral, 167–68; method of practiced in this study, xvi; political valence of, 2–3, 81–82, 100, 236n. 34; as secondary form of creativity, 27, 81, 84; theories of, 79, 81–82. *See also* entries for individual translators; language; originality

transnationalism, 7–13, 210, 214nn. 4–5, 215n. 7

transoceanic canal, 6, 11–12, 18, 38, 127, 164, 167–68, 171, 176, 186; overview of, 216n. 20

travel narratives: during discovery and conquest period, 85; of Latin American writers about the United States, 14, 45, 105, 162–63, 170–76, 188, 197–204; as metaphor for travels of texts, 13–14; of U.S. writers about Latin America, 14, 35, 68, 105, 223n. 18, 226n. 44, 231–32n. 6

Turla, Leopoldo, 146, 149, 163, 200–201

Turner, Frederick Jackson, 9

Twain, Mark, 12

United States of America: Civil War, 10, 11, 158–59, 177, 185; Gilded Age, 192; literacy rates, 22; national literary canon, 4, 25, 31, 90–91; monolingualism in, xvi, 4; Reconstruction, 185–86, 189; Revolution, 53–56. *See also* borderlands; expansionism; immigration; Latinos in the United States; Mexican War; transamerican relations

United States Review and Literary Gazette, 36, 52, 225n. 32

urbanism. *See* cities

Utopianism, 52, 90, 131

Vallejo, Mariano, xi, xv, 102, 206–7, 210

Varela, Félix, 12, 40, 52, 223n. 22. See also *Jicoténcal*

Vásquez, Tiburcio, 177

Venezuela, 15, 58, 105, 144, 203, 252n. 36

Venuti, Lawrence, 81–82

Verdad, La (New York City), 112, 145

Vidaurri, Santiago, 158–59

Vigil, José María, 177, 179–82 *passim*

Villaverde, Cirilo, 111, 112, 145–46, 153–54, 187, 200

Vingut, Javier, 223n. 22, 225n. 31, 240n. 9

Vitier, Cintio, 224n. 26

Walker, William, 136, 168–69

Wallerstein, Immanuel, 8

Washington, George, as iconic figure, 54, 58, 167–68, 202, 225n. 30

Webster, Daniel, 44

westward movement. *See* expansionism, U.S.

Whitman, Thomas Jefferson, 122, 124, 126, 225n. 39

Whitman, Walt: and African-Americans, 121, 128–31; and American language, 26; and Bryant, 243n. 35; and Civil War, 161–63; and Emerson, 5, 122, 235n. 33, 243n. 43; and expansionism, 38, 48, 90, 121, 133–36; as journalist, 121–22, 126–29; Latin American reputation, 47, 121; and Latin "race," 124–25, 134–36, 235n. 30; and Longfellow, 122, 124, 125, 235n. 30; and Martí, 121, 240n. 1; and Menken, 162, 194; in New Orleans, xiv, 109, 121–35; and originality, 20, 77, 81, 124; and sexuality, 121–22, 129–32, 239–40n. 1; and slavery, 122, 129–32; travels of, 123–24, 128; views on Mexican War, 17–18, 122–23

—"By Blue Ontario's Shore," 90, 244n. 50

—*Calamus* (general), 132

—"Crossing Brooklyn Ferry," 133

—"Facing West from California's Shores," 134

—"Inca's Daughter, The," 124, 134

—"I Saw in Louisiana a Live-Oak Growing," 132

—"I Sing the Body Electric," 131

—*Leaves of Grass* (general), 121, 128

—"Midnight on the Mississippi," 125, 127, 132

—*November Boughs* 122, 125, 135

—"O Magnet-South!," 132

—"Our Old Feuillage," 134